# The Languag
# Global Hip Hop

## Advances in Sociolinguistics

Series Editors: Professor Sally Johnson, University of Leeds
Dr Tommaso M. Milani, University of the Witwatersrand

Since the emergence of sociolinguistics as a new field of enquiry in the late 1960s, research into the relationship between language and society has advanced almost beyond recognition. In particular, the past decade has witnessed the considerable influence of theories drawn from outside of sociolinguistics itself. Thus rather than see language as a mere reflection of society, recent work has been increasingly inspired by ideas drawn from social, cultural, and political theory that have emphasized the constitutive role played by language/discourse in all areas of social life. The Advances in Sociolinguistics series seeks to provide a snapshot of the current diversity of the field of sociolinguistics and the blurring of the boundaries between sociolinguistics and other domains of study concerned with the role of language in society.

*Discourses of Endangerment: Ideology and Interest in the Defence of Languages*
Edited by Alexandre Duchêne and Monica Heller

*Linguistic Minorities and Modernity, 2ⁿᵈ Edition: A Sociolinguistic Ethnography*
Monica Heller

*Language, Culture and Identity: An Ethnolinguistic Perspective*
Philip Riley

*Language Ideologies and Media Discourse: Texts, Practices, Politics*
Edited by Sally Johnson and Tommaso M. Milani

*Language in the Media: Representations, Identities, Ideologies*
Edited by Sally Johnson and Astrid Ensslin

*Language and Power: An Introduction to Institutional Discourse*
Andrea Mayr

*Language Testing, Migration and Citizenship*
Edited by Guus Extra, Massimiliano Spotti and Piet Van Avermaet

*Multilingualism: A Critical Perspective*
Adrian Blackledge and Angela Creese

Semiotic Landscapes: Language, Image, Space
Edited by Adam Jaworski and Crispin Thurlow

*The Languages of Global Hip Hop*
Edited by Marina Terkourafi

*The Language of Newspapers: Socio-Historical Perspectives*
Martin Conboy

*The Languages of Urban Africa*
Edited by Fiona Mc Laughlin

# The Languages of Global Hip Hop

Edited by Marina Terkourafi

continuum

**Continuum International Publishing Group**

The Tower Building             80 Maiden Lane
11 York Road                   Suite 704
London SE1 7NX                 New York NY 10038

www.continuumbooks.com

First published 2010
Paperback edition first published 2012

**British Library Cataloguing-in-Publication Data**
A catalogue record for this book is available from the British Library.

ISBN:   978-0-8264-3160-8 (hardback)
        978-1-4411-4026-5 (paperback)

**Library of Congress Cataloging-in-Publication Data**
A catalog record for this book is available from the Library of Congress.

Typeset by Newgen Imaging Systems Pvt Ltd, Chennai, India
Printed and bound in Great Britain

*For my students*

# Contents

# Notes on Contributors

**Jannis Androutsopoulos** is Professor of German and Media Linguistics at the University of Hamburg, Germany. His research interests include sociolinguistics, media discourse, style, computer-mediated communication, youth and popular culture. He is editor of *HipHop: Globale Kultur – lokale Praktiken* (Transcript, 2003) and a special issue of the *Journal of Sociolinguistics* (2006) on sociolinguistics and computer-mediated communication.

**Endre Brunstad** is Associate Professor of Subject Related Didactics at the Department of Linguistic, Literary and Aesthetic Studies at the University of Bergen. His research interests include language and globalization, language planning, linguistic purism and language didactics. His current research concerns notions of 'good' language and conditions for learning and teaching Nynorsk. Brunstad also holds an adjunct position at The National Centre for the Teaching of New Norwegian.

**Jennifer Cramer** is a PhD candidate in Linguistics at the University of Illinois at Urbana-Champaign. She received BA degrees in French and Linguistics from the University of Kentucky and an MA in Linguistics from Purdue University. Her research interests include sociolinguistics, discourse analysis, Southern American English, language and identity, border identities, hip hop linguistics, world Englishes and English in the European Union.

**Cecelia Cutler** teaches at the City University of New York, Lehman College. Her work focuses on the sociolinguistic aspects of out-group language use, particularly the construction of Whiteness and authenticity within hip hop culture, and language ideologies and attitudes among teachers. Some of her recent studies explore the dynamics of identity formation among immigrant youth from Eastern Europe who affiliate with hip hop as well as the performance of authenticity among White rappers on reality television.

**Matt Garley** is a doctoral candidate in linguistics at the University of Illinois at Urbana-Champaign. He is in the process of completing a dissertation on linguistic borrowing in the German hip-hop community. His current research interests include the application of corpus methodology to questions of sociohistorical linguistics, contact-induced language change, language style and computer-mediated communication. He has been an avid fan of US and global hip hop since high school.

**Jill Hallett** is a PhD candidate in Linguistics at the University of Illinois and has been Assistant Editor for the journal *World Englishes* since 2008. Her research interests include sociolinguistics and second language/dialect acquisition, particularly with respect to American and world Englishes, classroom discourse, and language in the media and literature. Recent and upcoming publications include studies of varieties of English, language in the media, ethnography, Mayan linguistics, and several book reviews and notices.

**Samira Hassa** is a native of Fes, Morocco. She graduated from Université de Montpellier III in 2000 with a DEA (Diplome d'Etudes Approfondies) in French linguistics, and received her PhD in French Linguistics from the University of Illinois at Urbana-Champaign in 2005. She has taught at the College of William and Mary, the University of Illinois at Urbana-Champaign, and Rockford College. She is currently an Assistant Professor of French and Arabic at Manhattan College in New York.

**Franklin L. Hess** is the Coordinator of the Modern Greek Program at Indiana University and a lecturer in Western European Studies and American Studies. His current scholarly work examines twentieth- and twenty-first-century Greek popular culture – cinema, television and popular music – exploring the economic, geopolitical and geocultural contexts of its production. He has published on topics including early Greek cinema and the role of popular culture in Modern Greek Studies.

**Jamie Shinhee Lee** is Assistant Professor of Linguistics at the University of Michigan-Dearborn. She is co-editor of *World Englishes in Pop Culture* (2006) and *English and Asian Popular Culture* (forthcoming). Her research interests include world Englishes, language and popular culture, globalization and education, and Korean pragmatics and discourse analysis. Her articles have appeared in *Asian Englishes, Critical Discourse Studies, English Today, Harvard Studies in Korean Linguistics, Journal of Pragmatics, Language in Society* and *World Englishes*.

**John Littlejohn** is currently Visiting Assistant Professor of German at the University of West Georgia. His interest in ethnomusicology has led him to present and publish papers on Kraftwerk, Rammstein and German gangsta rappers and also to teach seminars on German music and culture. Most recently he served as guest editor (with frequent collaborator Michael Putnam) of a special edition of *Popular Music and Society* focusing on the Krautrock movement of the 1960s and 1970s.

**Toril Opsahl** completed her PhD thesis in 2009 on structural characteristics associated with Norwegian spoken among youth in multiethnic areas in Oslo. Her primary research interests are youth language (both in multicultural settings and in general), discourse markers and grammaticalization. She is currently working as a member of the editorial staff of the project Norsk Ordbok 2014 (Norwegian Dictionary 2014).

**Michael Putnam** is Assistant Professor of German and Linguistics at the Pennsylvania State University. In addition to syntax, semantics and morphology, he is actively engaged in sociolinguistics and ethnomusicology (focusing on modern German culture). He has taught seminars on hip-hop in German-speaking Europe and has published on the topic independently and with long-time collaborator, John Littlejohn. His article 'Teaching Taboos through Hip-Hop' was the American Association of Teachers of German's Article of the Year in 2006 for its contribution to the advancement of pedagogy.

**Unn Røyneland** is Associate Professor of Scandinavian Languages at the Department of Linguistics and Scandinavian Studies at the University of Oslo. Her research interests include language and dialect contact, language variation and change and youth language. Her current research concerns linguistic practices and the emergence of multiethnolectal speech styles among adolescents in multilingual urban contexts. She holds an adjunct position at University College Volda, teaching in the program for literacy, language planning and policy.

**Sarah Simeziane** completed an MA in linguistics from the University of Illinois at Urbana-Champaign and also holds a Maîtrise in linguistics from the Université Paris III, Sorbonne Nouvelle. Her current research interests include language and identity, (im)politeness, argumentation and public discourse. She spent two years in Hungary as an English lecturer as part of the Central European Teaching Program.

**Evros Stylianou** is currently studying English Language and Literature at the University of Nicosia in Cyprus. He has worked as a journalist for an English language newspaper on the island, writing independent music reviews with a focus on urban music. He has also contributed one of his own songs to the Cypriot Hip-Hop compilation album "The Rise of Cyprus Hip Hop, The Beginning".

**Marina Terkourafi** is Assistant Professor and Co-Director for Modern Greek Studies at the Department of Linguistics, University of Illinois at Urbana-Champaign. She specializes in theories of im/politeness, post-Gricean pragmatics, identity and language change, and the synchrony and diachrony of Cypriot Greek. She has published in the *Journal of Pragmatics, Journal of Politeness Research, Diachronica* and *Journal of Historical Pragmatics* among others. She is Associate Editor for the *International Review of Pragmatics* (Brill, 2009–).

**Angela Williams** is the Outreach Coordinator at the Center for South Asian and Middle Eastern Studies at the University of Illinois at Urbana-Champaign, where she designs programs focused on the Middle East for K-12 educators and community audiences. She completed her MA in Linguistics at the University of Illinois, during which time she also lived and studied Arabic in Egypt. Her research examines language usage in an American Muslim community, as well as Arabic hip hop in the Middle East.

# Introduction: A Fresh Look at Some Old Questions

Marina Terkourafi

## A (not so) personal encounter

A chance encounter with a fellow classmate from my high school days recently reminded me of the first glimpses of hip hop I got as a teenager at a public school in the medium-sized city of Heraklion in Greece. It was the mid-1980s, and a new student had just joined our class from Germany, where his family had emigrated a few years earlier. From Germany, the new classmate had brought back a new dress code – consisting mainly of hooded sweatshirts – a new style of 'calligraphy' (graffiti) – which we quickly adopted for the headlines of the class newspaper – and, last but not least, a new style of dance: breakdancing. Before our – and sometimes the teachers' – appreciative eyes, our new classmate would moonwalk and perform headspins, and it was not long before he had become famous in our small community for his skills, teaming up with another classmate to win first prize at a local breakdancing contest a few months later. That same summer, under a star-studded sky, together with a bunch of high school friends, we watched *Beat Street*, the 1984 movie, at the local open-air cinema, surrounded by the scents of jasmine and honeysuckle. Little did we know that a hip-hop revolution was under way and it was already making waves on the shores of faraway Crete . . .

This personal narrative is, I believe, not uncharacteristic of how many of us, especially outside of the United States, first came into contact with the phenomenon of global hip hop that is the focus of this book. Fast-forward a couple of decades, and I am sitting in a US university classroom debating with my graduate students the difference between 'rap' and 'hip hop'.[1] The hip-hop revolution has come (and gone?),[2] and hip hop is nowadays the subject of scholarly debate and academic writing. There is certainly a lot in hip-hop culture and the way it has spread to unsuspecting corners of the globe (from rural Norway to the Mediterranean island of Cyprus, and from Egypt to Korea; see Brunstad et al., Stylianou, Williams, Lee, this volume) for cultural historians, literary critics, anthropologists, sociologists and linguists to marvel at and write about. At the same time, one may wonder: In what sense does it make sense to talk about a global hip-hop culture? What are its determinants? And how is this public debate about hip hop in the media and in academia affecting and possibly changing the very phenomena it is attempting to elucidate? These are some of the broader issues I wish to touch upon in this introduction, before handing over to the volume contributors who, through painstaking analysis of the evidence on the ground, undertake the real task of putting together the pieces of the global hip-hop puzzle.

## What's so new about global hip hop anyway?

To those born after 1965,[3] hip hop may well be the only cultural phenomenon whose global spread they have witnessed firsthand. Cultural historians, however, are quick to point out that jazz and rock'n'roll pre-dated hip hop in achieving a similar feat, both reaching far beyond their respective birthplaces in the United States to hybridize with traditional musical styles and native tongues as far as Europe, Africa, Asia and Australia.[4] Both of those genres are now considered mainstream, and hip hop was so proclaimed even before the 1980s were over (Collins, 1988). Indeed, if performances at well-respected venues and dedicated museum exhibitions indicate at least some degree of societal engagement with – though not necessarily acceptance of – these genres, then these proclamations appear to be true.[5]

Nevertheless, societal engagement with these genres typically followed prior stigmatization, so again hip hop is not alone, nor the first, to get there. In fact, a distinction between sacred (or liturgical) and secular (or profane) music has been drawn in Western musical tradition (and *mutatis mutandis* elsewhere too) at least since late antiquity, with the latter often dismissed as 'pornographic', and even the playing of particular instruments condemned for aggravating a stupor brought on by wine.[6] More recently, ragtime, jazz and rock'n'roll are all examples of musical genres that have taken the heat for allegedly inciting bad behaviour.[7] It would seem, then, that hip hop as a cultural phenomenon is not unique, neither in its historical trajectory, nor in its current geographical expanse. If we want to understand the current fascination with hip hop by academics and the media alike – let alone the fans – we have to look elsewhere.

One possibility is hip hop's intensely political character. Hip-hop artists are known for being outspoken critics of the social realities around them, whatever those happen to be. In the United States, the debate has mostly centred around issues of race and gender,[8] while globally hip-hop artists offer incisive critiques of dominant cultures, engage with local issues of ethnicity and power, and address in different ways the legitimacy of their appropriation of what is traditionally deemed to be a Black genre – topics which are all examined in this volume. To capture this propensity for social engagement, Osumare (2007) introduces the concept of 'connective marginalities' to refer to the 'historic context of American racism' and the ability of global reinterpretations of blackness to 'signify parallel issues of marginality and difference marked already in other countries' (Osumare, 2007, p. 62).

However, when it comes to hip hop as a cultural phenomenon in its totality, it is possible that connective marginality is still not the 'glue' that binds it all together. Speaking in 2007 about the 'ways in which blackness metastasizes globally', Michael Eric Dyson struck a note of caution in this regard: outside the United States, he said, 'they need a form of rebellion to speak against the injustice of their culture there, . . . against forms of repression against which it is necessary to speak . . . while some of the hip-hop here . . . is celebrating the very things it should be criticizing.'[9] Intended as a rebuff against the violence and the misogyny portrayed in some of hip hop, Dyson's remark also underlines the fact that hip hop is not a monolith: polyphony and fragmentation can be found at its very core. While hip hop as practised globally may seem to have more similarities with US 'conscious rap', it is well-known that this is not the only kind of rap around, and that late 1970s hip hop was more akin to party music, while 1990s gangsta rap has typically been the *topic* of social critique rather than its exponent. Social critique and advocacy would, then, seem to be an element of only some of hip hop – both inside and outside the United States.

But social engagement and advocacy are not only *not necessary* to distinguish hip hop from other cultural phenomena; they are also *not sufficient*. In their quest to understand and deal with reality, artists of various media have engaged in social critique at least since Aristophanes and the West African griots, and often clashed with authorities who tried to police artistic expression in the process, with state control and sanction of Soviet-produced music and dance[10] and the excesses of the McCarthy years in the United States providing just two salient twentieth-century examples.

If hip hop defies delimitation and definition, perhaps this is not because it is in some way aberrant but exactly because, like other cultural phenomena, trying to reduce it to a set of *sine qua non* parameters is fundamentally misguided in the first place. Yet this is exactly what is often attempted, when lines are drawn around what hip hop *is* versus what *it is not* (conscious rap vs. gangsta rap, or underground hip hop vs. commercially successful hip hop), where it started (the Bronx vs. the Caribbean vs. the rest),[11] who has the right to produce it (the Beastie Boys and Eminem phenomena in the United States; see also Cutler, this volume), who has the right to consume it (inner city black youth vs. white suburban youth), and who may legitimately use its code (several incidents in recent years, culminating in calls for hip hop to 'clean up its act'; e.g., Franklin, 2007). One of the tasks of hip-hop scholarship is indeed to take note and try to make sense of these claims: What motivates them, and how effective are they?

Contrary to these often simplifying and reductionist assumptions, hip-hop scholarship is increasingly theorizing the genre in terms of 'transcultural' or 'global flows' (to borrow from the titles of two recent books, by Pennycook, 2007, and Alim et al., 2009, respectively), a move which seems befitting a genre that has at its heart the concepts of 'break' and 'flow', of 'sampling' and of 'mixing' (see next section). In fact, it is possible that Robert Farris Thompson was not far from the truth when he claimed, as early as 1988, that 'rap will remain a moving target. "Once America thinks it has got it right, rap will have moved on," he said adding, "I wouldn't be surprised if rap is going into the 21st century"' (quoted in Collins, 1988).

## A synergy of factors

To pin down the moving target that is hip hop – a prerequisite to theorizing about it – rather than look for its unique essence, it may be more useful to locate its singularity in a synergy of factors, none of which are unique to hip hop but all of which have left their imprint on it and continue to favour its spread. In terms of stylistic features, 'break', 'flow', 'sampling' and 'mixing' are central to hip hop's expressive code, whether realized as spoken word (MCing), instrumental sound (DJing), physical movement (break-dancing), or visual image (graffiti). These stylistic features compose a structural (or formal) framework that favours the incorporation of heterogeneous elements.[12] This in turn has allowed hip hop to take root in cultures and languages as diverse as North and South America, Africa, the Middle East, Europe, South and East Asia and Indigenous Australia. Moreover, as a historically situated product, hip hop itself may be thought of as a hybrid in its genesis, considering the multiple ethnic backgrounds and historical trajectories of its early exponents – even if they are all placed, according to the prevailing origin myth, in 1970s Bronx (cf. Kelley, 2006, p. xi; Alim, 2009, p. 8, and the references therein). In this sense, the stylistic features mentioned above are not coincidental but intimately tied to the socio-historical circumstances out of which hip hop emerged.

With sampling and mixing at its very core, hip hop provides an expressive vehicle that is flexible enough to accommodate the multiple origins and concerns of increasingly interconnected and mobile populations.

And increasingly interconnected and mobile is what we are, with both technological advances and socio-economic conditions conspiring to turn the planet into a (hotly debated) 'global village'.[13] Global telecommunications and the advent of the internet in particular have created a technological environment that has favoured the spread of hip hop as much by diffusing its products[14] as by enabling artists – especially those in smaller or newer markets – to upload their music directly making it instantly available on a global scale (Clarke and Hiscock, 2009, p. 243; Williams, Stylianou, this volume), and fans to form virtual communities of practice bound by their engagement with the genre (Garley, this volume).

At the same time, through presupposing this supra-local engagement with developments *elsewhere*, the expressive medium of hip hop endows its practitioners with a 'symbolic capital' (Bourdieu, 1991) that casts them as, at one and the same time, experts and outsiders in their own community. This dual role of *expert/outsider* places them in a privileged position from which to assume the role of social critic and respond to the challenges of the world around them, be those issues of racism, immigration and social inequality (Androutsopoulos, Hassa, Simeziane, Littlejohn and Putnam, this volume), terrorism and war (Williams, this volume), or life in a (post?)-capitalist era (Hess, Stylianou, this volume). It is not surprising, then, that this dual role is often assumed by immigrants and/or bilinguals, who naturally find themselves at the juncture between different communities and cultures, enabling them to function as conduits for the transmission of the genre (Androutsopoulos, Hassa, Lee, Stylianou, Brunstad et al., this volume).[15]

Placed against the context of technological advances and patterns of transnational movement and concomitant hybridization in the late twentieth/early twenty-first century, global hip hop appears to be a natural outcome of these processes, which have left their imprint on its form/structure, its function/content, as well as its modes of production and transmission. There is, however, one last element to hip hop that is not – or, at least, not as easily – traceable back to those processes, and that is its quest for authenticity. While at an abstract level 'keepin it real' may not be unrelated to the blurring of boundaries at several levels that goes on in hip hop, it is not obvious that any of these processes is directly involved in generating hip hop's current preoccupation with authenticity – what is probably the single theme to make an appearance in chapter after chapter of this volume.

**5**

## Deconstructing authenticity in hip hop

In a sense, authenticity is the hallmark of all great art. Collectors are wont to pay handsome sums of money to acquire original works of art, and the discovery of previously unknown works by artists long dead has the art world holding its breath.[16] Lack of authenticity, on the other hand, is dismissed as 'fake' and may even be punishable by law.[17] For these reasons, artists advance claims to authenticity on various grounds, including studying with the 'masters',[18] country of origin,[19] ethnic background,[20] and, last but not least, personal trajectory and lifestyle/attire.[21]

While authenticity has always been venerated across art forms, the current preoccupation with authenticity in hip hop is probably unprecedented. As Stylianou (this volume) is quick to remind us, the 'mantra of "keepin it real"' (Clarke and Hiscock, 2009, p. 244) is being echoed from several quarters: '"Keep it street", "stick to what you know", "do not sell out", "do not pander", "do not beat around the bush", "keep it Black", "show no fear", "avoid superfluity", "do not forget where you came from", "keep it gangsta", "never lose face", "be yourself", "don't back down", "express you"' (Stylianou, this volume). One may only speculate about the reasons why authenticity has become so central to the definition of hip hop.

One explanation may have to do with technical aspects of the genre. Typically, it has been possible to draw a distinction between the originator of the music (traditionally, an instrumental musician, though with the advent of composition by computer that need not necessarily be the case), and one who reproduces it later from a previous recording. In hip hop, notably through sampling, these two roles are fused into one, that of the DJ, who is now both reproducer (of materials from various sources) and originator of the music (responsible for fusing them into an original synthesis). It is possible that this fusion of the two roles into one results in a sense of contested 'authorship' or 'ownership' of the music, in response to which establishing authenticity becomes of paramount importance, if one is to establish the legitimacy of the new genre as more than simply a 'medley' of others' work.

Alongside this technically oriented justification, ideological aspects may also play a part. Specifically, it is possible that with transnational movement and cultural hybridization comes the undermining not only of previously clear-cut categories of race, ethnic background, national affiliation, and so on, but also of the certainties that emanate from these distinctions. The historical experience of the United States is a prime example of both the confusion that may result from these processes as well as of the vast array of ways of dealing with it and of new cultural

**6**

formations that may emerge in response. Establishing the authenticity of the genre, as well as of oneself as a representative of it, then, amounts to a gesture of emancipation from these multiple lineages, and a declaration of one's own unique identity and right to exist as an independent new entity.[22]

Whatever the reasons why authenticity has found itself at the epicentre of hip-hop culture, its effects are yet more interesting and far-reaching. What is important to highlight here is that, strong as the injunction to keep it real may be, it is not a monosemous (one-way) one. As will emerge from the chapters in this volume, hip hoppers around the globe are establishing their authenticity on (at least) two levels. At one level, they address local issues and social realities surrounding them directly, giving rise to the multiple 'Hip-Hop Cultures' celebrated in recent scholarship on the topic (see, e.g., Alim et al., 2009). Yet at another level, they enter into a dialogue with the whole of hip-hop culture, acknowledging its supra-local origins and drawing cultural capital from them (see previous section). At both levels, they claim authenticity through both *form* (music samples and language varieties used) and *content* (topics and genres referred to, and attitudes expressed), creating multiple – and sometimes conflicting (cf. Clarke and Hiscock, 2009, pp. 254–258) – authentici*ties* in the process.

In terms of form, keepin it real to the locale can be expressed in music, through sampling of local sounds and songs, as well as in language, through opting for local ways of speaking, which in turn may be: (a) *national languages* (Arabic in Egypt, French in France, German in Germany, Greek in Greece, Hungarian in Hungary, Korean in Korea, and so on; see chapters by Williams, Hassa, Androutsopoulos, Hess, Simeziane, Lee, this volume); (b) *regional, immigrant, or minority varieties* (the Greek Cypriot dialect in Cyprus, Verlan in France, Turkish in Germany, regional dialects in Norway, Romani in Hungary, Southern and Midwestern varieties of US English; see chapters by Stylianou, Hassa, Androutsopoulos, Brunstad et al., Simeziane, Cramer and Hallett, this volume); or, (c) *some combination of these through code-switching/ mixing* (see especially the chapters by Androutsopoulos, Hassa, Williams, Simeziane, Lee, Brunstad et al., Garley, this volume).

In terms of content, on the other hand, keepin it real to the locale can be expressed through the topics artists choose to address, as well as through the strategies they use to address them. As regards *topics*, references to local characters and placenames, and to broader social issues of local importance (migration, societal marginalization, consumerism, etc.) serve to anchor artistic production to its immediate surroundings both in the United States (Cramer and Hallett, this volume) as well as outside of it (Androutsopoulos, Hassa, Williams, Simeziane, Littlejohn and Putnam, Lee, Hess, Stylianou, Brunstad et al., this volume). In addition, at the level of *discourse strategies and styles*, native genres and rhetorical traditions, such as those of the 'cognate curse' in Egyptian Arabic, *chattistá* in Cypriot Greek, and the comedic genre of *epitheórisi* in Greece (see, respectively, Williams, Stylianou, Hess, this volume) can act as a bridge between hip hop and native audiences helping to decrease the distance between them and to inspire a sense of familiarity – making native audiences what one might call 'hip-hop ready'. In all of these ways, artists can capitalize on different aspects of local-ness to connect with and speak to their audiences.

At the same time, if global hip-hop artists are to establish their authenticity as worthy representatives of a genre they did not directly originate, keepin it real to the culture of hip hop is of paramount importance. This aspiration has, for the most part, been interpreted as a linguistic imperative to keep it real to the genre's Black inner city roots through the adoption of African American English (AAE) linguistic conventions, that have gone on to define a new global Hip Hop Nation Language (HHNL). Several of the chapters in this volume confirm this trend (see, e.g., Hassa, Lee, Brunstad et al.), adding how this 'invasion' of English 'from below' can generate quite different indexicalities and attitudes from those that usually accompany mainstream ideologies about the spread of (Standard) English 'from above' (see especially Hassa, Williams, Garley, this volume).

In addition, references to the concept of Blackness, real or imagined, are a recurring device by which homage is paid to the genre's Black roots (Williams, Simeziane, Lee, Hess, Brunstad et al., and especially Cutler, this volume). In this vein, Simeziane introduces the notion of a 'race metaphor' that

> serve[s] as convenient shorthand . . . a readily available and convenient 'source' domain in terms of which to conceptualize those more 'abstract' 'target' domains across which identification with hip hop occurs, namely 'culture, class, historical oppression, and youth rebellion' (Osumare, 2007, p. 15). (Simeziane, this volume)

Beyond these two trends that serve to unify local Hip-Hop Cultures under a larger umbrella at the level of form (through the adoption of HHNL) and content (through the 'race metaphor') respectively, I would like to propose a third way in which global hip-hop artists enter into a dialogue with the genre. This third way involves capitalizing on the historical lineage of hip-hop culture, specifically its situated roots in AAE practices of sounding (also known as snapping, and later the dozens, busting, capping, and other terms).

**8**

## Keepin it Real: The Third Way

According to Labov (1972), sounding in AAE assumes the canonical form given in (1):

> (1) 'T(B) is so X that P'
>
> where
> the Target [T] is a relative of the addressee [B] (mother, father, wife . . .)
> property X may be justly attributed (fat, skinny, old, . . .), and
> proposition P is *obviously untrue*
> e.g., 'your mama so old she got cobwebs under her arms.'

Sounds are immediately and overtly evaluated, either positively or negatively, by an audience, who are active participants in the action, and followed by a response by B which typically takes the form 'T(A) is so X′ that P′.' Moreover, sounds function as *ritual insults*. These are crucially *different* from personal insults – in which proposition P may be true – and may be used either purely for entertainment, or to gain an advantage over an opponent (Labov, 1972, p. 350). We may therefore describe sounding more aptly in Bauman's terms as a type of 'performance', that is, 'a specially marked mode of action, one that sets up or represents a special interpretative frame within which the act of communication is to be understood' (Bauman, 1992, p. 44). Given this rich semiotics, sounds constitute a powerful tool by which to create a sense of solidarity within a community and can by extension be used as a socialization device (cf. Garrett, 2005).

Interesting parallels can be found between sounds as a type of performance and Aristotle's definition of tragedy, which thus offers a useful framework for analysing them. This runs as follows:

> Tragedy, then, is an imitation of an action which is serious, complete, and of a certain magnitude – in language which is embellished . . . through dramatic enactment, not narrative – and which through the arousal of pity and fear effects the purification of such emotions. (Aristotle, *Poetics*, 1449b)

In this definition, tragedy is identified, first and foremost, as an *imitation* of an action. Similarly, Smitherman points out: 'the snap must not be literally true . . . if you take snappin out of the realm of play, you enter the real world, where ain nobody playin. Occasionally, though, players will go there, especially when they run out of clever snaps' (1995, p. 326). The second element of tragedy is *hyperbole*: the action depicted must be 'of a certain magnitude'; similarly, 'to signify is to . . . put on an act, [to] boast . . ., a contest in hyperbole' (Myers, 1990); the snap 'must be exaggerated, the wilder the better' (Smitherman, 1995, p. 326). *Language* is also important: it must be 'embellished', and so must sounds, which are 'expressed in metaphorical language, on time and in rhyme' (Smitherman, 1995, p. 326); 'calls, cries, hollers, riffs, licks, [and] overlapping antiphony are examples of signifying in hip hop music' (Caponi, 1999). Finally, 'through the arousal of pity and fear' tragedy aims to serve as an outlet for the emotions. And so it is with snaps, which 'for a people trying to survive under an oppressive racist yoke . . . functioned as an outlet for what countless blues people called "laughing to keep from crying"' (Smitherman, 1995, p. 324).

In addition to exhibiting all four features outlined by Aristotle as constitutive of tragedy, snaps also exemplify a fifth element central to this dramatic genre, that of a *contest* between an 'agonist' and an 'antagonist'. Thus, sounding has been described as 'speech the sole purpose of which is to put the orator's gifts on display (*epideixis*) . . . a battle for the respect of onlookers and rarely occur[ring] without spectators . . . intended to defuse conflict nonviolently' (Myers, 1990). Smitherman concurs:

> one upmanship is the goal of this oral contest, best played in a group of appreciative onlookers, who are secondary participants in the game . . . the dozens taught you how to chill . . . how to survive by verbal wit and cunning rhetoric rather than physical violence. (Smitherman, 1995, pp. 323–324)

These five elements – non literality, hyperbole, embellished language, an outlet for the emotions, and the notion of a contest – have arguably been inherited from African American sounding practices into hip hop as part of its lineage, making them available as a kind of 'genetic inheritance' that is able to generate the ever-changing understandings of authenticity that run through and link together all of hip hop – since its early days as dance music in the 1970s through the gangsta rap of the 1990s and through to its multiple transplantations around the globe today.

## Authenticity in flux

In the early days of hip hop in the US, keepin it real to the street meant doing 'dance music'. As Samuels notes, '[a]lthough much is made of rap as a kind of urban streetgeist, early rap had a more basic function: dance music . . .: the point wasn't rapping, it was rhythm, DJs cutting records left and right, [mixing] Led Zeppelin with a jazz record and some James Brown' (2004, p. 148). In 1984, as hip hop started making it into the mainstream, Run DMC were the first group to break through

**10**

to a mass white audience. However, 'unlike the first generation of rappers, they were solidly middle class. . . . Neither of them was deprived and neither of them ever ran with a gang, but on stage they became the biggest, baddest [*sic*], streetest [*sic*] guys in the world' (Samuels, 2004, p. 149). Soon after, in 1986, the Beastie Boys' (an all white group) album *Licensed to Ill* became the first rap record to sell one million copies. The mainstreaming of hip hop around that time has been frequently acknowledged (e.g., Collins, 1988; Samuels, 2004), and so have its effects: 'white demand indeed began to determine the direction of the genre, but what it wanted was music more defiantly black' (Samuels, 2004, p. 149).

With the mainstreaming of the genre in the United States – and its breakthrough around that same time to local markets worldwide (Hess, this volume) – came the first shift in the meaning of authenticity. Paradoxically, perhaps more so than before, hip hop was explicitly identified as a Black genre; however, this time, the indexicality of Blackness capitalized upon was no longer that of the 'oppressed' (Smitherman, 1995, p. 324) but a competing one held by White people: 'rap's appeal to whites rested in its evocation of an age-old image of blackness: a foreign, sexually charged, and criminal underworld against which the norms of white society are defined, and, by extension, through which they may be defied' (Samuels, 2004, pp. 147–148).[23] The 'cult of the thug' embodied in 1990s gangsta rap followed as a self-fulfilling prophecy. Once this new interpretation of authenticity was available, it also became available to hip hoppers worldwide, who capitalized on it in different ways, to different extents, and to multiple indexical effects – as analyses of references to violence and misogyny in their lyrics attest (Littlejohn and Putnam, Williams, Hassa, Brunstad et al., Stylianou, this volume).

Nonetheless, it is well-known among artists and scholars of hip hop alike that, contrary to perceived views, few rappers actually have first-hand experience of this criminally charged representation of the street, as has also been shown by ethnographic studies of teenage rappers (Hurt, 2006; Newman, 2009). As Newman points out, '[t]he idea that rappers should rap about what is real was fulfilled in the breach; their raps were always laden with what [one of them] called "concept"; that is, nothing real' (2009, p. 199). In other words, 'the cult of the thug was not, for the MCs, about being a thug but [about] holding up the thug as symbolically *compelling*' (ibid., p. 205; emphasis added) – which naturally leads to the question: Compelling to whom?

The answer to this last question brings us full circle to the role of the audience in shaping the product that is presented to them, including the understandings of authenticity that are projected onto this product. As is also acknowledged by several of the chapters in this volume, hip hop is not immune to marketability concerns (Williams, Simeziane, this volume); on the contrary, hip-hop artists may also detect such trends and actively seek to exploit them (Littlejohn and Putnam, this volume). As media backlash against the excesses of gangsta rap continues to feed public debate on the matter, paradoxically, this may also allow us a glimpse into the future. Increasing scholarly engagement with hip hop, as evidenced by the rising numbers of workshops and town-hall meetings, academic publications, and courses devoted to it,[24] represents an alternative market to which to respond. As scholars engage more closely with hip-hop culture worldwide, they are (re-)discovering the centrality of verbal skill that drives rappers' creative use of language – what Alim has called 'the cutting edge of the cutting edge' (2004, p. 396) – and alongside it hip hop's potential to play a role in social transformation. As Wa Thiongo put it, '[b]y making up your own words, you are freeing yourself from linguistic colonization' (1992, cited in Alim, 2004, p. 395). As a result, what started historically as a non-serious 'game' of verbally outwitting an opponent fit only for a select few may well be being re-constructed and re-read – through a 'backward projection' of intentions, as it were – as a conscious act of defiance, along the lines of contemporary conscious rap in the United States and elsewhere. However, we should be under no illusion: 'conscious rap' (a term coined only later) is no more 'real' than gangsta rap was in the 1990s or party rap before that. Rather, they all represent diverging interpretations of authenticity by different markets, and the genre's variable responses to each of them.

Authenticity, in other words, while central to hip hop, is a multivalent notion. Both keepin it real to the street and keepin it real to the genre can be multiply interpreted at several levels. Keepin it real to the street can depend on what is the reality of the street in each new locale, producing as many glocalized outcomes as there are regional scenes in hip hop – often with multiple scenes in the same country engaging in a second-order 'battle' over authenticity, as in the United States, France, Germany, and Norway, to name but some (see respectively, Cramer and Hallett, Hassa, Androutsopoulos, Brunstad et al. this volume). Keepin it real to the street can also be interpreted metaphorically with reference to a fictionalized 'street' that does not reflect rappers' own experiences, yet it corresponds to their perception of the genre, as in the 'cult of the thug' mentioned above. In this sense, the cult of the thug can also be justified as a way of keepin it real to the genre, taking into account the genre's hyperbolic, 'larger than life' and antagonistic elements (see previous section). In addition, keepin it real to the genre can serve to re-emphasize the elements of verbal skill and wit found in hip hop's lineage in African American sounding practices – but also in

**12**

corresponding traditions elsewhere – injecting the genre with a (renewed) potential for social critique that can also target itself, as in self-parody (Clarke and Hiscock, 2009). These multiple interpretations of authenticity are not either/or options; rather, they co-exist, often challenging one another, and serving as constant reminders that *reality is not one-way, but emergent and discursively constructed*. By the same token, given its gate-keeping potential, the debate over authenticity in hip hop is likely to rage on, as it constitutes the ultimate arena where the power to impose one's version of reality can be asserted.

## This volume

The chapters in this volume engage with all of the themes touched upon in this introduction, often moving them into new directions as outlined by Alim (2009, p. 16). Several of the chapters contain ethno-graphic material and interviews with the artists that meet the need for new 'hiphopographies' (Stylianou, Brunstad et al., Cutler), while others take up the challenge of delving into Androutsopoulos's (2009) 'third sphere', presenting analyses of hip hoppers' and fans' unscripted use of language (Garley, Cutler, Brunstad et al.). Three new regional scenes – Cyprus, Egypt and Roma rap in Hungary – are featured in this volume for the first time, while other, less researched ones, such as Norway and Greece, are also included alongside better-studied ones such as France, Germany, Korea, and the United States. A glossary of hip-hop terms is provided at the end of the volume as a quick reference for the most frequently used terms.

In the best of hip-hop traditions, this volume started out as a genuine grassroots endeavour. It was my students' enthusiasm about the topic that prompted me to organize, in November 2007, the workshop 'Language and Hip Hop Culture in a Globalizing World' at the University of Illinois at Urbana-Champaign, and soon after that a thematic panel on 'Hip Hop across the Globe: What Exactly is Going Global?' at the 17th Sociolinguistics Symposium (SS17) at the Vrije Universiteit in Amsterdam. Several of the chapters in this volume were first presented at these two venues, while others were explicitly solicited for this volume. I am grateful to all of the authors for their willingness to sub-ject their work to numerous revisions. Sarah Simeziane took on the daunting task of editorial assistant which she performed with brio into the small hours of the morning, and for that I would like to thank her. Thanks also go to the many colleagues who served as anonymous reviewers: this volume is decidedly better because of your input. Finally, I am grateful to Sally Johnson, series editor for *Advances in Sociolinguistics*, and Colleen Coalter on behalf of Continuum, for taking on board this project and for their support throughout. The journey has been fascinating, and it continues.

## Notes

1. 'Rap', the rhythmic delivery of spoken rhymes, is traditionally considered to be one of the elements of 'hip hop', which also comprises DJ-ing, break-dancing, graffiti, and an entire lifestyle (Alim, 2009, p. 2, and elsewhere). In other words, rap is the vocal part of the music which is produced by MCs, while hip hop embraces the whole of the culture, including all those who produce it and the fans who consume it (cf. Androutsopoulos's 2009 'three spheres'). Given the enduring centrality of rap in hip-hop culture, the two are often used interchangeably, and so they will be used in this introduction, save when the difference between them is at issue.

2. Cf. the title of American rapper's Nas 2006 release *Hip Hop is Dead*. While many interpreted Nas's title as critical of a certain kind of Southern rap (see Cramer and Hallett, this volume), to others hip hop had already died with the deaths of Tupac Shakur and Notorious B. I. G. in 1996 and 1997 respectively.

3. In his widely cited *The Hip Hop Generation: Young Blacks and the Crisis in African American Culture*, journalist Bakari Kitwana defines the 'hip hop generation' more narrowly as African Americans born between 1965 and 1984 (2002, p. xiii).

4. The phrase 'black innovation/white imitation' (Mercer, 1994) is sometimes used to underline perceived commonalities in the transmission of these cultural forms, of which hip hop is considered the latest example (cf. Collins, 1988; Samuels, 2004).

5. For some recent US examples, see: *Sympathy for the Devil: Art and Rock and Roll Since 1967*, an exhibition subdivided into six geographical sections (New York, West Coast/Los Angeles, the Midwest, the United Kingdom, Europe and The World) and organized by Chicago's Museum of Contemporary Art in 2007, that has since toured much of North America; *RECOGNIZE! Hip Hop and Contemporary Portraiture,* an exhibition organized by the Smithsonian's National Portrait Gallery in 2008; and *Hip-Hop Won't Stop: The Beat, the Rhymes, the Life*, a multi-year initiative to gather a broad collection on hip-hop culture launched by the Smithsonian's National Museum of American History in 2006.

6. To give just one example, with reference to early Byzantine attitudes to music, Touliatos-Miles writes, 'Although the Christian society of Byzantium placed constraints on the pagan music of Ancient Greece, Greek music and processional dancing continued but under the guise of secular music which was in constant condemnation by the Church Fathers. St. John Chrysostom of the late-fourth century CE referred to the music of the Byzantine symposia as "asmata pornika" (pornographic music) . . . for the songs accompanied with lyre are songs to the demons. . . . Basil [of Caesarea] especially condemned the practice of performing the Greek lyre and other instruments

from Antiquity at symposia, because it increased the drunkenness brought on by wine.' <http://www.geocities.com/hellenicmind/byzantium.html>, accessed 30 September 2009.

7. Jeff Ogbar, *The Hip Hop Revolution*. Book presentation on C-SPAN, 13 December 2007; <http://www.c-spanarchives.org/program/id/185051>, accessed 30 September 2009; cf. Collins, 1988.

8. These are, for instance, the two broad themes singled out for discussion on the website of Rap Sessions, a community initiative that has been organizing town-hall meetings across the United States since 2005, and is also responsible for two discussions on the same themes that aired on C-SPAN in 2005 and 2007 respectively; see <www.rapsessions.org>, accessed 30 September 2009.

9. Michael Eric Dyson, *Know what I Mean? Reflections on Hip Hop*. Book presentation on C-SPAN, 18 July 2007; <http://www.c-spanarchives.org/program/200193-1>, accessed 30 September 2009.

10. The stories of composer Dmitri Shostakovich (1906–1975) and Sergei Diaghilev (1872–1929), founder of the *Ballets Russes*, come to mind here.

11. For a recent take on the contested origins of hip hop, see Alim, 2009, pp. 7–9.

12. This incorporation of features from multiple sources is, of course, not unique to hip hop. Béla Bartók's (1881–1945) appropriation of traditional Hungarian folk tunes into his symphonic creations is a celebrated example of a parallel type of 'sampling' in the classical music world.

13. Media theorist Marshall McLuhan is credited with coining this term in the early 1960s as a way of capturing in a single term the increasing amount of interaction between people who are not physically co-present and the heightened social awareness and responsibility that emanates from this contact.

14. Several of the chapters in this volume contain references to websites where tracks, lyrics and information about the artists are equally available.

15. That is not to say, however, that immigrants/bilinguals are always involved in starting up new regional hip-hop scenes. From the countries represented in this volume, Greece exemplifies a scene that started out with minimal immigrant/bilingual involvement (Hess, this volume).

16. For a recent occurrence, see 'Two new Mozart compositions discovered', Press release, International Mozarteum Foundation, 2 August 2009; <http://www.mozarteum.at/00_META/00_News_Detail.asp?SID=6949377605140&ID=15287>, accessed 30 September 2009.

17. Forgery, in this sense, may be considered an extreme case of lack of authenticity.

18. A frequent occurrence at the workshops of famous Renaissance painters and sculptors.

19. As in the case of Argentine Tangueros.

20. As in the case of the Bauls of Bengal.

21. The examples of Irish-born Cretan lyra player Ross Daly, Australian Hokum Blues singer C. W. Stoneking, and white rapper Eminem all come to mind here. Ross Daly's personal page features photos of him sporting the long

hair and moustache characteristic of Cretan men standing alongside famous Cretan lyra players such as Xylouris and Mountakis and contains the following narrative of his life: 'Ross Daly's journey in the music of the world is inseparable from the course of his life. . . . In 1975 he travelled to Crete. . . . After a six month period of wandering from village to village encountering *local musicians*, he settled in the town of Hania on the west of the island and began studying the Cretan Lyra with its great *master* Kostas Mountakis. This *apprenticeship* was to last for many years. . . . After many years of intensive training in a variety of musical traditions, Ross Daly turned his attention largely to composition drawing heavily on the various *sources* that he had studied' (<http://www.rossdalymusic.com/biography.htm>; emphasis added, accessed 30 September 2009).

Similarly, the Wikipedia entry for C. W. Stoneking (<http://en.wikipedia.org/wiki/C._W._Stoneking>) refers to his American parents, and an August 2009 media release about him describes him as follows: 'C. W. Stoneking is as offbeat as they come, a baby-faced fellow in a *1920's delivery man's outfit, replete with little red bowtie and white shoes*, . . . Powered by influences like pre-war jazz, 1920s calypso music and jungle exotica, Stoneking creates a sonic wonderland world that halfway inhabits our reality and halfway inhabits a past that never quite existed' (<http://www.examiner.com/x-930-LA-Vinyl-Records-Examiner~y2009m8d12-CW-Stoneking-King-of-hokum-blues>; emphasis added, accessed 30 September 2009).

Finally, rapper Eminem's claims to authenticity rest on a similar premise: 'Shortly after his birth, his father *abandoned his family*. Until he was twelve, Mathers and his mother moved between various cities and towns in Missouri. . . . Although he was enrolled at Lincoln High School in Warren, he frequently participated in *freestyle battles* at Osborn High School across town, gaining the *approval of underground hip hop audiences*. After repeating the ninth grade three times due to truancy, he *dropped out of high school* at age 17. . . . [He] held a *minimum-wage job* of cooking and dishwashing. . . . Subjects covered in [his debut album] Infinite included his struggles with raising his newborn daughter Hailie Jade Scott while *on limited funds* and his strong *desire to get rich*. . . . After the release of Infinite, Eminem's personal struggles and *abuse of drugs and alcohol* culminated in his unsuccessful *suicide attempt*' (<http://en.wikipedia.org/wiki/Eminem>; emphasis added, accessed 30 September 2009).

22. This is not to deny the Black lineage of US hip hop but rather to identify this more closely with the experiences of a certain section of the African American community, situated in place and time. It is well-known that not all African Americans identify with hip hop, as shown by recent statements by Bill Cosby (<http://www.hiphopdx.com/index/news/id.4212/title./p.2>, accessed 30 September 2009), Oprah Winfrey (<http://www.mtv.com/news/articles/1534119/20060612/ludacris.jhtml>, accessed 30 September 2009) and Al Sharpton (<http://www.hiphopdx.com/index/news/id.5144/title.al-sharpton-takes-on-hip-hop-ocrites>, accessed 30 September 2009).

23. A similar view of the role of the mainstream and whatever they 'feel comfortable with' was expressed by TJ Crawford in a discussion of misogyny in hip-hop lyrics, C-SPAN, 2007 (available online from <http://www.rapsessions.org/flash/>, accessed 30 September 2009).
24. For an overview, see <http://www.hiphoparchive.org/university>, accessed 30 September 2009.

# References

Alim, H. S. (2004), 'Hip hop nation language', in E. Finegan and J. Rickford (eds), *Language in the USA: Themes for the Twenty-first Century*. New York: Cambridge University Press, pp. 387–409.

—(2009), 'Intro: Straight outta Compton, straight aus München: global linguistic flows, identities, and the politics of language in a Global Hip Hop Nation', in H. S. Alim, A. Ibrahim and A. Pennycook (eds), *Global Linguistic Flows: Hip hop Cultures, Youth Identities, and the Politics of Language*. Taylor & Francis Group: Routledge, pp. 1–22.

Androutsopoulos, J. (2009), 'Language and the three spheres of hip hop', in H. S. Alim, A. Ibrahim and A. Pennycook (eds), *Global Linguistic Flows: Hip Hop Cultures, Youth Identities, and the Politics of Language*. Taylor & Francis Group: Routledge, pp. 43–62.

Aristotle (*c.* AD 350/1986), *Poetics*. Translation and Commentary by Stephen Halliwell. London: Duckworth.

Bauman, R. (1992), 'Performance', in R. Bauman (ed.), *Folklore, Cultural Performances, and Popular Entertainments*. New York: Oxford University Press, pp. 41–49.

Bourdieu, P. (1991), *Language and Symbolic Power*. Cambridge: Polity.

Caponi, G. D. (1999), *Signifyin(G), Sanctifyin' & Slam Dunking: A Reader in African American Expressive Culture*. University of Massachusetts Press.

Clarke, S. and Hiscock, P. (2009), 'Hip hop in a post-insular community: hybridity, local language, and authenticity in an online Newfoundland group'. *Journal of English Linguistics*, 241–261.

Collins, G. (1988), 'Rap music, brash and swaggering, enters mainstream: black artists are not crossing over. Whites are coming to them'. *The New York Times*, 29 August 1988, p. C15.

Franklin, M. (2007), 'Simmons says 3 epithets should be banned', *The Associated Press*, April 24, 2007. Available online at: <http://www.washingtonpost.com/wp-dyn/content/article/2007/04/24/AR2007042400515.html>, accessed 24 January 2010.

Garrett, P. (2005), 'What a language is good for: language socialization, language shift, and the persistence of code-specific genres in St. Lucia'. *Language in Society*, 34, 327–361.

Hurt, B. (2006), *Hip Hop: Beyond Beats and Rhymes*. Northampton, MA: Media Education Foundation.

Kelley, R. (2006), 'Foreword', in D. Basu and S. J. Lemelle (eds), *The Vinyl Ain't Final: Hip Hop and the Globalization of Black Popular Culture*. Ann Arbour, MI: Pluto Books.

**17**

Kitwana, B. (2002), *The Hip Hop Generation: Young Blacks and the Crisis in African American Culture*. New York: Basic Civitas.

Labov, William (1972), *Language in the Inner City: Studies in the Black English Vernacular*. Oxford: Blackwell.

Mercer, Kobena (1994), 'Black hair/style politics', in K. Mercer (ed.), *Welcome to the Jungle: New Positions in Black Cultural Studies*. New York: Routledge, pp. 97–130.

Myers, D. G. (1990), 'Signifying nothing'. *New Criterion*, 8, 61–64.

Newman, M. (2009), '"That's all concept; it's nothing real": reality and lyrical meaning in rap', in H. S. Alim, A. Ibrahim and A. Pennycook (eds), *Global Linguistic Flows: Hip Hop Cultures, Youth Identities, and the Politics of Language*. New York: Routledge, pp. 195–212.

Osumare, H. (2007), *The Africanist Aesthetic in Global Hip Hop: Power Moves*. New York: Palgrave Macmillan.

Pennycook, A. (2007), *Global Englishes and Transcultural Flows*. New York: Routledge.

Samuels, D. (2004), 'The rap on rap: the "Black Music" that isn't either', in M. Forman and M. A. Neal (eds), *That's the Joint: The Hip-Hop Studies Reader*. Routledge: New York, pp. 147–153.

Smitherman, G. (1995), '"If I'm lyin, I'm flyin": the game of insult in Black language', in J. L. Percelay, S. Dweck and M. Ivey (eds), *Double Snaps*. New York: Quill. Reprinted in L. Monaghan and J. E. Goodman (2007, eds) *A Cultural Approach to Interpersonal Communication: Essential Readings*. Oxford: Blackwell, pp. 322–330.

# 1 Multilingualism, Ethnicity and Genre in Germany's Migrant Hip Hop

Jannis Androutsopoulos

## 1 Introduction

Multilingualism is a key issue in the sociolinguistics of hip hop, and multilingual rap lyrics have been examined in a variety of empirical settings across the world. Most researchers focus on the interplay between a country's native – national or vernacular – languages and English, the latter being both the original Hip Hop Nation Language (HHNL) (Alim, 2004) and a global language with varying sociolinguistic status. There is by now sufficient evidence that English is an important resource of transnational hip-hop discourse on a global scale (Androutsopoulos, 2009). However, local differences in the societal status of English – e.g., as 'foreign' language, official language, or de facto *lingua franca* – will also have an impact on – and provide interpretive backdrop for – the ways English is used in hip-hop discourse (see, e.g., Higgins, 2009, on Tanzania; Auzanneau, 2001, on Senegal; Pennycook, 2007, on Japan; Lüdtke, 2007, on Germany). Less attention has been paid to a second dimension of multilingual hip hop, i.e., the use of minority and migrant or 'community' languages. In Germany, the setting of this paper, recognized minority languages include Sorbian and Romani, while migrant languages are much more numerous, including Turkish, Italian, Greek, Russian and so on.

Young people of migrant descent have been an important force in the development of German hip hop in the last 20 years or so, and issues of ethnicity and migration are common topics of German rap discourse, reflecting the diverse ethnolinguistic background of parts of the German hip-hop scene (Güngör and Loh, 2002). Against that backdrop, the first question of this chapter is whether, to what extent, and how rappers of migrant background use migrant languages as a resource for their lyrics. The analysis, based on a sample of record releases reaching from the early 1990s to the mid 2000s, aims to offer insights into a lesser-studied constellation of linguistic diversity in hip hop, thereby complementing the main type of hip-hop multilingualism studied so far, i.e., the inter-play of national language(s) and English.

A second question addressed in this chapter concerns the study of multilingualism in rap lyrics generally. The relevant background to this question is the relation of multilingual lyrics to everyday multilingualism. More specifically, I argue against the assumption that multilingualism in rap lyrics reflects everyday multilingual talk – an assumption favoured by hip hop's language ideology, which views rap as capital-izing on 'authentic' vernacular speech (e.g., Potter, 1995), and explicitly expressed by some researchers and practitioners alike (see, e.g., Sarkar and Allen, 2007).[1] This is not to say that there is no relation between lyrics and conversational speech, but rather to question a simplistic equation between the two. I follow Bentahila and Davies who, in a study of Algerian/French *Rai* music lyrics, identify two main differ-ences between lyrics and conversational speech: audience and planning (2002, pp. 192–193). With regard to the latter, song lyrics may originate in spontaneous improvisation, but they subsequently go through sev-eral stages of editing, in which artists use literacy to optimize the rhyme and other formal properties of their lyrics and to tailor them to rhythmic constraints, thereby taking into account genre conventions and audience expectations. The final outcome of this process (i.e., the lyrics heard in a recording) may well incorporate traces of conversational and vernacular style, but its conditions of production distinguish it from spontaneous discourse. I therefore agree with Bentahila and Davies's suggestion that it would be problematic to use lyrics, or poetry, as evidence for code-switching patterns in a community.

Moreover, while everyday multilingual practices are usually set in private and informal situations, rap lyrics – at least on stage and in releases – are addressed to large and heterogeneous audiences, i.e., constitute public discourse. Language style in lyrics needs therefore to be studied as an outcome of strategic styling decisions within specific social and historical contexts. Bentahila and Davies (2002) found that *rai* recordings from the 1980s are rich in an 'insertion style' with fre-quent incorporation of French nouns and clauses in an Arabic matrix, which bears close resemblance to code mixing in urban Algerian com-munities. But in later productions the languages are more separated, their distribution bearing a 'more systematic relationship to the struc-ture of the song' (Bentahila and Davies, 2002, p. 202). This shift does not reflect language change on the part of the artists, but is rather moti-vated by a shift in their target audiences: as Algerian *Rai* music became more popular in France, artists and producers emphasized the use of French in the titles and refrains of their songs, hoping to increase their chances of exposure to a French audience. In such a case, a structural approach to code-switching is clearly not appropriate for the description of multilingualism in popular music. As Sarkar and Winer argue,

> code-switching in song lyrics is a very different phenomenon from code-switching in conversation, as it is neither spontaneous, nor is it intimate. . . . When code-switching moves into the arena of public discourse, discourse intended for large audiences of strangers and carefully pre-written at that, it requires a different approach to analysis. (Sarkar and Winer, 2006, p. 178)

In exploring such a 'different approach to analysis', this chapter engages with multilingualism in an inclusive sense, i.e., encompassing all discourse strategies involving the selection and distribution of two or more languages in song lyrics. Taking up the suggestion to examine 'the distribution of the switches' in relation to 'the structure of the song' (Benthalia and Davies, 2002, p. 202), I ask how the generic organization of a rap song may constrain language choices and shape their discursive meaning.

The structure of the chapter is as follows: The next section offers background on Germany's migrant hip hop. Rappers of migrant background have used hip hop as a means to express discourses of migration and ethnicity, thereby mobilizing immigrant languages, albeit in historically different patterns. Using concepts from multilingualism research, I then clarify the distinction between the base language and embedded languages in a song as well as the notion of symbolic language use. Following that, I discuss the organization of multilingualism in German migrant rap, outlining how the use of migrant languages is constrained by the typical generic structure of a song. I suggest that language choices tend to coincide with genre boundaries (e.g., between intro, stanzas, refrain and the like) and discuss some attested instances of code-switching and mixing within stanzas, to which I attribute an indexical, rather than symbolic, effect. In the concluding discussion, I develop an explanation of these patterns in terms of audience and market orientations, suggesting that a symbolic use of migrant languages allows artists to make ethnicity claims while targeting a mainstream, monolingual audience. I also discuss differences between the German case and the hip-hop discourse of other countries. Overall, the chapter aims at demonstrating that multilingualism in rap lyrics is a complex discourse process that cannot be properly understood without taking generic and institutional factors into account.

## 2 Migration and ethnicity in German hip hop

As elsewhere in Europe (and beyond), young people with a migrant background have been instrumental in the appropriation of hip hop in

Germany and the development of 'local' hip-hop discourses, in which ethnicity and migration constitute important topics from the very beginning. Both concepts are used here from an 'emic' perspective, drawing in particular on participants' own artistic discourse. In other words, assessing which artists and releases shall count as 'migrant' or 'ethnic' is based on discourse rather than demographics as such. The crucial point is an artist's explicit self-identification with an ethnic group (e.g., as 'German-Turkish', 'Sicilian', 'Afro-German') and their engagement with issues of ethnicity and migration. In that sense, 'migrant hip hop' is a cover term for narratives of migration and ethnicity, including the migration experience; testimonies of discrimination, exclusion and racist aggression in Germany; the pride and burden of ethnic heritage; the tension between dominant society and the ethnic group; and the search for new spaces or identity. Note, however, that hip-hop lyrics are fundamentally polythematic, and we shouldn't expect these topics to be addressed to the exclusion of others in a group's discourse.

Following Güngör and Loh (2002), Germany's migrant hip hop can be divided into three stages: Phase I: late 1980s and early 1990s, Phase II: mid to late 1990s, and Phase III: post 2000. The emergence of migrant hip hop in Germany dates back to the aftermath of German unification. It coincided with an increase in xenophobic discourse and a wave of assaults against migrants and asylum seekers. Migrant rap artists reacted against racist aggression and appropriated the tradition of protest or message rap to articulate their voices and viewpoints. The classic song 'Fremd im eigenen Land' ('A foreigner in your own country') by Advanced Chemistry epitomizes this movement. In the following years, some migrant rappers, especially of Turkish descent, developed a 'reactive nationalism' (Greve and Kaya, 2004) by aggressively affirming their ethnic identity and pride and calling to counter-aggression against neo-Nazis and even 'Germans' in general. The mid 1990s also saw artists exploring new symbolic resources in music and language: Rappers experimented with samples of arabesque/oriental music, giving rise to the marketing label *oriental hip hop*. And while German was the predominant language in the early years, this second phase witnesses a turn to migrant languages – sometimes exclusively in Turkish throughout a record, sometimes in several languages in the same record or song.[2] Characteristically, the mid 1990s have been termed the *linguistic Babylon* of German hip hop (Güngör and Loh, 2002).[3]

Since the turn of the century the German hip-hop market diversified increasingly, and rappers of migrant origin became successful on the mainstream as well as in niche and underground markets. However, migration and ethnicity were not always prominent among their chosen topics. Different trends need to be distinguished in this third phase. One of them is Brothers Keepers, a collaboration of Afro-German and international artists who came together after a series of racist assaults in 2000. Their music centres on issues of racism, discrimination and Afro-German identity. A second focal point is the Berlin rap scene, widely identified as battle or hardcore rap, featuring successful artists of migrant background such as Kool Savas, Eko Fresh and Bushido. These do not conceal their migrant origin, but do not turn it into a centre-point of their discourse either. In their non-political stance, localness (i.e., being a Berliner) seems a more valued identification than ethnic heritage.[4] They do, however, address issues such as the social exclusion of migrant youth, upward mobility, and achievement of status in the host society; Eko Fresh for instance raps about 'making dreams come true' and calls himself 'the German dream'. On the other hand, this phase witnessed successful rappers of migrant background – including Savas and especially Fler – appropriating Nazi metaphors and refer-ences, stirring controversy among critics and educators (see Putnam and Littlejohn, 2007, this volume).

## 3 Data and analysis

All three phases of migrant rap – the protest rap of the early years, the 'oriental hip hop of the 1990s' and the more recent wave of battle/hardcore rap – encompass bilingual and multilingual songs, albeit in different linguistic patterns. The analysis is based on a small sample of 15 CD releases (corresponding to approximately 220 songs) from all three phases of ethnic rap in Germany. This sample is not statistically repre-sentative, but it does include well-known migrant-background artists and releases and may therefore be regarded as qualitatively valid.[5]

My analysis makes use of concepts and categories familiar from soci-olinguistics and multilingualism research, drawing both on structural and especially conversational approaches to code-switching (Auer, 1998).[6] In general terms, each release was examined with respect to the amount of migrant languages used and their distribution across tracks. Based on the generic scheme discussed below, each track was examined with respect to the distribution of languages, patterns of juxtaposition in the lyrics, the semantics and pragmatics of minority language use, and resemblance to typical discourse functions of code-switching.

Two concepts with some relevance to my analysis are the notion of 'base language' and the 'symbolic function of language choice'. The notion of base language is usually applied to bilingual interaction (Auer, 2000) and transferred here to the song or the release as units of analysis. Identifying the base language of a song or release provides a background against which switches into other, locally minor codes can be interpreted. By and large, German is the base language of the rap songs in my data, with migrant languages switched into for shorter or longer portions of certain tracks. However, not all rap songs have a single base language. Some bilingual songs or even entire releases are characterized by a balanced distribution between two (or more) languages.

Assuming that understanding the lyrics of a rap song is important to hip-hop audiences, we may say that the base language of a rap song defines its primary audience. This might seem trivial for global languages such as English, but when it comes to the migrant languages of this study, the choice of a base language has obvious consequences: A rap song with, say, Turkish as the base language effectively restricts its main audience, as far as understanding the lyrics is concerned, to L1 or L2 speakers of Turkish.

But linguistic choices in music are relevant not only in terms of propositional content, but also with regard to the mere presence of a language. The notion of 'language as a symbol' is familiar from the sociology of language (Fishman, 1991), minority language policy (ÓReilly, 2003), and the semiotics of Roland Barthes (1967). In Barthes's terms, it implies that a language as a whole is understood as a signifier to which a new signified (in Barthes's terms, a 'connotation') is attached. A language comes to symbolize (to stand for) its speakers or the country in which it is spoken. In advertising, an arena where the notion of symbolic language choice has been repeatedly used (Piller, 2001; Cheshire and Moser, 1994), 'foreign' languages are interpreted as transferring positive attributes of their countries and/or people to the advertised product, while product 'facts' are conveyed in the majority/native language of the target audience. As researchers of advertising and popular music have argued, the symbolic meaning of language choice is understood even if audiences are oblivious to its communicative dimension, i.e., what is actually being said in that language (Bennett, 1999; Cheshire and Moser, 1994). In hip-hop scholarship, Bennett (1999) makes a telling observation to this effect:

> While working as a youth worker in Frankfurt, I was invited to sit on the judging panel of a talent competition for local bands in the neighbouring town of Schwalbach. As well as those bands taking part in the competition, a number of other local groups had been booked to provide entertainment . . ., including a Turkish rap group. Prior to the group's performance an incident occurred in which some of the young Turkish people who had come specially to see the group began hurling eggs . . . at a white group performing 'Deutsch-rock' (rock music with German lyrics). The Deutsch-rock group's performance had to be temporarily interrupted. . . . When

**24**

> the group returned to the stage their singer attempted to quell the situation by assuring the audience that, although the songs performed were in German, their lyrics were not racist and should not be regarded as such. Nevertheless, the Turkish youth remaining in the hall continued to act in a hostile fashion and accused the group of being Nazis. (Bennett, 1999, p. 85)

The notions of base and symbolic language choice offer an analytic angle on the use of migrant languages in rap lyrics. When these are non-base and their comprehension cannot be guaranteed, their meaning is sought not in their propositional content but in their function as a symbol of their groups of speakers. I identify three diagnostic features of symbolic language choice: amount, content and generic distribution.

1. Amount: the symbolic language is not the base language of a song/ release; its overall amount within that song/release is often quite limited. Even if a language is the base language of a particular song, it may be cast as symbolic on a larger scale, i.e., within the release as a whole;
2. Content: the propositional content conveyed by the symbolic language will typically refer to aspects of the respective ethnicity or minority group. In other words, there is a fit of form (minority language choice) and content (minority identity/culture). The precise content conveyed by the symbolic language, and the context in which it is embedded, will of course vary. For example, symbolic languages may be used to express the speaker's self-presentation as member of an ethnic group, or cultural key-words, or cultural resources; they may be embedded in narratives about the home country or the ethnic group in Germany or a critique of the ethnic group's lifestyle; etc.
3. Distribution: symbolic language choices tend to occur in particular parts of a rap song, as will be examined in detail below.

Many instances of migrant language use in my data exhibit these three features, which co-occur and yield distinctive patterns of multilingual lyrics.

## 4 Language choices and the generic organization of rap songs

I now move to the placement of migrant languages within a song. Figure 1.1 represents the parts of a record release and a song where migrant languages can be allocated in my data. Its mother node, the record release, is the largest unit of analysis. The left branch represents

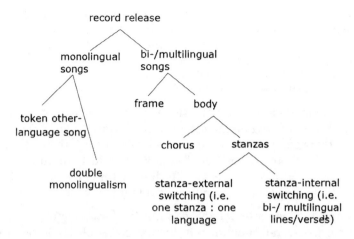

**Figure 1.1** Language choices and generic organization of rap songs

the juxtaposition of songs in different languages within a release. The right branch focuses on a bi- or multilingual song as a unit of analysis, including code-switching from the song's brackets to within a stanza.

It seems important to emphasize that this scheme does *not* suggest that artists actually decide about the distribution of languages in such a top-down fashion. What it does suggest is that choices of and switches between languages may take place on different levels of generic organization, ranging from the macro-textual level of an entire release to the micro-level of juxtaposing codes within a stanza. It also suggests that the shape of multilingualism in lyrics is constrained by genre: code-switches tend to coincide with boundaries between distinct parts of a rap song. In my data, for instance, switches between chorus and stanza or between stanzas are much more common than switching and mixing within a stanza. As a result, genre structure provides an orientation to the production as well as interpretation of multilingual lyrics.

At most levels of this scheme, languages appear in a compartmentalized way. A song may contain two, three or even four languages, but these remain neatly separated from one another. Code-switching in a narrow sense – here classically defined as *the use of two or more languages by the same speaker within the same turn/utterance* – is restricted to the bottom right of the scheme, i.e., within a stanza. However, 'stanza-internal code-switching' is rare as far as migrant languages are concerned, as opposed to English/German switching and mixing which is far more common.

I now move through this diagram, illustrating its elements with examples from all three phases of Germany's migrant rap. The left branch of the diagram represents record releases that contain monolingual songs in two or more languages; for example, the Berlin-produced *Fettfleck Sampler Volume One* consists of songs in German, Turkish and English. In some cases, there is just a single song in a language other than the base language of a release, and in my data this coincides with one migrant-language song on a German-language release. This 'token other-language song' repeatedly turns out to be an emblem of, and tribute to, the artist's ethnic origin. For example, the album *Der beste Tag meines Lebens* ('The Best Day of my Life') by Kool Savas (2002) features two skits with Turkish female voices from (as emerges through additional clues in the booklet) his mother and granny. Because these are only skits (of a duration of 1.00–1.30 min.), they establish Turkish-language niches within the German-language release.

The right branch of the diagram turns to bi- or multilingual songs and identifies potential locations of language choice and code-switching. The first one, in a sequential and narrative sense, is the song's bracket, i.e., the short sequences at the beginning and the end of the song. The notion of bracketing comes from Goffman who defines it as a process by which social activity 'is often marked off from the ongoing flow of surrounding events by a special set of boundary markers or brackets of a conventionalized kind'; he distinguishes 'opening and closing temporal brackets' (Goffman, 1986, pp. 251–252). In interactional socio-linguistics and discourse analysis, bracketing and the related notion of framing have been used in the study of bilingualism in the media, notably in ethnic newspapers, web guestbook messages and emails (see overview in Androutsopoulos, 2007). Hinrichs found Jamaican Creole appearing in the introductory and concluding greetings, terms of address and farewells of emails and web forum posts in English. Bracketing is rich in pragmatic and social meaning. Its constituents contextualize the enclosed discourse and frame the relationship between the partners in an interaction.

In rap, brackets typically draw on all sorts of audio material (e.g., street noises, media bits, casual conversation among artists, directly addressing the audience, ritual statements of time and place, etc.) and are intertextually (and indexically) related to the song content; for example, brackets may provide a stimulus to which the subsequent lyrics react, or they may offer cues for the interpretation of the lyrics (Androutsopoulos, 2007). Using another language for bracketing makes that language (and the ethnicity indexed by it) relevant to the topic discussed or the social identities performed in the song. In my data, the 2004 track 'Brandlöcher im Jersey' by Eko and Azra illustrates the distribution of Turkish and German to the brackets as opposed to other parts of the song. It features two friends smoking and talking in Turkish, while the song itself is about being overworked and 'falling asleep with the joint in one's hand'. Here the bracket stages the social setting that is being narrated in the song, and this setting is presented, by means of language choice, as a Turkish one. (The song itself is in German and Turkish, following the *one speaker/one stanza/one language* principle to be outlined below). Another example from the early phase of Germany's migrant hip hop is 'Telefonterror' by Freundeskreis (1996). The song is in German, but the opening bracket comes in the voice of a Jamaican sound-system DJ who introduces the song story in a Jamaican Creole English voice ('This is the story of a girl named Sue / she don't know what to do / fell in love with the MC, Maximi'). This prelude defines the identities of the song's characters and pre-empts the music style of that particular song. In another study, Kluge (2007) discusses an example from Argentinean hip hop: The frame is a sample of a 'welcome on board' statement, in Italian, on a flight to Rome and signifies the Italian origin of the band members. Another album by Kool Savas, from 2004, *Die Besten Tage Sind Gezählt* ('The Best Days are Counted') features skits and brackets which stage stereotypes of the hip hop world: the greedy club owner, the dumb fan, etc. Significantly, these voices speak the kind of stylized immigrant German one encounters in Berlin's multi-ethnic neighbourhoods and are thereby positioned as distant from the rapper and his own speech style. Thus skits and brackets do important indexical work, albeit not in full-blown songs but rather as 'side-dishes' that will be noticed but never receive popular attention on their own.

Moving on to the body of a song, a first pattern of code-switching is between chorus and stanza, in that the chorus is cast in a different language than the stanza that precedes or follows it (see examples 1 and 4 below). The discourse meaning of such code-switching draws on the conventional function of the refrain, which is meant to be the most memorable part of a song, summarizing its message. Having the refrain in a different melody and/or voice than the stanzas is part of wider pop music conventions. The chorus entails a pragmatic contrast to the stanza, and code-switching may enhance that contrast. Code-switching into English for the chorus is quite common in German rap, whereas the use of other languages depends on artist and topic. In the following 1997 track (from the 'oriental hip hop' phase), Turkish-German artist Aziza A. appropriates (what sounds like) a line from a traditional Turkish song as the chorus of her own song, which criticizes traditional gender roles in Turkish society.

(1) **Chorus**    *Daracik, Daracik sokaklar*    **'Narrow, narrow alleys where**
            *kizlar misket yuvarlar*            **girls are playing marbles'**

Stanza 1

1.      *Ich habe braune Augen,*          'My eyes are brown, my hair
        *habe schwarzes Haar*             is black

2.      *Und komm aus einem Land*         And I come from a land where
        *wo der Mann über der Frau*       man stands above woman
        *steht*

3.      *Und dort nicht wie hier ein*     Where no different wind is
        *ganz anderer Wind weht*          blowing, unlike here

4.      *In den zwei Kulturen, in*        In the two cultures I have
        *denen ich aufgewachsen bin,*     grown up in

5.      *Ziehen meine lieben*             My dear sisters are mostly on
        *Schwestern meist den*            the loser side
        *kürzeren*

6.      *Weil nicht nur die zwei*         Because not only do these
        *Kulturen aufeinander*            cultures collide
        *krachen*

7.      *Weil auch Väter über ihre*       But also because fathers are
        *Töchter wachen*                  watching over their daughters'

        . . .                             . . .

12.     *Du überlegst: ist es meine*      You are now reflecting: Is it
        *Pflicht*                         my plight

13.     *Das Leben meiner Eltern so zu*   To live my parents' life just as
        *leben, wie sie es bestreben?*    they want to?

14.     *Mit Autorität mir meinen*        To seal up my mouth with
        *Mund zu kleben?*                 authority?'

**Chorus**    *Daracik, Daracik sokaklar*    **'Narrow, narrow alleys where**
          *kizlar misket yuvarlar*            **girls are playing marbles'**

                                         Aziza A., 'Es ist Zeit'

Here, the Turkish chorus works interpretively on two levels. To those
who are competent in Turkish, the chorus may provide an additional
resource for meaning making (perhaps evoking intertextuality and asso-
ciative links between stanza and chorus). Those who are not competent
in Turkish will still interpret the chorus – based on knowledge of its
generic relationship to the stanza lyrics – as a symbol for one of the two
cultures the song is about. Another example of chorus-related code-
switching, again from the early phase, is 'Esperanto' by Freundeskreis,

a song about international friendship and understanding, with stanzas in German (and some Esperanto) and chorus in French and German. However, chorus-related code-switching may also work the other way around: My data includes the now defunct group Diaspora that was German-based but whose lyrics were predominantly in French. Their song 'Fuck Rassismus' used French for the stanzas and German for the chorus. The base language of that song is therefore French, even though it targets a German-speaking audience. Here it is the condensed message to the wider audience that is cast in the main language of that audience, the 'details' in the stanzas being in the rappers' native language.

Rap songs typically consist of two or more stanzas – defined as groups of (usually 8 or 16) verses typically delimited by the chorus – and these may well be cast in a different language each. This pattern of 'stanza external code-switching' affects by definition the communicative dimension of language use in lyrics, because a part of the lyrics will be incomprehensible to monolingual audiences. It is therefore common practice to find translations of non-German segments in the booklet or on the internet.

There are two sub-types of stanza-external code-switching in my data, depending on whether there is a change of speaker or not. The first (and by far most common) case is what I term the one speaker/one stanza/one language principle: songs delivered by two or more rappers, with each rapper delivering a stanza in their preferred language. The pattern occurs with multiethnic crews (such as Microphone Mafia from the 'oriental hip hop' phase), international co-operations (such as Brothers Keepers), or local collaborations among rappers of migrant background (e.g., Berlin-based, Turkish-background Eko Fresh and Frankfurt-based, Kurdish-background Azra). In code-switching terminology, these are instances of participant-related code-switching (Auer, 1998). This pattern is illustrated in example 2.

(2) Intro

| | | |
|---|---|---|
| Torch: | *Torchmann – es Africanos* | 'Torchmann – the Africans |
| | *Sékou – the ambassador, yeah* | Sékou – the ambassador, yeah' |
| Chorus | | |
| Sékou: | Three kings with the gifts we bring | 'Three kings with the gifts we bring |
| Torch: | *Wir benutzen unsere Zungen wie Schwerterklingen* | We use our tongues like sword-sounds |

| Blaise: | *Triple rois, triple foi, avale la polodringue* | Three kings, triple faith, swallow the ((unclear)) |
| Torch: | *Alle Feinde erstarren wenn unsere Stimmen erklingen* | All enemies freeze when our voices sound out.' |

Stanza 1

| Blaise: | *Cette révolution est plus que lyrics Nègre* | 'This revolution is more than Black words |
| | *Fier, les 144 là haut qu'ils aillent s'le mettre* | Proud, the 144 up there, |
| | *Kobo (noir) mixe le lait* | Kobo (black) mixes the milk |
| | *Dans le café s'il faut* | In the coffee/café, if he has to |
| | *Lynché au barbelé* | Lynched with barbed wire |
| | *La différence mais vraie ou faux?* | But is the difference true or false?' |

Brothers Keepers, 'Triple Rois'

This is a 2001 trilingual song that defies an easy identification of a single base language. Rather, it is designed in such a way that its multilingualism reflects the different origins and languages of the three collaborators, each of whom uses his 'own' language in the chorus as well as in his own dedicated stanza: Torch raps in German, Sekou in English, and Blaise in French. The only exception is the part by Torch (who is, so to speak, the host, since this is a German release) in the intro, where he uses English to introduce Sékou in his language (again, a participant-related code-switch) and Portuguese for the phrase *es africanos* ('the Africans'). This is the only instance of Portuguese in this song, going to show that linguistic choices in a song's bracket may well transgress the song's regular language choices. In this example, the meaning of code-switching is enforced by topical coherence: each rapper narrates a different take of the same story, i.e., the fate of African diaspora and pride in African ancestry. Multilingualism underscores that what is being narrated represents a collective experience that transcends linguistic borders.

The second subtype of stanza-external code-switching is Bakhtinian double-voicing in the delivery of the same speaker across two or more stanzas. This time code-switching coincides with a shift of voice, which is also a shift in narrative perspective. Example 3 is a 1993 classic from the early days of German migrant rap and fits well that era's main theme of protest against discrimination.

**31**

(3) End of Stanza 1

| | |
|---|---|
| 1. *Gestern ich komm von Arbeit, ich sitzen in der Bahn* | 'Yesterday I come from work I sit in the tram |
| 2. *Da kommt ein besoffen Mann und setzt sich nebenan* | There comes a drunken man and sits next to me |
| 3. *Der Mann sagt: Uff, du Knoblauch stinken* | The man says: Uh, you stink of garlic |
| 4. *Ich sage: Ach egal, du stinken von Trinken* | I said: oh whatever, you stink from drinking' |

Begin Stanza 2

| | |
|---|---|
| 5. *Nun den Spaß beiseite, hör gut zu, was ich meine* | 'Now joking aside, listen closely to what I'm saying |
| 6. *Lass uns Jeden Jeder sein lass Jedem doch das Seine* | Let's leave everyone as they are, each to his own |
| 7. *Ich kann das gut verstehen, wir haben andere Sitten* | I can surely understand, we have different customs |
| 8. *Ich weiß du magst das nicht ich möchte dich doch bitten . . .* | I know you don't like it but I want to ask you . . .' |

Fresh Familee, 'Ahmed Gündüz'

Here, the first stanza (of which only the last lines are reproduced here) comes in the voice of 'Ahmed', a stylized Turkish *Gastarbeiter*, and is cast in stylized interlanguage German. Besides a heavy non-native accent, these lines include morphosyntactic features such as violation of the verb-second word order in German (as in line 1), bare infinitives, omission of articles, prepositions and adjective inflections. The second stanza, by the same rapper, shifts to the rapper's own narrative voice in native colloquial German. The shift, enforced by a shift in beat and background instrumentation, is also obvious in the stanza's indexical grounding: while the first comes from the perspective of the immigrant character and encompasses a fictitious dialogue, the second features the rapper addressing the German audience. In Bakhtinian terms (as elaborated by Rampton, 1998 in his analysis of language crossing), this is an instance of unidirectional double-voicing, the speaker sympathizing with the staged voice and its concerns.

Language alternations within a stanza may come from different rappers or from the same rapper. In the first case (already illustrated in example 2 for the chorus) two or more rappers alternate or overlap, each in their preferred language. At the end of the song 'Brandlöcher im

Jersey' by Eko and Azra (2004), Azra keeps repeating *dunya dunyor* ('the world is turning round') in Turkish, while Eko raps on in German and English.

Stanza-internal code-switching by the same rapper is quite rare in my data, and I shall discuss this in more detail below. Using classic distinctions in code-switching analysis, we may first note a few cases of inter-sentential stanza-internal switching, as illustrated by the next two examples. In example 4 from 1998, stanza-internal code-switching is motivated by a shift in topic. A reference to Istanbul (line 5) triggers a four-liner in Turkish which keeps with the song's topic and gives it an ethnic take. This is the only instance of Turkish in this song; note that the chorus is in English, showing how different linguistic choices may apply to different parts of a song.

(4) Stanza 3

| | | |
|---|---|---|
| 1. | *ich rock die Party heut Nacht* | 'I rock the party tonight |
| 2. | *alles ist erlaubt was Spaß macht* | everything's permitted as long as it's fun |
| 3. | *frag nicht nach, sondern mach das was du willst* | don't ask, but just do what you want |
| 4. | *jeder ist bereit, keinen interessiert die Zeit* | everyone's ready, no one cares about time |
| 5. | *von Frankfurt bis nach Istanbul* | from Frankfurt to Istanbul |
| 6. | **hadi sende birisini bul** | **find yourself someone** |
| 7. | **bütün eller havaya** | **throw your arms in the air** |
| 8. | **herkes çıksın oynamaya** | **everybody get up and dance** |
| 9. | **bir sağ kalça bir sağ kalça** | **move your hips to and fro** |
| 10. | **çalkala güzelim çalkala** | **move, my beauty, move'** |

Chorus

'we like to party all night long' (3x)    'we like to party all night long' (3x)

Volkan, 'Funkfurt'

In other cases, the parts of a stanza delivered in a language other than German are more formulaic and bear an obvious referential or inter-textual relation to a specific ethnicity. In example 5 (from 1996), Afro-German rapper *Afrob* code-switches in line 4 to cry out *I selassie*, and in line 13 to declare 'I'm black and I'm proud'.

(5) Stanza 2 – Afrob

| | | |
|---|---|---|
| 1. | *Mein Afro ist Symbol für natürliches Wachstum* | 'My afro is a symbol of natural growth |
| 2. | *Nicht nur der Haare auch des geistigen Spektrums* | Not only of the hair, but of spiritual width |
| 3. | *Er ist der Vektor im Schaubild der Gleichung der Gleichheit* | It's the vector in the image of the equation of equality |
| 4. | *Ausdruck afrikanischer Weisheit **I Selassie*** | Expression of African wisdom: **I Selassie** |
| 5. | *Rocke Mikrophone nur für euch nicht für die Industrie* | Rocking microphones just for you not for the industry |
| 6. | *Der Löwe von Judäa Afrob Eriträer* | The Lion of Judea, Afrob from Eritrea |
| 7. | *King Salomon ist mir näher **yeah*** | King Salomon is closer to me **yeah** |
| 8. | *Meine Gedankenwege führen zurück zum Mutterland* | The paths of my thoughts lead me back to the motherland |
| 9. | *Wo Angie Davis kämpfte gegen Mr. Ignorant* | Where Angie Davies fought against Mr. Ignorant |
| 10. | *Ich nehm' ein Buch zur Hand und seh' nur Sand und Wüste* | I take a book in my hand, all I see is sand and desert |
| 11. | *Der weite Kontinent der für die weiße Herrschaft büsste* | The wide continent that had to pay for White domination |
| 12. | *Ruht in Frieden meine Helden weil die Welt nichts taugt* | Rest in peace my heroes the world is no good |
| 13. | *Doch euer Geist brennt immer noch **I'm black and proud*** | But your spirit is still burning **I'm black and proud'** |

Freundeskreis, 'Overseas/Übersee'

Both switches showcase ethnic/religious identity, as they intertextually connect the lyrics to the social/religious movements they index. The first originates in Ge'ez/Amharic, but is most commonly associated with the Rastafarian movement and its discourse. The second is, of course, English, but I would argue that the aspect of English at stake here is not as 'language of hip hop' but as the code of global African diaspora, of which Afrob counts himself as one. Here, as in other examples, we see how symbolic language choices may come restricted to just a few lexical items, which are linked, referentially, metonymically or intertextually, to a specific ethnic group.

However, example 5 also illustrates a different pattern of code-switching in rap lyrics: The discourse marker *yeah*, in line 7, is fairly typical of the kind of formulaic English code-switching frequently used by German rappers, even when German is their base language (see Androutsopoulos, 2009; Lüdtke, 2007). Such usage has wider currency in my data, as illustrated by examples 6 and 7, which include interjections, terms of address, or terms of abuse from migrant languages.[7]

In example 6 – a 1999 battle rap from the beginning of the third phase – we see a pattern of hip-hop multilingualism that is also described by Sarkar and Winer (2006) for Montreal rap: insertions from different languages are used as a resource to enhance rhyme, with lexical items from various sources being used precisely at the rhyming points in a verse (in example 6: Turkish: *Lan*/German: *Ballermann*, French: *Chassis*/German: *Haschisch*/Turkish: *Bakschisch*/German: *Spastis*).

(6) Stanza 3 – Scope

| | | |
|---|---|---|
| 1. | *Ich burn mit allen Sorten von Worten* | 'I'm burning with all sorts of words |
| 2. | *Dir fehlen die Eier im Sack also sauf mehr Verporten* | You're lacking eggs [i.e., balls] so booze more *Verporten* |
| 3. | *Ey fuck PC, ich kack auf Crews die Ärsche lecken* | Hey fuck PC, I shit on bootlicker crews |
| 4. | *STF kommt Ärsche tretend wie Tekken* | STF comes kicking ass like Tekken |
| 5. | *Auf Mixkasetten und in Plattenläden in allen Städten, **Lan*** | On mixtapes and in record stores in every city, **Lan** [Turkish: 'dude'] |
| 6. | *Wir und Savas gehören Zusammen wie Alk und Ballermann* | We and Savas go together like booze and party animals |
| 7. | *Drei Bass-Asis burnen massig Bass-Chassis wie Kiffer Haschisch* | Three bass freaks burning massive bass chassis like stoners hashish |
| 8. | *Also gebt uns **Bakschisch** ihr Spastis und quatscht nicht* | So give us **Baksheesh** [Turkish: 'bribe money'] you spastics and don't gab |
| 9. | *Ich hab Rap im Repetoire und tausend Gimmicks* | I've got rap in my repertoire and a thousand gimmicks |
| 10. | *Hi Mädels, ich laß die Zunge spielen wie Gene Simmons* | Hi girls, I let my tongue play like Gene Simmons' |
| | | STF feat/Kool Savas, 'Ihr müsst noch üben' |

**35**

In example 7 – from a Greek-Turkish collaboration project between Kool Savas and Illmatic – most Greek lexis in the first stanza is metonymic to Greek ethnicity. Note how a humorous effect is presumably aimed at through the juxtaposition of stereotypical Greek food/customs and hip-hop slang, indexing widely diverging social domains and lifestyles. The Greek discourse markers (interjection in line 6, term of abuse in line 8) index a mixed speech style. In the chorus, both country names come in their respective language, and the appeal to unite the two comes in English. The song also features an intermezzo in Greek (again talking about ethnicity and solidarity among migrants).

(7)  Stanza 1 – Illmatic

1. *dieser Vers ist für die Griechen, alle Griechen in Deutschland* — this verse is for the Greeks, all Greeks in Germany

2. *I-L-L ist ein Grieche in Deutschland* — I-L-L- is a Greek in Germany

3. *getrieben von Zeus' Hand und Held wie Odysseus* — driven by Zeus's hand, a hero like Ulysses

   . . .                                     . . .

6. *ich rechne meine Rhymes aus wie Archimedes* — I'm calculating my rhymes like Archimedes

7. *was das geht nicht.. Ich tanz **Syrtaki** du Bitch* — what, it' don't go, I'm dancing **syrtaki**, you bitch

8. *und mach dich zum **Saganaki** du Bitch . . . **opa!*** — turning you to **saganaki**, you bitch – **opa!**

9. *dein Rhyme ist zu weak Bro, meins ist **Pastizio*** — your rhyme is too weak bro, mine is **pastizzio**

10. *du flowst in meinem Crew Sau, **aide jamisu*** — You flow in my crew, pig, **aide jamisu**

11. *ich weiss das ist krass Alter, ich hustle weiter* — I know that's gross, mate, I keep on hustling

12. *die Heimat ist so weit und ich bin Gastarbeiter* — homeland is so far away and I'm a guest worker

Chorus

*Kopf hoch **Hellas**, Kopf hoch **Türkiye*** — Cheer up, **Hellas**, cheer up, **Türkiye**

*Wir teilen das gleiche Schicksal fern ab der Sonne des Südens* — We have a common fate away from the south sun

| | |
|---|---|
| *Vereint als Brüder in* | Together like brothers in |
| *Deutschland gebt euch die* | Germany, join hands |
| *Hand* | |
| *Umarmt euch und lebt* | Hug each other and live |
| *gemeinsam –* **united is one** | together – **united is one** |

Freunde der Sonne, 'Hellas
Türkiye'

The stanza-internal insertion of migrant language discourse markers that is illustrated in examples 6 and 7 is qualitatively different from the patterns identified at higher nodes of the generic diagram (see Fig. 1.1). It goes beyond the straightforward ethnic symbolism that predominates in the remainder of the data; rather, it indexes a speech style that is associated with speakers of migrant background in Germany. Significantly, this pattern is popular with younger rappers of the third phase associated with battle/hardcore rap, suggesting it represents a more recent development in German migrant rap. As a whole, however, intra-sentential switching/language mixing is rare in my data, and the only song in which I found it in abundance, i.e., example 7, is in a jocular key.

## 5 Discussion and conclusions

The analysis demonstrates that multilingualism in German rap lyrics is a complex mobilization of linguistic resources that goes beyond code-switching in a narrow sense. The rap lyrics examined involve choices and juxtapositions of languages on several levels of discourse organization. Lyrics in a migrant language are often restricted to a single generic part, notably the intro or chorus; in other cases, a release contains different patterns of language choice and code-switching: there is a 'token other-language song', while Turkish discourse markers occur in another song, and so on. In still other cases, a song features different linguistic choices for a number of its parts, resulting in a complex distribution of languages.[8] Despite the overall predominance of German, then, trilingual songs involving German, English and a migrant language are not uncommon, and the scheme introduced in this chapter helps us to understand their linguistic arrangement.

On the other hand, differences between artists and phases notwithstanding, migrant languages tend to concentrate on 'higher' nodes of the generic diagram. We noted a wealth of migrant language bracketing, as opposed to a scarcity of stanza-internal code-switching. German and migrant languages remain neatly separated in most of these songs, and switches to the latter tend to coincide with shifts between generic elements. This pattern stands in stark contrast to research findings on the speech of second and third generation migrant-background youth in Germany, in which switching and mixing prevail (Hinnenkamp, 2003; Kallmeyer and Keim, 2003). This is evidence against a simple equation of rap with conversational speech, at least with regard to migration-induced language contact.[9] An explanation of these rap lyrics as reflecting intergenerational language shift would be flawed. However, the absence of stanza-internal code-switching and language mixing between German and migrant languages in the data does not reflect a closure against multilingualism in the lyrics of these artists or in German rap generally. Quite the contrary, the same artists who work so sparingly with migrant languages are freely mixing English nonce borrowings and phrases in their German lyrics. This suggests that migrant languages have a different status from, and less value than, English in the pop music domain.

However, the picture is actually more complex, because some migrant rap in Germany does feature migrant languages as predominant codes of a song or release, i.e., as lyrical base languages. The 1990s 'oriental hip hop' phase was dominated by Turkish (and to a lesser extent by other languages), and some contemporary productions are bilingual (Turkish/German) or multilingual, selecting languages other than German as main means of expression. This seems to work mainly for Turkish, the language of the largest ethnic group in Germany, since there are no complete other-language productions in other languages.

In order to make sense of these patterns, we need to take into account the stratification of pop music markets and their different kinds of audience. The use of migrant languages documented in this chapter is the outcome of a marketing strategy for cultural commodities addressed to the German-speaking hip-hop market. From that point of view, migrant languages are elements of a 'double-bind' strategy, which combines a *selective foregrounding of ethnic difference* with a *maximization* of a mainstream, non-ethnic audience. This is consonant with the findings of Bentahila and Davies (2002) on the use of French in Algerian *Rai* music, as well as with findings from other sociolinguistic backgrounds (such as Cuba, Argentina, Italy, Hungary; see, e.g., Kluge, 2007; Scholz, 2003a, 2003b; Simeziane, this volume).

The widespread conjunction of form (language choice) and content in the examples suggests that migrant languages are strategically staged as 'we' codes (Gumperz, 1982). Their *raison d'etre* is their flagging of ethnic identities. Such a link is of course not ubiquitous in the everyday discourse of migrant communities, where different codes may serve as 'we' codes depending on context and narrative (Sebba and Wootton, 1998). Rather, it is constructed by migrant artists as a well-motivated part of a audience design recipient design addressed to 'they' code (i.e., majority) speakers. Positioning migrant languages as a minimally present 'we' code conveys a symbolic message that everyone is able to understand. I therefore read the prevailing distribution of migrant language choices in the rap lyrics examined here as an indicator of their mainly symbolic use: their contribution to propositional content is less relevant than their mere presence as ethnic identity symbols. They make ethnolinguistic otherness visible, without impeding the communicative value of lyrics to majority audiences.

Such a positioning seems characteristic for releases targeting the mainstream market, i.e., seeking to maximize their audience by being compatible to different output channels (e.g., 'radio-friendly'). It seems that Germany's mainstream music market will tolerate minority multilingualism only to a symbolic extent. A more extensive (base language-like) use of other languages is accepted only if these languages are globally prestigious codes, hence especially English and to some extent French and Spanish (note that the commercially successful multilingual project, Brothers Keepers, draw on precisely those languages). However, the mainstream market is complemented by niche/underground markets, which cater to smaller target groups and serve tastes that are diverging from the mainstream market. Such niche markets provide more leeway for linguistic experiment and, as a consequence, a predominant use of migrant languages in rap lyrics may persist. In other words, different segments of the popular music market may also be thought of as different linguistic markets. Moreover, the persistence of communicative uses of migrant languages in rap lyrics may be favoured by the orientation to another audience altogether. More precisely, we note that productions that are monolingual in the migrant language may target audiences in the home country. In fact, the most well-known representatives of oriental hip hop, Cartel and Islamic Force, had their commercial success in Turkey rather than Germany. However, this will work for monolingual releases only, since double monolingualism will risk disrupting the home community's monolingual expectations.

The linguistic consequences of this market divide are nicely illustrated by the release practices of German-Turkish rapper Eko Fresh: his commercially successful work is in German (except for the occasional migrant-language 'token song'), but he also does independent productions, in which German and Turkish are used in equal parts, i.e., in which Turkish stands on an equal footing with German.

Finally, it is worth pointing out that what ethnic German rappers do with multilingual resources seems strikingly limited when compared to rap lyrics from many other countries around the world, where stanza-internal code-switching and mixing are widespread (see, e.g., chapters in Alim et al., 2009; Higgins, 2009; Lee, 2004; Sarkar and Winer, 2006; Auzanneau, 2001). In the US, Latino rap artists seem to work with code-switching much more intensively than their German counterparts. A caveat to this comparison is that some of these cases involve English/national language contact, which I explicitly excluded from discussion, even though English is widely used in German rap lyrics, including those by migrant rappers. That said, I suggest that patterns of language contact in rap lyrics tend to index the status of multilingualism in a particular country. In other words, the absence of minority language switching and mixing from the German data indicates its status quo of a dominantly monolingual nation-state. In traditionally and officially monolingual societies such as Germany, minority and migrant artists who decide to use their language tend to prefer the functional compartmentalization and strategic 'we' code positioning of their languages as discussed in this chapter. By contrast, traditionally and officially multilingual societies provide more fertile ground for artists to exploit additional dimensions of language contact and to explore connections between lyrical discourse and everyday talk. However, more research is needed in order to check this hypothesis.

Popular music is an important arena for the public display of bilingual and multilingual practices. Examining rap lyrics contributes to the study of linguistic diversity in the domain of global entertainment discourses. Bentahila and Davies suggest that multilingual lyrics are increasingly accepted by audiences who 'seem more receptive to music using other languages than their counterparts of 20 years ago' (2002, p. 190). The multilingual discursive practices of German rappers, limited as they may be, imply that their audiences are expected to welcome linguistic diversity as an index of an artist's claimed 'authenticity'. However, it may be the case that this increasing acceptance goes hand in hand with a restriction of acceptable linguistic diversity to symbolic language usage. More comparative research is needed here, and I suggest that the generic analysis framework presented in this chapter can facilitate further exploration.

## Acknowledgements

This chapter originates in a paper presented in a panel on 'Multilingualism in hip hop lyrics' at the International Symposium of Bilingualism, 6 June 2007, Hamburg. I am indebted to panel co-organizer Mela Sarkar, to Marina Terkourafi for her editorial support and to two anonymous reviewers.

# Notes

1. But see also Sarkar (2009). According to Sarkar (personal communication), it is possible that the position that *on rap comme on parle* ('we rap as we speak') corresponds more closely to rapper ideology – what the rappers say and believe that they do – rather than practice – which in turn can only be assessed based on close ethnographic analysis of everyday conversational practices, which are likely to be highly localized.
2. This is in striking contrast to what has happened in France, where migrant-background rappers (especially of Maghreb origin) never turned away from the majority language, thus indexing their audience as the majority society as a whole. Verlan (2003) suggests that this is due to the fundamentally different understandings of the notion of citizenship in France and in Germany.
3. However, 'oriental hip hop' was an *etic* term, coined by the music industry, which ethnicized hip-hop artists, downplaying their musical and linguistic differences. Many mid-1990s productions that were marketed as 'oriental hip hop' in fact used many different kinds of samples and did not rap exclusively in Turkish (Güngör and Loh, 2002).
4. As Güngör and Loh (2002) point out, Kool Savas was from the very beginning *not* reduced to his ethnic origin, and indeed he blurred the line between *Deutschrap* and migrant hip hop.
5. An indicative discography is appended to this paper.
6. Although lyrics are not conversational speech (as discussed above), concepts from the study of bilingual interaction direct attention to sequential relations within a song and tie in well with an examination of the voices, i.e., social roles and positions, that are enacted in lyrics.
7. Cf. Turkish: *lan* (ex. 6), Greek: *opa* and *aide jamisou* ('fuck off'; ex. 7), and, in other lyrics, Turkish: *moruk, git lan, merhaba.*
8. In example 5, for instance, we have: speaker-related switching on the stanza level (German vs English); stanza-internal switching in the delivery of the same artist (switching from German to English); and chorus-level switching in French.
9. It might of course be the case that these particular artists are monolingual or dominant in German; but this is a different story, which cannot be investigated on the same empirical and methodological basis.

# Discography

Aziza A. (1997), 'Es ist Zeit'.
Brothers Keepers (2001), 'Triple Rois'.
Fresh Familee (1993), 'Ahmed Gündüz'.
Freunde der Sonne (2004), 'Hellas Türkiye'.
Freundeskreis (1996), 'Overseas/Übersee'.
STF feat. Kool Savas (1999), 'Ihr müsst noch üben'.
Volkan (1998), 'Funkfurt'.

# References

Alim, H. S. (2004), 'Hip Hop Nation language', in E. Finegan and J. R. Rickford (eds), *Language in the USA: Themes for the Twenty-first Century*. Cambridge: Cambridge University Press, pp. 387–409.

Alim, H. S., Ibrahim, A. and Pennycook, A. (eds) (2009), *Global Linguistic Flows: Hip Hop Cultures, Identities, and the Politics of Language*. Mahwah, New Jersey: Lawrence Erlbaum.

Androutsopoulos, J. (2007), 'Bilingualism in the mass media and on the internet', in M. Heller (ed.), *Bilingualism: A Social Approach*. Basingstoke, NY: Palgrave Macmillan, pp. 207–230.

—(2009), 'Language and the three spheres of hip hop', in H. S. Alim, A. Ibrahim and A. Pennycook (eds), *Global Linguistic Flows: Hip Hop Cultures, Youth Identities, and the Politics of Language*. New York: Routledge, pp. 43–62.

Auer, P. (1998), 'Introduction: bilingual conversation revisited', in P. Auer (ed.), *Code-Switching in Conversation. Language, Interaction and Identity*. London/New York: Routledge, pp. 1–24.

—(2000), 'Why should we and how can we determine the "base language" of a bilingual conversation?' *Estudios de Sociolingüística*, 1, 1, 129.

Auzanneau, M. (2001), 'Identités africaines: le rap comme lieu d'expression'. *Cahiers d'études africaines*, XLI, 3–4, 163–164.

Barthes, R. (1967), *The Fashion system [Système de la mode]*. Berkeley: University of California Press.

Bennett, A. (1999), 'Hip hop am Main: the localization of rap music and hip hop culture'. *Media, Culture and Society*, 21, 77–91.

Bentahila, A. and Davies, E. B. (2002), 'Language mixing in rai music: localization or globalization?' *Language and Communication*, 22, 187–207.

Cheshire, J. and Moser, L.-M. (1994), 'English as a cultural symbol: the case of advertisements in French-speaking Switzerland'. *Journal of Multilingual and Multicultural Development*, 15, 6, 451–469.

Fishman, J. (1991), *Reversing Language Shift: Theoretical and Empirical Foundations of Assistance to Threatened Languages*. Clevedon: Multilingual Matters.

Goffman, E. (1986 [1974]), *Frame Analysis: An Essay on the Organization of Experience* [with a foreword by Bennett M. Berger]. Boston: Northeastern University Press.

Greve, M. and Kaya, A. (2004), 'Islamic Force, Takim 34 und andere Identitätsmixturen türkischer Rapper in Berlin und Istanbul', in E. Kimminich (ed.), *Rap: More than Words*. Frankfurt/Main: Lang, pp. 161–179.

Gumperz, J. J. (1982), *Discourse Strategies*. Cambridge: University Press.

Güngör, M. and Loh, H. (2002), *Fear of a Kanak Planet: Hiphop zwischen Weltkultur und Nazi-Rap*. Höfen: Hannibal.

Higgins, C. (2009), *English as a Local Language: Post-colonial Identities and Multilingual Practices*. Bristol: Multilingual Matters.

Hinnenkamp, V. (2003), 'Mixed language varieties of migrant adolescents and the discourse of hybridity'. *Journal of Multilingual and Multicultural Development*, 24, 1/2, 11–41.

Kallmeyer, W. and Keim, I. (2003), 'Linguistic variation and the construction of social identity in a German-Turkish setting', in J. Androutsopoulos and A. Georgakopoulou (eds), *Discourse Constructions of Youth Identities.* Amsterdam/Philadelphia: Benjamins, pp. 29–46.

Kluge, B. (2007), 'Formen und Funktion von Sprachwahl und Code-switching in lateinamerikanischen Raptexten', in S. Stemmler and T. Skandries (eds), *Hip hop und Rap in romanischen Sprachwelten: Stationen einer globalen Musikkultur.* Frankfurt a. M.: Lang, pp. 137–154.

Lee, J. S. (2004), 'Linguistic hybridization in K-Pop: discourse of self-assertion and resistance'. *World Englishes*, 23, 3, 429–450.

Lüdtke, S. (2007), *Globalisierung und Lokalisierung von Rapmusik am Beispiel amerikanischer und deutscher Raptexte.* Münster: LIT.

ÓReilly, C. C. (2003), 'When a language is "just symbolic": reconsidering the significance of language to the politics of identity', in G. Hogan-Brun and S. Wolff (eds), *Minority Languages in Europe: Frameworks, Status, Prospects.* Basingstoke, NY: Palgrave Macmillan, pp. 16–33.

Pennycook, A. (2007), *Global Englishes and Transcultural Flows.* London: Taylor and Francis.

Piller, I. (2001), 'Identity constructions in multilingual advertising'. *Language in Society*, 30, 2, 153–186.

Potter, Russel (1995), *Spectacular Vernaculars: Hip-Hop and the Politics of Postmodernism.* New York: State University of New York Press.

Putnam, M. T. and Littlejohn J. T. (2007), 'National socialism with Fler? German hip hop from the right'. *Popular Music and Society*, 30, 4, 453–468.

Rampton, B. (1998), 'Language crossing and the redefinition of reality', in P. Auer (ed.), *Code-Switching in Conversation.* London: Routledge, pp. 290–320.

Sarkar, M. (2009), 'Still reppin por mi gente: the transformative power of language mixing in Quebec hip hop', in H. S. Alim, A. Ibrahim and A. Pennycook (eds), *Global Linguistic Flows: Hip Hop Cultures, Youth Identities, and the Politics of Language.* New York: Routledge, pp. 139–157.

Sarkar, M. and Allen, D. (2007), 'Hybrid identities in Quebec hip hop: language, territory and ethnicity in the mix'. *Journal of Language, Identity, and Education*, 6, 2, 117–130.

Sarkar, M. and Winer, L. (2006), 'Multilingual code-switching in Quebec rap: poetry, pragmatics and performativity'. *International Journal of Multilingualism*, 3, 3, 173–192.

Scholz, A. (2003a), 'Explicito Lingo' Funktionen von Substandard in romanischen Rap-Texten (Italien, Frankreich, Spanien)'. *Osnabrücker Beiträge zur Sprachtheorie*, 65, 111–130.

—(2003b), 'Rap in der Romania: "Glocal Approach" am Beispiel von Musikmarkt, Identität, Sprache', in J. Androutsopoulos (ed.), *HipHop: globale Kultur – lokale Praktiken*, Bielefeld: Transcript, pp. 147–167.

Sebba, M. and Wootton, T. (1998), 'We, they and identity: sequential vs. identity-related explanation in code-switching', in Peter Auer (ed.), *Code-switching in Conversation.* London: Routledge, pp. 262–289.

Verlan, S. (2003), *French Connection.* St. Andrä/Wördern: Hannibal.

# 2 Kiff my zikmu: Symbolic Dimensions of Arabic, English and Verlan in French Rap Texts

Samira Hassa

## 1 Introduction

Wine, cheese, berets, baguettes and Edith Piaf love songs are some of the stereotypical images of France. To the surprise of some, we may now include on this list rap music. Considered one of the largest producers and consumers of rap music in the world (Béthune, 1999; Krims, 2002), France has seen its list of native rappers extend to the point where the rap genre is regularly applauded by the music industry. In 2003, for instance, four rap singers/bands – Sniper, IAM, Gomez et Dubois and Diam's – were nominated for the *Victoires de la musique*, the French version of the Grammy Awards.

Rap is about rhythm, rhymes, beat and powerful words, but rap is also a sort of refuge in which a marginalized group or minority can express freely who they are, what they suffer from, and their dreams and hopes (Boucher, 1998). In France, rap artists generally are children of immigrants, for the most part of North African Muslim or of sub-Saharan African descent. (Prévos, 1998). Androutsopoulos and Scholz (2002, 2003) note that 92 per cent of rappers in France are of immigrant descent, the highest percentage in Europe in comparison to 60 per cent in Germany, 32 per cent in Spain, 4 per cent in Italy and zero per cent in Greece. The rise of hip-hop groups in France has been accompanied by an increase in CD releases; between 1990 and 1999, 331 albums were released, approximately three times as many as in Italy (118 albums) and six times more than Spain (52 albums) (Androutsopoulos, 2003). In their lyrics, rappers often refer to their places of origin (usually former French colonies), the postcolonial struggle (Omoniyi, 2009), and describe and express the difficulties related to migration, resettlement, assimilation, translocation and hybridization.

These phenomena are observable through analysis of the content of French rap discourse and the use of language in the lyrics. The objective

**44**

of this chapter is to analyse the context in which Arabic, English and Verlan[1] are used and to identify the function of each of these varieties in French rap lyrics. In this case, code-switching plays the role of an identity construction tool and an identity marker for numerous hip-hop artists in France.

In the United States of America, hip hop continues to attract scholars who endeavour to answer questions related to identity, multiculturalism and ethnicity (Alim, 2006; Krims, 2002). On the other side of the Atlantic, in France, scholarly research on hip hop has been somewhat slower to emerge (Bazin, 1995; Béthune, 1999; Lapassade and Rousselot, 1998; Prévos, 1996, 1998, 2003; Durand, 2002), perhaps due to the perception of rap as a trivial domain for research. But as Krims (2002) points out, there is a great need for research related to hip hop in the Francophone world where the colonial past is still very present in collective memory, and the interactions between the ex-colonizer and the ex-colonized are still being reconstructed and renegotiated (Auzanneau, 2001, 2002). In one track called 'Pourquoi' ('Why'), Sniper, a French multiethnic youth band, illustrates the parallel between their everyday struggles and the aftermath of the colonial past: [2]

> (1)  *Place au progrès, on nous*          'Time for progress, they are
>       *parle de mondialisation,*           telling us about globalization,
>       *Alors que dans nos têtes*           while in our heads, we are still
>       *on en est encore qu'à la*           dealing with colonization'
>       *colonisation*
>
>                                            Sniper, 'Pourquoi'

Boucher (1998, p. 183) has noted that the oppressed feeling of the multiethnic rappers is a result of denial by the French republican society, which continues to ignore the presence of the diverse community living on its soil. Rap discourse becomes a medium for the immigrant postcolonial descendants to remind France of its colonial past and to voice their anger about racism and discrimination. By studying rap discourse light can be shed on the interactions and language of youth; specifically, children of immigrants with their multilayered identities.

This chapter is a small contribution to the study of hip-hop culture in the Francophone world. It focuses on code-switching in French rap discourse, in which speakers make these language choices according to the symbolism of the language (Androutsopoulos, 2009, and this volume), or as Auzanneau puts it, its 'value and functions' (2002).

The languages used in hip-hop discourse in France consequently fulfil certain roles, represent distinct identities, and depict the social problems of youth in a context of immigration and postcolonialism.

## 2 The sociolinguistic context of rap music in France

The emergence of French rap goes back to the early 1980s when a Frenchman named Zekri, who lived in New York City and was supposedly the only white man who was able to walk the streets of the Bronx (Cannon, 1997; Prévos, 2002), imported rap music onto French soil (Alim, 2006; Prévos, 2002) after meeting Afrika Bambaataa, one of the pioneers of rap. Despite the fact that French rap is an imported product – meaning it was not born in the streets of France, in comparison to rap in the US that emerged from the streets of the South Bronx – they both flourished in an urban context. As Cannon (1997) explains, to understand the rap movement in France it is necessary to know the historical and social events in France that gave birth to this musical genre; in particular, the industrial boom in the 1960s that brought immigrant workers to France, mainly from North African ex-colonies such as Morocco, Algeria and Tunisia, as well as from places such as Senegal, Mali and the Caribbean. The rap movement was quickly adopted by youth of mixed origin living primarily in the suburbs around Paris and Marseille (Jacono, 2002; Prévos, 2002). It found its niche in the *banlieues* ('suburbs') and housing projects located outside the city called *cités* or *habitations à loyer modéré* (HLM) ('low-rent flats'). As Hargreaves and McKinney point out, the term *banlieue* has become 'synonymous with ethnic alterity, criminality and violence' (1997, pp. 12–13). The French rap scene, in turn, has become associated with the culture of the *banlieues*, notably immigrant families and the offspring of immigrant parents who are searching for identity, torn between two cultures and languages (cf. Auzanneau, 2002). It is not surprising to see the *banlieusards* ('youth from the *banlieues*') appropriate this musical genre to voice their resistance to social injustices.[3] Consequently, rap culture in France has become the oral, visual and artistic expression of the struggle and resistance of the immigrant youth of France (cf. Cannon, 1997). According to Calvet, the rap movement in France emerged as a result of a marginalized group who suffered from unemployment, school failure, and being torn between the culture of their immigrant parents and French culture (1994, p. 269). This socially and spatially marginalized youth group then created a *culture interstitielle* ('interstitial culture'), through their dress code, breakdancing and rapping, all of which served as a means of conveying their multi-cultural and multilingual identity.

## 3 Code-switching and popular music

### 3.1 Code-switching

No one would deny that the phenomenon of code-switching has been of great interest to linguists for the last few decades (Bokamba, 1989; Bentahila and Davies, 1992; Auer, 1998; Myers-Scotton, 1993). For the most part, however, code-switching has been analysed from a syntactic perspective with the ultimate aim of drawing universal constraints. This perspective has been criticized for not taking into adequate consideration speakers' social and psychological motivations (Bokamba, 1989; Bentahila and Davies, 1992). In addition, Bokamba (1989) makes a distinction between code-switching and code-mixing, limiting code-switching to the insertion of constituents between sentence boundaries, and using code-mixing to refer to the alternation of codes within the same sentence. This distinction is still open to debate. On the other hand, Myers-Scotton (1993) created a model that postulates that during code-switching there is a hierarchical relationship between the dominant or matrix language (ML), and an embedded language (EL), whose constituents EL are incorporated into the ML following the morphosyntactic structure of the ML. Gardner-Chloros, however disputes Myers-Scotton's search for grammatical constraints on code-switching; she perceives this approach as 'too rigid' and prefers a more flexible alternative (1993, p. 70).

Another important question concerns the distinction between code-switching and borrowing. Gumperz and Cook-Gumperz (1982) characterize borrowing as a word or a short sentence that is incorporated into a different code. Heath (1989), on the other hand, in his study of code-switching in Moroccan Arabic, recognizes the difficulty in distinguishing between a borrowed word and code-switching. For his study, the criteria of frequency and pronunciation proved problematic, leading him to suggest that a clear distinction between code-switching and borrowing could not be made. Analysing code-switching between French and Arabic in *Rai* (a genre of music from Algeria), Davies and Bentahila (2006) added to this rich debate by asking whether we can even analyse code-switching in song lyrics within previously established code-switching frameworks, given the fact that most of the work previously done on code-switching evaluated spontaneous speech. In other words, should we analyse code-switching in musical discourse according to previous scholars' orientations and research on code-switching, or should

**47**

we categorize research on lyrics differently given the fact that the discourse is artfully designed for a certain audience? (cf. Picone, 2002). Given the complexities that this research has revealed, this chapter neither attempts to answer these important questions nor to dispute them. Code-switching will simply be defined as the use of two or more languages within a conversation at a very broad level, since it is a 'fuzzy edged construct' as observed by Gardner-Chloros (1995, p. 70; quoted in Sarkar and Winer, 2006, p. 178).

## 3.2 Code-switching in popular music

Alternating languages within a song is not a new phenomenon. Davies and Bentahila note that this occurred already in songs in medieval Europe as well as in *muwashshah* songs, in which scholarly Arabic and Hebrew verses alternated with refrains in the quotidian language of the region (2006, p. 368). Mixing languages in hip hop likewise seems to be common. In studies of Quebecois rap, Sarkar and Winer (2006) and Sarkar (2009) suggest that the use of more than one language allows rappers to represent the cultural diversity of Quebec without the need to master the languages used. This dialectic between local and global culture (cf. Pennycook and Mitchell, 2009 and Alim, 2006) – confirms the idea that hip hop exhibits 'popular cultural production and practices that are as contradictory as they are conscious' (Alim, 2006, p. 3). The contradiction, or rather the convergence between the 'localness' of the identity and 'globalness', often conjoined into the term 'glocal' (Higgins, 2009; Roth-Gordon, 2009; Sarkar, 2009) is perceptible through this 'cocktail' of languages associated with French hip hop.

In French rap, code-switching is not as noticeable as in Moroccan or Quebecois rap. As Prévos writes: 'a few French rappers tried to record raps in English but they soon switched to French because they were aware that they did not sound as good as those African American models' (2002, p. 5).Their choice to sing mainly in French, however, did not stop them from incorporating lexemes from Arabic, Creole, English or other languages to spice up their texts and reject the 'imperialism of the standard French language' (Béthune, 1999, p. 191), resulting in what has been described by Omoniyi as 'an act of political subversion' (2009, p. 124). After a brief attempt at tossing in (American) English and imitating American rappers, French rap rapidly developed its own means of expression proper to the French *banlieue* by performing mostly in French (Pecqueux, 2007). French rap follows the tradition of French literary and philosophical culture (Calio, 1998), in which the author/performer masters the language well enough to use it as a 'weapon', as Diam's, a female rapper, declares in her track 'Suzy': 'j'manie le mic comme le fusil' ('I use the mic like a rifle'). Even though French rap is elaborated following the model of literary texts, the texts are still grounded in the oral culture of the street and the 'hood', producing what Zegnani describes as '*une forme orale standardisée*' (2004, p. 75), that is a standardized oral form where hip-hop discourse is 'constructed and transformed' (Androutsopoulos, 2009, p. 59).

## 4 The data

The data analysed in this chapter are taken from a collection of four albums for a total of 57 songs by rap artists that were nominated for the *Victoires de la Musique* in 2003. Using the *Victoires de la Musique* nominees allowed me to collect a sample of the most famous performers in the French music industry without bias towards personal preference. Surprisingly, the four bands/performers represented both the North and the South of France: Diam's and Sniper represent Paris and the northern region, while Gomez et Dubois and IAM represent Marseille in the South. The other striking phenomenon is the rise of the female performer, Diam's, in a field that is traditionally male-dominated (Boucher, 1998; Prévos, 2003).

As a native speaker of Arabic and French with near-native proficiency in English and a good knowledge of *Verlan*, I transcribed the Verlan in consultation with two other native speakers of French and Arabic who also have a strong command of Verlan. Once the text of the lyrics of all four albums had been obtained, Arabic, French and Verlan were chosen as the primary objects of study, as Creole, Spanish or other languages were virtually nonexistent in the four selected albums. In the texts analysed, French served as the matrix language, and Arabic, English and Verlan played the role of inserted languages, in Myers Scotton's (1993) terminology.

### 4.1 Languages

Moroccan, Tunisian and Algerian Arabic, also known as *Darija*, are the spoken varieties of Arabic that appear in the data. These forms of Arabic constitute low varieties in Ferguson's (1959) model of diglossia, and their morphology, syntax, pronunciation and vocabulary differ from Modern Standard Arabic. With regards to English, despite the fact that the variety taught in French schools is modelled on British English, in the hip-hop domain, the dominant variety of English seems to be American English, and more specifically African American English (AAE). Finally, Verlan is a spoken variety born in the working-class, immigrant suburbs of the wider Parisian region (Lefkowitz, 1989,

**49**

p. 313), and consists of inverting the order of the syllables to serve the role of a secret language (Calvet, 1994, p. 281). The term Verlan itself, for instance, is the 'Verlanized' version of *l'envers* ('the inverse').

## 4.2 Artists

Diam's (born Mélanie Georgiades) is a female rapper from Essonne (near Paris) who moved to Paris when she was four years old. Her father is Greek Cypriot and her mother is French.

Sniper are a hip-hop group from the Val-d'Oise department (near Paris). In 2004 the group faced legal action from then Interior Minister Nicolas Sarkozy for their violent lyrics that were perceived to be racist or anti-Semitic (Mouloud, 2003). The group consists of El Tunisiano (Bachir Baccour), who is of Tunisian descent; Aketo (Ryad Selmi), who is of Comorian descent; and Dj Boudj and Blacko (Karl Appela).

Gomez et Dubois is the pseudonym of two rap artists from Marseille, Eben and Faf LaRage (real name: Raphaël Mussard), who is of Malagasy and Reunionese descent. Gomez et Dubois's album *Flics & Hors La Loi* ('Cops and Outlaws') is a satire of the French police.

IAM are a French hip-hop group from Marseille who defend the culture of Marseille and the Mediterranean. They use Egyptian pseudo-nyms: Akhenaton (Philippe Fragione) is of Sicilian origin; Shurik'n (Geoffroy Mussard) is of Malagasy and Reunionese descent; Sultan Freeman (Malek Brahimi) is of Algerian descent; Khéops (Eric Mazel) is of Spanish and Marseille descent; Imhotep (Pascal Perez), born in Alger, is of Pied-Noir origin; and Kephren (François Mendy) is of Senegalese descent. [4] As further evidence of the link with French hip hop, it should be noted that the names of all the IAM members refer to Egyptian phar-aohs as a way of connecting with North African culture, the culture of the countries that are culturally closest to IAM's hometown of Mar-seille (Huq, 2006).

# 5 Analysis

## 5.1 Code-switching in Arabic

The Arabic language has a significant presence in the lyrics of French rap performers. In the corpus analysed, all rappers use some Arabic as opposed to other French music genres (e.g., pop), which use little to none. This may be due to the socio-cultural background of the rappers or to the genre itself, suggesting that rap is a genre used to express diverse sociolinguistic and cultural backgrounds. The use of Arabic in French rap suggests an identification with a North African community and/or a desire to increase awareness of the religious and cultural practices of the Berber and Arab communities living in France. The degree to which Arabic is used varies among rappers, and this variation does not seem to occur along geographical lines: if we compare Parisian and Marseille rappers, it is not easy to discern a clear trend. For instance, Diam's, from the Paris area, makes only one insertion in Arabic – **'wash'** ('are you?'), – while Sniper, also from Paris, uses more Arabic. In the South, Gomez et Dubois code-switch into Arabic to a significant degree, and invited Amine, a popular *Raï* singer of North African origin, to sing in Arabic (perhaps because they are not necessarily fluent in Arabic themselves). On the other hand, the occurrence of Arabic on IAM's album is very limited.

Arabic is solicited mostly in reference to the culture and practices of countries such as Algeria, Morocco and Tunisia, as exemplified in a passage by Akhenaton, the leader of IAM, in which he evokes his modest social class background as well as his Italian immigrant origin. In this passage, Akhenaton expresses his belonging to the North African community by referring to his children as a mix of Italian and North African cultures as symbolized by the word *douez*, a term describing the sauce of the *tagine*, a traditional North African dish, as seen in the following extract:

(2) *J'ai pas le sang bleu, gars, je*  'I don't have blue blood, man,
  *suis issu d'une famille modeste* I am from a modest family.

  *Immigrés de Naples*    Immigrants from Naples

  . . .          . . .

  *Mes gosses: honnête croisement* My kids: honest mix of a
  *d'un **douez** et d'une sauce*   **[North African] sauce** and
  *tomate*        tomato sauce'

               IAM, '21/04'

Born Catholic, and of Italian origin, Akhenaton converted to Islam (Swedenburg, 2002) and often refers to his Muslim religious praxis as in the following track, in which he calls for prayer and makes a reference to evil by using the term **ibliss** ('evil snakes'):

(3) *Et maintenant prions*   'And now let us pray

  *Car **bliss** [ibliss] s'est glissé* Because **evil** snakes in
  *dans nos artères, parade en* our veins, he parades, and
  *ville en triomphe*    triumphs in the city,

| | |
|---|---|
| *Projette la tyrannie d'nos embryons,* | Projects tyranny of our embryos |
| *d'puis les pyramides sur le reste* | From the pyramids to the rest |
| *Semant l'effroi dans les environs, sordide, timide sur le geste* | Sordid, shy moves, bringing fear in the surrounding' |

IAM, 'Tiens'

The fact that Arabic is the official language in North African countries and Islam the most practised religion also leads to Arabic often being used to refer to Muslim beliefs and cultural practices. It is common in French rap lyrics to read lexemes such as **hallal**, designating an object or an action that is permissible to use according to Islamic law and custom, and **ibliss** and **shetane**, both referring to an active force representing negative moral acts in the Muslim religion as seen in extracts 3, 4 and 5.

| | |
|---|---|
| (4) *J'essaie de ne pas péter les plombs* | 'I try not to blow a fuse |
| *Même si la chaîne me pousse à bouts* | Even if the system is pushing me to the limits |
| *Je ne casse pas, je ne plie pas, je reste au garde-à-vous* | I break nothing, I fold nothing, I stand at attention |
| *Eh, je garde la foi en tout* | I keep faith in everything |
| *Le monde devient fou, et tout le monde s'en fout* | The world is getting crazy, and people don't give a damn |
| *Ca se barre en illes-cou, le* **shétane** *est partout* | It's blowing up, **evil** is everywhere |
| *Retrouvons nos repères (eh)* | Let's get our points of reference back |
| *Il ne faut plus pleurer, nos mères* | Our mothers should no longer cry' |

Sniper, 'Pourquoi'

Other terms such as **hak'allah** ('I swear in the name of God') and **Inch'allah** ('God willing') allow French rappers to show their adherence to Islam and to express the struggles faced by Muslim communities. Expressing a connection to the Muslim faith goes back to contemporary rap's precursors, such as Afrika Bambaataa and the Nation of Islam, when Islam unified oppressed communities around the world, transcending geographical boundaries and skin colour (Boucher, 1998). Applying and emphasizing Islamic principles allows rappers to inject moral codes into their work, thereby transforming their rap into conscious rap (Lin, 2009). This transformation brings a message of both respect and recognition in an attempt to attenuate the tensions between maintaining a translocal orientation to Islam and demands to develop an Islam in line with *laïcité*, the principle of a secular society in France (Bowen, 2002).

In addition, in the corpus analysed, it appears that Arabic is often used in discourse related to religion, especially post September 11, as a way to confront 'Islamophobia' (Swedenburg, 2002). Extract 5 provides an example where Sniper denounces the stereotype of a Muslim as a terrorist by mentioning Robert Hue, a former French Communist Party leader with a beard, and Osama Bin Laden, the Islamic terrorist. The text also exposes their political views by condemning the Iraq war, and the political actions of Israel in the Israeli–Palestinian conflict.

(5) | *C'est Bush contre Sadam et Sharon contre Arafat* | 'It's Bush against Sadam and Sharon against Arafat |
|---|---|
| *Les combats éclatent son nom est douloureux* | Fights blow up, his name is painful, |
| *Mais à la fin du massacre aucun d'entre eux n'aura des bleus* | But at the end of the massacre none of them will have bruises |
| *Le dollar est en colère petit constat global* | The dollar is angry, little global remark |
| *T'as massacré les indiens persécuté les noirs* | You massacred the Indians and persecuted Blacks |
| *Après les **diab'** viennent les Arabes le tout en 200 ans d'histoire* | After the **devils**, come the Arabs in less than 200 years of history |
| *Dénonce un discours haineux dès l'départ tu nous en veux connard* | Denounce hateful speech from the beginning, you are going after us, asshole |
| *Qu'est c'tu compares le coran et Mein Kampf* | Why are you comparing the Koran to Mein Kampf? |
| *L'Irak attention, nouvelle cible des mythomanes* | Watch out Iraq, new target for compulsive liars |
| *Ça pue la coalition où Sadam se fait Sodom mal* | It stinks like the coalition where Sadam becomes bad Sodom' |

**53**

. . .                              . . .

*L'homme fabrique tout pour*  'Man prepares everything for his
*sa mort, l'enfant n'respecte*  death, Child no longer respects
*plus sa mère*  his mother'

. . .                              . . .

*Sexe au sommaire nos*  'Sex on the list, our mothers cry
*mères pleurent quand*  while **evil** is having a good time'
**shétane** *se marre*

Sniper, 'Visions chaotiques'

It should also be noted that Arabic words such as *khay, khti* ('brother, sister') are terms used in North Africa to establish social contact and solidarity among members of a group. In addition, Arabic in French rap discourse can also have a function of a mocking self-description as seen in the following passage by Gomez et Dubois:

(6)  *De toute façon c'est pas*  'Anyway it's not my section
     *mon secteur et je suis saoul*  And I am drunk

     *Des fois la nuit on a le*  In the night, sometimes, we have
     *blues comme dans Hill*  the blues like on Hill Street
     *Street*

     *Alors moi et Dubois on se*  So me and Dubois, we end up in
     *finit dans les bars à strip*  strip clubs

     *Gomez et Dubois* **ghirr**  Gomez and Dubois, they only
     **khabta ou zetla**  **drink alcohol** and smoke **weed**'

Gomez et Dubois, 'Ronde de nuit'

The two rappers, mimicking two corrupt cops in Marseille, use the words **ghirr khabta** ('alcohol'), and **zetla** ('marijuana'), terms from your culture, and thereby project the image of the hip-hop community, and specifically the *banlieusards*, as existing in a universe of alcohol and drugs. As Boucher (1998) points out, the youth of the *banlieues* use *drogue douce* ('soft drugs') as a way to forget the struggles of everyday life and create ties among group members. Code-switching in Arabic in this context refers to two actions forbidden by the socio-cultural background of the Muslim youth living in France, and the use of **ghirr khabta** and **zetla** becomes a code to refer to forbidden actions, thus enhancing the feeling of solidarity and creating a community of practice of its own. The hip-hop performers then come to represent a group of rebels who spend their time drinking and smoking drugs, an image that has very often been attributed to French youth living in the *banlieues*.

Finally, code-switching in Arabic, as shown in extract 7, is also used by rappers to express nostalgia towards the country of origin, while acknowledging the social problems of assimilation and hybridization. The second and third generations of immigrants are still considered foreigners or outsiders in their country of birth (France), and are persecuted because of their religious beliefs, yet are not able to integrate in the country of their forefathers either. Sniper's track 'Entre deux' ('Between two') reflects this search for identity, referring to the uncomfortable feeling of finding oneself between two seats symbolizing two cultures (in this case the French and Maghreb cultures).

(7) *J'ai pour pays d'origine la France*
'I have France as my country of origin

*Là où je crèche où on me reproche mes origines*
But where I live they hold my origins against me

*J'ai grandi loin de mon pays et on me l'a trop souvent*
I grew up far from my country and they too often

*Reproché on a trop souvent prétendu que je les avais trahis*
Held that against me, they claimed too often that I betrayed them

*Hé ma couille ici c'est pas l'**bled** où ça pue l'embrouille et*
Hey, shit here is not **my country of origin** where it smells like shady things and

*Même là-bas j'suis dans la merde, c'est comme*
Even there I am fucked, it's like

*Chaque été des que tu me vois tu dis **choukne** regards froids*
Each summer when you see me you say **who is he?** Cold looks

*Sifflotement v'là l'étranger dans le salon*
Whistling, here is the stranger in the living room

*Monsieur **Tounsi smahat manich jihane tek el hata***
Mister **Tunisiano listen I am not starving, I am fine**

*Ou **chabhtte l'hine emtaha l'jiraine** ici un danger*
**We are neighbours** Here a danger

*Là-bas j'suis un intru et là où j'aimerais m'ranger j'suis*
There I am an intruder and here where I would like to settle down

*vu comme un étranger donc j'suis perdu, et en plus j'suis*
I am seen as a stranger/foreigner, I am lost and on top of that I am

*pas le bienvenu où on se méfie des barbus*
Not welcome; they don't trust men who have beards

**55**

| | |
|---|---|
| *D' Oussama à Robert Hue* | From Osama to Robert Hue |
| *Toi aussi t'es dans mon cas?* | You are also in my shoes? |
| *un blème de pedigree* | A pedigree problem |
| *Vu que j'ai du mal à m'intégrer que ce soit ici ou là bas* | Seeing that it's is hard for me to integrate whether here or there |
| **Kalouli aarbi aha** | **They called me Arab** [in France], |
| **Menich fi bledi** | **You are not in your country** |
| **Kalouli roumi aha** | **They called me European** [in my country of origin] |
| **Yak fi bledi ya wildi** | **Go back home, my son** |
| **Khhouya bledi choufni rani aarbi manich roumi** | **Brother, look at me, I am an Arab, I am not European'** |

Sniper, 'Entre deux'

## 5.2 Code-switching in English

English is present to various degrees in the texts of all rap artists analysed. It is not clear if the distinction between Standard American English (SAE) and African American English (AAE) is well understood, perhaps due to the fact that French rappers do not master the English language well enough to capture the linguistic differences between SAE and AAE. In France, perceptions of the English language and American culture seem to be shaped by the media (i.e., television shows, sports, cinema and music). Consequently, it is not surprising to find in the corpus terms such as 'Hollywood', 'Harlem' and even reference to 'Starsky', a police hero of the 1970s US television show 'Starsky & Hutch', and the character JR from 'Dallas', a long-running TV drama from the 1980s. Besides these references, French rappers use the jargon commonly used by American rappers, who were the pioneers of the hip-hop movement, including terms such as 'beat', 'vibe', 'flow', 'man', 'crew' (see extracts 8 and 9).[5]

| | |
|---|---|
| (8) *Moi j'veux qu'on dise que j'suis d'la bombe* | 'I want them to say that I am the bomb |
| Big up *à ceux qui ont kiffé l'époque de* time *bombe* | Big up to those who liked the era of the time bomb |
| *Rappelle-toi quand ça* kick*ait sec à Paname* | Remember when it kicked hard in Paris |

*Tu suis l'école où tu ne* kick   You follow the school, where if
*pas si tu n'as pas l'âme*        you don't kick, you have no soul

*Concours de* flow *de*           Competitions of flow, explosive
*phases de balle de larmes*       sentences, tears'

Diam's, 'Mon repertoire'

In French rap, code-switching into English becomes some sort of a reminder of the origin, the base, the lingua franca by which French rappers build solidarity with the larger, global hip-hop community while rearticulating and localizing it to attest to the authenticity of the *banlieue* culture. In the corpus analysed, English language in rap texts tends to be linked to violence or the degrading of women using sexual references (Boucher, 1998). Words such as 'bitch', 'fuck', 'fucking', 'kick*ait*' – where the verb is conjugated as a regular French verb form in *-er* – 'shoot', 'dead', 'gangs', 'gun' are now part of the regular lexicon of French rap music, as noted by Androutsopoulos and Scholz (2003, p. 473) and seen in IAM's track below.

(9)  Yeah, I hear a lot of kick in this
       bitch
      Turn the music up in this
       motherfucker
      Other side of the track niggaz
      Method Man, Redman, IAM
      Let's get it dirty
      Yeah, we back live again
      It's the world wide niggaz
      Ladies and germs, it's
      pandemonium, brick Napoleon
      Doc and Meth, all in ya girl
       fallopian
      Fuck you up, like a double-
       stacked Pokemon
      Peek-at-you/Pikachu, your puss
       (Dat slowly man?)
      I'm from the brick, where there's
       real car thieves
      Rock this funky joint, like
       P.R.P.'s
      Tricks up my sleeve, just give me
       an hour
      I bang two women, on the Eiffel
       Tower

| | |
|---|---|
| *Mes dits saignent, y'a tempête, voici un son d'compet'* | 'My words are bleeding, there is a storm, here is a sound of competition |
| *Pour l'occas', Rho, on ramène sur la poudrière l'allumette* | For the occasion, Rho, we bring on the explosives and matches |
| *Celle qui régénère, la base, et les crimes qu'on n'a pu commettre* | Those that regenerate, the base, and the crimes that we were not able to commit, |
| *Sur disque pour la peine v'là 5 comètes* | As punishment, here are five comets on a disc' |

IAM, 'Noble art'

The violence reflected in the lyrics of French rap may result from the strong impact of the 'gangsta' imagery of the American ghetto, as suggested by the rappers' Americanized choice of pseudonyms, such as Sniper, Freeman, Blacko and many others. This influence is perhaps nurtured by the media scandals of some famous American rappers such as Tupac, Snoop Dogg and others. This trend is reflected in the use of English words describing violent acts – as in extract 9 – by the band IAM, in which the text in English is very explicit, referring to vandalism and sexual acts, whereas the lyrics in French have a much more poetic and softer tone. Code-switching in English may imply a need to reproduce an image of violence associated with the *banlieue* lifestyle, to which rap is intrinsically linked; an image of youth involved in drugs and illegal activities, following the path of American rap as an act of rebellion. The use of English may then allow rap artists to transcend certain socio-cultural taboos as it sounds easier to talk about explicit physical violence such as rape and other violent acts in English, a foreign language in France, rather than in French. English provides a certain linguistic camouflage whereby singing in English becomes mimicking without being really responsible for the content of the lyrics. Depicting physical violence, vandalism and sexual acts in French rap songs could also be interpreted as a verbal, symbolic and cathartic expression of anger and hate (Béthune, 1999) as well as an ironic, sarcastic self-description of the youth of the *banlieue* who are often perceived as youth who speak funny, riot, and deal and use drugs. This stigmatized image of the *banlieusards* projected by the media seems to be reproduced by the rappers themselves through the use of English, possibly as a way to criticize indirectly the negative clichés of the *banlieue* lifestyle. Rappers often call themselves '*lascars*', a term defined as a youth who struggles in the *cité* because of his origin and skin colour, often dealing with delinquency (Zegnani, 2004, p. 78).

## 5.3 Code-switching in Verlan

The last variety analysed in the corpus of French rap is Verlan. Verlan is a sociolect, a variety spoken by a group aimed at excluding certain people from the conversation. Verlan initially functions as encryption used in playful contexts and as an in-group identity marker in the *banlieue*. As mentioned before, this variety emerged out of the immigrant experience in the Northern suburbs of Paris (Lefkowitz, 1989), so it is not surprising that Sniper and Diam's, who are rap artists from Paris, incorporate it into their lyrics, while IAM and Gomez et Dubois – all from Marseille – hardly use it. While in the United States the rivalry in the hip-hop industry is between East and West Coasts, in France this geographical rivalry is between North and South, and more precisely, between Paris and Marseille (Boucher, 1998; Prévos, 2003). This geographic division in French rap is what Prévos describes as the emergence of a 'regionalization of rap in France' (2002, p. 15) and is visible in the degree to which Verlan is used in French rap lyrics. As for the topics that occur with code-switching into Verlan, the analysis shows that this variety is often used to depict social and economic aspects of suburban life in France (Calio, 1998), and more precisely the struggles of a generation of descendents of immigrants who face social problems related to assimilation, as exemplified in extracts 10 and 11:

(10) *J' vis dans la crainte*      'I live in fear

     *Que dans mon verre il y ait*    That in my glass there is a drug
     *de la drogue*

     *J'évite les rues la nuit car le*   I avoid streets in the night
     *viol est à la mode*           because rape is in style

     *Sinik m'a dit tu sais ici c'est*   Sinik told me here it's shit
     *la merde*

     *Pour t'en sortir il faut une*     If you want to get by you need
     *patate d'enfer*              a lot of luck

     *Ou un grand frère*          Or a big brother

     *J' vis dans la crainte*        I live in fear

     *Ma bombe lacrymaux dans*    My Mace in my pocket
     *la poche*

     *J' suis parano*              I am paranoid

| | |
|---|---|
| *Car y'a trop de haine quand on m'approche* | Because there is too much hate close to me |
| *Y'a trop de mecs **fonce-dés** au crack dès le matin* | There are too many guys **fucked-up** on crack early in the morning |
| *Il veut sa dose* | He wants his fix |
| *Donc j'suis victime de l'arrachage de sac à main* | So I am a victim of a purse snatching |
| *J' vis la violence au jour le jour en attendant demain* | I live violence day after day while waiting for tomorrow. |
| *D'ailleurs les **keufs** ils étaient où pour mon histoire de sac à mains?!* | By the way, where were the **cops** at the time of my mugging?! |
| *Tu me traites de 'chienne', de **tinpe**, de salope* | You call me a bitch, a **whore**, a slut |
| *Mais mec pourquoi tu t'énerves j' t'ai juste dit* | But man why do you get angry, all I said is |
| *Que j'ai pas de clopes* | That I have no smokes' |
| | Diam's, 'Incassable' |

| | | |
|---|---|---|
| (11) | *J'parle pour les **reufs** qui **béton*** | 'I am speaking for the **brothers** who **go to jail** |
| | *Une fois qu'ils sortiront* | Once they get out |
| | *C'est soit ils s'calmeront* | Either they will cool it |
| | *Ou bien ils récidiveront* | Or they will relapse' |
| | | Sniper, 'Pourquoi' |

Rap performers turn to Verlan to articulate the complex social reality of life in the *banlieue*, which is characterized by high unemployment, delinquency, frustration and racial tensions, as shown by the most frequently used lexemes in Verlan: ***Ivé*** (*vie* 'life'), ***Du-per*** (*perdu* 'lost'), ***Car-pla*** (*placard* 'jail'), ***Beu-her*** (*herbe* 'marijuana'), ***keufs*** (*flics* 'cops'), ***beurs*** (*arabe* 'Arab'). This idea was confirmed by Lefkowitz's definition of the context of use of Verlan as 'words [in Verlan] used for money, clothes and cigarettes; words used as insults, playful or otherwise; words associated with relationships, and also words referring to drugs or criminal activities' (1989, pp. 116–119). As an in-group identity marker, Verlan offers a wide range of terms describing the strong ties between members of the group such as ***refré*** or ***reufs*** (*frère* 'brother') and **reus** (*soeur* 'sister'), which allow youth to forge close interpersonal relationships. This collective identity transcends their diverse countries of origin, religion and sociolinguistic factors as a response to the economic and social conditions they all share. Moreover, in the corpus analysed, one of the most loaded words associated with French Prime Minister Nicolas Sarkozy, the word *racaille* ('scum'), occurs:

(12) *Fille de la rue ne veut pas*      'Girl from the street does not
*dire* **caillera** *dans l'âme*        mean **scum** in the soul

*Ne connaît pas la flicaille*           Doesn't know the cops

*Mais a déjà vu des tas d'*             But she saw a lot of dirty girls in
*filles crades en larmes*               tears

*Elle connaît le* **ce-vi** *et*        She knows the **vice** and the
*l'instinct d'survie*                   survival instinct'

                                        Diam's, 'Cruelle la vie'

Nicolas Sarkozy famously used this word to describe rioters in one of the Parisian *banlieue* in 2005 while he was Minister of the Interior (Dumay, 2005). In extract 12, the word *racaille* in Verlan (**caillera**) is used an ironic, sarcastic way to describe how the *banlieusards* believe they are perceived by the French people. This identity construction is shaped around the dialectic of *banlieusards* versus non-*banlieusards*; us, the youth of the *banlieue,* and them, those who have an easy and happy life. The concept of us and them, the in-group versus the out-group, is expressed by a reaffirmation of the identity of a *banlieusard* that could be qualified as a form of pride in being an outsider, a sense of belonging to the *cités*, bringing authenticity to their texts (Calio, 1998).

This spatial identification is notable in Sniper's song '*Panam All Starz*' in which rappers shout the names and numbers of their *départements* – for instance, 93 for Seine-Saint-Denis, 95 for Val d'Oise – which are well-known Parisian suburbs to mainstream French people, often portrayed by the media as dangerous places to live. In response to this often biased representation of the *banlieue*, rappers are starting to claim their connection to a specific *département* and *banlieue* in order to fight the negative stereotypical representations of the *banlieue* and the resulting exclusion and spatial segregation.

## 6 Conclusion

In this chapter, I have described the context and the symbolic dimensions of instances of Arabic, English and Verlan in French hip hop. An analysis of 57 songs, represented here by selected passages from

11 tracks, revealed that Arabic is often used to refer to family, religion or conflict of identity with respect to assimilation and hybridization among second- and third-generation North African Muslim immigrants. The use of English, on the other hand, centres mostly around topics pertaining to violence, reflecting the American gangsta hip hop image of the discourse of rebellion. Finally, Verlan is associated with the youth culture of the *banlieue* (i.e., poor housing conditions, lack of jobs and an uncertain future), and also delimits the boundary between the North and the South, as opposed to Arabic and English, which seem to be familiar languages in all French suburban working-class immigrant communities.

Despite the fact that French rappers claim to rap only in French, it is possible that rap music in France is a genre where mixing two or more codes is less likely to be criticized for not respecting the grammatical and stylistic norms of the French language. French rappers alternate languages to various degrees, which may be associated with rappers' multicultural and multilingual ethnicity but also at a higher level with the genre itself. One may even say that it is a necessity to be from a diverse ethnic background in order to become a French rapper. Diam's, for instance, a white Caucasian French female rapper from a Greek Cypriot father and a French mother, describes herself as a '*petite métisse à la peau d'or*' ('an inter-racial woman with golden skin'), which shows that despite the fact that many white rappers are on the scene, the notion of whiteness is still somewhat represented as 'Other' (Boyd, 2002; cited in Cutler, 2009, p. 80). Rappers in France project a multicultural, multi-racial identity that allows them to align themselves with a diverse immigrant community as is perceived to be the norm in French hip hop. The use of various languages in rap lyrics is a provocative mirror of the multicultural, multi-layered identity of the French rappers and the youth of the *banlieue* as well as a reflection of ideologies held by hip-hop artists and youth about these languages. The linguistic patchwork described in this chapter acts as an identity marker for the youth of the *banlieue*. Using code-switching allows rappers to construct a cryptic discourse where the language used plays a poetic, aesthetic and tran-scultural role as well as serves as a riposte to the dominant sociocultural norm in place. The fertile ground for research represented by the hip-hop culture in France may help overcome the sociocultural challenges of assimilation where numerous government policies have failed.

## Acknowledgements

I would like to thank Christopher Stewart for his valuable comments on the very early draft of this chapter.

# Notes

1. Variably characterized as a sociolect or youth slang, Verlan is a form of verbal wordplay that involves flipping the syllables of a word.
2. The coding criteria in the song extracts are: French is in italics, Arabic in bold, English in Roman, and Verlan in bold and italics.
3. The term *banlieue* is sometimes used with a pejorative connotation, much like 'inner city' in the United States.
4. The term *pieds-noirs* (lit., 'black feet') refers to French nationals born in Algeria under French colonialism up until Algerian independence in 1962.
5. The expression *Paname* in extract 8 is slang for 'Paris'.

# Discography

Diam's (2003), *Brut de femme*. EMI.
Gomez et Dubois (2003), *Flics et hors la loi*. BMG.
IAM (2003), *Revoir un printemps*. EMI.
Sniper (2003), *Gravé dans la roche*. EMI.

# References

Alim, H. S. (2006), *Roc the Mic Right: The Language of Hip Hop Culture*. New York: Routledge.

Androutsopoulos, J. (2009), 'Language and the three spheres of hip hop', in H. S. Alim, A. Ibrahim and A. Pennycook (eds), *Global Linguistic Flows: Hip Hop Cultures, Youth Identities, and the Politics of Language*. New York: Routledge, pp. 43–62.

Androutsopoulos, J. and Scholz, A. (2002), 'On the recontextualization of hip hop in European speech communities: a contrastive analysis of rap lyrics', *PhiN: Philologie im Netz*, 19, <http://web.fu-berlin.de/phin/phin19/p19t1.htm>, accessed 24 January 2010.

—(2003), 'Spaghetti funk: appropriations of hip hop culture and rap music in Europe'. *Popular Music and Society*, 26, 4, 463–479.

Auer, P. (ed.) (1998), *Code-switching in Conversation*. New York: Routledge.

Auzanneau, M. (2001), 'Identités africaines: le rap comme lieu d'expression'. *Cahiers d' études africaines*, 163/164, 711–734.

—(2002), 'Rap in Libreville, Gabon: an urban sociolinguistic space', in A. P. Durand (ed.), *Black, Blanc, Beur: Rap Music and the Hip Hop Culture in the Francophone World*. Oxford: The Scarecrow Press, pp. 104–123.

Bazin, H. (1995), *La culture hip hop*. Paris: Desclée de Brouwer.

Bentahila, A. and Davies, E. (1992), 'Code-switching and language dominance'. *Advances in Psychology*, 83, 443–458.

—(2002), 'Language mixing in Rai music: localisation or globalisation?' *Language and Communication*, 22, 187–207.

Béthune, C. (1999), *Le rap: une esthétique hors la loi*. Paris: Editions Autrement.

**63**

Bokamba, E. (1989), 'Are there syntactic constraints on code-switching?' *World Englishes*, 8, 3, 277–292.

Boucher, M. (1998), *Rap, expression des lascars: Signification et enjeux du rap dans la société française*. Paris: L'Harmattan.

Bowen, J. (2002), 'Islam in/of France: dilemmas of translocality', Paper presented at the *13th International Conference of Europeanists*. Chicago, March 14–16, 2002. <http://www.ceri-sciencespo.com/archive/mai02/artjrb.pdf>, accessed 13 March 2010.

Calio, J. (1998), *Le rap: une réponse des banlieues?* Lyon: Aléas Editeur.

Calvet, L.-J. (1994), *Les voix de la ville*. Paris: Editions Payot & Rivages.

Cannon, S. (1997), 'Paname city rapping: B-boys in the banlieues and beyond', in A. Hargreaves and M. McKinney (eds.), *Post-colonial Cultures in France*. London: Routledge, pp. 150–166.

Cutler, C. (2000), '"Chanter en yaourt": pop music and language choice in France'. *Popular Music and Society*, 24, 177–133.

—(2009), '"You shouldn't be rappin', you should be skateboardin' the X-games": the coconstruction of whiteness in an MC battle', in H. S. Alim, A. Ibrahim and A. Pennycook (eds), *Global Linguistic Flows: Hip Hop Cultures, Youth Identities, and the Politics of Language*. New York: Routledge, pp. 79–94.

Davies, E. and Bentahila, A. (2006), 'Code-switching and the globalisation of popular music: the case of North African rai and rap'. *Multilingua*, 25, 367–392.

Dumay, J.-M. (2005), 'Violences et vigilance, le face-à-face des banlieues', *Le Monde*, 8 November 2005.

Durand, A.-P. (ed.) (2002), *Black, Blanc, Beur: Rap Music and Hip hop Culture in the Francophone World*. Oxford: Scarecrow.

Ferguson, C. A. (1959), 'Diglossia'. *Word*, 15, 325–340.

Gardner-Chloros, P. (1995), 'Code-switching in community, regional and national repertoires: the myth of the discreteness of linguistic systems', in L. Milroy and P. Muysken (eds), *One Speaker, Two Languages: Cross-disciplinary Perspectives on Code-switching*. New York: Cambridge University Press, pp. 68–89.

Gumperz, J. and Cook-Gumperz, J. (1982), 'Introduction: language and the communication of social identity', in J. Gumperz (ed.), *Language and Social Identity*. Cambridge: Cambridge University Press, pp. 1–21.

Hargreaves, A. G. and McKinney, M. (1997), 'Introduction: the post-colonial problematic in France', in A. Hargreaves and M. McKinney (eds), *Post-colonial Cultures in France*. London: Routledge, pp. 3–25.

Heath, J. (1989), *From Code-switching to Borrowing: Foreign and Diglossic Mixing in Moroccan Arabic*. London: Kegan Paul.

Higgins, C. (2009), 'From Da Bomb to *Bomba*: global hip hop nation language in Tanzania', in H. S. Alim, A. Ibrahim and A. Pennycook (eds), *Global Linguistic Flows: Hip Hop Cultures, Youth Identities, and the Politics of Language*. New York: Routledge, pp. 95–112.

Huq, R. (2006), *Beyond Subculture: Pop, Youth and Identity in a Postcolonial World*, London: Routledge.

Jacono, J. M. (2002), 'Musical dimensions and ways of expressing identity in French rap: the groups from Marseille', in A. P. Durand (ed.), *Black, Blanc, Beur: Rap Music and the Hip Hop Culture in the Francophone world*. Oxford: The Scarecrow Press, pp. 22–32.

Krims, A. (2002), 'Foreword: francophone hip hop as a colonial urban geography', in A. P. Durand (ed.), *Black, Blanc, Beur: Rap Music and the Hip Hop Culture in the Francophone World*. Oxford: The Scarecrow Press, pp. vii–x.

Lapassade, G. and Rousselot, P. (1998), *Le rap ou la fureur de dire*. Paris: Editions Loris Talmart.

Lefkowitz, N. (1989), 'Verlan: talking backwards'. *The French Review*, 63, 312–322.

Lin, A. (2009), '"Respect for da chopstick hip hop": the politics, poetics, and pedagogy of Cantonese verbal art in Hong Kong', in H. S. Alim, A. Ibrahim and A. Pennycook (eds), *Global Linguistic Flows: Hip Hop Cultures, Youth Identities, and the Politics of Language*. New York: Routledge, pp. 159–177.

Mouloud, L. (2003), 'L'Affaire Sniper: La mauvaise cible de Sarkozy?'. *L'Humanité*, 11 November 2003.

Myers-Scotton, C. (1993), *Duelling Languages*. Oxford: Clarendon Press.

Omoniyi, T. (2009), 'So I choose to do am Naija style: hip hop, language, and post colonial identities', in H. S. Alim, A. Ibrahim and A. Pennycook (eds), *Global Linguistic Flows: Hip Hop Cultures, Youth Identities, and the Politics of Language*. New York: Routledge, pp. 159–177.

Pecqueux, A. (2007), *Voix du rap: Essai de sociologie de l'action musicale*. Paris: Editions de l'Harmattan.

Pennycook, A. and Mitchell, T. (2009), 'Hip hop as a dusty foot philosophy: engaging locality', in H. S. Alim, A. Ibrahim and A. Pennycook (eds), *Global Linguistic Flows: Hip Hop Cultures, Youth Identities, and the Politics of Language*. New York: Routledge, pp. 25–42.

Picone, M. (2002), 'Artistic codemixing'. *University of Pennsylvania Working Papers in Linguistics*, 8, 191–207.

Prévos, A. (1996), 'The evolution of French rap music and hip hop culture in the 1980s and 1990s'. *The French Review*, 69, 713–725.

—(1998), 'Hip hop, rap, and repression in France and in the United States'. *Popular Music and Society*, 22, 67–84.

—(2002), 'Two decades of rap in France: emergence, developments, prospects', in A. P. Durand (ed.), *Black, Blanc, Beur: Rap Music and the Hip Hop Culture in the Francophone World*. Oxford: The Scarecrow Press, pp. 1–21.

—(2003), '"In it for the money": rap and business cultures in France', *Popular Music and Society*, 26, 445–461.

Roth-Gordon, J. (2009), 'Conversational sampling, race trafficking, and the invocation of the gueto in brazilian hip hop', in H. S. Alim, A. Ibrahim and A. Pennycook (eds), *Global Linguistic Flows: Hip Hop Cultures, Youth Identities, and the Politics of Language*. New York: Routledge, pp. 63–77.

Sarkar, M. (2009), 'Still reppin por mi gente: the transformative power of language mixing in Quebec hip hop', in H. S. Alim, A. Ibrahim and

A. Pennycook (eds), *Global Linguistic Flows: Hip Hop Cultures, Youth Identities, and the Politics of Language*. New York: Routledge, pp. 139–157.

Sarkar, M. and Winer, L. (2006), 'Multilingual code-switching in Quebec rap: poetry, pragmatics and performativity'. *International Journal of Multilingualism*, 3, 173–92.

Swedenburg, T. (2002), 'Islamic hip hop vs islamophobia', in T. Mitchell (ed.), *Global Noise: Rap and Hip hop Outside the USA*. Wesleyan University Press, pp. 57–85.

Zegnani, S. (2004), 'Le rap comme activité scripturale: l'emergence d'un groupe illégitime de lettres'. *Language et Societé*, 110, 65–84.

# 3 'We ain't Terrorists but we Droppin' Bombs': Language Use and Localization in Egyptian Hip Hop

Angela Williams

## 1 Introduction

Within the past two decades rap music and hip-hop culture have widely expanded from being an American production and commercial export to a worldwide movement mediated by global communications.[1] This genre of music has at its core linguistic conventions – phonological, lexical, syntactic and pragmatic – prominent in African American communities which combined with rhythmic beats to give structure to lyrical expression representing the shared experiences of community members. Although hip hop originated among African American communities in the United States of America as an expression of their struggle against racial oppression and economic disparity, rap music and hip-hop culture is combined with local linguistic, musical and political contexts to become a vehicle for youth protest and resistance around the world (Mitchell, 2001). It has been put forward that the artists who create this style of music relate to African American culture through the history of oppression and disenfranchisement. Osumare (2007) suggests that rap artists around the world share a 'connective marginality' which allows them to produce music as a commentary on their social situations.

Various theories have been proposed to examine the global spread of hip-hop music and culture. The spread of hip hop was initially attributed to globalization as an American commercial export (Perry, 2004, p. 19) and 'a culture of the African American minority' (Bozza, 2004, p. 130). Others have described the existence of hip hop outside of the US as being 'already local', meaning that the music has emerged from indigenous communities and oral traditional practices (Pennycook and Mitchell, 2009), therefore making hip hop a means for the revival and spread of local culture. An alternative theory, *mondialisation* (Mattelart, 2005), examines the economic and social interconnectedness of communities in order to analyse the spread of hip-hop culture and understand how local hip-hop artists in one country are connected to artists in another country. According to Darling-Wolf, *mondialisation* allows for the notion of the global sphere to be conceptualized as a 'collection of locally connected, socio-cultural arenas intersecting with nation-states and national culture in multiple and fluid ways and engaged in relationships of differential power' (2008, p. 197). Examining the spread of hip-hop culture through the lens of *mondialisation* provides a more comprehensive understanding of the socio-cultural situations in which the artists exist, as well as how they relate to other artists around the world.

The spread of rap music and hip-hop culture cannot only be understood as an American cultural import that has been acquired by youth around the world. Nor is it solely the manifestation of an indigenous art form and local expressive traditions. Rather, inquiry into global hip-hop movements must begin with the examination of local-to-local relationships and the development of global racial identity politics which affect claims to authenticity. This chapter examines the construction of a local Egyptian hip-hop identity through Egyptian Arabic language use and conventions, as well as through local themes expressed in English and Arabic, by analysing the work of four mainstream and underground groups. Specifically, I seek to examine the process of localization of hip hop in the Egyptian context, focusing on the themes of nationalism, Pan-Arabism and connective marginality and how these are expressed in songs addressing both local and global audiences. I will argue that each of the groups have become localized and examine how one group in particular resist established usage conventions and adapt a traditional practice of verbal one-upmanship to redefine language ideologies. In demonstrating that language choices in hip-hop lyrics do not merely reflect the social norms and language ideology, it will emerge that English, which usually functions as an 'elite code' in Egypt, is actually used in the lyrics to express resistance against the English-speaking world. Through the making of music, the groups change and transmit local traditions, as well as create a space (via the internet, media and album sales) for these traditions to spread (Pennycook, 2007, p. 139). Through the localization of hip-hop culture, the artists are redefining what it means to be Egyptian in terms of language choice and self expression.

## 2 Language use in Egypt

### 2.1 Arabic in Egypt

Before examining how hip-hop culture is becoming legitimized and localized in Egypt, it is necessary to first establish an understanding of language use in the country. The sociolinguistic landscape of Egypt is complicated both in terms of the uses of Arabic language varieties, which symbolize different social and political views in Egypt (Suleiman, 2006), as well as certain historical and political events that have given preference to the use of such foreign languages as English, French and German. Arabic variation in Egypt, as well as other Arabic-speaking countries, has been described as 'diglossic' between a high (H) form of language, which carries prestige within a society, and a low (L) form, which does not (Ferguson, 1959). However, scholars have argued for the existence of more intermediate varieties of Arabic (El-Hassan, 1978; Mitchell, 1986; Meiseles, 1980; Harry, 1996), and have actually defended up to five different levels (Badawi, 1973; Blanc, 1960).

Haeri argues that one must take a critical look at 'the role and place of Arabic' within the hierarchy of the 'linguistic repertoire of Egypt' (1997, pp. 159–160) in order to reach an understanding of the stylistic variation and language use. To this end, Haeri employs Bourdieu's (1991) notion of the linguistic market, which stresses the importance of symbolic capital for access to the labour market. According to the conventional understanding of the linguistic market, especially those in Western societies, knowledge of the standard is like a valuable piece of currency. In turn, this has led to linking greater use of the standard variety of a language to dominant groups who belong to the upper classes. In contexts such as Cairo, however, this is not the case. Haeri argues that speakers' bi- or multi-lingualism, rather than their use of Classical or Modern Standard Arabic, secures better access to the labour market, upward mobility and belonging to the upper class. She observes that the linguistic market of Cairo requires multiple 'currencies' and that the 'currency' of Modern Standard Arabic is by no means the only currency, nor is it the most prominent. The variety of Arabic that is the focus of this chapter is the Arabic vernacular of Egyptian youth, which has not been previously investigated in the context of hip-hop language research.[2]

## 2.2 English in Egypt

Kachru (1992) places English in Egypt in the 'Expanding Circle', due to increasing recognition of it as a universal second language. English continues to have significant use in popular culture in Egypt, as seen in advertising, television, clothing and music, as well as international businesses (Schaub, 2000). Due to President Sadat's 'Open Door Policy', or انفتاح (*infitah*, 'opening'), import and export business has expanded. As a result, English is not only a spoken *lingua franca*, but also the language of correspondence and documentation.

The Open Door Policy, funded mainly by the US, Germany, France and Japan, ushered in a new era in Egypt which allowed rich foreigners to gain more power and control in the country in the 1970s and 1980s and created a class of wealthy Egyptians (Cochran, 2008). While this specific policy was unique to Egypt, the outcomes of the increased foreign involvement and economic privilege given to those who acquired the English language are not uncommon throughout postcolonial societies in Africa and the rest of the world. Today, English use continues to be profitable in terms of tourism and international business and is regarded as a code used for accommodating foreign interests. In the linguistic market, it has gained a higher value and prestige than any other language in Egypt.

## 3 The Egyptian hip-hop scene: profiling the artists

Hip hop in Egypt is a fairly recent cultural phenomenon that has been steadily on the rise for the past five years. One of the most popular hip-hop groups in Egypt is MTM, whose name stands for the group members' initials, as well as the acronym for *Mezzika Tilakhbat Mukhak* ( 'Music Messes up your Mind'). The group is from Alexandria, but its music is popular in Cairo as well. The group's songs, which are in Egyptian Arabic, concern social issues, especially those involving youth in Egypt, and are often in a light-hearted tone. According to group member Takki: '[Rap] is really close to young people because it speaks their language and it speaks about their real-life problems and social life from their point of view. We really needed this in the Arab world.'³ The Arab hip-hop scene is gaining in popularity with MTM, who have produced two CDs – *Omy Mesafra* ('My Mother is Travelling') in 2003, and *Telephony Biren* ('My Phone is Ringing') in 2004 – and were awarded the prize for best modern Arab act at the Arab Music Awards in 2004. MTM use Egyptian Arabic almost exclusively as their mode of reaching youth, but more recently the use of English by other groups within the Egyptian hip-hop community has emerged.

The use of African American English (AAE), which has been called the 'default code' (Androutsopoulos, 2009) of hip hop, is a symbolic gesture that evokes identification with the global hip-hop community. A newer group from Cairo, the Arabian Knightz, whose composition includes E-Money, Getto Pharaoh, Sphinx and Saifullah, use both English and Egyptian Arabic in their lyrics. Still very much an underground group, the Arabian Knightz released their first independently-produced mix-tape in 2008, entitled *Desert Saga*. This album has 19 tracks, with some songs predominately rapped in English and others in Egyptian

**70**

Arabic. Their lyrics often address socio-political themes. Their use of English creates the potential for their music to reach non-Arabic speaking listeners, while their use of Egyptian Arabic keeps them authentic to their Arab identity and also makes their music popular among the bilingual youth in Egypt.

Another group who rap in both English and Arabic, Y-Crew, consists of MC Omar Boflot, winner of MTV Arabia's Season 1 *Hip Hopna* Middle East reality talent show in 2007, and Alien-X, who are from Alexandria. Before going on *Hip Hopna*, Boflot self-recorded, produced and released his tracks online. While his talent had initially been underground, winning *Hip Hopna* has brought him more recognition. In 2001 he formed the group Y-Crew with Alien-X. According to the group's Myspace page, the letter 'Y' in the group's name symbolizes the shape of the Nile River as it flows throughout Egypt into the Mediterranean Sea.[4]

Another group who advanced to the final round of MTV Arabia's *Hip Hopna* is Asfalt. The two MCs of the group are from Cairo, and they rap almost exclusively in Egyptian Arabic, with the group's logo represented in Arabic orthography as أسفلت (*asfalt*). The group gained the support of Egyptian clothing label Al-Fikrah Couture, with whom they collaborated to create a limited edition T-shirt bearing the logo written in bold letters that was sold in Egypt in 2008. Although Asfalt is one of the newest groups on the hip-hop scene in Egypt, it is quickly gaining recognition and support through networking websites such as Myspace and Facebook, as well as public performances.

Each of the groups introduced above has performed at such reputable venues as *El Sawy Culturewheel*, a cultural centre located in Zamalek, an upscale business and residential district in Cairo. Groups have also performed outside of *Bibliotheca Alexandrina*, the new Library of Alexandria, as well as at various clubs and hotels throughout Egypt. While each of the groups is unique in regards to their position, particular involvement and development of hip-hop culture, they share similar language conventions within their lyrics that facilitate the construction of an Egyptian hip-hop community.

## 4 Language use in Egyptian hip hop

To analyse language use in Egyptian hip-hop music, I examined 85 songs from these four groups: MTM, Y-Crew, Arabian Knightz and Asfalt. I chose these artists because they represent both the mainstream and underground hip-hop movements in Egypt. Of these, 17 songs are from the two recorded albums by MTM, *Omy Mesafra* and *Telephony Biren*.

**71**

The remainder are independent releases, uploaded online by the artists between the years 2005–2009. I obtained transcriptions of MTM's songs from www.mtmclub.tk, a fan-based website which may or may not have official affiliation with the group. The remaining songs I downloaded or accessed online from www.soundclick.com, an online community for independent artists of all genres of music, as well as from www.egy-rap.blogspot.com, a blog devoted to Egyptian underground hip-hop artists, and from the artists' Myspace pages. Nine songs by the Arabian Knightz were first accessed from the group's Myspace page in 2007 as part of a pilot study I conducted on the Egyptian hip-hop scene and language use. Of these nine songs, only one, 'AKKKAAAAYYYYY', appears on the group's mix-tape, *Desert Saga*, which was released independently in 2008. I have included the Arabian Knightz's earlier songs in the data as well as their newer ones in order to examine language use changes in their lyrics. I discovered that while their earlier songs tended to be predominately in English with some degree of Arabic, their newer songs include collaborations with other artists, such as Egyptian rapper MC Amin and Tamer Nafar of the Palestinian group DAM. The group's recent collaborations and extended network of other artists in the region have had an impact on the choice of language in their lyrics.

I analysed the lyrics to identify instances of code-switching from the matrix language (Myers-Scotton, 1993), either Egyptian Arabic or English, into the embedded language. For some songs, two native Egyptian Arabic speakers assisted me with the transcription of Arabic lyrics. To analyse the lyrics, I adopted Kahf's (2007) framework, which analyses Arabic hip hop as a genre that authenticates itself based on three dimensions: social-political, emotional-experiential, and rhetorical. I will explore the extent to which these groups have localized rap music and hip-hop culture in terms of their songs' themes and language forms, including adapting local language traditions such as the cognate curse in Egyptian Arabic (Stewart, 1997), which provides a background to the artists' use of English – the code of the oppressor – as a code of resistance *against that very same oppressor*. Also, I use the framework of Davies and Bentahila (2008) to examine the use of code-switching as an aesthetic device which may be motivated by either the structure or the meaning of the lyric. In the examples throughout this chapter, Egyptian Arabic lyrics are transliterated in a line of text to the right of the Arabic text. The English translation is then located to the right of the transliteration, and titles of songs appear in quotation marks. The analysis proceeds in a top-down fashion, as I first explore the scope of hip hop's localization in Egypt, and then move to an examination of switching patterns between languages.

## 4.1 Trajectories of localization

In this section, I will explore the localization of rap music and hip-hop culture in Egypt by examining themes and messages in lyrics. According-ing to Pennycook, localization occurs when the artists 'us[e] a particular register that is local, generational, cultural and distinctive' (2007, p. 105). Hip-hop culture is localized by the situated use of conventions that are known throughout global hip-hop communities, as well as through the transmittal of local traditions and verbal expressions. Evidence of localization in the first sense is seen in Egyptian artists' use of conventions, such as lexicon and speech acts, that are typical of global hip-hop artists. Furthermore, the artists' self-identification with 'Blackness' lays claim to an identity as authentic participants of hip-hop culture. Evidence of localization in the second sense, on the other hand, is found in the language choices of Egyptian artists which exemplify Egyptian Arabic youth language, as well as in their use of English for resistance, which carries echoes of the local tradition of the cognate curse (Stewart, 1997), that is, using a previous speaker's own words to fashion an insult hurled back at him or her. In addition, hip hop is localized in Egypt based on the use of local themes that authen-ticate the artists' Egyptian and Arab identity: the themes of patriotism and Pan-Arabism are themes through which the artists lay claim to an Arab identity, even when using English to communicate these concepts.

### 4.1.1 Hip-hop language conventions localized

According to Mitchell, hip hop is a 'vehicle for global youth affiliations and a tool for reworking local identity all over the world' (2001, pp. 1–2). In Egyptian hip-hop culture, first and foremost, the term 'hip hop' has been appropriated and assimilated into the local language. This is evident in the title of MTV Arabia's reality TV show, *Hip Hopna*, whose title and logo exemplify the blending of cultures and languages. Written as Hip Hop ـنا (-*na*, first person plural possessive), it symbolizes the participation of Arab youth in hip-hop culture, laying simultaneous claims to both authenticity and possession (*our* hip hop). A similar television series began in May 2009, entitled بيت الهب هوب (*bayt al-hip hop*, 'house of hip hop'). In this title, the Arabic language orthography is retained, despite the fact that the language lacks a /p/ grapheme. The Arabic letter ب (/b/) is used instead. Often in Arabic orthography, for-eign words containing /p/ will be written with a ب (/b/) with three dots. The omission of the three dots, as well as the use of (ب) for 'hip hop' may signify that 'hip hop' is no longer a foreign word, but has gone

**73**

through a process of Arabization. Therefore, artists who participate in هب هوب ('hip hop') seem to have localized both the word and the concept, and made them their own.

Another way of localizing concepts that are characteristic of hip-hop music and culture is to translate them directly into Arabic. Y-Crew do this in their song 'Melook Eskinderia' ('Kings of Alexandria'), using the term تحت الأرض (*taht al-ard*, 'underground') to describe their music.

| (1) موجودين **تحت الأرض** بس | *Mawgudin **taht al-ard*** | 'We are here |
|---|---|---|
| أكيد حانطلع فوق | *bas akid hantla fo* | underground but for |
| | | sure we will climb to |
| | | the top' |

Y-Crew, 'ملوك الأسكندرية', 'Melook Eskinderia'

Examples (2)–(4) additionally contain lyrics that illustrate both the localization of Hip Hop Nation Language (HHNL) conventions (Alim, 2004), as well as local youth language. Language practices are localized by means of speech acts that hip-hop artists commonly use. Androutsopoulos and Scholz (2006) identify seven such speech acts, which include 'self-referential speech', 'listener-directed speech', 'boasting', 'dissing', 'place and time reference', 'identification' and 'representation'. Example (2) by Y-Crew, which bears the same name as the reality show mentioned earlier, makes reference to the hip-hop competition organized by MTV Arabia and contains both self-referential and listener-directed speech as well as boasting.

| (2) حيب حوبنا | *hip hopna* | 'Our Hip Hop' |
|---|---|---|
| MTV, Y-Family's on the screen | | |
| Turn up the volume, it's the | | |
| aggressive machine | | |
| أفتح | *iftah* | 'Open' |
| MTV Arabia | | |
| خالي بالك | *khali balak* | 'Watch out' |
| From the words that I say to ya | | |
| Boflot is the winner in, in your area | | |

Y-Crew, 'حيب حوبنا', 'Hip hopna'

Another common feature is the spelling feature, which occurs when artists spell either a proper name or other word. MTM use this feature in their songs. For example, in (3) from 'Zay ma inta a'aiz' ('As you like'), each artist spells out his name, Mahmoud and Taky.

**74**

(3)   د – و – م – ح – م   *meem, haa, meem, wa, daal*   'M-H-M-W-D'

ي – و – ك – ا – ت   *tay, alif, kaf, wi, yay*   'T-A-K-W-Y'

MTM, 'زاي ما أنت عايز', 'Zay ma inta a'aiz'

Identification speech is used in a song by the groups Asfalt and El Zero, another underground rap group who is also increasing its participation in the hip hop scene in Egypt. In example (4) from the track 'Al-senario we Al-huwar' ('The Discussion'), the artists ask one another to identify themselves. Each says that they have been participating in the hip-hop scene in Egypt for years and that they are well-known.

(4)   يا عم اسفلت مين؟   *ya 'am asfalt min?*   'Oh, man, who is Asfalt?'

يا عم الزيرو مين؟   *ya 'am al zero min?*   'Oh, man who is Zero?'

معرفين معالمين   *ma'rfin ma'almin*   'We are well-known'

أحنا بدأنا من سنين   *ehna beda'na min senin*   'We started years ago'

أنتو مين أنتو مين   *intu min, intu min*   'Who are you, who are you?'

طب قولي أنتو اللي مين   *Teb 'uli intu ili min*   'Tell me who are you?'

فاكسلين فاكسنين   *faksenin, faksenin*   'Failures, failures'

أنتو اللي فاكسنين   *intu ili faksenin*   'You are the failures'

Asfalt, 'السينارو و الحوار', 'Al-senario we al huwar'

Example (4) also contains an instance of 'dissing' involving the use of a lexical item exclusively used by youth in Egypt. The word فاكسنين (*faksenin*, 'failures') is derived from the word فاكس, (*faks*) meaning 'failed' or 'empty', and, according to native speakers, entered the lexicon of Egyptian youth as recently as 2007. Use of language conventions characteristic of HHNL, as well as the appearance of hip-hop terminology in Arabic, show how the music and the culture are in the process of localization.

### 4.1.2 Artists' use of local themes: patriotism and Pan-Arabism

The ideals of patriotism are strong in Egypt and play a large role in the education and socialization of youth. From an early age, children are taught about the wealth of Egypt's ancient history. In Egypt's public schools, each morning young students line up side by side outside of the school, recite the national anthem and listen to the morning's headline news broadcast over a loud speaker. As in many countries, males are required to serve in the army for two years, except in special circumstances. It is evident that patriotism and love for the country is instilled in young people at an early age. The young people who are members of hip-hop groups in Egypt are no exception. This nationalism is often displayed in their lyrics, such as in example (5), from MC Amin's song 'Tahha al Gumheria' ('Long Live the Republic'). The first line of the song resembles the anthem that is spoken each morning before school. The second line exalts the Egyptian people, describing them with an adjective that is popular in Egyptian colloquial Arabic, *mia mia*, which originates from the word for 100 (مية , *mia*).

| (5) | تحي الجمهورية العربية المصرية | *tahya al gumheria* | 'Long live the Arab |
| | | *al-'arabia al-masria* | Republic of Egypt |
| | اللي ناسها كواسين اللي ناسها مية | *ili nas-ha kwaysin* | Whose people are good |
| | مية | *ili nas-ha mia mia* | and perfect' |

MC Amin, 'تحي الجمهورية', 'Tahya al gumheria'

Other patriotic songs also exist that are predominately in English. Getto Pharaoh of the Arabian Knigthz raps an anthem about Egypt, with the chorus, 'Lemme tell you where I'm from: *Masr, masr*' ('Egypt'). Example (6) by the Arabian Knightz also displays pride in the artists' Egyptian origins. The song is not only patriotic but also hints at the group's ideals of Pan-Arabism.

| (6) | From the M-I-D-D-L-E-E-A-S-T | | |
| | Ain't no Israel it's فلسطين | *Philistine* | 'Palestine' |
| | Straight outta | | |
| | أم الدونية | *Om* | 'Mother of the world' |
| | | *a-dunia* | |
| | These niggas running things | | |

Arabian Knightz, 'C-A-I-R-O'

In the song 'C-A-I-R-O', we begin to see the artists' multiple allegiances to the Middle East, or Arabia, and also to what has been typically understood as Black American culture. Although their lyrics do not directly address the problem of race, they reconcile 'Arabness' and 'Blackness' in songs such as this one. Juxtaposing the location – أم الدونية (*Om a-dunia*, lit. 'Mother of the world', fig. 'Egypt') – with 'these niggas', who are presumably themselves, they are creating a new space, or new world, in terms of the theory of *mondialisation*. In this new space, 'Arabness' and 'Blackness' coexist and become a hyphenated identity. The artists' self-referential speech, which identifies them as 'these niggas' is further dealt with in section 4.1.4 below.

For the Egyptian artists, then, local themes are not restricted to what happens within Egypt's borders, but also concern what occurs in other areas in the region. The Palestinian struggle is a common theme and concern both in Egyptian society and in the artists' lyrics. Throughout the twentieth century until the present, Egypt has been involved in peace processes in the region, and many Palestinians have been given refuge in Egypt. Although Egypt has offered aid to Palestinian people, at times the government has been criticized by other Arab nations for not doing enough to assist Palestinians. By indexing the Palestinian struggle, the artists legitimize themselves as real 'Arab rappers' equally sensitive to these struggles as their fellow Arabs. In all cases, even when rapping in English, the artists retain the Arabic pronunciation of Palestine as *Philistine*. The mainstream group MTM also mentions the Palestinian situation. As this group is mainstream, and therefore subject to censorship, their lyrics appear to be less controversial and almost jest-like when they mention Palestine in example (7), '*Ay Kalam*' ('Nonsense'). In this song, the artist dreams that he meets a ghost who grants him three wishes. His first wish is that Israel would withdraw from Palestinian land.

| | | | |
|---|---|---|---|
| (7) | ده عفريت بجد لالالا | *da afreet begad la la la* | 'Is that really a ghost, no, no, no |
| | عفرييييييييت | *afreeeeeet* | Ghooooost |
| | قرصت نفسى ودعكت عنيا | *arest nefsi wa da'kt 'anaya* | I pinched myself and rubbed my eyes |
| | عفريت طلع لى بقى بين ايديا | *afreet tala' li ba bain idaya* | The ghost appeared between my hands |
| | أعدت افكر شوية هى تبقى اية أول أمنية | *a'adt afuker shwaya heya tiba eh awul amnia* | I began thinking about my first wish |
| | أول حاجة جات فى بالى | *awul haga gat fi bali* | The first thing that came to my mind |
| | فلسطين فى الوضع الحالى | *filisteen fil wada' al hali* | Palestine's current situation |
| | أسرائيل خالتها تلالى | *israil khaliha telali* | Israel has really worn her out |

| | | |
|---|---|---|
| قلت للعفريت شيلها لى | *qalt lil'afreet sheelha li* | I told the ghost to remove Israel |
| لاعايز فلوس ولا قصر | *la aiz faloos wa la asur* | I don't want money or a castle |
| أصل ديونا مالهاش حصر | *asl diyuna maluhash hasur* | Our debts are limitless |
| قلت للعفريت سددها بس أبقى هات لى بيهم وصل | *qalt lil'afreet sadedha bas hat li bihum wasl* | I said to the ghost to pay them and bring me a receipt |
| وشوف أية اخر أمنية دى اكيد حاجة هتبقى ليا | *wa shuf eh akher amnia di akeed haga liya* | Look what the last wish was for me |
| خلصت فترة الصلاحية والنبى هات لى كارت بمية | *halst futra al-sulahia wa an-nabi hat li kart bi-mia* | The time has run out, so please bring me A (phone) card for 100 (minutes)' |

MTM, 'اي كلام', 'Ay Kalam'

The music of MTM has become localized as their lyrics discuss topics that are authentic in Egyptian society. As in many countries throughout the world, mobile phones have become quite prevalent in Egypt. Young adolescents begin carrying a phone as early as 11 or 12 years of age. Most people have rechargeable SIM cards in their phones, which means that they must purchase phone cards for 10, 20, 50 or 100 minutes, and when the card runs out, a new one must be purchased. In this song, the artist parallels his wishes, that Israel would cease to occupy Palestinian territory, and that he would obtain a new phone card. Whereas the former may be a valiant request, and the latter a trivial whim, when the two are paralleled, they create a unique picture – and critique – of Egyptian society that the artists help to construct. MTM, the only group who has been signed to a mainstream record label, represent a variety of hip hop that is less socially-challenging, and therefore the majority of youth may readily accept and relate to it. Although the group express concern for Palestinians, they are not overly political. They maintain a light sense of humour in their lyrics that is typical and desirable in Egyptian society. Other groups' lyrics, however, are extremely more direct in their assessment of the Palestinian struggle.

Y-Crew also discuss the Palestinian struggle in extract (8), 'Filiseen' (Palestine'). The artist uses English to communicate resistance against the oppression directed towards Palestinian people. In this song, the Arabic lyrics seem to provide religious commentary, while the artist speaks graphically in English against Israel.

(8) فلسطين فلسطين

'Philisteen, Philisteen'

'Palestine, Palestine

جوها ما فيش أمان

Gowaha mafish aman

Inside there is no security

صوت قنبولة والرصاص في كل مكان

sot qanbola wa al risas fi kul makan

The noise of bombs and bullets everywhere

أحساسنا في القلبنا

ahsasna fil qalb

Our feelings in our hearts

بس أطالع من لسان

bas atala' min lisan

Just appear from on tongues

مدفون جوانا بس

medfun gowana bas

A cemetery inside of us

دة من أضعف الإمان

da min ada'f al-aman

Is the weakest security

سألت نفسي لية مافيش مافيش أمان

saelt nufsi li mafish mafish aman

I asked myself where is there no peace

علشان كلنا نعيش

ashan kulena na'esh

For all of us to live'

So please throw your guns away 'cause we got to live in peace
So what's it gonna be
This song's dedicated to Philisteen

. . .

فاكرين أحنا نامين مش محناش صحين

fakrin ehna naming mish mahnash sahin

'They think that we're asleep and will not awake'

All I see now is murder-kill gear
And we're about to crush the star of Israel
Muslims unite together there's no

more fear
And we're about to
make the Jews
disappear
There's no need to
make the innocent see
more blood
We shall take back
our land with the help
of our gun

| من زما في الحرب | *min zaman al-harb* | 'Since the past, there is war |
| بين الخير و بين الشر | *bain al-khayr wa bain al-shar* | Between good and evil |
| ألله اكبر | *Allahu akbar* | God is great |

Our victory's possible
We just wanna fight
who is responsible

. . .

| حزن في عينينا | *hozn fi 'aeenayna* | Sadness in our eyes |

When I see these
people die

| أصمدوا يا أبطال | *asmedu ya abtal* | Endure, oh heroes |

I know that you can

try

| ربنا وعدنا نصر | *rabina wa'adna nasr* | God promised us victory |

We will win in the
end

| دي مزكورة في القرآن | *di muzkura fil Quran* | This is remembered in the Qur'an |

You don't believe me
ask your friend
Only time will tell

| حان وقت احرب | *han waqt-al harb* | Now is the time of war |
| | | |

One day they will
burn in hell
A stone in my hand is
the weapon that I
need

| و نفسي أمدايد | *wa nufsi amed 'id* | I want to reach out my hand and die |
| و باخلم أموت شهيد | *wa bahlem amot shadid* | And dream of dying a martyr' |

Y-Crew, 'فلسطين', 'Philisteen'

In example (8), the Arabic lyrics seem to seek to provide justification for what is expressed in the English lyrics. While the English lyrics assert such notions as opposition and vengeance, the Arabic lyrics offer an explanation and context to the historical and cultural background. Using English as a language of resistance goes against the language ideology that wants English to be a vehicle that caters to foreign desires, such as tourism, international business and trade. The group has such strong feelings for the Palestinian struggle, that the artist claims in his lyrics that he would be willing to die a martyr for the sake of the struggle. These Pan-Arab sentiments are a local theme that these mainstream and underground artists in Egypt address in their lyrics.

Example (9), 'Electric Chair' by the Arabian Knightz, contains equal lyrics in English and Arabic. The song mentions situations that the artists deem have unjustly oppressed the Arab world. Among these are: Zionism, the prison at Guantanamo Bay, and the Iraq War. The chorus of the song goes, 'If I had my way, I'd put you all in the electric chair.' The lyrics metaphorically refer to the death of Sadam Hussein, who was executed in Iraq during a religious holiday in 2007. The artists compare the execution to that of an American leader being killed on Christmas day. The lyrics, which are exceedingly direct, are most effective at communicating resistance by comparing an actual event with a hypothetical occurrence to show how horrific it would be. The artist 'flips' the situation in order to express his resistance to the infamous prison camp and Zionism, as well as an execution on a religious holiday.

(9)  If I had my way, I'd open the gates of
     Guantanamo Bay

Zionism would die today

Bush would feel Iraqi pain

Die like Sadam Hussein on Christmas Day

> Arabian Knightz,    'Electric Chair'

The Arabian Knightz also express sentiments of Pan-Arabism in example (10), as the lyrics literally support the movement. In the song 'Da Knightz', the artist Sphinx, promotes the USA – that is the 'United State of Arabia', and refers to this area as 'the land of the brave'. The lyrics create an image of a unified Arab State. The first verse is in English, the second in Arabic, and the third in a mixture of English and Arabic. The chorus of the song is the chorus of the song 'Arabian Nights', the soundtrack of the Disney film *Aladdin*.

(10) عربي, مصري, أصلي            *arabi, masri,*      'Arab, Egyptian,
                                  *asli*              original'

The land of the brave

Good ol' USA

United State of Arabia

Where the AKs reign

The rarest of strains

Sphinx, best beware of his

Arabic rage

His Arabic is crazed

The blood of Mangorian

slaves

Go to war and erase

The disgraced race

Replaced by the Arabs

Take Jerusalem back,

Lebanon and Iraq

All assassins attack

For the red, white and

black

The vision of Pan-Arabism

is back

In the form of **kufi** rap

The new **khalifat** dynasty

Arab league

Ramadan's over, tonight

we feast.

Arabian Knightz, 'Da Knightz'

In the first verse, Sphinx introduces the USA by using the same references that are commonly used for America, such as the 'good ol' USA, the land of the brave'. The artist makes explicit reference to Arabic rap music as being part of a new movement of Pan-Arabism which may be able to unite Arab nations together. By also mentioning images that are well-known throughout the Arabic-speaking world, the artist, although rapping in English, again makes claims to his Arab identity. *Kufi*, a style of Arabic calligraphy, and *khalifat* ('caliphate'), which refers to the political leadership in various eras of Islamic history, symbolize a rich heritage within Arab civilization.

The theme of Pan-Arabism is constructed throughout the artists' lyrics in order to authenticate them as Arab rappers and express shared marginality with Arab nations who may be suffering under foreign occupation. At the same time, this marginality legitimizes their participation in hip-hop culture. In the English lyrics, the artists use Arabic borrowings that call to mind Arab civilization, such as *kufi* and *khalifat*. Also, the language ideology of English is reversed, making it a code to express resistance.

### 4.1.3 The cognate curse in Egyptian Arabic and English as resistance

In the Arabian Knightz's song 'Da Knightz', Sphinx's introduction of the 'United State of Arabia' by means of the same references commonly used for America, such as the 'good ol' USA, the land of the brave', may be interpreted as a rhetorical move of 'script flippin' (Smitherman, 1997) through which the artist attempts to get back at an opponent by using that opponent's language to attack him (for another instance of script flippin', see section 4.1.4). Throughout various hip-hop cultures, the element of a verbal duel remains central and language is seen as a crucial means of authenticating artists and giving them a 'one up', as it were, that trumps verbal opponents. Hip hop may be said to have inherited this element from the practice of 'signifying', an African American folk notion for constructing meaning based on inference drawn from the context and shared knowledge or experience (Mitchell-Kernan, 1972). The rap lyrics of US artists frequently draw on the practice of

**83**

'signifying' to insult other artists or other public figures. These insults may not always be easily understood by lay audiences and often take a fair amount of background knowledge of the artist's history to understand.

Signifying is similar to the cognate curse in Egyptian Arabic in that it requires shared knowledge or experience. Stewart defines the cognate curse as an instance of cognate paronomasia that uses 'a single sentence with an optative verb, either explicit or understood, in which a keyword echoes the root-letters of a keyword in the initiator phrase to which it responds' (1997, p. 331). The effectiveness of cognate parono-masia lies in the implication that it is the initial speaker's statement that contains its own fulfilment or refutation, enabling him or her to be affirmed or ridiculed by his or her own words (Stewart, 1997, p. 331). The cognate curse may thus be said to constitute a local rhetorical tradi-tion that resonates through Sphinx's usage in example (10), at once endowing it – for those listeners familiar with the practice – with a rich indexical meaning, and winning him kudos in the verbal game of one-upmanship. This is, then, another way in which hip-hop culture becomes localized to Egypt, as the hip-hop practice of 'signifying' awak-ens echoes of a local tradition and a new, hybrid practice is born.

At the same time, applying the principle of cognate paronomasia to the level of an entire language code and using this code to attack its own (native) speakers has the effect of transforming English, tradition-ally an elite code in Egypt, into a language of resistance. The use of English for resistance is further indexed by artists' choice of Hip Hop Nation Language (HHNL), the vernacular English that the musicians identify as part of hip-hop culture. The use of a vernacular variety of English to rebel against social and political forces clashes with the traditional view of English in Egypt as being a commodity for greater economic gain and stability. In their music, the lyrics are composed in English not to accommodate but to express political dissent and oppo-sition to events often orchestrated by the English-speaking world. The musicians use a particular style of English that has historically been used as a medium to express resistance. In addition, in using this code, they are broadening their audience base.

### 4.1.4 Resisting local racial norms: being and becoming 'Black'

As it has been seen, Egyptian rappers self-identify as Arabs and, more generally, as Middle Eastern. The Arabian Knightz, especially, repeat-edly in their songs refer to the Middle East as the 'Middle Beast'. Through their lyrics, they express their resistance to the conflicts in the region. At the same time, the rappers in the underground scene also self-identify with perceived concepts of 'Blackness'. This is made evident in the artists' frequent referrals to themselves and other artists as 'niggas', a word that carries with it a great deal of controversy among African Americans.

Smitherman (1997) discusses the 'script flippin' that occurs with 'nigger' and 'nigga', the latter pronounced with the deletion of the post-vocalic /r/. According to her, the latter usage of the word has a variety of positive meanings related to camaraderie. On the contrary, when used in a negative context the word refers to social behaviour rather than to race, so that white people or those of non-African decent, can also be 'niggers'. Still, any use of the word remains controversial and sensitive, as it continues to be a racialized term shaped within a history of racism in the US.

In hip-hop lyrics, it has been argued that the term is an important signifier of political dissent and oppositional consciousness that pre-supposes the social and economic marginalization of those who use it (Perry, 2004; Quinne, 2005; Rivera, 2003). Although Wermuth (2001) mentions that Dutch rappers of African Caribbean background use the word 'nigger' in reference to one another, there has been little work devoted to the usage of the word in hip-hop cultures outside of the US. Ibrahim (1999) examines the adoption of 'Blackness' by means of par-ticipation in hip-hop culture and appropriation of 'Black Stylized English' by African youth who are refugees in Quebec. He describes how the youth 'become Black' by entering a *social imaginary* discursive space, in which their identities are already constructed, imagined or positioned by dominant groups. The youth acquire Black Stylized Eng-lish, which includes the self-referential term 'nigga'. A similar process can be seen to be at work in the lyrics of Egyptian rappers, which include the usage of 'nigga' as well as other Black Power images and elements familiar to Black Stylized English. The Black Power symbol of a raised fist, popularized during the Civil Rights Movement of the late 1960s, is invoked in examples (11), 'Bettah', and (12), 'Ha haha ha', by the Arabian Knightz.

(11)  I got the revolutionary area of Arabia with they fist up,

Fist up, then they clipped up

Flip the script, nobody move

This a stick up

Now for to quip up

The big picture, turbaned up

Sand nigga

Sphinx, what?

Arabian Knightz, 'Bettah'

In this song, Sphinx uses Black Stylized English exemplified by the feature of copular deletion (*This Ø a stick up*). He also refers to himself as a *sand nigga*, which, according to the online *Urban Dictionary*, is 'a person of Middle Eastern descent due to the various desert regions there; usually meant in a disparaging and demeaning way'.[5] By means of 'script flippin' (Smitherman, 1997), the term, which originated as a racial slur, goes through the phonetic change of final /r/ loss, and is given a positive connotation in the context of the lyrics.

In another example, the image of a fist in the air is mentioned in the lyrics again, this time with reference to the October War, which began on 6 October 1973. For 17 days, Egyptian forces engaged in combat to reclaim the Sinai Peninsula, which had been occupied by Israel. 6 October 1973 is a day heralded in Egyptian history.

> (12)   Yo, throw up your fists like it's October the Sixth
>
>   If you down with this Arabic, rock to this hit, rock to this hit
>
>   Rock in your hip hop with a twist
>
>   AK we got this
>
>   Arabian Knightz, 'Ha haha ha'

The image of the salute used in the Black Power movement juxtaposed with 6 October 1973 localizes the struggle described in the artists' lyrics. By emphasizing resistance and identifying with Blackness, the artists construct and demonstrate a connective sense of marginality that is both uniquely 'Black' and 'Arab' at the same time.

## 4.2 Code-switching in relation to lyrical structure

Artists creatively use Arabic and English to construct an Egyptian hip-hop identity, making conscious switches between English and Arabic as a poetic device. Since the basis of rap music and lyrics is the rhythm, language choices are governed by both communicative function as well as lyrical structure. Switching between languages has the potential to both widen the groups' audiences, as well as to maintain an in-group identity. Switches in sections 4.2.1–4.2.3 will be examined in terms of: switches that constitute rhyme, switches within and between lines and those in song choruses and introductions.

### 4.2.1 Switches that constitute rhyme

Like many other genres of popular songs, the lyrics of rap music often employ rhyme at the ends of the lines. Examples of various types of rhyme schemes are couplets, as well as alternating rhymes. These are seen in example (13):

(13)   Couplets – AA, BB, CC                 Alternating – AB, AB

A third rhyme scheme consists of a single-end rhyme that occurs at the end of a line after a long preceding stretch of words. This rhyming prose, known as *saj*, is a pattern characteristic of Classic Arabic poetry. Unlike the couplets and alternating rhymes, *saj* rhymes lack a consistent meter or rhythm.

Even with lyrics which are almost entirely in Arabic, there may be minimal switches to English. This especially occurs in the lyrics of MTM, whose albums have been produced to be marketed exclusively to an Arabic-speaking Egyptian audience. It is common in their songs for a switch in languages to occur at the end of the line, making this word the focus of the line. In example (14), from their song 'Omy Mesafra' ('My Mom is Travelling'), the first Arabic verse ends in the English expression 'cool' (i.e., 'awesome', 'agreeable'), which is paralleled in the same line with Arabic expressions that convey similar meanings.

| | | |
|---|---|---|
| (14)   كلمت كل أصحابى على طول | *kelemt kul ashabi 'ala tool* | 'I called my friends right away' |
| ما كانش فيهم مشغول | *ma kansh fihum mushgul* | 'None of them were busy' |
| كله كان يرد يقول | *kulu kan yerud b'ul* | 'They all answered saying,' |
| يا قشطة يا بية يا قمة cool | *ya qishta ya bey ya ima cool* | 'Sweet, man, cool!' |

MTM, 'أمي مسفرة', 'Omy mesafra'

Rhymes across languages may also occur in the middle of a verse when a code-switched word is used at the end of a line. One such instance occurs in MTM's song, 'Ihsibha Sah' ('Think About It'), as the artist switches to a word in English and continues with the same rhyming scheme in the remainder of the Arabic verse.

| | | |
|---|---|---|
| (15)   صباح الخير يوم جميل | *sabah al khayr yom gamil* | 'Good morning; it's a beautiful day |
| اقعد في البيت دا مستحيل | *a'ad fil bayt da mustahil* | It's impossible to sit at home |

| كلمت تاكي اشوف ايه ال deal | *kelmt taky ashul eh al deal* | I called Taky to see what was the deal |
| لقيته نايم نوم الفيل | *le'atu naym nom al fil* | I found him sleeping like an elephant' |

MTM, 'احسبها صح', 'Ahsibha sah'

MTM is the most popular mainstream rap group in Egypt, so it is no surprise that the majority of their lyrics are in Arabic, as this is the language that appeals to the masses in terms of intelligibility. Since their themes are generally non-controversial, their songs would not be subject to censorship. Even though English is a linguistic commodity in Egypt, popular music is almost always in Egyptian Arabic. Underground hip-hop artists, though, are more likely to use English for different reasons, and in various contexts.

### 4.2.2 Switches within and between lines

Code-switching may also occur within the line-structure of the song. These patterns are often regular in the lyrics of underground artists. A line may begin in Arabic and continue in English. Davies and Bentahila (2008) have also observed patterns of switching between lines. Sometimes there may be a pattern created when a series begins in one language and continues in the other language, as in example (16) by Y-Crew, entitled 'Tadmeer Shamel' ('Total destruction'), which describes the sky and environment during times of war.

| (16) كل أنتو شيفو | *kulu intu shafu* | 'All that you (all) see |
| Is turning into ashes, and dust, ashes and dust | | |
| بني أدم بالخاس | *beni adam bil-khas* | Especially humans |
| ما لوش حال | ma lush hal | There's no solution' |

Y-Crew, 'تدمير شامل', 'Tadmeer shamel'

In other instances, the switches distinguish lines of text from each other, as the languages alternate with one another among the lines of the verse. So for instance in example (17), we find the pattern A E A E A E E A A E.

| أحنا ملوك الأسكندرية (17) | *ehna meluk asskendriya* | 'We are the Kings of Alexandria |
|---|---|---|
| We be the kings of your city | | |
| كلمتكو قبل كدة | *kelmtku abla kada* | I have told you (all) before |
| From day one | | |
| لحد دالوقتي | *Li had dilwati* | Up until now |
| We can make 'em run | | |
| Nothing can make the world go round | | |
| زاي الراب العربي | *Zay al rap al-'arabi* | Like Arabic Rap |
| لما ينزل عايكو | *lema yenzil 'alayku* | That comes upon you' |
| Poverty | | |

Y-Crew,'ملوك الأسكندرية', 'Melook Eskinderia'

Once again, the first line of English is not the variety of English that is perceived as the standard variety, as it employs the variant known as 'habitual be', a feature found in African American Vernacular English (Rickford and Rickford, 2000; Green, 2004).

### 4.2.3 Language switches in introductions and choruses

Switching between languages also occurs in larger sequences of lyrics. There are many examples of a theme of a song being developed completely in Arabic, whereas the refrain will occur either predominately or entirely in English. Introductions and closings of songs often use English, even if the entire remainder of the song is in Arabic. This phenomenon is true for the mainstream artists, such as MTM, as well as the underground ones, such as Y-Crew and Arabian Knightz. Bentahila and Davies (2002) suggest that a refrain performed in a language other than Arabic makes the song accessible to an audience that is not familiar with the colloquial Arabic used in the body of the song. It also enables an Arabic-speaking audience that may not be familiar with English to grasp the meaning of the refrain, which often points to the underlying theme.

The mainstream artists MTM use English in such a way in their lyrics. Even if their audience do not speak English, the Arabic lyrics in the body of the song which convey the main story or theme will appeal to them. Likewise the novelty of English would also be attractive to some Arabic-speaking listeners. In example (18) from the track 'Li Teshky' ('Why Complain?'), the artists describe various scenarios that will be familiar to youth in Egypt. In the song, a young man does not score high enough on his high school exam to go the university he chooses. Another falls in love with a woman, but is not allowed to marry her since he is already betrothed to his cousin. Finally, a third travels to America and becomes disillusioned with the lifestyle and what he describes as a lack of moral values. After the last verse, the refrain is sung in English, 'Why are you not satisfied?'

| | | |
|---|---|---|
| (18) مكنتش عارف رايح فين | *makuntsh 'arif raeeh fain* | 'I didn't know where I was going |
| او هجيب فلوس منين | *ow hagib falus minayn* | Or where I was going to get money |
| كل اللي انا كنت عايزه | *kul ili ana kunt aizo* | All that I wanted |
| اني اتصرف في قرشين | *ini atsarf fi urshin* | Was to get some small change |
| كنت حاطط في دماغي اني اعيش يومين | *kunt hututu damage ini 'aish yomain* | It was my plan to live a little |
| كنت فاكر اني هعمل من الالف الفين | *kunt faker ini ha'ml min alaf alfain* | I thought that I would make thousands |
| و دوخت على شغل | *wa dukhat 'ala shughl* | I made myself dizzy from work |
| و رحت و جيت كتير | *wa rahet wag it katir* | I came and went too much |
| و دقت هناك المر | *wa do't hunak al mur* | I tried it out |
| و شفت اني اسير لناس | *wa shuft ini asir linas* | I saw the procession of the people |
| ملهاش كبير لناس ملهاش ضمير | *malihash kabir inas malihash damir* | People have no consciousness |
| لناس ما بتتمناش لحد غيرها خير | *linas ma batetimanash lihad gher ha khayr* | They do not wish any good on others |
| و كانت ضربة قاضية يوم | *wa kant dareba qadia yom* | And it was the fatal blow one day' |

. . .

Why are you not

satisfied?

In yourself, will only

make you cry

In this game that we

call life

Take your time, make

up your mind

MTM,'لي تشكي', 'Li Teshky'

In the predominately Arabic Egyptian songs, English lyrics may also take on the form of an announcement, as they introduce the artist or the theme of the song in English. Y-Crew's 'Al-Bint al- Masriya' ('The Egyptian Girl') praises Egyptian young women. The song is performed entirely in Arabic, except for the extract in (19),which is spoken in the beginning of the track.

(19) Eh, yo, this song is dedicated to all Egyptian girls around the world

And especially in Egypt, you know.

This story tonight, it's all about you.

Yo, Khalid Samy, break it down for me.

Y-Crew, 'البنت المصرية', 'Al-Bint Al-Masreya'

The introduction to example (19), though in English, sets the context for the remainder of the lyrics, which are in Arabic. Switching throughout the songs not only depends on the audience, but also on the position of the lyric in the song.

## 4.3 Switching in English-dominant lyrics

As mentioned earlier, switching to Arabic in English-dominant lyrics has been used primarily by the Arabian Knightz in their earlier songs (2005–2007). As these songs predated the mix-tape, the group's only form of dissemination of their music was via the internet, making their audience a global one. Perhaps for this reason more of their earlier songs are predominately in English. With these early songs, the group were able to increase their audience to English-speaking listeners, and still maintain their Egyptian identity. The song 'C-A-I-R-O' contains 'self-referential speech', 'boasting' and 'place and time reference', which are examples of speech act patterns Androutsopoulos and Scholz (2006) have identified as characteristic of hip-hop culture. In the first verse, the artist code-switches to Arabic when making reference to the groups' origins, Egypt. By referring to Egypt as *um a-dunia* ('Mother of the world'), a popular nickname for Egypt, in example (20), the group acknowledge their origins and boast about their Egyptian heritage.

(20)  Straight outta

أم الدونية                    *Om a-dunia*              'Mother of the world'

Arabian Knightz., 'C-A-I-R-O'

Other songs by the Arabian Knightz that are predominately in English incorporate Arabic words that may or may not be recognized by a non-Arabic speaking audience. These words when sung in the lyrics maintain the Arabic pronunciation, such as words that contain the Arabic emphatic /h/. For instance *Mohamed* and *Hezbollah* are pronounced with the Arabic pronunciation even when the words occur in the context of English lyrics. The common Arabic discourse marker *yani* is also used in (21), 'Whatchu Know', as the artist metaphorically refers to Arab hip hop as his weapon on a battlefield.

(21)  Hip hop my battle field, I'm armed
      to the tee
      Using Arab hip hop, droppin'
      bombs, يعني                    *yani*  'I mean' [discourse marker]
      Using slang as a tool to reach the
      ears that hear

Arabian Knightz, 'Whatchu Know'

By using Arabic terms in songs that are predominately English, the rappers increase their listening audience to English-speakers, while still maintaining an Arab identity. Language switching in the lyrics occurs to various degrees. Language choice is motivated by the structure of the song as well as the song's theme and intended audience. While uses of English may broaden the listening audience, the Arabic usages function as identity markers.

# 5 Conclusion

Youths' participation in hip-hop culture in Egypt causes local traditions to be changed and transmitted in new forms. Localization of hip hop in Egypt can be realized in terms of the themes of patriotism, Pan-Arabism, and the artists' self-identification with 'Blackness' as constructed through language use and images from African American culture that evoke resistance. Furthermore, the application of traditional Arabic language conventions such as the cognate curse, which produces insults by using an opponent's words against him/her, is extended to the English language. Traditionally, English is regarded as an elite code which leads to economic gain, due to historical-political circumstances. However, a stylized English variety that has been associated with hip-hop culture is used as a medium of expressing resistance. Even though the artists are speaking English, they are not doing so to accommodate, but to criticize and oppose political and social issues that affect their communities. A more complete understanding of hip-hop culture and its spread in contexts outside of the US is needed to further examine the processes of localization in terms of youth language, local themes and claims to connective marginality. Through the involvement with hip-hop culture, Egyptian youth construct their identities as Middle Eastern, Arab and Egyptian, and continue to shape the face of global hip hop.

## Notes

1. In this chapter, I will use 'rap' in reference to the style of music and 'hip hop' as an all-encompassing term denoting the music, fashion and culture that is comprised of the elements of emceeing, DJing, breakdancing and graffiti art.
2. In the remainder of this chapter 'Arabic' will be used as shorthand for this colloquial Egyptian Arabic spoken by youth.
3. 'Arabs Rap to a Different Beat.' <http://english.aljazeera.net/archive/2004/05/20084916165312193.html>, accessed 5 May 2007.
4. <http://www.myspace.com/eltofan>, accessed 18 September 2009
5. <www.urbandictionary.com>, accessed 18 September 2009.

## References

Alim, H. S. (2004), 'Hip Hop Nation language', in E. Finnegan and J. R. Rickford (eds), *Language in the USA: Perspectives for the 21st Century*. Cambridge University Press, pp. 387–409.

Androutsopoulos, J. (2009), 'Language and the three spheres of hip hop', in H. S. Alim, A. Ibrahim and A. Pennycook (eds), *Global Linguistic Flows:*

*Hip Hop Cultures, Youth Identities, and the Politics of Language.* New York: Routledge, pp. 43–62.

Androutsopoulos, J. and Scholz, A. (2006), 'Recontextualization: hip hop culture and rap lyrics in Europe', in A. Linke and J. Tanner (eds), *Attraktion und Abwehr: Die Amerikanisierung der Alltagskultur in Europa.* Koln; Weimar; Wien: Bohlau Verlag, pp. 289–305.

Badawi, E. S. (1973), *Mustawayaat al-'arabiyya al-mu'asira fill misr.* Cairo: Dar Al-Ma'arif.

Bentahila, A. and Davies, E. (2002), 'Language mixing in rai music: localisation or globalisation?' *Language and Communication*, 22, 2, 187–207.

Bourdieu, P. (1991), *Language and Symbolic Power.* Harvard University Press.

Bozza, A. (2004), *Whatever You Say I Am: The Life and Times of Eminem.* New York: Three Rivers Press.

Cochran, J. (2008), *Educational Roots of Political Crisis in Egypt.* Lanham, MD: Lexington Books.

Darling-Wolf, F. (2008), 'Getting over our "illusion d'optique": from globalization to mondialisation (through French rap)'. *Communication Theory*, 18, 2, 187–209.

Davies, E. and Bentahila, A. (2008), 'Code-switching as poetic device: examples from rai lyrics'. *Language and Communication*, 28, 1, 1–20.

El-Hassan, S. A. (1978), 'Educated Spoken Arabic in Egypt and the Levant: a critical review of diglossia and related concepts'. *Archivum Linguisticum*, 8, 2, 112–132.

Ferguson, C. A. (1959), 'Diglossia'. *Word*, 15, 325–40.

Green, L. (2004), 'African American English', in E. Finnegan and R. Rickford (eds), *Language in the USA: Perspectives for the 21st Century.* Cambridge University Press, pp. 76–91.

Haeri, N. (1997), *The Sociolinguistic Market in Cairo: Gender, Class and Education.* New York: Columbia University Press.

Harry, B. (1996), 'The importance of the language continuum in Arabic Multiglossia', in A. Elgibali (ed.), *Understanding Arabic: Essays in Contemporary Arabic Linguistics in Honour of El-Said Badawi.* Cairo: The American University in Cairo Press, pp. 69–90.

Ibrahim, A. (1999), 'Becoming black: rap and hip hop, race, gender, identity, and the politics of ESL learning'. *TESOL Quarterly*, 33, 3, 349–369.

Kachru, B. (1992), 'The second diaspora of English', in T. Machan and C. Scott (eds), *English in its Social Contexts. Essays in historical linguistics.* New York: Oxford University Press, pp. 230–252.

Kahf, U. (2007), 'Arabic hip hop: claims of authenticity and identity of a new genre'. *Journal of Popular Music Studies*, 19, 4, 359–385.

Matterlart, A. (2005), *Diversité culturelle et mondialisation.* Paris: La Découverte.

Meiseles, G. (1980), 'Educated Spoken Arabic and the Arabic language continuum'. *Archivum Linguisticum*, 11, 2, 118–148.

Mitchell, T. (1986), 'What is Educated Spoken Arabic?' *International Journal of the Sociology of Language*, 61, 7–32.

—(2001), *Global Noise: Rap and Hip Hop Outside the USA.* Middleton: Wesleyan University Press.

Mitchell-Kernan, C. (1972), 'Signifying and marking: two Afro-American speech acts', in J. Gumperz and D. Hymes (eds), *Directions in Sociolinguists*. New York: Holt, Rinehart and Winston, pp. 161–179.

Myers-Scotton, C. (1993), *Duelling Languages: Grammatical Structure in Code-switching*. New York: Oxford University Press.

Osumare, H. (2007), *The Africanist Aesthetic in Global Hip Hop: Power Moves*. New York: Palgrave Macmillan.

Pennycook, A. (2007), 'Language, localization, and the real: hip hop and the global spread of authenticity'. *Journal of Language, Identity, and Education*, 6, 2, 101–115.

Pennycook, A. and Mitchell, T. (2009), 'Hip hop as dusty foot philosophy: engaging locality', in H. S. Alim, A. Ibrahim and A. Pennycook (eds), *Global Linguistic Flows: Hip Hop Cultures, Youth Identities, and the Politics of Language*. New York: Routledge, pp. 43–62.

Perry, I. (2004), *Prophets of the Hood: Politics and Poetics in Hip Hop*. Durham, NC: Duke University Press.

Quinne, E. (2005), *Nuthin' but a 'G' Thang*. New York: Columbia University Press.

Rickford, J. and Rickford, R. (2000), *Spoken Soul: The Story of Black English*. New York: John Wiley & Sons.

Rivera, R. (2003), *New York Ricans in the Hip Hop Zone*. New York: Palgrave Press.

Schaub, M. (2000), 'English in the Arab Republic of Egypt', *World Englishes*, 19, 2, 225–238.

Smitherman, G. (1997), 'The chain remain the same: communicative practices in the Hip Hop Nation'. *Journal of Black Studies*, 28, 1, 3–25.

Stewart, D. J. (1997), 'Impoliteness formulae: the cognate curse in Egyptian Arabic'. *Journal of Semitic Studies*, XLII, 2, 327–360.

Suleiman, Y. (2006), 'Egypt: from Egyptian to Pan-Arab nationalism', in A. Simpson (ed.), *Language and National Identity in Africa*. Oxford University Press, pp. 26–43.

Wermuth, M. (2001), 'Rap in the Low Countries: global dichotomies on a national scale', in T. Mitchell (ed.), *Global Noise: Rap and Hip Hop Outside the USA*. Middletown: Wesleyan University Press, pp. 149–170.

# 4 Roma Rap and the *Black Train*: Minority Voices in Hungarian Hip Hop

Sarah Simeziane

## 1 Introduction: why hip hop?

As hip hop has grown into a global phenomenon it neither changes completely nor remains the same (Pennycook and Mitchell, 2009, p. 27).[1] The genre has been described as 'black music, of and for blacks' (Costello and Wallace, 1997, p. 21), but this characterization has become too simplistic as hip hop has been adopted and appropriated around the world and artists have contributed and shaped it into a broader cross-cultural community of practice (Alim, 2009, pp. 4–5).[2] While retaining recognizable features associating it with African American urban culture, global hip hop has been appropriated in such a way that it also reflects the local culture of wherever it is produced (Androutsopoulos, 2009, pp. 43–44; Mitchell, 2001a, pp. 1–2). Hip-hop artists around the world use the genre to speak about the social, cultural and political conditions they live in. Their language choices also stem from their linguistic practices and environments, employing the various linguistic varieties they have at their disposal in order to achieve the artistic and commercial ends they seek.

Global hip hop provides an arena in which to investigate globalization phenomena as well as the interplay between language and identity construction (Androutsopoulos, 2009; Darling-Wolf, 2008). A great deal of ethnographic background work is necessary when examining how language use indexes identity. We find this ethnographic groundwork already partially laid down, as hip-hop lyrics can be examined alongside interviews or other discourse in which artists discuss the identity they wish to project and/or fans discuss the identities they perceive. This complementary discourse often provides more concrete evidence for the specific ways artists use language to establish identity and whether or not these identities are ratified by the audience.

The language of hip hop is also of interest to sociolinguists for the multitude of variation phenomena that occur, such as style-shifting, code-mixing and code-switching (Alim, 2009, p. 5). The distinct verbal style associated with rap has motivated a particular focus on the linguistic aspects of the genre, whether it be lexical choices (Cutler, 2009; Mitchell, 2001b), rhythmic patterns and prosody (O'Hanlon, 2006; Fagyal, 2007), or language choice and code-switching (Higgins, 2009; Sarkar and Allen, 2007).

The global spread of hip hop, described by Androutsopoulos and Scholz (2003) as 'the productive use of an originally imported cultural pattern', can be viewed through Lull's (1995) framework of the movement from *deterritorialization*, 'the loss of the "natural" relation between culture with geographic and social territory' (García Canclini, 1989, p. 288) to *reterritorialization*, where 'the foundations of cultural territory . . . are all open to new interpretations and understandings' and 'culture is constantly reconstituted through social interaction' (Lull, 1995, p. 159). Through these processes hip hop has been taken up from its original habitat in African American urban culture, introduced to other cultures around the world, and fused with their linguistic and musical traditions and local experiences to the point that it eventually becomes recognized as a local art form (Androutsopoulos and Scholz, 2003, pp. 467–468).

This chapter seeks to contribute to current debates about global hip hop as succinctly formulated by Alim in the following three questions:

(a) Just how is it that 'Hip Hop Culture' has become a primary site of identification and self-understanding for youth around the world?
(b) . . . what linguistic resources do youth manipulate, (re)appropriate, and sometimes (re)create, in order to fashion themselves as members of a 'Global Hip Hop Nation'?
(c) . . . in doing so, what challenges do they face and pose, within distinct, local scenes, which privilege their own often competing, locally relevant categories of identification? (Alim, 2009, p. 5)

More specifically, I will examine language and identity construction in the lyrics of a popular late-1990s Hungarian Roma hip-hop group known as Fekete Vonat ('Black Train') and the various factors and constraints that determine the final product. The Roma, more commonly known as gypsies, are a highly marginalized population within Hungary.[3] I will look at how Fekete Vonat linguistically construct their identity and establish authenticity, paying particular attention to language choice. I will also examine an incident with the band's recording label that raises questions of filtering and marketability, highlighting the importance of viewing hip hop as a discursive construct and a collaborative process. Based on these observations, I will consider more broadly what the experiences of this group signify about the establishment of authenticity within the Global Hip Hop Nation (GHHN) and in terms of sociolinguistic constraints on code choice in hip hop.

## 2 Hip hop as a locus of globalization

Hip hop has been embraced around the world as a formidable instrument for the expression of youth, minority, political and class issues. The foundations of hip hop – such as rapping, scratching and break-beats – have been fused with various global musical and linguistic traditions that put a new spin on the genre. The choice of language varieties varies from country to country. Pennycook and Mitchell (2009) note that linguistic localization in hip hop 'is subject to the cultural politics of local language use' (2009, p. 36). More vernacular forms and 'lower' varieties of languages tend to occur. Androutsopoulos and Scholz (2003) surveyed hip hop across a number of European countries and found that a great deal of code-mixing and code-switching between dominant and migrant languages is also used, although the dominant language of a country also tends to be dominant in the hip hop produced there (2003, p. 473). Similarly, Omoniyi (2009) notes that in Nigerian hip hop 'in some environments hip hop artists deploy linguistic convergence in performing in the dominant official language of the cosmopolis' (2009, p. 124; see also Androutsopoulos, this volume). Why should the dominant language emerge as the default language of hip hop, particularly among groups such as immigrants or ethnic minorities, who might not use it as their primary language? We will see in Section 4 that the pattern that emerges from Fekete Vonat's code choices (and the dictates of their management) indicates that audience design (Bell, 1984), as it relates to market forces, plays a primary role in defining the default.

When code-switching and/or code-mixing do occur in hip hop, these phenomena need to be analysed as a form of public discourse. Sarkar (2009) characterizes rap as 'highly scripted, prewritten forms of language that differ in important ways from normal conversational speech' (2009, p. 147). Davies and Bentahila (2006) suggest that even among communities for whom unmarked code-switching is the norm, occurrences of code-switching in public discourse, such as music or speeches, represent a marked choice due to the preparation and planning inherent in these public genres. They believe such instances of code-switching to be 'a more or less conscious, considered decision . . . for which some motivation must be sought' (2006, p. 368). Occurrences of code-switching in public discourse can provide insight into the common mechanisms speakers and the communities they address use to explicitly construct identity through language.

Language and globalization is not limited to the spread of a specific language; it also involves the appropriation of 'specific speech forms, genres, styles, and forms of literacy practice' (Blommaert, 2003). This is exactly what happens in global hip hop, where artists appropriate and recontextualize features of hip hop – including language variety, rhyming patterns, or the themes addressed – rather than simply repro-ducing what comes out of the United States, resulting in 'hybrid co-productions of languages and cultures' (Pennycook, 2007, p. 6).

Androutsopoulos and Scholz (2003) put forward that 'rap in Europe follows traditions established by US rap, but is not identical to it, because one of the imperatives of rap discourse is to express local concerns and to reflect local social realities' (2003, pp. 475–476), and these local concerns and realities will vary from place to place. Alim (2009) ties global hip hop to broader questions of 'glocalization', the local appropriation and recontextualization of global resources (cf. Robertson, 1995). He suggests that 'when local practices of music, dance, story-telling and painting encounter diversifying forms of globalized hip hop, they enable a recreation both of what it means to be local and of what then counts as the global' (Alim, 2009, p. 27).

In her chapter on rap in Hungary, Éva Miklódy suggests that the appropriation of hip hop by other, non-African American cultures is simply taking the essence of hip hop further. She quotes Dick Hebdige as saying

> the hip hoppers 'stole' music off air and cut it up. Then they broke it down into its component parts and remixed it on tape. By doing this they were breaking the law of copyright. But the cut 'n' mix attitude was that no one owns a rhythm or a sound. You just borrow it and use it and give it back to the people in a slightly different form. (Hebdige, 1987, cited in Miklódy, 2004, pp. 198–199)

Miklódy considers that international hip-hop artists have simply applied the same formula to hip hop itself by cutting and mixing African American hip hop and adapting it to their own sound and their own experiences: 'Hungarian youth . . . create a Hungarian version of African American rap by reflecting Hungarian reality – as they view it – and by cutting and mixing basic elements of black rap with the idiosyncrasies of Hungarian musical and linguistic traditions' (Miklódy, 2004, p. 199).

Tony Mitchell characterizes hip hop and rap as 'a vehicle for global youth affiliations and a tool for reworking local identity all over the world' (2001a, pp. 1–2). Although far more American hip hop is exported to other countries than is imported from them, the extensive popularity of hip hop around the world cannot be viewed as simply another example of Americanization or 'US cultural domination', but rather as 'driven as much by local artists and their fans' (Mitchell, 2001a, p. 2). Although there is arguably little influence of global hip hop on American hip hop, the global spread of hip hop does redefine and (re)create the genre: 'the echoes around the world of new hip-hop cultures may be understood not so much as subvarieties of global hip hop, but rather as local traditions being pulled toward global cultural forms while those traditions are simultaneously reinvented' (Pennycook and Mitchell, 2009, p. 30).

Darling-Wolf (2008) discusses how French hip hop is redefining the question of what it means to be French and what constitutes French music. French hip hop is associated with the *banlieues* (suburbs) and immigrant culture and highlights the mixing of French culture with that of France's former colonies. These local renegotiations of French identity eventually go global and are seen around the world as expressions of French identity, due to the success of French rap as a 'cultural export' (2008, pp. 197–201). Like many globalization phenomena, such as world Englishes, global hip hop is not simply a matter of hip hop radiating out from the United States: 'Global hip hops do not have one point of origin . . . but rather multiple, copresent, global origins' (Darling-Wolf, 2008, p. 40).

The question of the true origins of hip hop is a complex one.[4] The general public tend to associate hip hop with African American urban culture, and for the purposes of this chapter, I will also embrace the notion of New York City as the birthplace of hip hop, as it is such a salient assumption for fans (and non-fans) of hip hop around the world. However, while remaining an undeniable part of global hip hop, this association of the genre with African American urban culture is no longer its central or sole determinant: French hip hop is French, and it distinguishes itself from Egyptian hip hop, which in turn distinguishes itself from Hungarian hip hop, and so on and so forth.

## 2.1 Hip hop, race and authenticity

Although there are a number of aspects to one's identity (race, gender, class, nationality, ethnicity, age, etc.), race occupies a particularly prominent position for theorists, artists, and fans of hip hop alike. Raphael-Hernandez (2004) characterizes the emergence of hip hop in Hungary as a 'blackening' of the youth culture that embraces it (Raphael-Hernandez, 2004, p. 6). Similarly, Roth-Gordon (2009) shows how hip hoppers in Brazilian *favelas* fashion the differences between themselves and the dominant culture as a Black vs White divide which in reality is based more on economic factors. Following on from these remarks, we might ask: What exactly is the glue that holds hip-hop communities together? Is it really race, or does race merely serve as convenient shorthand, a metaphor for the various locally relevant identities hip-hop artists wish to project and problematize?

Although often linked to race by artists, fans and the general public, hip hop seems in fact to be a locus of identification for groups who feel, or seek to be, outside some aspect of mainstream culture; groups who are 'along the separation from the values of the dominant culture and in the integration into a community' (Nagy, 2003, p. 130). Pennycook and Mitchell (2009) note that 'for many hip hop artists around the world, there is an identification not only with aspects of the music, style, and language of U.S. hip hop, but also with the racial politics that surround it' (2009, p. 37). This is not to say that global hip-hop artists rap primarily about US race relations, but rather that their identification with the genre is heightened by, and in turn heightens, their perception of issues of racism and discrimination in their own local communities. Omoniyi (2009) acknowledges the 'extensively racialized' nature of hip hop at its inception, and raises the question 'whether or not race and class politics are on the agenda worldwide' (2009, p. 119). In his study of code-switching in Nigerian hip hop, he concludes that ethnicity seems to be a more salient identity marker in that context, and proposes to 'conceive of hip-hop identities as belonging to a global complex within which performers may move freely for whatever reasons they considered salient in the moments of identification in which they find and attempt to define themselves' (2009, p. 129).

According to the cognitive linguistic tradition, speakers construct, and hearers interpret, metaphor by envisaging a comparison between a 'source domain' and the 'target domain' which is metaphorically construed in terms of the former (Lakoff and Johnson, 1980/2003; Croft and Cruse, 2004, p. 55). In the case of Roth-Gordon's (2009) Brazilian hip hoppers, race serves as the source and wealth as the target domain, with a poor vs rich distinction metaphorically construed as a 'Black' vs 'White' one. Metaphor is not simply a substitution of one term for another for the sake of embellishment; rather, a metaphorical expression has 'a character that no literal expression has' (Croft and Cruse, 2004, p. 194). Neither is metaphor limited to individual linguistic items; rather, it can be a property of conceptual domains shared by members of a speech community: in the case of conceptual (well-established) metaphors, '[t]he correspondences between domains are represented

**101**

in the conceptual system, and are fully conventionalized among members of a speech community' (Croft and Cruse, 2004, pp. 194–197).

We can view the Global Hip Hop Nation as a community of practice (Lave and Wenger, 1991) that shares the discourse of race as a basic conceptual metaphor for thinking and talking about locally relevant aspects of falling victim to (social) inequality. This is not to deny that the category of race is itself a socially constructed one. Nevertheless, in the case of race, this socially constructed character is frequently forgotten, and, until challenged as such, race is often treated as easily identifiable and static over time. It thus serves as a readily available and convenient 'source' domain in terms of which to conceptualize those more 'abstract' 'target' domains across which identification with hip hop occurs, namely 'culture, class, historical oppression, and youth rebellion' (Osumare, 2007, p. 15). These four domains may, then, be seen as different facets of (specifically African American) race, which becomes the most salient and the default feature of hip-hop identity to artists, fans and detractors alike.

## 2.2 Hip hop in Hungary

The case of hip hop in Hungary provides another argument in favour of the universality of hip hop beyond a US-centric and racialized form of expression, as Hungary has never had a significant Black population similar to those of the UK, France or Germany, nor was hip hop in Hungary immediately embraced by ethnic minorities (Miklódy, 2004, p. 188). The common thread between the development of hip hop in Hungary and the United States, however, is that it 'emerged from a common socioeconomic background' as it did in the United States (2004, p. 189). Hip hop has enjoyed widespread popularity in Hungary; Miklódy (2004) characterizes this phenomenon as a 'blackening' of Hungarian youth, where identification with hip hop equates to identification as Black, and 'Blackness' remains the essence of hip hop (2004, pp. 188–189). Nevertheless, I would argue that as we examine the emergence of hip hop in Hungary within the broader global context, the widespread adoption and adaptation of the genre points more to its universality and expression of an identity that is not bound to race, as hip hop is often – though not exclusively – embraced by or associated with urban socioeconomically disadvantaged populations, such as *banlieue* youth in France or the residents of Brazil's *favelas*.

Hip hop was introduced to Hungary in the early 1980s via Germany through breakdancing, but the use of the Hungarian language in rap did not enter in full force until the early to mid 1990s after the fall of communism. At the time of Miklódy's 2004 article, she estimated that approximately 300 rap groups were active in Hungary, with approximately 50 experiencing widespread success in the country. In a country of 10 million inhabitants, over half of which are estimated to be elderly, such spread is not only extensive in terms of the size of the country but also clearly specific to youth culture (2004, p. 189). The conditions following the overthrow of communism in Hungary allowed Hungarian hip hop to flourish not only because the country was opened up to Western media, but also because new Hungarian media and entertainment industries were allowed to develop.

The development of hip hop in Hungary follows the progression of phases proposed by Lull (1995). There is a certain fuzziness to the boundaries between Lull's three categories of (i) transculturation, 'a process in which cultural forms literally move through time and space' (1995, p. 153); (ii) hybridization, 'the fusing of cultural forms' (1995, p. 155); and (iii) indigenization, where 'imported cultural forms take on local features' (1995, p. 155). The evolution of hip hop in Hungary, however, can help clarify some of these different phases also embraced by Androutsopoulos and Scholz (2003): we can observe a progression from rapping by Hungarians to rapping in Hungarian to Hungarian rap. In the initial phase of transculturation, Hungarian hip-hop artists imitated African American hip-hop artists and rapped in English. Artists then moved into a hybridization phase, highlighted by the translation of lyrics from popular and influential American hip-hop songs into Hungarian, notably Ganxsta Zolee's translation of 'The Message' by Grandmaster Flash. In the mid-1990s original lyrics began to appear in Hungarian, as the genre passed into the final phase of indigenization (Miklódy, 2004, pp. 194–195; Androutsopoulos and Scholz, 2003, pp. 467–468). The progression of group and MC names followed a similar pattern, beginning with names that were in English and/or reflected African American hip-hop culture of the time and gradually became more and more Hungarian: from early names such as Boyz in Da Getto, to Ganxsta Zolee és a kartel ('Gangsta Zolee and the Cartel' – Zoli being a typical Hungarian first name) to Fekete Vonat ('Black Train'), which is not only completely in Hungarian, but also carries a specific cultural reference (see Section 4 below). Though this was not necessarily a uniform naming pattern across the country, we can observe a significant shift from English to Hungarian names throughout the period from the late 1980s to the mid 1990s. The type of music sampled and the song topics also followed a similar path as more and more Hungarian folk and popular music was integrated with rap, and lyrics began to draw on life experiences in Hungary rather than abroad (Miklódy, 2004, pp. 195–196).

Miklódy notes two major parallels between Hungarian and American hip hop, the first being a division between 'underground' and 'mainstream' rap, currents which have sprung up in similar ways in both the United States and Hungary, where membership in the mainstream can result in a loss of authenticity (2004, p. 196).[5] The second parallel is more interesting for our current purposes, as it concerns the socioeconomic origins and influences on hip-hop content. Miklódy views hip hop as 'acts of symbolic resistance against the pressures of a capitalist ideology' (2004, p. 196). The African American struggle against 'ideological racism and discrimination in capitalist America' is reflected in and provides fuel for rap lyrics and hip-hop culture. Miklódy compares these conditions to Hungary, where rappers address 'the dire social, cultural, and human consequences of a newly established, rough, capitalist, economic system' (2004, pp. 196–197). She describes a sort of 'push-and-pull' between Hungarian rap artists both distancing and aligning themselves with African American hip hop, mixing local references and distinct styles of dress with references to ghettoes and 'the socioeconomic and cultural roots of black rap' (2004, p. 191). On the other hand, she also notes artists that specifically localize their work to Hungary (Animal Cannibals: 'From the middle of Central-Europe, it's Budapest speaking') and even make a clear distinction between themselves and American hip hop, with lyrics such as K. A. O. S.: 'This is Hungary and not America,' and 'This is Szolnok Country and not Chicago,' or Animal Cannibals: 'This country is not New Jack City' (Miklódy, 2004, p. 191).

Fekete Vonat were notably left out of Miklódy's (2004) article, despite the fact that the group had already released three albums, including one that had gone platinum, by that time.[6] I would argue that an additional socioeconomic parallel can be drawn between African American and Hungarian *Roma* hip hop, which has also been born out of a culture that experiences not only economic hardship but also deep-seated racism and discrimination. These conditions have clearly inspired much of the work of Fekete Vonat, as we shall see in Section 4.

## 3 The Roma in Hungary

Central and Eastern Europe have included extensive Roma populations ever since the Middle Ages, when large numbers of Roma were forced eastward out of Western Europe (Imre, 2007, p. 272). Their status differs from other minority groups: 'neither a regional minority nor an immigrant minority; [the Roma] are . . . one of the indigenous ethnic groups of Europe' (Halwachs, 2003, p. 192). Roma minorities demonstrate varying degrees of assimilation across Europe. Even 'assimilated' groups preserve traces of Roma culture, in particular 'their binary conception of the world: the Roma and the non-Roma' (Halwachs, 2003, p. 192).

The Roma people constitute a significant minority in Hungary, a population estimated at around 500,000. They have faced massive, widespread discrimination and racism since the Hapsburg rule, discrimination which continues on a daily basis in Hungary today (Imre, 2007, pp. 271–272). Improvements have been made – particularly as a condition of Hungary's 2004 accession to the European Union: official Roma institutions have been established and some Romani language media have emerged both through private and state-run media channels. A daily 2-hour program is now broadcast on state-run radio as well as a weekly show on television (Matras, 2005, p. 15). In addition, in 2001 the first Roma radio station in Hungary, Rádió C, went on the air. It features both Hungarian and Romani language programming that centres around Roma culture and issues.

Despite these improvements, the Roma continue to suffer large-scale discrimination, in the form of violent attacks and police indifference to (and sometimes sanction of) such attacks; lack of access to education, with children often segregated into Roma classes that are treated as remedial classes; high unemployment rates, which have risen sharply since the overthrow of communism; and discrimination in housing and public services. Although activists and organizations are working hard to improve these conditions, the Roma face racism from the general Hungarian population that is 'reinforced by media representations and state policies' (Imre, 2007, p. 271) and have generally been 'kept out of the respectable professions that defined citizenship' portrayed instead as 'only good at playing music and dancing' (Imre, 2007, p. 272).

Roma music and hip hop seem to be a natural match, as the Roma have a strong tradition of incorporating the folk music of various other ethnic groups 'while maintaining a strong connection to Roma identities' (Imre, 2007, p. 272). In fact, much of the popular traditional music that tourists associate with Hungary often contains more Roma influence than features of original Magyar music (Imre, 2007, p. 272).

## 3.1 Romani

The Romani language has been spoken in Europe for centuries, 'the only Indo-Aryan language . . . that has been spoken exclusively in Europe since the Middle Ages' (Matras, 2005, p. 1). Although the number of Romani speakers in Europe has not been reliably established, conservative estimates put this at (at least) 3.5 million, constituting 'probably the second-largest minority language (after Catalan) in the

European Union since its enlargement in May 2004, with the prospect of becoming the largest minority language once Romania and Bulgaria join' (Matras, 2005, p. 2).[7]

Romani can be described as a 'non-territorial language' and shows a great deal of dialect diversity with respect to the geographical distribution of its speakers (Halwachs, 2003, p. 196). Communication between speakers of these dialects is impeded due to factors not directly linked to significant structural differences among them. The factors that affect cross-dialect communication stem primarily from the fact that 'all Romani speakers are bilingual' and tend to code-switch or code-mix between Romani and their other respective mother tongues. Romani is a dominated language; borrowings from the dominant language are extensive (Halwachs, 2003, p. 196). Another factor that affects cross-dialectal communication is a lack of communication between the speakers of the various dialects. Until more recent exchanges among Roma intellectuals and activists were initiated, communication in Romani was limited to within the family and the community, with little contact between Roma groups from different regions or countries (Matras, 2005, pp. 4–5). Romani remains linked to specific domains, used primarily as an in-group or intimate language (Matras, 2005, p. 196). Speakers therefore do not have experience of communicating with those who use different varieties of the language. In this type of situation, there are no standard forms to fall back on, as are available for speakers of, for instance, American and Australian English or Mexican and Costa Rican Spanish. Halwachs (2003) characterizes Romani as 'a heterogeneous cluster of varieties without any homogenizing standard' (2003, p. 192).

That is not to say there have been no attempts at codification and standardization of Romani, particularly as 'a symbol of political unity [and] as a token of loyalty to a centralised policy of cultural emancipation' (Matras, 2005, p. 11). These attempts at standardization have not garnered the support they need. In the linguistic choices Fekete Vonat make in their music, we will see a similar pattern, where although Romani is used as an in-group marker, it is not exclusively used as a means of asserting Roma identity. The most notable impediment to the establishment of a standard is the primacy of a local over a more widespread global community. Roma activists seek to work first of all for their local communities; it is their support they seek above others'. Political unity is an important goal for Roma activists across Europe, yet the lack of a standard language is not considered 'as an obstacle to unity' (Matras, 2005, p. 11). In a similar vein, Fekete Vonat's lyrics indicate that they also do not see Romani as a necessary vehicle for the expression of their political and social concerns. In fact, they use

Hungarian to get those messages across, whereas Romani is reserved for directly addressing Roma, for intimate, in-group communication.

The use of Romani in media across Europe is typically more symbolic rather than representative of a major shift from a state language to Romani.[8] These emblematic uses include journals, magazines, albums, or songs with Romani titles, but content in the official language of the country in question. Their function is twofold: marking a space as Roma, and simply demonstrating that 'written culture' in Romani is possible, that Romani is a legitimate language alongside the state language, and by extension the Roma people are legitimate as well (Matras, 2005, p. 12).

Not all Roma communities have maintained the language as a marker of identity: 'some Roma groups have given up Romani without . . . losing their ethnic awareness' (Halwachs, 2003, pp. 196–197). For non-Roma, however, Romani is a highly salient identity marker, according to Halwachs (2003) perceived as 'the Roma's primary cultural identity factor' (2003, p. 203).

## 4 Fekete Vonat

The name Fekete Vonat means 'Black Train', referring to the trains that Roma workers took between their homes and places of work in Budapest during the communist period. The group formed in the late 1990s, and disbanded in 2001. One member, L. L. Junior, continues to enjoy success as a performer and celebrity in Hungary. Fekete Vonat seem to be the only breakthrough Roma hip-hop group in Hungary; the website www.allmusic.hu has a category for *Roma Rap*, however the only artists listed are Fekete Vonat and L. L. Junior. They also enjoyed a measure of international success; their Romani-language single '**Bilako**' ('**Without Her**') made it onto French charts. The group were also cited in a 2001 CNN report on global hip hop.[9]

Their (inter)national success with both Roma and non-Roma audiences did not necessarily represent a victory for Roma equality in Hungary; their recording label, EMI Hungary, refused to release any songs containing Romani on the group's third album under contract with them (Imre, 2007, p. 274). The group recorded a fourth album in 2004 under a new label. The description on the website www.allmusic.hu makes a point of noting that there are gypsy-language songs on the album (in fact, there is only one).[10]

The three members of Fekete Vonat identify themselves as Roma and are bilingual in Hungarian and Romani. Their lyrics are primarily in Hungarian, a tendency in keeping with the general trends across Europe, where 'the language of rap lyrics [. . .] is almost categorically native speech or, with regard to artists of migrant descent, the dominant language of the society the rappers live and work in' (Androutsopoulos and Scholz, 2003, p. 473), but also reflective of the everyday linguistic practices of the artists in question: in interviews they have said they consider Hungarian to be their $L_1$. Fekete Vonat's body of work thus far contains three notable exceptions: two songs from the album *A város másik oldalán* ('On the Other Side of Town') and one from *Még várj* that are entirely in Romani, one being the aforementioned international single '**Bilako**'; and a fourth song that contains a few instances of code-switching between Romani and Hungarian. The topics of these songs are very different; the songs in Romani are more light-hearted, and always address other Roma directly, whereas their most political songs are rapped in Hungarian.

Although Fekete Vonat address the political and social conditions for Roma in Hungary, they are not a purely political group. They rap about their career, hanging out, brother/sister-hood (in Hungarian, these two concepts can be expressed by the same word, literally 'sibling-hood') and love, as well as issues regarding discrimination and racism directed against Hungarian Roma.

I examined the lyrics of 39 songs by Fekete Vonat from four albums and independent releases, focusing on their most successful release: *A város másik oldalán* ('On the Other Side of Town') from 2001. Lyrics were obtained from the published album jacket and from the Hungarian online lyric database www.dalszoveg.hu. Romani lyrics were translated by a native Romani speaker fluent in both Hungarian and English, and Hungarian lyrics were translated by the author in consultation with native Hungarian speakers. In the examples, Romani lyrics appear in bold, as do their English glosses. Lyrics in Hungarian appear in italics in the original. Titles of songs appear in quotes.

## 4.1 Fekete Vonat and hip-hop identity

Fekete Vonat emerged out of circumstances similar to African Americans' – in terms of poverty, discrimination and racism – and their more politically charged songs evoke the aspects of their identity common to the GHHN. In the song 'Flamenco Rap', they describe their Roma music as *az igazi fekete zaj* ('the real Black noise') and refer to the Roma's dark skin:

> (1) *hé barna kislány*       'Hey little brown girl, I am kissing your
> *csókolom a szád*       lips'
>
> 'Flamenco Rap'

Similarly, in 'Mondd miért' ('Say why'):

(2)   *Barna bőröm ez én vagyok*       'Brown skin is what I am

     *Megváltozni nem fogok*       I will not change'

                                     'Mondd miért'

These references to skin colour indicate that Fekete Vonat do racialize their identity to a certain degree. At the same time, though, they also ground their lyrics in their own experiences as Roma, rather than aligning themselves with African Americans, stating that what they do is fresh, as in the following excerpt from their track 'Reggeltől estig olaszosan' ('From morning till night, going commando').

(3)   *Tudod ilyen a stílusunk*       'You know this is our style

     *Mi nem az amerikai*       We don't steal from American
     *filmekből lopunk*       movies

     *És büszkék vagyunk rá*       We're proud to be Roma'
     *hogy romák vagyunk*

                              'Reggeltől estig olaszosan'

Topography plays an important role in the identity Fekete Vonat express through their music as a way of establishing their own specific urban identity. Whether this identity is constructed deliberately as a means of claiming membership in the GHHN or simply stems from the group's personal experiences in Budapest is unclear; however the urban experience is central to many of their lyrics. The song 'Reggeltől estig olaszosan', for example, depicts a day cruising around Budapest, meeting up with other Roma youth in specific Budapest neighbourhoods. Neighbourhoods all around the city are simply identified by name without additional description or reference to who lives there; rather, the song portrays the city as the rappers' playground. Fekete Vonat's songs are very much rooted in Budapest, with constant references to the neighbourhoods they are from and frequent, in particular the 8th district, also known as *Józsefváros*, known for its significant Roma populations for well over a century. The neighbourhood is often characterized as a slum, although gentrification projects have been implemented over the past few years (Hodgson, 2005, p. 7).

The title song of their third album, 'Harlemi éjszakák' ('Harlem Nights'), refers to their neighbourhood as 'Harlem'. However, this is not a creative use of this nickname by Fekete Vonat as a way of drawing a parallel with the ghettoes of New York; rather, it is a well-established nickname for the neighbourhood that was already widely used.[11] Although Fekete Vonat could be playing on this traditional association of *Józsefváros* with Harlem, there are no other lyrics in the song to suggest that this reference is intended by the artists to draw a parallel with African Americans. In addition, the slums that Fekete Vonat describe are not the typical violent or dangerous 'ghetto' often found in American gangsta rap. Rather, what is described is a neighbourhood where children and adults learn to be strong and get by in the face of adversity rather than in the face of violence. The historical use of the name 'Harlem' for this neighbourhood does, nevertheless, indicate that the general public associate the Roma with being Black. Fekete Vonat do not seem to need the additional boost of casting themselves as Black, contrary to other Hungarian acts, such as Ganxsta Zolee and Klikk who incorporate more stereotypical gangsta rap ghetto imagery and direct references to African American culture. Such references are absent from Fekete Vonat's work.

Instead, Fekete Vonat address a number of specific problems that the Roma face in Hungary in 'Mondd miért' ('Say why'), their strongest denouncement of racism against the Roma in Hungary. They describe the general disdain that most Roma experience in Hungary:

(4) *Miért kerülnek az emberek*     'Why do people avoid/shun (us)

   *Gúnyos szemek tekintete*     Looking with scornful eyes'

                              'Mondd miért'

They also express pride in their ethnicity, through reference to skin colour (see extract (2) above). They continue with the more institutionalized racism that they face, such as limited access to education and lack of security:

(5)   *Gyermekeink nevessenek*     'Our children should laugh

     *Iskolába mehessenek*     They should go to school

     *Biztonságban vígan éljenek*     They should live cheerfully
                              in security'

                              'Mondd miért'

By painting a picture of the Roma experience as one of social injustice, Fekete Vonat make clear the parallels with the African American experience for all to see without for that matter needing to draw these parallels explicitly. It is perhaps for this reason that Fekete Vonat do not need to rely too heavily on the race metaphor via explicit references to African Americans in order to portray themselves as authentic members of the GHHN. Instead, they use references to skin colour, bringing in a hint of the race metaphor as a way of categorizing the ethnic distinction between the Roma and the general Hungarian population.

## 4.2 Roma identity and code choice

We have seen that the dominant language tends to serve as the default in European hip hop, but why? In Fekete Vonat's work the message and the intended audience seem to stand out as the deciding factors in language choice. All of Fekete Vonat's songs that address social and political issues are in Hungarian. By not addressing themselves exclusively to other Roma (through the medium of Romani) in their more political songs, their lyrics appeal to Hungarians to understand the plight of the Roma and change their attitudes towards them.

When Fekete Vonat *do* rap in Romani or code-switch between Romani and Hungarian, they are addressing Roma more directly. These songs are more light-hearted and have virtually no political overtones. In '**Bilako**' ('**Without Her**'), they directly address other Roma:

(6)  *Haj romale, T'aven tume baxhtale!*  'Hey Roma people, may you be greeted!

*O Kalo Zibano akanak gilyabarel*  The Black Train is singing now

*tumenge variso, Shunen athe:*  something for you, listen up'

'Bilako'

The rest of the song is a light-hearted love song about meeting a girl and wanting to take her home and be with her.

In 'Numa Romanes II' ('Only in Romani II'), they also directly address other Roma as the in-group and non-Roma as the out-group:

(7)  *Shunen athe, avel e vorba tumenge,*  'Listen up, this message is going out to you

*le romendar devorta le rakhlenge*  From Roma to the non-Roma

*Ame gilyabarasa thaj tume khelen*  We will sing and you will dance

*Mukhav le rakhlen vi von shaj shunen*  I will let non-Roma listen as well'

'Numa Romanes II'

**111**

Although they are actually addressing non-Roma in Romani, this case is interesting as they say 'we [Roma] will sing and you [non-Roma] will dance', so the non-Roma do not need to understand the Romani lyrics. These lyrics also sound like a declaration of power, in that they suggest the non-Roma will be dancing to the music the Roma provide, and also that these artists will give non-Roma permission to participate. Interestingly, this declaration of power over the non-Roma is rapped only in Romani, therefore making it more an instance of 'symbolic language use' (Androutsopoulos, this volume) reserved for in-group communication.

Our only examples of code-switching between the two languages come from another love song, Flamenco Rap. The rapper is speaking to a Roma girl, identified as dark-skinned, as we saw in example (1) above. In (8), he wants to know whether she understands Romani, but reassures her that it is not a shortcoming if she does not:

(8) *nem tudom **romnyi** mennyire érted*  'I don't know **wife** how much you understand'

*de megkérdem tőled **sar zhanes romanes?***  'but I am asking you **if you know Romani**?'

*ha nem nát nem nincs semmi baj*  'If not, then not, no problem'

'Flamenco Rap'

This second declaration is made only in Hungarian, while the question is asked in a mixture of the two languages. This song reflects that for the Roma in Hungary, speaking Romani can, but does not have to, be an essential defining feature of being Roma.

In a 1998 online interview, Fekete Vonat were asked explicitly about their code choices and what gives their music an identity as *Roma Rap*.[12] They described their Romani lyrics as the result of messing around and mixing Romani words into Hungarian lyrics and integrating Roma folklore into their songs. Junior noted that Hungarian is typically the jumping off point, adding that translations into Romani do not always yield rhythmically pleasing results. They saw rap as a tool for expressing the problems they and their fellow Roma experience and saw a market for that type of rap, pointing out that if they were not able to sell their music, they would not have obtained a recording contract. They also did not view their *Roma Rap* as an exclusively Roma product – noting that they would like the participation of other Roma on future albums, in addition to their previous non-Roma collaborators.

**112**

## 4.3 Filtering and marketability: the record label scandal

A 2001 press release from EMI Hungary stated that songs entirely in Romani would have to be accompanied by a recorded Hungarian version in order to avoid provoking 'resentment in the average listener'.[13] This surprising decision, as Fekete Vonat's previous use of Romani did not seem to hurt sales, caused the group to break their contract with the label. Interestingly, it is the medium, and not the message that was deemed potentially offensive. As noted above, Fekete Vonat's most politically charged songs were all released in Hungarian, thus accessible to the 'average listener'. No objections were raised, however, to the content of the messages – just to their form.

Such a move indicates that code-choice in hip hop, or indeed any form of public discourse, is not always a matter of artistic freedom; at various levels, marketability and mutual intelligibility are definitely taken into consideration. Fekete Vonat were not asked to make their lyrics inauthentic by using standard Hungarian, but they were required to abandon a language that carries with it particular cultural significance, one deemed undesirable. This experience highlights the need to keep in mind that language in hip hop is a collaborative effort in which decisions are made at a number of different – and not necessarily cooperative – levels. The perception by EMI Hungary that Romani lyrics would lead to feelings of hostility among potential audiences underscores the perception among the general population – if not among the Roma themselves – that the Romani language is a strong aspect of Roma identity. Simply not understanding popular music lyrics in a foreign language is certainly not the heart of the matter: music in English, German, Serbian, and a number of other languages is massively popular in Hungary, especially when it comes to hip hop. The recording label's problem seemed to be more with what the language choice indexes, rather than with the idea of selling music in a language foreign to the majority of the population.

# 5 Code choice and audience design

We have seen that Fekete Vonat use language to appeal to local Hungarian and/or Roma populations, depending on the subject matter. The Hungarian group Realistic Crew, on the other hand, acknowledge that they compose lyrics in English in order to gain an international audience:

> 'It's really strange to me,' says Dalma Berger, the singer . . . 'My lyrics are important for me, and I want people to understand. If I write in Hungarian, only Hungarians can understand. Why would

this music be more interesting if we sing in Hungarian than in English?' (Batey, 2008)

This perspective provides further evidence of audience design as the basis for language choice, and consequently the trend that the dominant language of a country serves as the matrix language of hip hop. The dominant language of Fekete Vonat's intended audience is Hungarian, while Realistic Crew appear to desire an identity as a more international group, choosing English as their matrix language.

Switching between varieties of a language or between two languages is more common than not around the world. As long as the majority of the population is familiar with or has at least accepted the codes in question, code-switching may not serve as a deterrent to or restrict the artist's potential audience. Mitchell notes that although word play, varieties, or codes can be employed as 'resistance vernacular' strategies, if they are not widely used or understood within the target community 'their limited accessibility in both linguistic and marketing terms largely condemns them to a heavily circumscribed local context of reception' (Mitchell, 2000, p. 52). The social indexicality of linguistic forms, and, by implication, of entire codes also plays a role. Even if certain immigrant groups are devalued in various European cultures, in many countries their languages still have the exotic quality of being from a far-off land, and this exotic quality can be put to artistic use. Romani and the Roma do not have this same exotic aspect of being *foreign*: in Hungary they are simply *other*, an other that is not valued. We see, however, that the pattern of rapping in the dominant language also holds true for Roma rap in Hungary, following the same general tendency as immigrant languages across Europe.

In their examination of North African hip hop, Davies and Bentahila (2006) found that code-switching can be used to achieve two opposing ends: 'it may be a device for closing off discourse to outsiders, localizing it firmly with a specific community' or 'it may be a means of opening up the text, offering points of entry to various audiences and resisting too rigid a specification of whom the text belongs to and whom it is addressed to' (2006, p. 390). In Fekete Vonat's case, they seem to make their language choices to perform the former: the songs entirely in Romani are clearly intended to address their fellow Roma or, as in the case of our example that contains code-switching, they are intended to represent the form a conversation among Roma would take.

The juxtaposition of experiences and productions by Fekete Vonat and Realistic Crew above suggests that the intended audience plays the primary role in language choice, a consideration that affects not only how lyrics are written, but also which lyrics ultimately get released.

**114**

Fekete Vonat seek to appeal to a wider Hungarian audience in order to address the conditions for Roma in Hungary, as evidenced by their choice of the dominant language to deliver social messages, and this goal can partially account for their use of Hungarian. We must not neglect, however, that market forces affect and very often determine language choice – especially when the choice is between languages with very different indexicalities, whether it be on a local or international scale.

## 6 Conclusion

The global hip-hop sphere provides an interesting domain in which to examine identity construction through language both because of the prominent role of language in hip-hop culture as well as because we can compare the linguistic content of lyrics with additional sources that confirm the identity artists seek to establish. The interview with Realistic Crew revealed their desire to be an internationally accessible group, which they accomplish linguistically through the use of English rather than Hungarian in their lyrics. On the other hand, the 2001 EMI Hungary press release indicated that the use of Romani was perceived by the record label as indexing an undesirable identity, and their actions highlight the need to take into consideration the multiple filters an artist's work may pass through before it reaches the public.

As we return to Alim's (2009) three questions cited at the outset, we find that Fekete Vonat have appropriated hip hop in a way that highlights the shared experiences between Hungarian Roma and the GHHN with respect to socioeconomic conditions and racism and by evoking the race metaphor through references to skin colour. Fekete Vonat manipulate their linguistic resources, choosing Romani or Hungarian (or mixing the two) as a way of identifying their target audience and highlighting different identities with respect to the subject matter at hand. Their strategies of using both languages to index different identities or address different audiences have clearly met with resistance that stems from the clash of recording labels' concerns for marketability and the (perceived) intolerance for the Roma among the general Hungarian population. A comparison with Roma communities in Hungary and abroad would be useful in examining how the popularity of global hip hop has affected Roma identity as well as how code-switching between Romani and majority languages is employed beyond the realm of hip hop in Hungary and across Europe.

On a broader scale, we have seen that global hip hop exhibits a universality that goes beyond characterizing artists as *Black*, but also that, if only as a metaphor, 'blackness' remains an integral part of authenticity in hip hop. Although as observers we may discover that race is not a defining feature of different hip-hop communities around the world, we cannot totally disregard its influence; it does remain a salient point of reference for theorists and fans alike, and the primary property of authenticity. The notion of a race metaphor in hip hop does not mean that all artists try to portray themselves as Black in order to gain authenticity, but simply that race is a salient reference point around which most hip-hop artists seem to construct their identity. Further research on hip-hop identity construction around the world should take into account perceptions of race, and potentially ethnicity, even when they may not seem to be the most relevant criteria for establishing authenticity, to further enhance our understanding of the unfolding dialogue between the local and the global that lies at the heart of global hip hop.

## Notes

1. The precise definitions of rap and hip hop themselves are subject to an extensive, sometimes heated, debate. Samy Alim makes the following distinction: 'hip hop means the whole culture of the movement. When you talk about rap you have to understand that rap is part of the hip hop Culture' (2006, p. 4). 'Hip hop' is generally considered to comprise an entire lifestyle – fashion, dancing and art as well as politics and worldviews – while 'rap' designates a specific lyrical musical style: 'the aesthetic placement of verbal rhymes over musical beats' (Alim, 2004, p. 388 and 2009, p. 2). The equation of the two terms is a consequence of rap's centrality in hip-hop culture as its most recognizable element (Alim, 2004, p. 338). As Androutsopoulos (2009, p. 43) also points out, rap has become the aspect of hip hop most commonly associated with the genre and is often considered the most representative of it. For the purposes of this chapter, I will use the terms 'rap' and 'hip hop' interchangeably when referring to the music, as many of the authors cited have done, leaving the final verdict on the distinction up to the performers, producers, record labels and fans.
2. '"Serious" rap – a unique U.S. inner-city fusion of funk, technified reggae, teen-to-teen "hardcore" rock, and the early 1970s "poetry of the black experience" . . . – has . . . always had its real roots in the Neighbourhood, the black gang-banger Underground, like trees over skeptics. Black music, of and for blacks' (Costello and Wallace, 1990, p. 21).
3. The ethnic group of interest will be referred to as *Roma*, rather than the often pejorative English term *gypsy*, and their language as *Romani*. Sometimes referred to as *gypsy languages*, the term Romani has been used in academia since the 1800s as a neutral, non-pejorative term. Although the designation *cigány* ('gypsy') in Hungary can encompass groups in addition to the Roma, such as the *Boyash*, because the band in question self-identify

as Roma and claim Romani as one of their languages, I will use these terms throughout this chapter.

4. For a discussion on multiple origins and influences on the emergence of hip hop, see Pennycook and Mitchell (2009).

5. For similar distinctions drawn within the Cypriot and Egyptian hip-hop scenes, see Stylianou (this volume), and Williams (this volume), respectively.

6. <http://www.mahasz.hu/m/?menu=arany_es_platinalemezek&menu2=ada tbazis>, accessed 30 September 2009.

7. Romania and Bulgaria have since joined the EU in January 2007.

8. For an application of the distinction between base and symbolic language use in hip-hop lyrics, see Androutsopoulos (this volume).

9. The full text of the report can be viewed at: <http://archives.cnn.com/2001/ SHOWBIZ/Music/01/15/wb.hiphop/index.html>, accessed 30 September 2009.

10. <http://www.allmusic.hu/index.php?SID=&oldal=albumlista&h_ id=3447>, accessed 30 September 2009.

11. <http://www.c3.hu/othercontent/linkbudapest/site9901/archives/menes_ bio.htm>, <http://epa.oszk.hu/00000/00003/00024/varga.html>, accessed 30 September 2009>, <http://www.balaton-zeitung.info/Hohe-Kriminalitaet-in-Budapester-City>, accessed 30 September 2009.

12. <http://www.amarodrom.hu/archivum/98/vonat.html>, accessed 30 September 2009.

13. <http://groups.yahoo.com/group/balkanhr/message/2029>, accessed 30 September 2009.

# References

Alim, H. S. (2004), 'Hip Hop Nation language', in E. Finegan, and J. Rickford (eds), *Language in the USA: Themes for the Twenty-first Century*. Cambridge: Cambridge University Press, pp. 387–409.

—(2006), *Roc the Mic Right: The Language of Hip Hop Culture*. London: Routledge, Taylor & Francis Group.

—(2009), 'Intro', in H. S. Alim, A. Ibrahim and A. Pennycook (eds), *Global Linguistic Flows: Hip Hop Cultures, Youth Identities, and the Politics of Language*. New York: Routledge, Taylor & Francis Group, pp. 1–22.

Androutsopoulos, J. (2009), 'Language and the three spheres of hip hop', in H. S. Alim, A. Ibrahim and A. Pennycook (eds), *Global Linguistic Flows: Hip Hop Cultures, Youth Identities, and the Politics of Language*. New York: Routledge, Taylor & Francis Group, pp. 43–62.

Androutsopoulos, J. and Scholz, A. (2003), 'Spaghetti funk: appropriations of hip hop culture and rap music in Europe'. *Popular Music and Society*, 26, 4, 463–479.

Batey, A. (2008), 'In Hungary – we don't have stars'. Guardian.co.uk. 29 February. <http://www.guardian.co.uk/music/2008/feb/29/electronicmusic. popandrock>, accessed 24 January 2010.

Bell, A. (1984), 'Language style as audience design'. *Language in Society*, 13, 2, 145–204.

Blommaert, J. (2003), 'Commentary: a sociolinguistics of globalization'. *Journal of Sociolinguistics*, 7, 4, 607–623.

Costello, M. and Wallace, D. F. (1997), *Signifying Rappers: Rap and Race in the Urban Present*. New York: Ecco Press.

Croft, W. and Cruse, D. A. (2004), *Cognitive Linguistics*. New York: Cambridge University Press.

Cutler, C. (2009), '"You shouldn't be rappin", you should be skateboardin' the X-games: the coconstruction of Whiteness in an MC battle', in H. S. Alim, A. Ibrahim and A. Pennycook (eds), *Global Linguistic Flows: Hip Hop Cultures, Youth Identities, and the Politics of Language*. New York: Routledge, Taylor & Francis Group, pp. 79–94.

Darling-Wolf, F. (2008), 'Getting over our "illusion d'optique": from globalization to *mondialisation* (through French rap)'. *Communication Theory*, 18, 187–209.

Davies, E. E. and Bentahila, A. (2006), 'Code switching and the globalisation of popular music: the case of North African rai and rap'. *Multilingua*, 25, 367–392.

Fagyal, Zs. (2007), 'Syncope: de l'irrégularité rythmique dans la musique rap au dévoisement des voyelles dans la parole des adolescents dits "des banlieues"'. *Nottingham French Studies*, 46, 2, 119–134.

García Canclini, N. (1989), *Culturas Híbridas: Estrategias para Entrar y Salir de la Modernidad*. Mexico City: Grijalbo.

Halwachs, D. (2003), 'The changing status of Romani in Europe', in G. Hogan-Brun and S. Wolff (ed.), *Minority Languages in Europe: Frameworks, Status, Prospects*. New York: Palgrave, pp. 192–207.

Higgins, C. (2009), 'From Da Bomb to *Bomba*', in H. S. Alim, A. Ibrahim and A. Pennycook (eds), *Global Linguistic Flows: Hip Hop Cultures, Youth Identities, and the Politics of Language*. New York: Routledge, Taylor & Francis Group, pp. 95–112.

Hodgson, R. (2005), 'Rebuilding a district block by block'. *The Budapest Times: m²*, 1, 5, 4–7.

Imre, A. (2007), 'Hip Hop nation and gender politics'. *Thamyris/Intersecting: Place, Sex & Race*, 18, 265–286.

Lakoff, G. and Johnson, M. (1980/2003), *Metaphors We Live By*. University of Chicago Press.

Lave, J. and Wenger, E. (1991), *Situated Learning: Legitimate Peripheral Participation*. New York: Cambridge University Press.

Lull, J. (1995), *Media, Communication, Culture: A Global Approach*. New York: Columbia University Press.

Matras, Y. (2005), *The Status of Romani in Europe*. Report submitted to the Council of Europe's Language Policy Division, October 2005.

Miklódy, É. (2004), 'A. R. T., Klikk, K. A. O. S., and the rest: Hungarian youth rapping', in H. Raphael-Hernandez (ed.), *Blackening Europe: The African American Presence*, New York and London: Routledge, pp. 187–215.

Mitchell, T. (2000), 'Doin' damage in my native language: the use of resistance vernaculars in hip hop in France, Italy and Aotearoa/New Zealand'. *Popular Music and Society*, 24, 3, 41–54.

—(2001a), 'Another root – hip hop outside the USA', in T. Mitchell (ed.), *Global Noise: Rap and Hip Hop Outside the USA*. Wesleyan University Press, pp. 1–38.

—(2001b), 'Fightin' da faida', in T. Mitchell (ed.), *Global Noise: Rap and Hip Hop Outside the USA*. Wesleyan University Press, pp. 194–221.

Nagy, T. (2003), 'The appearance of an underground electromusic subculture in the cultural sphere of the city'. *Acta Ethnographica Hungarica*, 48, 1–2, 123–138.

O'Hanlon, R. (2006), 'Australian hip hop: a sociolinguistic investigation'. *Australian Journal of Linguistics*, 26, 2, 193–209.

Omoniyi, T. (2009), 'So I choose to do am Naija style: hip hop, language, and post colonial identities', in H. S. Alim, A. Ibrahim and A. Pennycook (eds), *Global Linguistic Flows: Hip Hop Cultures, Youth Identities, and the Politics of Language*. New York: Routledge, pp. 159–177.

Osumare, H. (2007), *The Africanist Aesthetic in Global Hip Hop: Power Moves*. New York: Palgrave Macmillan.

Pennycook, A. (2007), *Global Englishes and Transcultural Flows*. New York: Routledge.

Pennycook, A. and Mitchell T. (2009), 'Hip hop as dusty foot philosophy', in H. S. Alim, A. Ibrahim and A. Pennycook (eds), *Global Linguistic Flows: Hip Hop Cultures, Youth Identities, and the Politics of Language*. New York: Routledge, Taylor & Francis Group, pp. 25–42.

Raphael-Hernandez, H. (2004), 'Making the African American experience primary', in H. Raphael-Hernandez (ed.), *Blackening Europe: The African American Presence*. New York and London: Routledge, pp. 187–215.

Robertson, R. (1995), 'Glocalization: time-space and homogeneity-heterogeneity', in M. Featherstone, S. Lash and R. Robertson (eds), *Global Modernities*. London: Sage, pp. 25–44.

Roth-Gordon, J. (2009), 'Conversational sampling, race trafficking, and the invocation of the *Gueto* in Brazilian hip hop', in H. S. Alim, A. Ibrahim and A. Pennycook (eds), *Global Linguistic Flows: Hip Hop Cultures, Youth Identities, and the Politics of Language*. New York: Routledge, Taylor & Francis Group, pp. 63–78.

Sarkar, M. (2009), 'Still reppin' por mi gente', in H. S. Alim, A. Ibrahim and A. Pennycook (eds), *Global Linguistic Flows: Hip Hop Cultures, Youth Identities, and the Politics of Language*. New York: Routledge, Taylor & Francis Group, pp. 139–157.

Sarkar, M. and Allen, D. (2007), 'Hybrid identities in Quebec hip hop: language, territory, and ethnicity in the mix'. *Journal of Language, Identity & Education*, 6, 2, 117–130.

# 5 Empowerment through Taboo: Probing the Sociolinguistic Parameters of German Gangsta Rap Lyrics

John T. Littlejohn and Michael T. Putnam

## 1 Introduction

Hip-hop music has long exploited linguistic and cultural taboos, especially since the advent of 'gangsta rap' in the late 1980s and early 1990s. Volumes have been written about violent, misogynist and homophobic lyrics in hip-hop music, while the frequent appearances of 'bitch' and especially 'nigga' in rap have raised heated debate both within and outside the hip-hop community. The usage of taboos serves any number of purposes: to sell music through shock or titillation, for the sake of linguistic authenticity, or simply for artistic reasons.

As hip hop gains prominence beyond the boundaries of the United States, especially in a culture where English is not the dominant language, new rules apply. For instance, even though the word 'nigger' exists in Germany – the country that will be focus of this chapter – the word does not bear the same weight or carry the same stigma as in American culture with its deep history of racial oppression of Black people.[1] Norms vary across different societies; so too must taboos.

Perhaps the most culturally specific taboo within Germany, and the one most personal to Germans, is the use of references to and analogies with Hitler and the Third Reich. During the last ten years, a form of German gangsta rap has evolved in which artists have repeatedly used Nazi imagery and language. The two Berlin record companies Royal Bunker and Aggro Berlin in particular have fostered these artists, achieving in the first decade of the millennium a lesser but similar success and infamy to American rap label Death Row records ten years prior.

Current and former Aggro Berlin artists have released music with anti-woman, anti-gay, or anti-Black lyrics,[2] though none of these have met with the same backlash as texts with Nazi references. One possible explanation for this is that the public views Germans' use of misogy-nist, racist (against Blacks), or homophobic imagery in their German gangsta rap as nothing more than a borrowing of prevalent themes in American gangsta rap, themes which appear to have been popular long before the home-grown variety became successful in Germany. As such, these 'hate' lyrics would then be viewed as nothing more than a copy of the thematic patterns in the original, and not a true reflection of the artists or German culture in general.

Some Old School German traditionalists have reacted negatively to Nazi themes and the general gangsta-ism of hip-hop music in the last several years. Hip-hop activists Hannes Loh and Murat Güngör clearly display their distaste for this music in a June 2005 interview in the *Süddeutsche Zeitung* (Rühle and Peitz, 2005),[3] while Loh and Sasha Verlan (2006) express how they disapprove of it in their book *25 Jahre HipHop in Deutschland*. In Putnam and Littlejohn (2007), an examina-tion of the furore surrounding this music, we argued that the public initially saw Nazi imagery in rap music as a simple attempt to instigate controversy and sell records. Soon, however, the media began to see such imagery as part of a dangerous new movement in German society, and thus instigated controversy that eventually did help these artists sell records. In our earlier work dealing with right-wing themes in recent German hip-hop music, we introduced the idea that Hitler and his henchmen represent gangstas due to their toughness, success in achieving power, and ruthlessness in dealing with enemies. In the present work, we explore this idea in detail set against the background of current trends in German national identity, both the *Bio-Deutschen* (White Germans with German ancestry) and the *Migranten* (immigrants). In this chapter, we take German gangsta rappers' role as cultural critics and cultural theorists seriously in connection with the notion of 'hiphopography' (Spady, 2004) in the Hip Hop Nation (HHN).

The key question, of course, centres on the function of linguistic taboos in language communities in general. In this chapter, we shall pay particular attention to two separate but connected language com-munities: 'German' culture (to whatever extent this is definable) and global hip-hop culture as generally described in works on the HHN. As hip-hop artists in Germany, these artists live at the axis of these cultures, forming a 'glocalized' community. Making the problem more complex is the fact that many rappers in Germany[4] come from a migrant background (Androutsopoulos and Scholz, 2002, p. 6), including some of the best-known German rappers such as Kool Savas, Eko Fresh and Bushido. Such a course of study underlies the central focus of *Hip Hop Linguistics* (HHLx; Alim, 2006, 2009). In the words of Alim, 'since lan-guage ain't neva neutral, HHLx interrogates the development of unequal power relations between and within groups in an effort to make a con-tribution to our understanding of the world around us' (2006, p. 8).

What emerges from our analysis, which grants these artists the rights attributed to cultural critics, is that their usage of linguistic and cultur-ally specific taboos can best be understood as 'flippin' the terms' (Alim, 2006, p. 13) to provide an opportunity for social empowerment and the locus of cultural criticism by minorities who themselves feel oppressed in modern-day Germany. In this chapter we address the following questions, which stand at the crossroads of the HHN and modern German identity: what, if anything, does the use of National Socialist (i.e., Nazi) references in German hip-hop music symbolize both among the performers and consumers of this form of German-language gangsta rap? Is German national identity in flux as the first post-Reunification generation grows up and finds itself in a state of what seems to be con-stant transition? Or is this merely a crass and calculated attempt by a small group of musicians to stir up controversy and sell as many records as possible? Furthermore, have these artists been successful in their unit-shifting endeavours? The structure of this chapter is as follows: in the next section we will briefly examine the socio-economic back-ground of some of the gangsta rappers in Germany and how they relate to the minority rappers in America. The following section develops the core argument of our chapter, which elaborates on German rappers' usage of the ultimate taboo: Adolf Hitler and references to his hench-men and other atrocities associated with the Third Reich. The use of taboos in German gangsta rap has a double impact in that they not only draw upon a cultural taboo, Hitler and the Nazis, that has been present in the German psyche for four generations, but they also reflect Germans' individual and collective social unrest in coming to terms with their sense of identity, in particular their national identity.

## 2 The backdrop

Like the United States of America, German culture has its own lengthy history of racial oppression. Most infamous, of course, is the extermina-tion of millions of Jews and other groups under Hitler during the 1930s and 1940s. The events of the Third Reich and the *Endlösung* ('Final Solution') hang over the German collective consciousness well over half a century later. The Germans' history with the *Gastarbeiter* is less known internationally. These foreign 'guest workers' came to Germany to help with the labour shortage between 1955 and 1973, with a large number of people coming from Turkey beginning in 1961. Many guest workers have stayed in the country and raised families there. Legally, these families are foreigners – even children who were born in Germany and have lived there their entire lives – as German law decides citizenship by right of blood (*ius sanguinis*) rather than right of birth (*ius soli*).[5] As 'foreigners', these immigrants and their children and grandchildren have lived a second-class existence in which they are often labelled *Türken* ('Turks') regardless of their national background. But as Eva Kolinsky notes, '. . . the second generation has become more sensitive about injustice and discrimination, but also more able to defend itself and stand its ground' (2002, p. 214).

While US hip hoppers have made allusions to America's centuries-long tradition of slavery, these allusions have not brought US artists the infamy of the German hip hoppers who have referenced the Holocaust in their music. There are, of course, many reasons for this. Institutionalized slavery in the United States lasted much longer than the Holocaust, measurable in centuries rather than years; however, the latter is closer to the present day. An older generation that remembers the Third Reich and its atrocities are still living, whereas there are few people alive today who could have ever known former slaves in the United States. Furthermore, and connected to the previous point,[6] the National Socialist past is a much more emotional topic to the majority of *Bio-Deutschen*. In today's Germany, which considers people of non-German ancestry 'migrants' even if their families have perhaps lived in the country for two or three generations or longer, hip hoppers who raise racial issues have much to gain. German hip-hop music and art has the ability to raise awareness about their treatment both socially and legally. This fits naturally within the discourse goals of HHLx to connect to a larger community, namely, the HHN. It may come as no surprise that the children of migrant workers in Germany would emerge as the forerunners and pioneers of hip-hop culture in their 'homeland'.[7]

## 3 Adolf Hitler: straight gangsta mack

In their 2002 book *20 Jahre HipHop in Deutschland*, Sascha Verlan and Hannes Loh remarked upon increasingly aggressive and militaristic raps during battles, and provided (anonymous) sample lyrics from such battles:

> (1) *ich bomb dich wie vietnam / verbaler fremdenlegionär, erober dich wie militär / ich bin der disco-diktator, pate der partys, regiere mikrofone durch stile, wie regime auf kuba und chile / ich verbrenn dich wie die inquisition*
>
> 'I'll bomb you like Vietnam'/'Verbal foreign legionnaire, conquering you like the military'/'I am the disco-dictator, Godfather of the parties, and govern the microphone through styles, like

> the regimes in Cuba and Chile'/'I'll burn you like the inquisi-
> tion'. (Verlan and Loh, 2002, p. 246)

One notes a variety of usages here. These artists employ threats ('I'll bomb you like Vietnam', 'I'll burn you like the inquisition'), report ('Verbal foreign legionnaire, conquering you like the military'), and bragging ('I am the disco-dictator, Godfather of the parties'). They also refer to events both political and religious, in the present, the recent and the remote past.

While the usage of more violent lyrics may have been a disturbing trend within the hip-hop community – it certainly was for Verlan and Loh (2002) – it was only when the references to National Socialism became common that society at large became outraged, and the rappers became famous. Verlan and Loh (2002, p. 246) also supply the follow-ing lyric: *ich schalt die radios gleich, wie die fuckin' nazis* ('I control the radio like the fuckin' Nazis'). The structure is similar to the rhymes cited in example (1) above, particularly as they all use a simile with *wie* ('like'), which is a common lyrical technique in German as well as English rap. The image, in fact, does not prove as violent as many of the other lyrics above, i.e., no bombing, burning or even conquering. The inflammatory material here – much more so than the pedestrian use of the English word 'fuckin' – is the mention of the Nazis.

The increased usage of more violent imagery in German hardcore rap in an attempt to emulate the American gangsta rap model, while shocking and troubling to traditionalists such as Verlan and Loh (2002), is not surprising. What perhaps is shocking is the upsurge in National Socialist references, especially references to Adolf Hitler. Examples of German hip-hop lyrics playing on aspects of Nazi Germany culture and/or Adolf Hitler have become quite commonplace: Bass Sultan Hengzt raps that *Ich schlachte Kinder wie Hitler* ('I butcher children like Hitler'), and MC Basstard rhymes about fellow rapper Taktlo$$: *T-A-K-T-L-O-SS . . . er ist der Battlerap-Führer . . . also sieg ihm heil!* ('T-A-K-T-L-O-SS . . . he's the battle rap-Führer . . . so greet him with "Sieg Heil!"'; Güngör and Loh, 2002, p. 301). Other examples of references to Nazi Germany are not difficult to find in contemporary German hip hop: the Turkish-German rapper Kool Savas raps that he is 'Nazi' and that Adolf Hitler is his father (*Ich bin ein Nazi. Adolf Hitler ist mein Vater*),[8] while rapper Ronald Mack Donald from *M. O. R.*, who is also of Turkish-German ancestry, warns his foes that after any sort of confrontation with him he will usher them off to the 'gas show-ers' and that he also chases children into concentration camps. Such allusions to Germany's Nazi past, whether indirect (e.g., Bushido's reference to 'the leader like A') or quite transparent (e.g., Kool Savas's

'I am a Nazi'), have been sharply criticized by the German media, scholars and hip-hop activists. In our 2007 analysis of the German media's reaction to Aggro Berlin rappers Bushido and Fler's controversial lyrics and overall personae, we made a clear distinction between rappers who openly embrace a right-wing, nationalist agenda (such as Dissau Crime) and rappers such as Bushido, Fler, Kool Savas and Ronald Mack Donald. The fact that Bushido, Kool Savas and Ronald Mack Donald all hail from multi-cultural backgrounds suggests that these references and allusions to National Socialism, and in particular Adolf Hitler, are not an attempt to further promulgate extreme right-wing ideology. On the contrary, in Putnam and Littlejohn (2007) we advanced the hypothesis that references to Adolf Hitler, and Germany's Nazi past in general, function as an articulation of a German identity in flux, reconstructed through a complex engagement with the collective German past and American culture (i.e., gangsta rap). Our discussion here expands upon this core argument by adopting Quinn's (2005) analysis of a gangsta split-identity between 'dynamic badman' and 'trickster-pimp' present in contemporary gangsta rap that transcends mere recent trends in hip-hop culture.

Before the National Socialist and Neo-Nazi references began appearing in Battle Rap in the late 1990s, gangsta rap had never played a prominent part in German hip-hop history. In fact, as late as 2003, Jannis Androutsopoulos and Arno Scholz (2003, p. 469), examining hip-hop culture and rap music in German, remarked that gangsta rap '. . . did not really "catch on" in Europe, i.e. it is consumed but not productively appropriated'. To date, many reporters and critics have observed how rappers have used Nazi imagery in their raps and come to the conclusion that Neo-Nazis and other right-wingers have begun to use rap music to spread their political message (Rühle and Pietz, 2005; Elkins, 2005). This view is untenable, partly because many of the hip-hop artists in question deny any fascist political intention, but mainly because so many of the accused gangsta rappers are so-called 'immigrants', making neo-Nazi membership a de facto impossibility. We make an alternative, and contrary, assertion: far-right politics did not make an entry into the mainstream by co-opting American-style gangsta rap, but rather German-language gangsta rap gained great prominence (and airplay) by evoking Nazism. In this chapter we put forward the hypothesis that German-language rappers have been grafting National Socialist allusions onto American gangsta rap, a practice in which Adolf Hitler et al. take their position as substitute gangsters. As such, Hitler is framed by these rappers as the embodiment of the gangster ethos. Following Quinn (2005), we concur that the embodiment of the two dominant types of gangsta – 'dynamic badman' and 'trickster-pimp' – taps into much older distinctions in Black expressive culture. According to Quinn,

> Contemporary incarnations of the gangsta drew on the images of cinematic black gangsters of the 1930s and 1940s; and they drew even more heavily on themes and stories from African American oral culture. . . . At the risk of shunting disparate characters into two overarching types, the *badman* in gangsta rap is characterized by stylishly violent, emotionally inarticulate, politically insurgent, and socially alienated personas (the crazy nigga, insurrectionary badman, nihilistic bitch, 40-drinking baller, and so on). By contrast, gangsta's *pimp/trickster* serves to represent the more socially mobile and verbally dexterous hustler (the golden-tongued mack, money-hungry hoe, flashy drug dealer, and also, as we have already seen, the publicity image of many gangsta artists/entrepreneurs themselves). (Quinn, 2005, p. 93)

Our argument is that the allusions to Hitler, his henchmen and the Holocaust are an attempt by German gangsta rappers to draw upon these traditional African American oral traditions and map them onto culturally relevant topics in their own sphere of reality. To illustrate our point, we will provide a brief, yet concise analysis of two contemporary German hip-hop songs: Fler's (2005) 'NDW 2005' and Bushido's (2004) 'Electro Ghetto'. The former, the quasi-title track to Fler's first album, *Neue Deutsche Welle*, has attracted much attention from the media both at home and abroad.[9]

As witnessed in virtually all forms of hip hop, Fler establishes his lyrical superiority, declaring himself a 'Hip-hop Tsunami' that can 'overpower others':

(2) *Ich bin ein Hip-Hop-Tsunami, weil ich Leute überschwemme*
   'I am a Hip-Hop-Tsunami, because I deluge people'

In discussing his locale, Berlin, Fler is quick to point out illegal activities (such as boxing: *Komm nach Berlin und du siehst wie sich die Leute hier boxen*, 'Come to Berlin and you'll see how the people here box') that he supposedly frequents, or at the very least, recognizes. Fler establishes himself as an 'outsider' (*Ihr holt die Bullen, wir sind die Außenseiter, wir sind Aggro Berlin*, 'You call the cops, we are the outsiders, we are Aggro Berlin') that seeks revenge (*Ich hab's gesagt, man ich werd mich rächen*, 'I've said it, man, I'll get my revenge') – although this revenge is never clearly specified in the song lyrics.

Fler goes on to provide some further insight into his frustration. As noted in the lyrics, Fler (as well as others) seeks to establish a hip-hop scene in Germany that builds upon German culture and is exclusively

**126**

in German. By labelling this music as *Volksmusik* that is 'loved by the German people', Fler establishes a form of national (or at the very least, local) pride in this form of music (*ne neue Ära beginnt, das ist wie Volksmusik / Die Medien boykottieren mich, doch ich werd' vom Volk geliebt*, 'A new era is beginning, that is like folk music / The media boycott me, but I'm loved by the people'). Fler further explicates his frustration, as well as the likely frustration of many Germans, having, up to this point, had to play second fiddle to 'Ami-rap' which 'no one understands a word of' (*Es gibt nur Ami-Rap, weil man da kein Wort versteht* / 'There's only American rap, because nobody can understand it'). Fler then once again refers to his music and the music of his contemporaries as *deutsche Mucke* (*Deutsche Mucke ist kastriert und ihr seid gegen uns* / 'German music is castrated and you are against us'). A succinct pattern emerges from these lyrics: Fler's lyrics promote some form of national and local pride, a fact which some in the media would come to recognize as nationalistic and, in some cases, supportive of right-wing ideology. Fler continues to play on these images of national pride by referring to the 'flag in the sky' and the 'national anthem' (*Die Neue Deutsche Welle guck, man sieht die Fahne am Himmel / Die Nationalhymne kommt heut mit Schlagzeug und Bass!*, 'The new German Wave, look, you can see the flag in the sky / The national anthem is coming today with drums and bass!'), symbols which played a part in the media uproar examined by Putnam and Littlejohn (2007).

Receiving almost as much negative media coverage, though one may suppose these rappers did not consider any media coverage negative, was Fler's former label-mate, Bushido – a rapper who has now become one of the most successful entertainers in Germany. In his 'Electro Ghetto' (2004), Bushido cleverly introduces an ambiguous (potential) reference to Adolf Hitler in the song's chorus:

(3) *salutiert steht stramm ich bin der Leader wie A*
    'salute, stand tall, I am the leader like A.'

From the outset of this song, Bushido desires to associate both him and his music to criminal activities such as drug trafficking and the prison yard (*Ich mach den Sound für den Hof im Knast / ich bin der Grund warum du nie deine Millionen machst / ich hab den Sound für die Dealer im Park*, 'I make the sound for the prison yard / I am the reason why you'll never make millions / I have the sound for the dealers in the park'). He appears to insinuate that such an approach to hip hop, as well as life in general, has nothing to do with a surface-level commitment to this sort of gangsta mentality; rather, this success is maintained by 'keepin' it real' (*denn ohne mich wird Deutscher Rap schon wieder*

**127**

*nicht hart / schon wieder ein tag an dem ich eure Lieder nicht mag,*
'Cause without me German rap won't be hard again / Already another
day, and I can't stand your songs'). These sentiments are echoed strongly
in the music of Fler presented above. The (possible) reference to Hitler
in this song can be found where Bushido admonishes his listeners 'to
salute and stand tall' because he is 'the leader like A'. In his defence,
Bushido touts that the reference to 'A' is in actuality a reference to his
friend and colleague in the hip-hop industry, Azad. Another sense of
ambiguity is employed in the crowd's reaction to 'A' in the form of
cheering from the crowd in the background on the song.

The development of the German hip-hop scene, as well as most other
variants of global hip hop, embraced the battle culture also found in the
original American scene (Verlan and Loh, 2002, p. 55). This was a way
of sifting the proverbial wheat from the tares, of establishing who the
best performers were in the region at any specific point in time. Those
who did not produce a superior product in competition with other
performers at a local jam were soon to be forgotten. Much like its
American counterpart, German rap – as noted by Güngör and Loh
(Rühle and Peitz, 2005), among a host of others[10] – has also undergone
a shift in which more violent and descriptive lyrics now appear in
German battle rap culture.

Androutsopoulos and Scholz (2003) remark that up to that point
gangsta rap had not caught on in Germany and the rest of Europe. They
produce a compelling rationale for this popular sub-genre not establishing itself there:

> We suggest that the reason for this is the fundamentally different
> social base of hip-hop culture in Europe. In particular, the living
> conditions reflected in gangsta rap hardly have a direct equivalent
> in the lives of European rap artists and fans. . . . While European rap
> artists may listen to (and look up to) U.S. gangsta rap, their own
> lyrics are expected to represent their own social environment. If an
> essential aspect of rap discourse is to reflect 'urban lived experi-
> ence' (Rose 102), then simply copying an imported narrative will
> clearly not meet the expectations. (Androutsopoulos and Scholz,
> 2003, p. 472)

Hip hoppers in Germany found a prominent equivalent: Adolf Hitler,
a figure who could embody both the 'badman' and 'pimp'/'trickster'
persona of the traditional gangsta in African American oral tradition.
In 'That's all Concept; It's Nothing Real' Michael Newman (2009,
p. 211) examines the complexities involved in rappers' attempts to
establish authenticity, which he characterizes as a '. . . constant hip-hop
preoccupation'. David Gordon Smith sees the sense in evoking the

Nazi past: '. . . if you are a German rapper suffering from a street credibility deficiency, how do you manage to get yourself noticed?' (Smith, 2006, p. 2). Neo-Nazi imagery is the obvious answer. Nothing is more guaranteed to shock middle-class parents and win the respect and, more importantly, the disposable income of the key market of disgruntled teenagers. Newman (2009, p. 205) notes that 'there was simply no evidence that rap influenced the MCs in this study to adopt the thug lifestyle they idealized.' The sentiment works equally well when one substitutes 'Nazi' in Germany for 'thug' in Newman's study, as in the following statement: '. . . the cult of [the] thug was not, for the MCs, about being a thug but holding up the thug as symbolically compelling' (Newman, 2009, p. 205). As Newman (2009, p. 210) notes, '. . . outlaws and outlaw icons predate rap by millennia, as do controversies over the relations between the two'. Interest in outlaw icons has not only enjoyed a long history, but also a wide spread.

Hitler was the ultimate gangsta. In terms of scale, he out-performed the American gangsters operating (roughly) contemporarily. Whereas gangsters such as Al Capone and Dutch Schultz fought for power over neighbourhoods and cities, Hitler gained absolute control of an entire country, and vied for control of an entire continent. Furthermore, where American gangsters, from the early twentieth century well into the present, wanted to make their own rules and do whatever they wanted, Hitler literally made his own laws. Even during his 'downfall' he remained in control of his personal fate. He decided when he would die and the means by which he would do it. He even retained a measure of personal control beyond his death; he had his body burned, thereby avoiding indignities for himself and Eva Braun similar to those suffered by the Italian dictator Benito Mussolini and his mistress. By committing suicide, he furthermore avoided incarceration, unlike Capone, or death at the hands of others, as was the fate of Mussolini, Schultz and John Dillinger.[11]

The notion and mythology of gangsters has remained strong with the American public for decades, just as Hitler and the National Socialist past has stayed prominent in the German psyche. An initial wave of gangster films enjoyed immense popularity during the years preceding the adoption of the Hays code,[12] while decades later the television show *The Untouchables*, focusing on the gangland era, would run for four seasons in the late 1950s and early 1960s. In 1977, Randy Newman would release the album *Little Criminals*, the title track of which criticized the glorification of gangsters in popular culture, which was clearly still strong in mid-1970s society (Schütte, 2004, p. 127). In the following decade, Brian De Palma reused this powerful material in *Scarface* and *The Untouchables*, the former updating the story and the

**129**

latter staying in period. De Palma released these films in the mid 1980s (1983 and 1987, respectively) the same time that gangsta rap was beginning to come into existence. The 1983 film *Scarface*, which updates an early gangster classic into the modern era, still holds a prominent place in hip-hop lore, with one gangsta rapper from the Geto Boys even taking its title as his stage-name.

Hitler and Nazism similarly take a prominent position in German consciousness. Not only do the stigma of Germany's defeat in World War II and the atrocities of the Holocaust linger, but so do the physical scars of buildings not yet rebuilt after the bombing in the 1940s. The existence of Neo-Nazis in Germany, as well as abroad, further testifies to Adolf Hitler's continued infamy. Although Hitler and the National Socialists are part of Germany's political history and collective conscious, there has been little open debate about their legacy among the greater public. There is no black and white: Nazi = bad. Not misunderstood, not misled, not victims of egregious social circumstances; bad. *Mein Kampf* is still banned in Germany, as is the National Socialist Party (NSDAP). But the memory of Hitler and his era are not only alive in small right-wing collectives. In our young century, two prominent films focusing on Hitler have already come out of Germany and gained great popularity with the German public: *The Downfall* (*Der Untergang*, 2004) and *My Führer: The Absolutely Truest Truth About Adolf Hitler* (*Mein Führer: Die wirklich wahrste Wahrheit über Adolf Hitler*, 2007). [13] It is unlikely that either of these films would have been produced 20 or even 10 years prior, the first showing Hitler as a human instead of a monster or evil incarnate, the latter an actual comedy about him.

The mere existence of these films demonstrates a change in attitude in the German public towards Hitler, the National Socialists, and the Second World War: an emotional dissociation from them. Many factors contribute to this apparent dissociation. Time plays a considerable role in this process; it has been more than six decades since the end of the Third Reich, and there are now few Germans who were alive and conscious of it. Furthermore, millions of 'immigrants'[14] who have come from Turkey, Morocco and other countries have no association with a Nazi past.

It is striking that the nascent gangsta rap in America began to enjoy growth and financial success at the same time that interest in gangsters, the gangster lifestyle, and its modern-day equivalents was high in the public consciousness, demonstrated by the success of the films *The Untouchables* and especially *Scarface*. German-language gangsta rap, using images harkening back to the National Socialist era also went mainstream just as the German public exhibited a similar upsurge of interest in the existing Nazi legacy. Just as hardcore rap embraced a gangster tradition and gangster lore to play on in its music, the hardcore rap from Germany, which did not have a gangster tradition, used Hitler and the Nazi mythology to graft onto the music in a corresponding manner. Such a move should not be surprising. At least one artist from the greater hip-hop world has publicly admitted (a form of) admiration for Hitler, despite the stigma which would be attached to such an assertion, and about the same time so-called 'Nazi-Rap' was hitting the German mainstream. In December 2002, rapper Nas made the following remark about the track 'Masterminds' from his album *God's Son:*

> It's telling about people I look up to . . . [people like] Genghis Khan, Hitler, Nat Turner, J. Edgar Hoover, Huey Newton, all different types of mother@#*$ers. Some demonic, some of them are children of God. You gotta be a mastermind to survive in this world. (Triviño, 2002)

As mentioned in Putnam and Littlejohn (2007, p. 464), Nas received an immense amount of backlash, prompting him to almost immediately issue an explanation and claim that the interviewer had taken his word out of context: [15]

> I hate Hitler, because he hated my people . . . but, as an enemy if you don't respect a smart, evil genius you are going down. . . . First of all, this [reporter] makes out my song to be a song for Hitler. My music has nothing to do with Hitler. I hate Hitler. He hated my people. He killed my people as well as Jews and any other person that came after his army. The guy makes my song out to be something it has nothing to do with because he wanted his audience to say, 'How do we discredit Nas? How do we get Nas to look like he's crazy?'

Adolf Hitler wielded massive power and reigned terrible destruction over those whom he perceived as his enemies. It is therefore not very surprising that a hip-hop artist would 'respect' his 'evil genius', and it is unlikely that Nas is the only American rapper to whom this thought has occurred. Nas was simply impolitic enough to make the comment, and he furthermore was unfortunate enough to make it to a reporter who would publish the remark.[16]

Some Germans, however, are using the aura and taboo around Hitler to their advantage, using *Kunst als Waffe* ('art as a weapon') to quote prominent anti-Hitler propagandist Friedrich Wolf. The 'immigrants' are able to use such imagery. Their relatives had nothing to do with Hitler, Nazism or the Holocaust; therefore this language would not be as emotionally laden to them as to others with a German heritage. Inasmuch as hip-hop competitions[17] in Berlin – where the Nazi imagery within immigrant rap developed – were often drawn between citizens and non-citizens as early as the mid-1980s (Pennay, 2001), these immigrant rappers need not fear reprisal from many of these *Bio-Deutschen*. The emotional connection is there for the latter, and with white skin and Germanic features they bear the Nazi taint, even if members of their families had to flee from Germany or became anti-Nazi fighters. This treatment is a reversal of and a parallel to the treatment of people with dark skin or non-Germanic features in Germany who are labelled foreigners and outsiders from their mere appearance. Furthermore, if *Bio-Deutschen* rappers used Nazi symbols in battle rap or hip-hop lyrics against outsiders, they would force themselves into a racially oppressive position similar to that of the National Socialists. It would also raise a public furore, which it in fact did when White, Germanic rapper Fler flirted with Nazi imagery. This also directed attention to the problem of German racism in general, which would also be advantageous to these 'immigrants'.

The success of these attempts to achieve authenticity through the use of references to Hitler and the Nazis is an open issue. However, the grasp on any success gained through this means seems tenuous. Because these rappers presented themselves as larger than life, perhaps not always successfully, they were prone to imitation and lampooning. In 2007, the German rap/comedy group Aggro Grünwald (also known as Die Stehkrägen) mocked Aggro Berlin[18] as well as the ghetto aesthetic. Royal Bunker itself provided mockery of Berlin gangsta rap, bringing joyously puerile rappers K.I.Z.[19] to the public at almost exactly the same time, releasing their album *Hahnenkampf* in August 2007. In the wake of such mockery and the undermining of Berlin Gangsta, the head of Royal Bunker, arguably the most influential German hip-hop label of the first decade of the twenty-first century (Riesselmann, 2008), announced in early 2008 that the label would complete its imminent obligations and fold. Whether this occurred despite or because of the success of K.I.Z. is debatable.

Aggro Berlin – *Staatsfeind Nummer 1* ('public enemy number one') for parents, teachers and censors (Spiegel, 2009) – would close its doors in April 2009. By that time, however, its artists were, perhaps, already turning to other ways of establishing credibility than using Nazi symbolism. Three masked men armed with knives attacked Fler in November 2007, outside the MTV studios in Berlin (Pletl, 2007). Two months later, unknown assailants shot at Massiv, a Sony artist with strong Aggro Berlin connections, a week before his major label debut (Müller, 2008).

In conclusion and in concord with our previous work on this topic (Putnam and Littlejohn, 2007), we hope to have shown that a premature dismissal of these artists' lyrics as mere 'hate music' is unwarranted, especially if we wish to grant them the status of 'cultural theorists' according to Spady's (2004) definition of hiphopography. What remains fascinating is that these hip-hop artists, 5,000 miles removed from the birthplace of this cultural movement, were able to tap into and exploit an understanding of 'gangsta' that has roots in African American oral traditions much older than hip hop. In future studies of global hip hop, it will be interesting to note whether other cultures also make use of these discussions through local figures and constructs unique to their own culture and society. Speaking specifically about the hip-hop scene in Germany, future studies must also focus on the interpretation and opinions of the consumers of hip hop to gain a deeper understanding of the impact these artists have had in contributing to the debate on German national identity and in speaking to injustice and oppression within this society.

# 4 Final thoughts and directions for future research

In this chapter we hope to have shed some light on references to Adolf Hitler and the Third Reich in contemporary, and very popular, German hip-hop lyrics. These extremely controversial themes, used almost exclusively by racial minorities in Germany, can best be understood as a weapon (our *Kunst als Waffe* analogy in the previous section) by these minority groups who '. . . have a relatively poor command of the German language and occupy minor positions in the labor market . . .' (Bennett, 2004, p. 183). As such, hip hop represents the same opportunity for these minorities as for others in similar situations in other countries: the music industry has the potential to provide a better life and cause a rise in social standing in and outside of their communities. Bennett (2004, p. 183) further explicates that 'two thematic issues that appear regularly in German-language rap songs concentrate respectively upon the fear and anger instilled in ethnic minority groups by racism and the insecurity experienced by many young members of such groups over issues of nationality'. Not surprisingly, these communities latched onto a set of taboos that would most assuredly grab the attention of the dominant culture: references to Nazi Germany. Given Germany's unique cultural past, to put things lightly, this study and future studies like it have the unique opportunity to study the interplay of linguistic taboos used in hip-hop culture with other debates and controversies in society as a whole.

Research in hip-hop studies has a responsibility to investigate this complex network of the employment of linguistic taboos and issues of societal/cultural identity in flux. Focusing exclusively on the German scene, the time to gain a deep perspective on these issues, at least with regard to references to the Third Reich in gangsta hip hop in Germany, may be dwindling, as indicated by comments from prominent artists such as G-Hot and K.I.Z. who find this form of rhetoric to be 'laughable'. Second, a more thorough investigation probing the differences and similarities in meaning and usage of the terms 'nigger' and 'nigga' in the American hip-hop scene compared to the usage of the term *Kanake* (a derogatory term for people with a foreign appearance) to refer to minorities in the German hip-hop community is sorely needed. Third, what could prove to be most revealing and of immediate interest for scholars involved in studies of German nationalism and national and ethnic identity, is the response and reaction of not only the media (Putnam and Littlejohn, 2007), but also the opinions of the consumers and 'regular' Germans who might not necessarily be aware of these recent controversies in German hip hop. In the spirit of Lin (2009), we note the necessity for research into the way 'migrant' German rappers create their own discursive space through the use of Gangsta rap and National Socialist imagery. Research in this area has the potential to reveal aspects of German identity in flux and expose the connections between 'mainstream' culture and the German hip-hop scene. There are, of course, a litany of other related issues that warrant more in-depth treatment, such as the comparison of the systematic usage of rapping in English vs rapping in German and the adaptations of the German language to conform to HHLx and African American English (AAE) in particular.

## Acknowledgements

We would like to thank all of the participants at the Language and Hip-Hop Culture in a Globalizing World conference held at the University of Illinois Urbana-Champaign. We are particularly grateful to Marina Terkourafi for the invitation to present our work at such a venue. We are also thankful to comments and discussions pertaining to this chapter by Awad Ibrahim. All remaining errors are our own.

## Notes

1. However, due to prolonged exposure to American culture and the word itself, the word 'nigger' is starting to take on the negative effect of the English usage in Germany too.
2. Among others, Sido's '*Arschficksong*', G-Hot's '*Keine Toleranz*' and B-Tight's '*Neger, Neger*' respectively.
3. The third interviewee was Bushido, a former Aggro Berlin rapper who has become one of the best-selling German recording artists. He, naturally, did not share the Loh's and Güngör's opinion on this matter.

4. Following Verlan and Loh's *20 Jahre HipHop in Deutschland* and *25 Jahre HipHop in Deutschland*, we prefer to use the phrase 'hip hop in Germany' instead of 'German hip hop' as the latter carries implications about the race of the artists and the language of the texts which are often misleading.

5. The German government changed the law regarding this matter, the German Nationality Law, in 1999 and made further progress by passing an Immigration Law in 2004 (Loentz, 2006, p. 46). However, Templeton notes that the '. . . traditional attitudes that German national identity is related to German blood . . . still exist' nonetheless (2005, p. 158).

6. The Nazis committed atrocities in a more modern technological age which allowed the filmed and sound-recorded documentation not only of the concentration camps and the stories of their victims, but also the propaganda efforts which led up to these events.

7. This statement invites some controversy that goes beyond the scope of this article; namely, how minorities (such as the members of Advanced Chemistry) affiliated with German hip hop's Old School scene take serious issue with the lyrics of the younger generation of gangsta rappers' lyrics.

8. Westberlin Maskulin, 'Bass', *Hoes, Flows, and Moneytoes* (Bunker Records, 1999).

9. See Putnam and Littlejohn, 2007 for a more detailed rundown of the various treatments and analysis offered by the media of Fler's music (as well as others affiliated with the now defunct Aggro Berlin label).

10. Trenkamp (2004), Gross (2004), Rühle (2006), Tzorztis (2005), Boser (2006).

11. It bears mentioning that Dutch Schultz mentioned Hitler among a famous series of incoherent utterances in his last hours after being fatally shot in 1935.

12. Three prominent examples are *Little Caesar* with Edward G. Robinson (1930), *Public Enemy* with James Cagney (1931), and Howard Hawks's *Scarface* (1932).

13. The director of *My Führer: The Absolutely Truest Truth About Adolf Hitler* is Swiss-born Dani Levy. Other German films, such as *Before the Fall* (*Napola*, 2004) and *Sophie Scholl: The Final Days* (*Sophie Scholl: Die letzten Tage*, 2005) have also dealt recently with the Third Reich.

14. . . . and their children, many of whom, due to German law, are not German citizens, though they were born and have possibly lived their entire lives within German borders.

15. 'Nas says Hitler quote taken out of context', AllHipHop.com, 12 December, <http://allhiphop.com/blogs/news/archive/2002/12/13/18127672.aspx>. Last accessed September 2009.

16. This was by no means Hitler's only connection with English-language popular music. John Lennon had suggested that Hitler appear as one of the 'audience' on the cover of the Beatles' *Sgt. Pepper's Lonely Hearts Club Band*. The idea was later rejected, along with two other Lennon choices: Jesus and Gandhi. Hitler being on the cover was still viable late in the

**135**

artistic process; his cut-out can be seen in the booklet for the album's 1987 CD release (Lewisohn and Wilkinson, 1987, p. 7, 9).

17. Here: dance-offs. Before the 1990s, dancing played a much more prominent role within German hip-hop culture than did rap music.

18. Grünwald is a small suburb of Munich. The contrast between this Bavarian community and cosmopolitan Berlin is acute.

19. The name K.I.Z. is reminiscent of the abbreviation KZ: *Konzentrationslager* (concentration camp). As *K.I.Z.* has been evasive about the real meaning of its name (Kedves, 2007), the connection to concentration camps appears to be intentional.

## Discography

Bushido, 'Electro Ghetto', *Electro Ghetto*. ersguterjunge/Universal, 2004.
Fler, 'NDW 2005', *Neue Deutsche Welle*. Aggro Berlin, 2005.

## References

Alim, H. S. (2006), *Roc the Mic Right: The Language of Hip Hop Culture*. New York: Routledge.

—(2009), 'Intro: straight outta Compton, straight aus München: global linguistic flows, identities, and the politics of language in a global hip hop nation', in H. S. Alim, A. Ibrahim and A. Pennycook (eds), *Global Linguistic Flows: Hip Hop Cultures, Youth Identities, and the Politics of Language*. New York: Routledge, pp. 1–22.

Androutsopoulos, J. and Scholz, A. (2002), 'On the recontextualization of hip-hop in European speech communities: a contrastive analysis of rap lyrics'. *PhiN: Philologie im Netz*, 19, 1–42. <http://web.fu-berlin.de/phin/phin19/p19t1.htm>, accessed 20 September 2009.

—(2003), 'Spaghetti funk: appropriations of hip-hop culture and rap music in Europe'. *Popular Music and Society*, 26, 4, 463–479.

Bennett, A. (2004), 'Hip-Hop am Main, rappin' on the Tyne: hip-hop culture as a local construct in two European cities', in M. Forman and M. A. Neal (eds), *That's the Joint!: The Hip-Hop Studies Reader*. New York: Routledge, pp. 177–200.

Boser, U. (2006), 'And now . . . aryan rap'. *U.S. News and World Report*, 23 January. <www.usnews.com/usnews/news/articles/060123/23berlin.htm>, accessed 20 September 2009.

Elkins, R. (2005), 'Rap music and the far right: Germany goes gangsta'. *The Independent*, 17 August. LexisNexis.

Gross, T. (2004), 'Der Bauch Berlins'. *Die Zeit*, 7 September. <http://zeus.zeit.de/text/2004/32/Sido>, accessed 20 September 2009.

Güngör, M. and Loh, H. (2002), *Fear of a Kanak Planet: HipHop zwischen Weltkultur und Nazi-Rap*. Höfen: Hannibal.

Kedves, J. (2007), 'Vier gegen den Rest der Welt'. *Welt am Sonntag*, 26 August. LexisNexis.

Kolinsky, E. (2002), 'Migration experiences and the construction of identity among Turks living in Germany', in S. Taberner and F. Finlay (eds), *Recasting German Identity: Culture, Politics, and Literature in the Berlin Republic.* Rochester, NY: Camden House, pp. 205–218.

Lewisohn, M. and Wilkinson, P. (1987), 'Booklet', *Sgt. Pepper's Lonely Hearts Club Band.* Capitol: The Beatles.

Lin, A. (2009), '"Respect for da chopstick hip hop:" the politics, poetics, and pedagogy of Cantonese verbal art in Hong Kong', in H. S. Alim, A. Ibrahim and A. Pennycook (eds), *Global Linguistic Flows: Hip Hop Cultures, Youth Identities, and the Politics of Language.* New York: Routledge, pp. 159–177.

Loentz, E. (2006), 'Yiddish, *kanak sprak*, klezmer, and hiphop: ethnolect, minority culture, multiculturalism, and stereotype in Germany'. *Shofar*, 25, 1, 33–62.

Müller, D. (2008), 'Ein zynischer Zufall'. *die tageszeitung*, 17 January. LexisNexis.

Newman, M. (2009), '"That's all concept; it's nothing real": reality and lyrical meaning in rap', in H. S. Alim, A. Ibrahim and A. Pennycook (eds), *Global Linguistic Flows: Hip Hop Cultures, Youth Identities, and the Politics of Language.* New York: Routledge, pp. 195–212.

Pennay, M. (2001), 'Rap in Germany: the birth of a genre', in Tony Mitchell (ed.), *Global Noise: Rap and Hip-Hop Outside the USA.* Middletown, CT: Wesleyan University Press, pp. 111–133.

Pletl, S. (2009), 'Angriff auf Musiker'. *Die Welt*, 29 November 2009. LexisNexis.

Putnam, M. T. and Littlejohn, J. T. (2007), 'National socialism with Fler? German hip hop from the right'. *Popular Music and Society*, 30, 4, 453–468.

Quinn, E. (2005), *Nuthin' but a 'G' Thang: The Culture and Commerce of Gangsta Rap.* New York: Columbia University Press.

Riesselmann, K. (2008), 'Besser, man geht kraftstrotzend'. *Die Tageszeitung*, 7 January. LexisNexis.

Rühle, A. (2006), 'Die rassistischen Vier'. *Süddeutsche Zeitung*, 13 May. Factiva.

Rühle, A. and Peitz D. (2005), 'Die Härte der Texte und die Härte der Nazis'. *Süddeutsche Zeitung*, 28 June. Factiva.

Schütte, U. (2004), *Basis-Diskothek Rock und Pop.* Stuttgart: Reclam.

Smith, D. G. (2006), 'Germany's wannabe public enemies: nasty is the new nice'. *Expatica*, 28 June. <http://www.expatica.com/de/leisure/arts_culture/germanys-wannabe-public-enemies-nasty-is-the-new-nice-23524.html>, accessed 20 September 2009.

Spady, J. (2004), 'The Hip Hop Nation as a site of African-American cultural and historical memory'. *Dumvoices revue*, 154–166.

Spiegel, S. (2009), 'Adieu, Staatsfeind Nr. 1'. *die tageszeitung*, 15 April. LexisNexis.

Templeton, I. H. (2005), *What's So German About It?: Cultural Identity in the Berlin Hip Hop Scene.* Diss. University of Stirling.

Trenkamp, O. (2004), 'Gewalt ist nur eine Inszenierung'. *die tageszeitung*, 28 June. Factiva.

Triviño, J. (2002), 'Nas looks up to Hitler?' *Sohh.com*, 11 December, <http://www.sohh.com/articles/article.php/4117>, accessed 20 September 2009.

**137**

Tzortzis, A. (2005), 'Germany's rap music veers toward the violent'. *The New York Times*, 9 August. Factiva.

Verlan, S. and Loh H. (2002), *20 Jahre HipHop in Deutschland*. Höfen: Hannibal.

—(2006), *25 Jahre HipHop in Deutschland*. Höfen: Hannibal.

# 6 Glocalizing *Keepin' it Real*: South Korean Hip-Hop Playas

Jamie Shinhee Lee

## 1 Globalization and localization of hip hop: res and verba

Globalization is no new topic in academia; in relation to hip hop, however, it has recently entered the realm of sociolinguistic scholarly debate. While Smitherman contends that 'hip-hop refers to urban youth culture in America' (1997, p. 3), this is a questionable limitation for what hip hop is now and has become around the world – a global youth phenomenon, as is recognized by several scholars (see e.g., White, 2004; Chang, 2007; Taylor and Taylor, 2007). Hip hop's influence goes beyond music and has an impact particularly on youth and their speech style, as demonstrated in Cutler's (2009) discussion of Hip Hop Speech Style (HHSS). Chang argues that 'hip hop is evolving into a truly global art of communication' (2007, p. 58). Global youth culture 'emerges as a transnational market ideology' (Kjeldgaard and Askegaard, 2006, p. 235), rap music and rap artists being generally recognized as marketable commodities (Smith, 2008). However, the marketability of hip hop, especially in the 'peripheries' of globalization, is closely connected to the local. Chang asserts that 'hip hop is a lingua franca that binds young people all around the world, all while giving them the chance to alter it with their own national flavor,' and its being 'a vital progressive agenda that challenges the status quo' is pointed out as one of the consistent themes across cultures (2007, p. 60).

The prevalence of the hip-hop genre in the music industry around the world is indicative of its global presence, but one should not expect to encounter homogeneous hip hop across the board as 'all hip hop is local' (Watkins, 2007, p. 64). The interplay between the global and the local components in hip hop is clearly addressed in Androutsopoulos's observation that hip hop is 'paradigmatic of the dialectic of cultural globalization and localization' (2003, cited in Pennycook, 2007, p. 103). Such inevitable connection between the global and the local is discussed under different names – 'grobalization' (Ritzer, 2004) and 'glocalization' (Robertson, 1995). Condry's (2006, p. 208) notion of 'deepening (global) connectedness' and 'widening (cultural) diversity' sums up the complicated dynamics between globalization and localization.

The entertainment industry is an area in which we observe an intriguing interaction between globalization and location. As Shim notes, 'globalization, particularly in the realm of popular culture, breeds a creative form of hybridization that works towards sustaining local identities in the global context' (2006, p. 39). The idea of 'think globally and act locally' is often viewed as synonymous with glocalization. Kjeldgaard and Askegaard summarize it as 'a coexistence of dimensions of similarity and difference' (2006, p. 245). Söderman and Folkestad argue that 'hip hop is a glocal culture' (2004, p. 324). They demonstrate that creating music can be handled globally through the internet, but those involved in this creation process, for instance, beatmakers with different linguistic and cultural backgrounds, often join forces and contribute uniquely to collaborative projects. Kjeldgaard and Askegaard also support the importance of the 'dialectical process of glocalization' (2006, p. 235) in global youth culture. As Mitchell (1998) articulates, the global and the local are not polarized opposites; rather, they intersect, each defined by the other. Thus, the global becomes localized and the local globalized (Thompson and Arsel, 2004).

Glocalization enables a simultaneous attachment to, and detachment from, the local (Roudometof, 2005). The global music industry is now experiencing increasing hybridization in visual, aural and lyrical dimensions of music production and performance, which is an interesting outcome of glocalization. Shim observes that 'cultural hybridization has occurred as local cultural agents and actors interact and negotiate with global forms, using them as resources through which Koreans construct their own cultural spaces, as exemplified in the case of rap' (2006, p. 38). Omoniyi argues that Nigerian hip-hop artists have made modifications 'in their resistance to wholesale assimilation by global hip hop culture and to carve out an independent glocal identity' (2006, p. 198). Pennycook seems to concur by stating that 'such locally emerging scenes are neither mere reflection of a global culture nor nationally bound local appropriations, but rather participants in a much more dynamic flow of linguistic and cultural influences' (2009, p. 332). I argue that 'global-local musical syncretism', to borrow Mitchell's (2001) term, exists both in the *res* and *verba* of hip hop, affecting its several components ranging from linguistic elements such as social issues and language use to non-linguistic factors such as attire, hairdos and 'bling bling'.[1]

**140**

Hip hop as a form of social commentary against the status quo or the establishment may be a global phenomenon. On the other hand, specific defiant discourses presented in hip-hop lyrics may not and cannot be homogeneous in nature, since the status quo and impending social issues vary from country to country. Pennycook maintains, 'for many hip hop artists, then, the first move toward localization is a rejection of aspects of rap from the United States and a turn toward overtly local themes' (2007, p. 106). Themes such as 'police brutality, racial profiling, gang violence, and political apathy' are common in American hip hop (Chang, 2007, p. 62), while discourses against 'homogeneity of Tokyo urban retailscapes' and 'conscripts from the South Korea army' are featured in Japanese hip hop and Korean hip hop (Watkins, 2007, p. 65). Diverse themes vocalized in hip hop are not necessarily due to the East versus West dichotomy. Even in Africa, whose oral traditions supposedly influenced rap music, social issues featured in music are quite different from those in American hip hop. For instance, Omoniyi's study of Nigerian hip hop shows that it 'departs from mainstream norms by excluding features such as gangsta, heavy sexualization, misogyny, politics and monolingualism' (2006, p. 198).

The need for authenticity in performance seems to be quite widespread in hip hop. Pennycook (2007) notes that there is the 'global spread of authenticity' in the hip-hop world, while globalization itself challenges the idea of authenticity in hip hop: what is real and what is not real. 'Keepin' it real' epitomizes 'the hip hop ideology of authenticity' (Pennycook, 2007). Keepin' it real is construed as 'the hip hop mantra' (Morgan, 2005) and is often viewed as 'real talk' and 'straight talk' (Alim, 2007). As Alim astutely remarks, the authenticity of hip hop is manifested through 'not only is you expressin yoself freely (as in "straight talk"), but you allegedly speakin the truth as you see it, understand, and know it to be' (2004, p. 86). According to Taylor and Taylor, youth culture, which is often discussed in close connection with hip hop, understands being 'real' as 'an unabashed, raw reflection of things adults would prefer not to admit' (2007, p. 211); moreover, 'hip hop culture represents some ugly truths about everything society is and is not' (p. 213). Pennycook (2007) notes that 'global real talk, while easily glossed as keepin' it real, is better understood as a global ideology that is always pulled into local ways of being' (p. 112). He further argues that 'this emphasis on being true to oneself might nevertheless be seen as the global spread of a particular individualist take on what counts as real. The notion of authenticity, however, can be understood not so much as an individualist obsession with the self [but] rather as a dialogical engagement with community' (Pennycook,

**141**

2007, p. 103). As argued in White (2004), 'the authenticity of experience is related to locations' (p. 166).

## 2 South Korean hip-hop playas[2]

Smitherman notes that 'rap music is rooted in the Black oral tradition of tonal semantics, narrativizing, signification/signifyin, the dozens/ playin the dozens, Africanized syntax, and other communicative practices' and the rapper is 'a postmodern African griot, the verbally gifted storyteller and cultural historian in traditional African society' (1997, p. 4). Modern hip hop, however, does not fit this description anymore since its performers and their stories are no longer limited to 'Black', 'American' or 'African'. Hip hop as 'the latest example of African Americanization' (White, 2004) has been disseminated to and accepted by non-African Americans in the US and beyond as a popular art form. Because of this derivative nature of hip hop outside the US, those who view hip hop mainly as the lived experience of African Americans often argue that hip hop appropriated by non-Blacks is not authentic.[3]

Utilizing English expressions in non-English medium pop music is a fairly common practice these days, including J-pop in Japan (Moody, 2000, 2001 and 2006; Stanlaw, 2000 and 2004), K-pop in Korea (Lee, 2004, 2006 and 2007), and Cantopop in Hong Kong (Chan, 2009). An important globalized and yet localized element in hip hop is the issue of authenticity in language use (Pennycook, 2007). In particular, outside the so-called English speaking countries, the use of several different languages seems to be in fashion. English, Swahili and Kikuyu are used in Kenyan hip hop (Watkins, 2007) and Cantonese, English and Mandarin co-occur in Hong Kong hip hop (Chang, 2007). This practice could be view as a way of staying true to who they are – hip-hop artists who have access to the transnational community called the Hip Hop Nation (Alim, 2004) and yet firmly grounded in a local scene.

Cullity (2002) notes indigenization of MTV India in Hinglish – a mixture of Hindi and English – and its less seditious image. In discussing the English lyrics by the Malaysian rappers Too Phat, Pennycook asserts that their language may be global but their register is 'local, generational, cultural, and distinctive' (2007, p. 105). Adelt observes that

> [the] processes of hybridization and indigenization are played against an identification with a global hip hop scene by European rappers and fans. A good example of this dualism is the simultaneous use of local dialects and English expressions as a way of signifyin(g) to the hip hop community. (Adelt, 2005, p. 290)

**142**

Omoniyi, for instance, shows that Nigerian hip hoppers use Yoruba and English in their performance and explains that these bilingual lyrics allow the Nigerian hip hopper to express 'the glocal self' as a 'new self [which] is made manifest in fusion code' (2006, p. 202). In discussing the German band Die Ärzte's performance of the song 'Ich bin der rock'n'roll-übermensch' ('I am the rock'n'roll superman'), Adelt demonstrates that German identity takes the form of a 'multicultural hybrid of Nietzschean *übermensch* theories, Japanese monster movies, US rock'n'roll, and remnants of Caribbean reggae – quite a contrast to Rammstein's Teutonic heavy metal, but "German" nonetheless' (2005, p. 289).

The main objective of this study is to discuss the global-local syncretism in the South Korean hip-hop scene and address its glocalizing practice of the hip-hop ideology of authenticity: keepin' it real. The chapter presents a textual analysis of social issues voiced by South Korean hip-hop playas and uncovers what is depicted as their 'lived' experiences.

## 3 The data

This study examines 68 songs by four major South Korean hip-hop artists whose albums appeared on the top ten yearly album sales chart on http://hiphopplaya.com in December 2007. Hip-Hop Playa is one of the most frequented hip-hop music websites in South Korea and is the self-proclaimed 'No.1 Black Music Portal Site'. The tracks analysed in this study are from four albums listed in the Discography at the end.

### 3.1 Playas

The hip-hop artists featured in this study are South Korean nationals, but most of them use English stage names. When their Korean legal names are known, they are presented in parentheses. Background information about these artists was compiled from newspaper and magazine articles and their homepages, which often are maintained by their managing companies.

**Table 6.1** Profiles of playas

| Group name | Members | Main home page URL | Years active |
|---|---|---|---|
| Epik High | Tablo (Lee Sun Woong)[4] Mithra Jin (Choi Jin) DJ Tukutz (Kim Jung Sik) | www.epikhigh.com | 2003–Present |

(*Continued*)

**143**

**Table 6.1** (*Continued*)

| Group name | Members | Main home page URL | Years active |
|---|---|---|---|
| Dynamic Duo | Choiza (Choi Jae-ho)<br>Gaeko (Kim Yoon-sung) | www.dynamicduo.co.kr | 2004–Present |
| Drunken Tiger[5] | JK (Jung Kwon Suh)[6] | www.drukencamp.com | 1998–Present |
| Soul Company | Kebee<br>The Quiett<br>Jerry.k<br>Makesense<br>RHYME-A<br>화나 (Hwana)<br>D.C.<br>Planet Black<br>Mad Clown<br>DJ Silent<br>P & Q<br>Loquence | www.soulcompany.net | 2004–Present |

The majority of these artists were born and raised in South Korea but some groups either have a member educated outside Korea or had non-Korean members at the beginning of their music careers. For example, the original members of the group Drunken Tiger had a Filipino and an Italian-Korean band member. Most hip-hop playas currently working in South Korea are young males in their twenties. Those featured in the study fit this profile as well, with the exception of Tiger JK in Drunken Tiger, who is in his early thirties.

Among these groups, Drunken Tiger in particular stands out. The front man Tiger JK, who grew up in Los Angeles, caught people's attention back in 1992 when he performed in reaction to Ice Cube' song 'Black Korea'. 'Black Korea' featured racially charged, unflattering lyrics about Koreans such as 'Oriental one-penny-countin' motherfuckers' and 'little chop suey ass'. A Korean shop owner killed a 15-year-old African American girl who was allegedly caught shoplifting. This incident aggravated the tension between Korean Americans and African Americans in LA. Forrest (2000) explains the situation as follows:[7]

> [N]ot many from the Korean community responded to the song. However, it inspired one young Korean to break the stereotype. After hearing the song, Tiger JK (at the time 18) made it his responsibility to show that these stereotypes were untrue and had to be broken. At a hip hop show that promoted racial harmony, JK spoke

his feelings in lyrics rather than a speech, and despite the criticisms he received from that crowd, he still caught the interests of some Korean record labels.

JK was reported to have said 'Ice Cube, he was mad racist' and 'Chop suey isn't even Korean' (Forrest, 2000). Furthermore, he asserted that

> something needed to be said . . . If I put my heart into it they would get the message that Koreans can do it, too. The crowd was going, 'Chung-ching-chung,' the good old stereotypical diss. They were booing, but when I started flipping my Korean, I saw fools with their mouths open. (Forrest, 2000)

JK's statement indicates that he was painfully aware of racial stereo-types against Asians in his adopted home, the United States, and seriously intended to rebel against them.[8] He accomplished this by utilizing his heritage language, Korean, which suggests that he embraced his Korean identity and did not shy away from his original ethnic and linguistic background. He used his bilingual and bicultural status to his advantage to position himself as an authoritative orator who is familiar with social issues in both worlds.

## 4 South Korean hip-hop playas' keepin' it real

### 4.1 Ageism

The idea of keepin' it real seems to be equated with down-to-earth lyrics and up-front attitudes. The following statement about Drunken Tiger's contribution to the Korean hip-hop world is a revealing example of what is valued by the music industry and aspired to by hip-hop artists.

> Drunken Tiger challenged the system with their unique hip hop sound and *realistic lyrics*. Although their *straightforward attitude* made them one of the most controversial figures in Korea's con-servative media, without their willingness to *challenge musical and societal conventions*, Korean hip hop would not be where it is today. (http://drunken camp.com/ spin.htm, accessed 21 September 2009; emphasis added)

Because the statement above was made by their managing company, we may accept it as an objective remark or question its validity. Never-theless, what is unequivocally expressed in this statement is the band's 'marketed' identity as a maverick to challenge conventions and experi-ment with something new and controversial.

The South Korean hip hoppers in this study talk about keepin' it real with reference to the kind of hip hop *they* perform and the kind of hip hop *others* do. They often launch attacks on rivals, emphasizing the importance of doing 'real' hip hop and condemning 'fake' hip hop. Inauthentic hip hop is mocked as 'blah' done by those caring only for fame with no true passion and love for hip hop, as articulated by Soul Company on *Official Bootleg Vol. 2*. In P & Q's contribution to the album, *Cikhye polkkey* ('I'll be watchin' you'), real hip hop is revered in stark contrast with *kacca* ('fake') hip hop, which is linguistically ridiculed as *kay cicnun soli* ('dog barking nonsense') or *ipman salasse* ('rambling with no substance'), the literal translation meaning that only the mouth is alive and everything else is dead. Fake hip hoppers are identified as young, inexperienced, self-proclaimed gangsta hip hoppers pretending to be tough and acting like thugs but afraid of authorities such as cops. In an attempt to embarrass fake hip hoppers, P & Q belittle them as *elinay* ('child') or *kkomayngi* ('kiddo') and consider them to be not as good as *cincca hyengtul* ('real older brothers'). A noteworthy point is that these South Korean hip hoppers are sensitive to the age hierarchy common in mainstream society and tend to treat an older age as synonymous with more experience.

Any discriminatory action and prejudice solely on the basis of age is ageism. In the West, ageism is generally discussed regarding negative bias against old age. On the other hand, in the East, old age is often a sign of wisdom and experience. The South Korean hip hoppers in the study seem to validate this view. 五倫 (*olyun*) in Korea refers to ethics or moral guidelines governing five fundamental human relations; among these relations, 丈幼有序 (*cangyuyuse*) makes specific reference to a proper relationship between the old and the young. It literally means that there should be an order between the adult and the child. In other words, the younger should give precedence to the elder. Along with this general principle, excerpt (1) also draws upon the common Korean saying *hyengmanhan awu epsta* ('Younger brothers never can be as good as older brothers'). Two hip hoppers are often treated as brothers in the same family, although they are not related by blood. Their competition is viewed as sibling rivalry in which the older brother knows and does better than the younger brother. The fact that younger hip-hop playas are labelled various lexical items representing 'the child' is a noteworthy reminder of their subordinate position.[9]

(1) ... you got no love for this     '... **You got no love for this**. You
넌 힙합인척                           pretend to do hip hop
누가 가짜 또 누가 진짜 real     Who is a fake and who is a **real**
thug                                    **thug**
가사가 어쩨 flow가 첫쩨     What about lyrics, **flow** first and
rhyme은 두번                     then **rhyme**

| | |
|---|---|
| ... blah 말만 떠벌릴뿐 개소리들로괜한 언더와 오벌 갈라놓네 | **... blah** blah dog barking nonsense, alienating underground hip hop from mainstream hip hop |
| ... stop being wannabe be real mc | **... stop being a wannabe be real MC** |
| 자칭 갱스터 힙합 코스프레쯤 될걸 위험한 척 유난을 떨면서 | self-proclaimed gangsta acting like a dangerous man but actually hip hop cosplay |
| ... 너 경찰을 무서워해 여전히 어린애진짜 형들의 반에 반도 못가 | ... you are afraid of cops still kids not even a quarter as good as real older brothers' |

Soul Company (P & Q), 'Cikhye polkkey'

The term 'cosplay' is telling. It is shortened from the expression 'costume play', referring to a character playing performance based on elaborate costumes and accessories. These characters are normally from comic books, anime[10] and videogames. By being labelled 'hip hop cosplay', these pretenders are dismissed as 'wannabes' who may look like hip hoppers but have no real talent or substance. P & Q's attack against American gangsta hip-hop copycats is evocative of two Korean idiomatic expressions *kethkwa soki taluta* ('The inside and the outside are different') and *enhayngi ilchihacianta* ('Word and actions do not match'). These expressions are often used to disapprove of disingenuous behaviour or hypocrisy. P & Q criticize young inexperienced hip hoppers for superficially mimicking gangsta rap and acting tough but actually being weak inside and behaving cowardly towards law enforcement.

Perseverance and tenacity are key elements often praised in South Korean hip hop. Playas lacking these characteristics are labelled 'hip hop kidz' with no substance and are criticized for taking an easy road to fame and for creating nonsensical controversies. Excerpt (2) from Soul Company's 'A macta' ('Oh, right!') is a case in point.

| | | |
|---|---|---|
| (2) | Soul company 수많은 Hiphop kidz 그들이 걱정돼 안스러워 | 'We **Soul Company** worry about many **hip hop kidz**' |
| | 손쉬운 방법으로 그저 관심을 원해 | 'They just want the public's attention' |
| | Issue maker의 컨셉, 대중의 의식을 훔쳤네 | 'With the concept of "**issue maker**", they are robbing the public of its consciousness' |

> Straight up me and ma soul.   'Straight up me and ma soul.'
>
> Soul Company (Kebee), 'A macta'

## 4.2 Meta-hip hop: career, global ambition and work ethic

In addition to the age-related hierarchy, the dichotomy between 'real' and 'fake' hip hop is discursively constructed in relation to work ethic and passion. The playas in the study seem to be primarily concerned with their artistic identity; their success, failure and struggle with their music career are recurring themes. All four groups express their desire or belief to be the best in the industry. There is a certain sense of dichotomy between *us* and *them*; often *our* supremacy is contrasted with *their* mediocrity. The ways in which these hip-hop playas promote the authenticity of their music and boast superb 'flow' or 'rhyme' are not necessarily connected to natural talent but have more to do with an incredible amount of dedication and sacrifice that goes into their craft. The hip-hop texts in this study suggest that playas themselves view work ethic and passion as greater virtues than god-given talents. In short, perspiration counts more than inspiration. In pursuit of successful music careers, these artists often emphasize how important it is to persevere, not to give up hopes and dreams, and not to compromise their artistic vision and integrity.

When promoting their music career, the hip-hop playas in this study often voice their global ambition, which is reflective of South Korea's globalization drive called *Segyehwa* (Kim, 2000). South Korean hip hoppers' desire to be successful beyond Korea is also closely related to *Hanlyu* (the Korean Wave), which refers to widely reported increasing appreciation of Korean pop culture in Asia and beyond. Their career ambition includes not only local and national success but also global and world recognition. Vales argues that 'hip hop is all about aspiration' (2005, cited in Smith, 2008, p. 88). In particular, global career aspirations seem to manifest themselves more strongly among artists in the peripheries of globalization than those in the centre. There is a clear indication that the South Korean playas in this study have global career aspirations and consciousness, which are linguistically represented by the use of place names outside Korea, for example, ocean names (e.g., the Atlantic), country names (e.g., Germany), or city names (e.g., San Francisco). Dynamic Duo express the band's global expansion ambition in two different songs. In one, they portray themselves as *nolayhanun haycek* ('singing pirates') who travel in the ship called 'beat' and steal everything with the sword of 'language' and 'destroy the order of the sea'. They want to 'destroy' the hierarchy of the world through their beat and lyrics.

**148**

(3) 지금부터태평양대서양인도양       'From now on, we handle the
    다우리들이접수한다              entire Pacific, Atlantic, and
                                Indian'

                      Dynamic Duo, 'Haycek' ('Pirates')

When addressing their global ambition, the South Korean hip hoppers in this study remind audiences that hip hop is a 'universal language', 'breaking down national boundaries' as expressed in excerpt (4). The so-called *cikwupon* music ('globe music'), which literally refers to the globe itself, is presented as a tool to build a common ground between two distant unrelated spaces and is praised as 'the best' kind of music.

(4) This is 지구본 music            **'This is** globe **music**, the best in
    세상에서가장 근사한 Music       the world, connecting two dots
    (지 지구본에 선 선을 그어       from **San Francisco to Seoul** on
    점 두 개를 연결해 frisco to     the globe
    seoul)

    . . . 노래로 국경을 부셔         . . . Breaking national
                                boundaries with songs

    . . . 음악은 감정의 통역기 내   . . . **Music** is a translator of
    꿈을 싣고 높이 날아가는 고무    emotions, a balloon carrying
    동력기 이제 조금씩 더 높이      my dream high. I am gonna fly
    날려볼래 더 멀리 From US to     higher **from US to Germany'**
    Germany

                      Dynamic Duo, 'Cikwupon Music'

Hip-hop music in the data is depicted not only as a universal language but also as a language promoting equality. When artists burn out from their gruelling performance schedule and feel they hit a creativity plateau, they seek opportunities to refuel their passion and to be inspired. In the song 'Cikwupon Music'('Globe music'), Dynamic Duo describe their need to be away from people's expectations and to escape to New York and California for artistic rejuvenation. They explain how 'the language called music' enabled them to become one with non-Korean artists and to feel equal 'in a foreign territory'.

(5) 영혼의허기를새로운열기로       'We wanted to feed our spiritual
    우고파서 찾아간 곳은            hunger and fill us up with passion'

    New York and Cali let's        **Let's ride.** So we went to **New**
    ride                           **York and California**

    낯 선 땅에서 먼저 느낀 건      The first thing we felt in the
    음악이란 언어 앞에 모두         strange land was that we were one
    하나인 것                      in the name of music

| 악수를 할 수 있다면 모두가<br>동등해 | If we can shake hands, we are<br>equal |
| 거짓없이 우리도 서로를<br>존중해 | We respect each other with no<br>hypocrisy' |

Dynamic Duo, 'Cikwupon Music'

Along with global ambition, the South Korean hip-hop playas in the study assert the importance of work ethic in achieving a successful music career. The general message is that great hip hoppers are not necessarily born but are made through hard work. This view is contrastive with freestyle hip hop in the US, which does not appreciate rehearsed, contrived predictable rap. For instance, several MCs in Soul Company assert that they work harder than their competitors and take their hip-hop career very seriously; they read rhyme books and write lyrics while their competitors watch games on TV.

| (6) 니들이 Game TV를 볼 때 나는<br>Rhyme Book을 볼래 | 'When you watch **Game TV**,<br>I'll read my **rhyme book** |
| 니들이 개인기를 연습할때면 난<br>글을 적네 | When you work on your<br>trivial talent, I'll write |
| 깨있지 못한 자는 바른 말들을<br>못해 | Those not awake cannot say<br>the right things |
| 니들이 괜히 시비를 걸 때마다<br>마이크를 쥐었네 | Whenever you pick a fight<br>with me, I grab a microphone |
| 난 토하고 토해. 또 뱉어내고<br>뱉어내 | I speak out and speak out<br>again I rap out and rap out' |

Soul Company, 'Ruff Enuff'

In addition, the concept of keepin' it real is manifest in various social issues and concerns that are locally relevant and ring true, including Confucianism-inspired filial piety, the notoriously difficult college entrance exam, and obligatory military service for all men.

## 4.3 Family

Family is a theme that appears quite often in the data and is depicted in ambivalent ways. It is mentioned positively in the context of a tight-knit support system, such as a hard-working mother and sacrificing aging parents, or negatively in terms of pressuring, pushy and conservative parents who disapprove of their children's choices including, but not limited to, their hip-hop career. For example, Epik High rap about aging parents' suffering and parental sacrifice and dedication in

**150**

'Silecung' ('Aphasia'), and conflict with their parents over religion and behaviour problems in 'Paykya' (lit., 'White night', meaning 'night with the midnight sun').

Furthermore, familial obligations, particularly duties to parents, seep into the lyrics. In Confucian thought, filial piety 孝 (*hyo*) represents respect and love for parents and ancestors, which is considered to be a great virtue and a child's duty. The desire to take care of suffering *emma* ('mom') is expressed in the song 'Haycek' ('Pirates') by Dynamic Duo. They use the synecdoche of 'gold badges' to represent South Korean parliament members and express their desire to take all the gold badges from corrupt politicians and melt them into gold magnet bracelets for their parents, considered to be effective in alleviating rheumatic pain. Here we see a glimpse of 孝 (*hyo*) in conjunction with condemnation against corrupt politics.

## 4.4 Overwork

Hip-hop artists rap about what they actually experience such as 'the Korean problem' and 'the Malaysian scene' (Pennycook, 2007, p. 106). As argued in Pardue, 'local contexts and concerns are not epiphenomenal but actually shape the meaning of hip hop' (2007, p. 675). The theme of overwork, for example, is arguably more local than global to many Koreans; it has arisen as a very serious social issue in the region including Korea and Japan, more so than in the rest of the world. In a country where six days a week and 12 hours a day are considered the 'norm' and where there is even a name for death from overwork – 過勞死 (*kwalosa*) – insane work schedules and overworked employees are appropriately problematized in South Korean hip hop. For example, Dynamic Duo's '출Check' ('Chwul Check', 'Attendance Check') describes an average workweek as 월화수목금금금 ('Monday, Tuesday, Wednesday, Thursday, Friday, Friday, Friday'), with Saturday and Sunday conspicuously missing. Later in the song, phrases like 'blistered lips' and 'life like war' further depict the fatigue-plagued, tough work environments many South Korean 'salarymen' (corporate employees whose income is salary based) are subject to.

## 4.5 Education

A great emphasis on academic achievement has produced good results for South Korea, which boasts one of the highest literacy rates in the world, a large number of college graduates, and a highly educated work force. Seth notes that the most contributing factor to prestige and social class in South Korea is likely to be education, asserting that 'education

**151**

is a national obsession in South Korea' (2002, p. 1) and reasons that 'the preoccupation with the pursuit of formal school was the product of the diffusion of traditional Confucianist attitudes toward learning and status, new egalitarian ideas introduced from the West and the complex, often contradictory ways in which new and old ideas and formulations interacted' (2002, p. 6). The education fever, however, has also generated problems such as notoriously difficult college entrance exams, expensive test prep courses, excessive competition among students, and parent–child conflicts regarding school choices, just to name a few. Some hip-hop playas in the study reminisce about their own high school days and the parental and social pressure they were subject to when they were younger. 'Still life' by Epik High is a case in point, featuring a defiant discourse about education-oriented society and parental pressure about academic success.

(7) 왜 내가 무슨 이유로 색안경 끼언른들이 택한울타리 밖에 묶인 희생양이 됐나    'How come I became a scapegoat tied to a fence built by adults wearing tinted glasses

. . . 같은 감옥 속에서 6년을 구속해    . . . confined for 6 years in a prison-like life

. . . 나는 일류 대학 석사보다 더    . . . more than a first-rate school Master's degree holder

나는높고 높으신 그 박사보다 더    more than an esteemed Ph.D.

오직 비트위에 낙서하는 작사가가 더    I'd like to be a lyricist scribbling only (rap) beats'

Epik High, 'Still Life'

They rap about stifling school life and feeling trapped in 'a prison' called school. They feel victimized within the boundaries set by 'adults' who are judgemental and overly critical. Junior and senior high school days are viewed as equivalent to six years of imprisonment. Later in the song they talk about their decision to become hip hoppers at the age of 16 and their rebellion against their parents' wish for them to go to Korean Ivy League schools pursuing MA and PhD degrees. They rap that academic success does not interest them as much as advancement in a music career; it is clearly indicated in the text that they would rather be serious lyricists than serious scholars.

Another common education experience is the notoriously difficult college entrance exam and its gruelling preparation process in the 12th grade, often dubbed 'hell'. Test jitters are expressed by Soul Company member Kebee in the song 'Ko 3 hwuki' ('Epilogue to the 12th grade').

He raps about how nervous he was, how supportive his friend was, how hesitant he was, and how unsure he was.

| (8) | 알 수 없는 긴장감에 사로잡힌 시험 전날 | 'The day before the exam indescribable anxiety came over me |
|---|---|---|
| | 여태껏 서로를 지탱해주던 친구와 전화 붙잡고 | I talked to a friend who was supportive all this time |
| | 대체 우리가 지금껏 무엇을 찾고 있었던가에 대해서 얘길했지 | We wondered what in the world we were looking for |
| | 이건 누가 우리에게 품고 있는 기대치 때문이 아닌 나 자신을 위한 일이겠지 | Are we doing this to please others or for ourselves? |
| | . . . 익숙한 골목이 오늘따라 괜히 낯설어 | . . . Even familiar alleys look totally strange today |
| | . . . 내 발걸음은 제자리에서 망설여 | . . . my feet lingered hesitantly' |

Soul Company (Kebee), 'Ko 3 hwuki'

## 4.6 Military service

Whenever two or three Korean men gather, they need to talk about military service. This is a complaint often made by Korean women who lightheartedly point out their partners' countless retelling of their *kwuntay saynghwal* ('life in the military'). Korean men, on the other hand, often think that talking about their military service is a major bonding experience with other men. Since every Korean man has to go through it, mandatory military service is also a recurring theme in Korean hip hop, as a South Korean DJ in Pennycook's (2007) study asserts. Some hip-hop playas in this study talk about their disillusionment after completing the service with respect to readjusting back into mainstream society. For example, in 'Yeypiyek' ('The army reserve'), Loquence, D. C. and Planet Black from Soul Company lament the unwelcome responses they received from society and how utterly crushed they felt after their military service.

| (9) | 2년이라는 터널을 건너고 나면모든 게 분명해지고 뭐든 할 수있을 줄알았어 | 'I thought I would be more certain about things and feel I could do anything when I went through two years of tunnel |
|---|---|---|
| | 허나 벗어난 순간부터 모든게 쉽지 않았어 | But as soon as I was released, nothing was easy |

**153**

세상은 쓸모 없는 날반기지  Society did not welcome useless
않았어                  me'

Soul Company (Loquence, D. C. & Planet Black), 'Yeypiyek'

Most Korean men take a leave of absence from school when they are freshmen or sophomores to complete their compulsory military service and resume their study afterwards. Many argue that unimaginative, repeated routines and brainwashing regularly reinforced through disciplinary actions dull their intellect while they serve in the military. Consequently, they find it challenging to do well when they go back to school.

## 4.7 Badass: pirates and dictators

Uncompromising viewpoints about their artistic pursuit are also discursively constructed as essential to the ideology of keepin' it real in the data. When it comes to improving the quality of music and gaining influence in the hip-hop world, 'badass' attitudes are considered desirable qualities by these playas. Unattractive titles such as 'pirate' and 'dictator' become attractive when they are used by South Korean hip hoppers for self-referencing, where obduracy and inflexibility are greatly appreciated.

Building upon the notion that pirates are associated with adventures, exploring new territories and accumulating possessions on their journey, the group Dynamic Duo voice an urgent need to transform current Korean hip hop into mould-breaking new hip hop in the song 'Haycek' ('Pirates'). These artists attach the pioneer spirit to pirates and stress the importance of breaking fresh ground in the K-hip-hop scene. Also, it is significant that the word 'hatchery' is used to refer to a relatively young history of South Korean hip hop and its underdeveloped status. Similar to the disrespect affiliated with young hip hoppers discussed earlier in the chapter, in excerpt (10) the current K-hip-hop scene is equated with a 'hatchery' which serves merely as a commercial site where young hip hoppers are concocted and incubated.

(10) . . . hatchery 파헤쳐           '. . . Tear up the **hatchery**
    take off the barrack k-hip hop  Take off the barrack k-hip hop
    신대륙개척               Open up a new continent'

Dynamic Duo, 'Haycek'

In the same song, Dynamic Duo's global ambition is expressed in the phrase 'travelling all over the world', which echoes the *Segyehwa* spirit – the drive for globalization – discussed earlier in this chapter.

**154**

(11) 우리는노래하는해적     'We are singing pirates travelling all over the world

세상구석구석다니며원하는건다뺏어     We plunder whatever we want

건들면 다돼져     If you touch us, you will get killed

넌나와대적할수 없어     You can't fight me'

Dynamic Duo, 'Haycek'

Pirates' feared and formidable presence is reimagined as a sign of success and reputation beyond comparison in the realm of hip hop. Also, the artists appear to be fully aware of market ideology in the music industry as the idea of possession is incorporated into their lyrics. What is implied is that someone else's proud possession can easily be theirs as they aspire to be globally successful. Later in the song, they list the things they want to steal: fame and fortune. Several references in the song are about American celebrities and their famous possessions. South Korean hip-hop playas' remarks on American pop culture, either celebrities or Hollywood movies, indicate that American cultural influence is quite powerful in Korea. For example, Hugh Hefner's Playboy mansion, Steve Jobs's Apple, and Paris Hilton's engagement ring are mentioned. Their wish list, however, is not composed only of superficial materialistic possessions. They hope to seize North Korean leader Kim Jong Il's personal chef to feed the hungry crew on the ship, criticizing Kim Jong Il's lack of effort to alleviate North Korea's infamous food shortage and his own alleged decadent lifestyle. Thus, in addition to their awareness of global cultural icons, South Korean playas utilize their knowledge of local politics in the lyrics, in this case, North Korean issues. By articulating their desire to punish the 'Dear Leader', they express their brotherly sympathy towards North Korean citizens. Pirates in this song are not portrayed as heartless thieves; rather, they are presented as modern-day socially and politically conscious Robin Hoods, robbing the rich and famous in order to help the poor, fighting against tyranny and injustice.

In addition, these playas claim to be uninterested in pleasing people. In their song 'Tongcen hanniph' ('A penny'), Dynamic Duo tell audiences to listen to their music if they like and turn it off if they don't like it, indicating that they are not going to change their music for the people. They proudly announce that their passion is a fire bottle (gasoline bomb), a major weapon in radical student demonstrations against the dictatorial government of the 1980s in South Korea. These hip-hop playas view themselves as dissidents and depict their music as a weapon to fight the establishment.

**155**

| (12) | 니가 좋으면 들어 그리고 싫으면 꺼 | 'If you like it, you listen. If you hate it, turn it off. |
|---|---|---|
| | 계속 음악을 할 테니깐 | I will continue my music. |
| | 내게 타협은 절대 no 열정은 내 화염병 | Never will I compromise. **No**. My passion is a fire bottle' |

Dynamic Duo, 'Tongcen hanniph'

The theme of 'no compromise' in their music is also often equated with anti-commercialism, yet ironically they want fame and fortune. In the same song, Dynamic Duo say that they are not businessmen, hustlers, or crooks who cheat, lie and act cowardly and compromise just to sell albums. In another song, 'Dictator', the same band take pride in their *ttongpayccang* ('foolhardiness'/'daredevilry'), doing their music as they please. The idea of keepin' it real is closely tied to maintaining artistic integrity and not succumbing to commercialism or pressure from competitors and fans, as illustrated in excerpt (13) below.

| (13) | 나는 내 뜻대로 우겨대는 똥 배짱 | 'I'm a stubborn hardass. I do as I please' |
|---|---|---|
| | 거침없이 노래를 불러온 지 오래다 | 'I've been singing my song without any constraints for a long time' |
| | 나는 두려움 따윈 삼켜버린 고래다 | 'I am a whale who swallowed fear' |
| | 나는 내 일을 지배하는 독재자 | 'I am a dictator who is in charge of my own business' |

Dynamic Duo, 'Tongcen hanniph'

The same artists appear to present seemingly conflicting views on dictatorship. They position themselves as protesters fighting against dictators with 'a fire bottle' of hip hop in excerpt (12), whereas excerpt (13) portrays them as dictators who reign over the hip-hop world and dominate all the others in the same industry. In other words, political dictatorship is criticized but artistic dictatorship is praised.

## 5 Conclusion

The four South Korean hip-hop groups featured in this study demonstrate that they subscribe to the hip-hop ideology of keepin' it real, which indicates that they are part of the global ideology of authenticity in hip hop. However, specific ways in which they *practise* this ideology are localized. Behaving just like American gangsta hip hoppers is not real, but not incorporating some features from the global hip-hop scene is likewise not real. Thus, hip-hop playas who are not in the so-called centre of globalization feel the need to strike a balance between the global and the local more than those in the centre. I would argue that hip-hop playas in the centre of globalization, like those in the US, are not pressured to incorporate the global, because the local for them can be accepted and identified as the global when their music goes to the peripheries or in-betweens of globalization.

Common themes emerging from the lyrics in the study suggest that South Korean hip-hop playas' practice of keepin' it real demonstrates global-local syncretism. Like most hip-hop artists, they serve as critical social commentators and incorporate global components, for example, English and hip-hop style outfits and accessories in their performance. At the same time, they stay true to who they are – South Korean artists, not American artists – by problematizing 'Korean' issues. Their glocalization of the hip-hop ideology of authenticity is in operation with respect to several social aspects of South Korea including ageism, career, family, education and military service. Although these themes deal with separate issues, they all provide helpful clues as to what it is like to live a life as a young male in South Korea, which happens to be a very hierarchically oriented society where age, family background, academic sectarianism and occupation define who you are and dictate enduring patterns of social behaviour and relations. The South Korean hip-hop playas in the study individually construct and present their own versions of reality, yet they all collectively participate in stereotypically characterizing Korean men's common experience.

The South Korean hip hoppers in the study reject *kacca* ('fake') hip hop which is claimed to be performed by inexperienced, superficial, 'young' rappers who lack passion and work ethics. In contrast, *cincca hyengtul* ('true older brothers') are respected as real artists. This is a prime example of the types of Confucianism-based, age-sensitive hierarchical relationships routinely implemented in South Korea. The influence of Confucianism goes beyond their relationships with fellow hip hoppers. Some of the lyrics make specific reference to Confucianism-inspired obligations to family. Furthermore, widely identified 'Korean' social issues such as the notoriously dreadful college entrance exam prep dubbed *ipsiciok* ('exam hell'), compulsory military service and overwork are articulated with great concern in the data.

The hip-hop lyrics featured in this study are often quite meta-hip hop, i.e., hip hop about hip hop. South Korean hip hoppers rap about hip hop or other topics pertinent to the genre including their music careers: ups and downs, artistic integrity and passion, skills and work ethic. While these themes may not be truly unique to the South Korean

**157**

hip-hop scene, the ways in which they self-praise their music are rather localized. For instance, 'practising' and working hard on crafting skills are more valued than natural god-given talents. This is quite a departure from the more improvisation-oriented, freestyle hip hop in the US, where rehearsed prefabrication is significantly devalued. With respect to their careers, South Korean hip-hop playas reveal global consciousness in their lyrics. This is evident in their desire to be successful beyond local contexts as well as through their belief that music is a universal language which allows them to freely cross cultural and national boundaries and provides a platform for an equal footing for any playa who shares love and passion for it. Their dream of global expansion is in line with the South Korean government's drive for globalization, *Segyehwa*, and is indicative of their desire to be part of *Hanlyu*, the Korean Wave, which refers to the recent surge in popularity of Korean entertainment products in Asia and beyond.

These playas' global aspirations are sometimes depicted rather aggressively, for example, as being on a pirate ship, plundering whatever they can get their hands on, feared by their enemies. Similar to American hip hop, being an outlaw or acting tough is portrayed as 'a cool thing' in South Korean hip hop. Another negative term that is used positively in the data in relation to their career ambition is 'dictator'. For a country such as South Korea that was governed under dictatorship until the 1980s, it is surprising to see the term 'dictator' have any redeeming qualities. What is interesting, however, is the fact that the playas in this study frame that term in two opposing senses. When it comes to their own monopoly of artistic success, being a dictator is viewed positively. On the other hand, dictatorship in a political sense is utilized negatively. Arguably, the dual use of the term itself is an example of localization of keepin' it real. As citizens of a former dictatorship, these South Korean hip-hop playas are aware of the negative consequences of this type of rule, but at the same time they have experienced firsthand the incontestable authoritative power of dictators, a coveted quality in dominating the hip-hop world.

The findings of the study suggest that the hip-hop ideology of authenticity – keepin' it real – is articulated in South Korean hip hop, but what it means to South Korean hip hoppers diverges from how hip hoppers from other cultures understand and practise it. Hip hop is all about lived experience. Local concerns and issues occupy local hip hoppers' minds and are expressed through their creative musical outlet. At the same time, hip hoppers in the peripheries and in-betweens of globalization inevitably incorporate global elements into their artistic creation.

**158**

## Notes

1. According to Wikipedia, 'Bling-bling (or simply bling) is a slang term popularized in hip-hop culture, referring to flashy or elaborate jewelry and ornamented accessories that are carried, worn, or installed, such as cell phones or tooth caps. The concept is often associated with either the working and lower middle classes or the newly wealthy, implying that the concept of riches and shiny items is something new to them. Used in this sense, it can be derogatory, suggesting lack of good taste.' <http://en.wikipedia.org/wiki/Bling-bling>, accessed 29 September 2009.
2. The term 'hip-hop playas' in this chapter refers to those actively participating in hip-hop music production and performance.
3. See, for instance, Farrow (2004).
4. He was born in Korea but lived in Indonesia, Switzerland, Canada and the United States of America.
5. Drunken Tiger originally consisted of DJ Shine ,Tiger JK, DJ Jhig, Micki Eyes (Half Korean half Italian) and Roscoe Umali (Filipino). When their sixth album was released in 2005, DJ Shine left the group, leaving JK as the main front man of the group.
6. He was born in Korea but raised in Los Angeles.
7. <http://www.drunkencamp.com>, accessed 21 September 2009.
8. For an excellent recent study of such stereotypes, see Reyes and Lo, 2009.
9. Switches into English are indicated in bold in the English translation.
10. Anime is animation that originated in Japan around 1917. Both hand-drawn and computer-animated anime exist. It is used in television series, films, video, video games, commercials and internet-based releases, and represents most, if not all, genres of fiction. Anime has a large audience in Japan and high recognition throughout the world.

## Discography

Drunken Tiger (September 5, 2007), *Sky is the Limit.* 정글('Jungle') Entertainment (20 tracks).
Dynamic Duo (May 20, 2007), *Enlightened.* Amoeba Culture (15 tracks).
Epik High (January 23, 2007), *Remapping the Human Soul.* 울림('Wulim') Entertainment (14 tracks).
Soul Company (February 20, 2007), *Official Bootleg Vol. 2.* Soul Company (19 tracks).

## References

Adelt, U. (2005), '*Ich bin der rock'n'roll-übermensch*: globalization and localization in German music television'. *Popular Music and Society*, 28, 3, 279–295.

Alim, H. S. (2004), *You Know My Steez: An Ethnographic and Sociolinguistic Study of Styleshifting in a Black American Speech Community.* Durham: Duke University Press.

—(2007), 'Critical hip hop language pedagogies: combat, consciousness, and the cultural politics of communication'. *Journal of Language, Identity, and Education*, 6, 2, 161–176.

Chan, B. and Hok-Shing (2009), 'English in Hong Kong Cantopop: language choice, code-switching and genre'. *World Englishes*, 28, 1, 107–129.

Chang, J. (2007), 'It's a hip hop world'. *Foreign Policy*, Nov/Dec, 58–63.

Condry, I. (2006), *Hip Hop in Japan: Rap and the Paths of Cultural Globalization.* Durham: Duke University Press.

Cullity, J. (2002), 'The global *desi*: cultural nationalism on MTV India'. *Journal of Communication Inquiry*, 26, 408–425.

Cutler, C. (2009), 'Yorkville crossing: white teens, hip hop, and African American English', in N. Coupland and A. Jaworski (eds), *The New Sociolinguistics Reader.* New York: Palgrave Macmillan, pp. 299–310.

Farrow, K. (2004), 'We real cool? On hip-hop, Asian-Americans, Black folks, and appropriation'. <http://www.nathanielturner.com/werealcoolkenyon.htm>, accessed 29 September 2009.

Forrest, B. (2000), 'Silence makes the beat grow stronger'. *SPIN*, 154–160.

Kim, S. S. (2000), 'Korea and globalization (Segyehwa): a framework for analysis', in S. S. Kim (ed.), *Korea's Globalization.* Cambridge: Cambridge University Press, pp. 1–28.

Kjeldgaard, D. and Askegaard, S. (2006), 'The glocalization of youth culture: the global youth segment as structures of common difference'. *Journal of Consumer Research*, 33, 231–247.

Lee, J. S. (2004), 'Linguistic hybridization in K-Pop: self-assertion and resistance'. *World Englishes*, 23, 3, 429–450.

—(2006), '*Crossing* and *crossers* in East Asian pop music: Korea and Japan'. *World Englishes*, 25, 2, 235–250.

—(2007), '*I'm the illest fucka*: an analysis of African American English in South Korean hip hop'. *English Today*, 23, 2, 54–60.

Mitchell, T. (1998), 'Australian hip hop as a "glocal" subculture'. Paper presented at the Ultimo Series Seminar, University of Technology, Sydney, 18 March.

—(2001), 'Dick Lee's transit lounge: Orientalism and Pan-Asian pop'. *Perfect Beat*, 5, 3, 18–45.

Moody, A. J. (2000), 'Beyond "shooby-dooby-doo-wah": an examination of English lyrics in Japanese pop music'. *Gengo Bunka* [Language and Culture], 8, 1–8.

—(2001), 'J-Pop English: or, how to write a Japanese pop song'. *Gengo Komyunikeeshon Kenkyuu* [Language Communication Studies], 1, 96–107.

—(2006), 'English in Japanese popular culture and J-Pop music'. *World Englishes*, 25, 2, 209–22.

Morgan, M. (2005), 'After . . . word! The philosophy of the hip hop battle', in D. Darby and T. Shelby (eds), *Hip Hop and Philosophy: Rhyme 2 Reason.* Chicago: Open Court, pp. 205–211.

Omoniyi, T. (2006), 'Hip hop through the world Englishes lens'. *World Englishes*, 25, 2, 195–208.

Pardue, D. (2007), 'Hip hop as pedagogy: a look into "heaven" and "soul" in São Paulo, Brazil'. *Anthropological Quarterly*, 80, 3, 673–709.

Pennycook, A. (2007), 'Language, localization, the real: hip-hop and the global spread of authenticity'. *Journal of Language, Identity, and Education*, 6, 2, 101–115.

—(2009), 'Refashioning and performing identities in global hip hop', in N. Coupland and A. Jaworski (eds), *The New Sociolinguistics Reader*. New York: Palgrave Macmillan, pp. 326–347.

Reyes, A. and Lo, A. (eds) (2009), *Beyond Yellow English: Toward a Linguistic Anthropology of Asian Pacific America*. New York: Oxford University Press.

Ritzer, G. (2004), *The Globalization of Nothing*. Thousand Oaks, CA: Pine Forge Press.

Robertson, R. (1995), 'Glocalization: time-space and homogeneity-heterogeneity', in M. Featherstone, S. Lash and R. Robertson (eds), *Global Modernities*. London: Sage, pp. 25–44.

Roudometof, Victor (2005), 'Transnationalism, cosmopolitanism and glocalization'. *Current Sociology*, 53, 1, 113–135.

Seth, M. J. (2002), *Education Fever: Society, Politics, and the Pursuit of Schooling in South Korea*. Honolulu, Hawaii: University of Hawaii Press.

Shim, D. (2006), 'Hybridity and the rise of Korean popular culture in Asia'. *Media, Culture & Society*, 28, 1, 25–44.

Smith, D. C. (2008), 'Language in hip hop', in D. Smith, *The Words Unspoken*. Durham, NC: Carolina Academic Press, pp. 75–94.

Smitherman, G. (1997), 'The chain remains the same: communicative practices in the Hip Hop Nation'. *Journal of Black Studies*, 28, 1, 3–25.

Söderman, J. and Folkestad, G. (2004), 'How hip hop musicians learn: strategies in informal creative music making'. *Music Education Research*, 6, 3, 313–326.

Stanlaw, J. (2000), 'Open your file, open your mind: women, English, and changing roles and voices in Japanese pop music', in T. J. Craig (ed.), *Japan Pop!: Inside the World of Japanese Popular Culture*. Armonk, NY: M. E. Sharpe, pp. 75–100.

—(2004), *Japanese English: Language and Culture Contact*. Hong Kong: Hong Kong University Press.

Taylor, C. and Taylor, V. (2007), 'Hip hop is now: an evolving youth culture'. *Reclaiming Children and Youth*, 15, 4, 210–213.

Thompson, C. J. and Arsel, Z. (2004), 'The Starbucks brandscape and consumers' (anticorporate) experiences of glocalization'. *Journal of Consumer Research*, 31, 631–42.

Watkins, S. C. (2007), 'Why hip-hop is like no other'. *Foreign Policy*, Nov/Dec, 63.

White, R. (2004), 'Sign of a black planet: hip hop and globalisation', in N. Campbell, J. Davies and G. McKay (eds), *Issues in Americanisation and Culture*. Edinburgh: Edinburgh University Press, pp. 163–177.

# 7 From American Form to Greek Performance: The Global Hip-Hop Poetics and Politics of the *Imiskoumbria*

Franklin L. Hess

## 1 Introduction

In November 1987, the rap group Public Enemy embarked on its first European tour with L. L. Cool J., Eric B. and Rakim. Although small in scope, covering only London, Amsterdam, Norway, Sweden, Denmark and Germany, the tour had a major impact on rap music as an art form by transforming the way Public Enemy conceived its message and audience. As lead rapper Chuck D. explains, the group realized that even if they 'never dominated the U.S. market', they could still 'take the markets that nobody else wanted – the rest of the world' (Chuck D., 1997, p. 94). As a result, Public Enemy set about cultivating an international audience for its music. Extended international tours followed in 1992 and 1994 bringing live American rap music to southern Europe, Africa, Australia and Asia. Although in most places where they toured imported rap recordings had been available for some time and small communities of rap fans had emerged, Public Enemy's tours played a transforming role in the evolution of rap music as a global phenomenon by introducing large numbers of fans to rap music as live performance and demonstrating the power of rap music's international appeal to both American artists and aspiring artists working within other national contexts. They provided, in other words, the impetus for the development of outposts of hip-hop culture around the world.

Greece was one of the countries Public Enemy visited on their 1992 international tour. Although rap music had appeared on American Armed Forces radio in Greece and had begun to make its way into record stores around 1983, Greece's rap scene was still very limited: a few radio programs on low-wattage stations and a small, but dedicated core of fans who understood both the social context and historical development of the genre. A rap group, Fortified Concept, even formed

in 1986, but they had no recording contract and a limited public following. Public Enemy's 1992 Athens concert expanded rap music's fan
base in Greece to the point where it reached a critical mass.[1] Soon after
the concert, new Greek rap acts began to surface: Active Member,
Terror-X-Crew, Going Through, and the Imiskoumbria (*Ημισκούμπρια*,
'Semi-Mackerels'). Of these groups, the Imiskoumbria and Active
Member have been among the most commercially successful and enduring. They also represent two strikingly different approaches to the
musical genre.

Active Member – the brainchild of Mihalis Mitakidis, who performs
under the pseudonym B. D. Foxmoor along with fellow bandmates
Sadahzinia or Yiolanda Tsiambokalou and, until recently, X-Ray or
Nikitas Klint – have followed a bottom-up, locally grounded approach
to both the music business and the music itself. In the process, they
have cultivated an extremely dedicated fan base. The term 'low bap'
was coined by the group following its third album as a means of distinguishing Greek rap from its American counterpart and 'emphasizing
the immediate connection of the music to life' (Low Bap Foundation,
2008). Musically, low bap is characterized by a move away from sampled material towards instrumental accompaniment, an understated
vocal style, and a hard message. Lyrically, the songs tend to be political.
They are, in other words, 'protest-oriented' (Androutsopoulos and
Scholz, 2003, p. 465) and very much engaged with both national issues
as well as the local affairs of Perama, the working-class neighbourhood
where Active Member are based.

By way of contrast, the Imiskoumbria – composed of rappers Dimitris Mentzelos, Mithridatis and DJ Pritanis (the Dean) – have been less
neighbourhood-grounded, more commercially oriented, and less overtly
political. Since forming in 1994, the group have released seven albums
of original material and a greatest hits compilation. Their first two
records, the tongue-in-cheek *Thirty Years of Hits* (*Τριάντα χρόνια
επιτυχίες*, 1996) and *The Disk You Advertise* (*Ο δίσκος που διαφημίζετε*,
1997), both achieved gold record status. Singles such as 'The Bucolic'
('*Το βουκολικό*'), 'At the Discotheque' ('*Στη ντισκοτέκ*'), 'Public Sector
Forevah' ('*Δημόσιο* Forevah') and 'Early' ('*Νωρίς*') have cracked video
and radio playlists. As Kolovos (2000, p. 48) has noted, the Imiskoumbria's sales have substantially outstripped those of other rap artists. The
popular appeal of the group, whose humorous songs deal with the
ironies of contemporary Greek experience, has occasionally even transcended the barriers of age and tradition. Older Athenians are often
intimately familiar with the lyrical content of songs such as 'Public
Sector Forevah' and 'Early', which satirize Greece's public and private
sectors, and the group even played 15 sold-out dates in 1997 at

**163**

Thessaloniki's *Mylos*, a club that is normally a bastion of traditional Greek *laïkí* ('folk') music.[2] The Imiskoumbria have paid a price for their popularity. They were rejected by devotees of the low bap movement as well as hard-core rap fans, who opted, in the late 1990s and early 2000s, for the politically charged anger of Terror-X-Crew and, more recently, have turned their attention to the gangsta rap-based rage of the hard-core group, Zontaní Nekrí (*Ζωντανοί Νεκροί*, 'Living Dead').

Although both Active Member and the Imiskoumbria deserve scholarly attention, I will focus in this essay on the Imiskoumbria, who, in my opinion, constitute a particularly rich linguistic and critical phenomenon. The Imiskoumbria represent a distinctly Greek version of hip-hop consciousness. By employing mimicry (cf. Bhabha, 1994) to challenge the attempts of political and economic powers, both internal and external to Greece, to regulate the behaviour of local populations, and by manipulating the formal conventions of American rap music and reformulating its linguistic and political content, they produce a hybrid, poetic reconfiguration of Greek identity and a transnational critique that addresses contemporary Greek society and its relationship to both the United States and Europe.

## 2 The politics of rap and rap criticism in an era of globalization

Rap music and hip-hop culture pose acute critical challenges due to the multiple spatial frames of reference – local, national and transnational/ global – in which they operate culturally and politically. This polyvalent spatiality, in turn, has contributed to a somewhat fractured critical discourse. Virtually all critics agree that hip-hop culture and rap music are, at heart, local phenomena. There has been less agreement, however, whether the broader political significance of the discourses that they generate should be interpreted within a narrowly national (i.e., African American), a limited transnational (i.e., African diaspora), or a fully transnational framework that is not limited by racial identity.

Initially, there was significant support for a limited transnational framework. Early commentators (e.g., Toop, 1984; Fernando, 1994; Brennan, 1994) emphasized the global origins of rap music, tracing its roots to the confluence of Jamaican DJing conventions and local music content that occurred in New York City's African-Caribbean immigrant neighbourhoods in the mid- to late-1970s. Additionally, other scholars argued for a diasporic understanding of rap music and hip-hop culture. For instance, Gilroy (1993, pp. 33–34) suggested that hip hop should be understood as a hybrid form of cultural expression that 'flaunts and

glories in its own malleability as well as its transnational character'
and, as such, resists appropriation as a narrow 'expression of some
African American essence'. Likewise, Lipsitz characterized hip hop as
a post-colonial art form and as part of 'an international dialogue built
on the imagination and ingenuity of slum dwellers from around the
globe' that constitutes a 'crucial force for opening up cultural, social,
and political space for struggles over identity, autonomy, and power'
(1994, p. 27).

This initial tendency towards a transnational framework, however,
gradually gave way in the mid-1990s to studies that constructed rap
music and hip-hop culture as specifically African American and framed
them as part of a national politico-cultural debate. In large measure,
this shift can be attributed to political exigency. The commercialization
of the genre led to increasing popularity with young white audiences in
the United States (Samuels, 2004). This increased popularity, combined
with the emergence of controversial genres such as dirty and gangsta
rap, in turn led to increased political oversight and culminated in public controversies over violence, indecency and misogyny in rap lyrics.
As a result, rap criticism was forced to turn inward and focus its
energies on defending the genre against domestic critics. Many of the
resulting studies were landmarks that succeeded by providing the
music with a much-needed political voice. For example, Rose's *Black
Noise*, in addition to providing much needed perspective on the genre's
tendency towards misogyny (1994, pp. 146–182), also made the broader
case that hip hop 'articulates the shifting terms of black marginality in
contemporary American culture' and that it 'replicates and reimagines
the experiences of urban life and symbolically appropriates urban space
through sampling, attitude, dance, style, and sound effects' (1994, p. 3).
Similarly, Kelley argued that gangsta rap should be seen as a form of
'social realism' and 'street ethnography' and explored how it constitutes a 'window into, and critique of, the criminalization of black youth'
in the United States (1996, p. 121). Baker (1993) and Dyson (1997) also
made important contributions to this wave of scholarship, focusing on
the ethical and political controversies surrounding the much publi-
cized attempts of figures like Tipper Gore and Bob Dole to censor the
content of rap records. These scholars and others, in the words of Krims,
sought to validate 'rap music against the cultural biases which inform
against it' (2000, p. 13). By cultivating a historical sensibility about rap
music, they have made it much more difficult for public figures – Gore,
Dole, Susan Baker, Charlton Heston and Bill Cosby, among others – to
dismiss rap music's social vision or political impetus based on impres-
sionistic understandings constructed from the commercial and stylistic
extremes of the genre.

**165**

As the political controversies of the 1990s subsided and rap music established a tentative truce with mainstream culture in the United States, rap scholarship turned outward again. The past decade has witnessed a flourishing of English-language scholarship – by musicologists, cultural anthropologists and sociolinguists, among others – that focuses on rap music and hip-hop culture as fully transnational, global phenomena, unified in their emphasis on reclaiming and reimagining the local. Included in this body of work are studies of rap in the Netherlands and on Canada's Indian reservations (Krims, 2000), in France (Prévos, 1996, 1998, 2001, 2003; Helenon, 2006) and the Francophone world (Durand, 2003), in Britain (Hesmondhalgh and Melville, 2001), in Japan (Condry, 2001, 2006; Fink, 2006), in Australia and New Zealand (Mitchell, 2001b, 2003, 2006; Maxwell, 2001), in Italy (Androutsopoulos and Scholz, 2003; Mitchell, 2001a, 2003) and in Germany (Brown, 2006; Kaya, 2001; Pennay, 2001; Androutsopoulos and Scholz, 2003; Androutsopoulos, 2007), among others. As Alim points out, this wave of scholarship represents an innovative and important move away from a 'monolithic' notion of 'Hip-Hop culture' towards a fuller appreciation of the diversity of 'Hip-Hop cultures' (2009, p. 3). Building on the work of Spady et al. (2006), he envisions the plurality of hip-hop cultures worldwide as a global 'cipha' – rap's circular exchange of ideas and perspectives through verse – where 'language, ideologies, and identities are shaped, fashioned, and vigorously contested, and where languages themselves are flexed, created and sometimes (often intentionally) bent up beyond all recognition' (2009, p. 2). Along similar lines, Pennycook and Mitchell, borrowing from an album title by Canadian/Somalian rapper K'naan, argue that hip hop constitutes a global community of 'dusty foot philosophers' who are 'both grounded in the local and the real, and capable of articulating a broader sense of what life is about' (2009, p. 25). These dusty foot philosophers, they continue, 'benefit from and participate in the rapid flows of music and ideas made possible in the digital age, and yet they remain highly critical of Western ways of viewing the world, and of the bias in particular forms of historical reasoning' (2009, p. 26).

Perhaps the most thorough articulation of this new, fully transnational approach to hip hop can be found in Pennycook's *Global Englishes and Transcultural Flows* (2007). Pennycook rejects the traditional binaries that have animated discussions of globalization in both sociolinguistics and cultural studies, arguing that we need to transcend arguments about homogeneity or heterogeneity (2007, p. 5), imperialism and nation states (2007, p. 5), modernity and postmodernity (2007, p. 43), and the centre and the periphery (2007, p. 46). Instead, he proposes a transgressive approach (2007, pp. 36–57) to both global Englishes

**166**

and the cultures of global hip hop that, building on Appadurai (1996), focuses on 'translocal and transcultural flows' (2007, p. 6). From this perspective, neither language nor culture is viewed as indelibly linked to place or permanence. Instead, they are seen as fluid locations for negotiating identity and articulating critiques of both conceptions of the real – i.e., 'taken-for-granted categories such as man, woman, class, race, ethnicity, nation, identity, awareness, emancipation, language, [and] power' (Pennycook, 2007, p. 39) – and the ontologies that support them. This 'critical philosophy of transgression', argues Pennycook, 'is not a set of anarchist incursions, tokenistic border-crossings or haphazard critiques of what is deemed to be wrong with the modern world, but rather a continuous questioning of how we come to be as we are, how our ways of understanding have been set, and how this could look differently if we started to think otherwise' (2007, p. 56).

The possibilities of Pennycook's critical philosophy of transgression are tantalizing. At a certain level, though, they remain largely unrealized, chiefly because the privileging of the local and singularity within this analytical schema curtails the possibilities of political discourse. Power in the contemporary world may, indeed, be multidimensional and diffuse, and it certainly is experienced in very different ways by different groups of people. At the same time, political discourse is empty if it does not share a common target or targets. Political discourse, in other words, exists in the moment and, as such, must concretize the entities that it seeks to change. This is not to say that the targets of political discourse should be viewed as permanent and unchanging. Quite the opposite, they are transient due to the plasticity of power, which is always expanding, contracting and morphing. Rather, it is an acknowledgment that the complex and multiple realities that shape our experiences need to be made concrete in order for shared understanding and political action to emerge. What I am proposing, then, is a strategy that is capable of bringing a transgressive approach to scholarship more into line with the principles of bottom-up knowledge that undergird both the global 'cipha' and the legion of dusty foot philosophers. I believe that a close examination of the content of rap music and hip-hop culture reveals that concretized understandings of the world are already circulating within global hip hop. The job of the scholar, then, is to identify these concretized understandings, elucidate them, and, when the barriers of language impede communication, facilitate their transmission.

A detailed analysis of the music and lyrics of the Imiskoumbria reveals the utility of a concept of US imperialism as a potential vehicle for linking both hip-hop cultures worldwide and scholarship of these cultures in a common discourse about the politics of locality in an era

**167**

of rapid globalization. This is not to say that US imperialism is the only concept capable of facilitating a meaningful exchange of ideas between hip-hop communities and scholars of hip-hop culture. Nor is it a claim for the permanent centrality of this object of analysis. Rather it is a pragmatic move designed to facilitate conversations that, in the future, may evolve into a very different sort of discourse. It is also an acknowledgement that understanding the centrality of the United States and US-based neo-liberalism in the economic, political and social transformations that local cultures around the world are experiencing remains one of the key political challenges of the present era. In concert, I will also be arguing for the utility of Bhabha's (1994) notion of 'mimicry' as a tool for unlocking the political dimensions of the language and performance styles of many rap artists. In contrast to its attendant term 'hybridity' (Bhabha, 1994), which represents more of a state of being, mimicry is a dynamic strategy for performing and, by extension, politicizing identity.

## 3 From the poetics of hybridity to the politics of mimicry: the Greek variant

As one of the first studies to examine rap music as a form that 'has been globalized well beyond African communities and . . . passed into a number of both commercialized and hybrid social contexts' (Krims, 2000, p. 9), *Rap Music and the Poetics of Identity* represents a milepost for rap scholarship that pushed beyond both the narrowly national and the limited transnational, African-diasporic frameworks. Eschewing traditional approaches to academic music criticism that isolate musical form from social and cultural theory, Krims attempts to 'outline the poetics of [rap music] functioning in the formation of ethnic and geographic identities' (2000, p. 1), bringing various regional rapping styles in the US into a dialogue with rap music in the Netherlands and within Cree populations in Canada.

Krims provides valuable insight into the social dynamics of rap consumption abroad. The weakness of his study, to the extent that there is one, is found in the rather static conception of politics that he employs. Dutch and Cree rap music, in his narrative, respond passively to political issues – racism, economic underdevelopment, the cultural primacy of the United States – but they have little to offer in terms of an active, transformative political vision that is capable of changing mindsets and contributing to the creation of movements. If, as he argues, international variants of 'rap music and hip-hop culture owe much of their character to complex determinations of local and global forces'

(2000, p. 177), then it should follow that international variants of rap music attempt to address and transform both local and global political discourses.

Krims's struggle to identify an active politics of identity is reflected in a theoretical problem in his argument. He explores rap music poetics as a mode of being in the world and not as a strategy for transforming the world. His emphasis on *being* as opposed to *becoming* may be traced to the use of Bhabha's notion of 'hybridity', defined as a liminal form of identity that 'may . . . lead to new possibilities for political action' (Krims, 2000, p. 156). The problem is not Krims's use of the term per se, but the fact that he isolates hybridity from an attendant term, 'mimicry', that translates identity into political action. In *The Location of Culture*, Bhabha describes mimicry as a bi-directional discourse between the colonizer and colonized that plays on 'the desire for a reformed, recognizable Other, as *a subject of difference that is almost the same, but not quite*' (1994, p. 86, original emphasis). Arguing that 'the discourse of mimicry is constructed around an *ambivalence*' (ibid.) and that, in order to be effective, it 'must continually produce its slippage, its excess, its difference' (ibid.), he suggests that mimicry takes part in 'a discursive process by which the excess or slippage produced by the *ambivalence* of mimicry . . . does not merely "rupture" the discourse, but becomes transformed into an uncertainty which fixes the colonial subject as a "partial" presence' (ibid., original emphasis). Bhabha's notion of mimicry, then, is a double-edged sword that cuts both the colonized and the colonizer. 'The *menace* of mimicry', he thus concludes, 'is its *double* vision which in disclosing the ambivalence of colonial discourse also disrupts its authority' (1994, p. 88, original emphasis), thus suggesting that 'fetishized colonial culture is potentially and strategically an insurgent counter-appeal' (1994, p. 91).

Bhabha's (1994) notion of mimicry puts political teeth on the analytical framework that Krims developed for explicating international variants of rap music and hip-hop culture. Its application, however, to the Greek context – and specifically to the music of the Imiskoumbria – raises a methodological issue that must be answered before the analysis proceeds. Bhabha (1994) uses the term to describe relations between the self and other in colonial and postcolonial societies. It might thus be judged to have value for a place such as the Netherlands that, although economically affluent and – traditionally at least – relatively tolerant socially, is actively grappling with the demographic repercussions of its colonial past, as citizens of its former territories have opted to immigrate to the land of their former colonizer. Its value, however, for a country such as Greece is less readily apparent. Though Greece, which acquired nation-state status in 1829, pursued irredentist policies for its first 100 years aimed at incorporating Greek populations in neighbouring territories, the country never collectively saw itself as a colonizer and only rarely attempted to exert administrative control over non-Greek populations external to its borders. Consequently, Greek society's relationship with its non-Greek immigrant populations, which started arriving in significant numbers only after the dissolution of the Eastern Bloc, has not been shaped by the same history of colonizer-colonized relationships that marks immigration to Great Britain, France and the Netherlands. As a result, the Greek rap scene has evolved along very different lines, and immigrant participation has been very limited.[3]

The absence of this type of history of colonizer-colonized relations, however, does not mean that Greek rap is entirely isolated from the cultural dynamics of colonialism. Quite the opposite, Greeks routinely identify with the experiences of the victims of Western European colonialism, viewing their past in terms of a long history of invasions and external political control that begins with Arab, Genoese and Venetian incursions during the Byzantine Empire, continues through four centuries of Ottoman dominance in the region, and, during the nation-state period, includes a series of foreign monarchs as well as periods of British and American tutelage. This perception is not inaccurate. Since its founding, Greece, like many nations, has rarely acted with complete independence, experiencing significant levels of external control over local political, economic and cultural life. Accordingly, mimicry has been an enduring strategy for displacing alterity and resisting this external control. For instance, beginning in the Ottoman Empire and continuing well into the national period, the *Karagkiózis* (Greek shadow theatre) satirized both Greco-Turkish and Greco-Western relations through characters such as Hatziavatis, a servile Greek who does the bidding of the Pasha, and Sir Dionysios, a Westernized Greek from the Ionian Islands. Similarly, the *epitheórisi* (Greek theatrical revue), which began in the late 1800s and continues through the present, frequently targeted relations between Westernized urban elites and more traditional cohorts of the population, seizing on events such as the controversy that erupted in the first decade of the twentieth century, when the ladies of Athenian society, fearing stray whiskers in their food, began to demand that their cooks shave their moustaches, in order to create a complex mimicry of Greek social relations (Hatzipantazis, 1977, p. 154, p. 167, pp. 207–208).

It is within this tradition of mimetic resistance to external authority that the poetics of Greek rap should be placed. The Imiskoumbria employ a medium non-indigenous to Greek culture – rap music – to both critique and celebrate the arbitrariness of contemporary Greek culture, articulating, in the process, a systemic critique of global power

**170**

relations as they manifest themselves at a local level. Mimicry within their music thus operates within both local and global registers, articulating a politics of identity that targets manifestations of the prevailing system of global power relations, a system that may be subsumed, following the lead of Kaplan (1993) and Pease (1993), under the rubric of United States imperialism.

# 4 The Imiskoumbria's polyvalent critique of United States imperialism

## 4.1 Tradition and modernity

My use of the term United States imperialism to describe the geopolitical context of the Imiskoumbria's music does not mean that the United States dominates Greek political, economic and cultural life to the exclusion of other geopolitical entities. The United States, to be sure, never directly dominated Greece. It has been forced to vie for influence with Britain, France, Germany, and most recently the European Union. Nevertheless, through its military presence in the region, and its insistence on a global neo-liberal economic system, the United States has played the leading role in shaping the parameters within which local sovereignty operates. In line with Kaplan (1993, p. 18), then, my use of the notion of United States imperialism reflects the determining role that the United States played in Greece during the second half of the twentieth century through instruments such as the Truman Doctrine, NATO, Hollywood film, television programs and American-style consumer culture.[4]

Building on the aforementioned tradition of resistance to external authority, the Imiskoumbria respond to a political context in which the role that the United States plays is determining, but not total. As a result, the mimetic counterdiscourse that the group deploys is polyvalent. It has multiple targets that build from a local to a global political critique. The political critique of the Imiskoumbria and of Greek rap in general is based on stylistic parallelism, an aesthetic mode and approach to mimicry that recognizes the inevitability of *being* modern and begins to explore the process of *becoming* modern, that is, of continually reinventing oneself and one's culture within the realm of the modern. Rather than accepting modernity as a homogeneous, amorphous totality dominated, in this instance, by standardized versions of English and standardized music, stylistic parallelism initiates the search for difference within the modern as voiced through hybrid linguistic and musical formations. Since its inception, Greek rap has been dominated by this aesthetic mode. Although a few of the early groups sang a song or two in English and many adopted English-language names, they quickly moved towards rapping in Greek and began to place a 'Greek' stamp on their content. The 'reterritorialization' (Androutsopoulos and Scholz, 2003, p. 463) of the form, in other words, was almost immediate.

The Imiskoumbria, as the first rap group to obtain commercial success, played a key role in defining this aesthetic of parallelism and establishing its political and linguistic content. The group signals its adherence to an aesthetic of parallelism by creating lyrical and sampling disjunctions within a musical foundation that otherwise largely conforms to the formal qualities and production values of American rap music. For example, the sonic content of the 1997 song 'The Cat on the Roof' ('Η γάτα της σκεπής') appears to conform to the Death Row Records gangsta-rap sound that was created by Dr. Dre and Snoop Dogg and reached its peak in popularity in the early to mid 1990s. The Death Row Records sound has three audio signatures: (1) a high-pitched synthesized melody, (2) a Bootsy Collins-derived loose, reverberating bass and (3) samples from George Clinton songs.[5] In 'The Cat on the Roof' the Imiskoumbria replicate this sound, minus the George Clinton samples. In so doing, they signal their cotemporaneity – that is, their technological standardization – with Dr. Dre and Snoop Dogg. Their lyrics, however, create a disjunction that signals their difference and, by extension, their parallel status.

(1) Είμαι ένας γάιδαρος που κουβαλάει βάρη | 'Me, I'm a donkey, heavy loads I carry,

Από την Χολαργάρα ίσαμε την Βάρη. | From Holarghara all the way to Vari.

Μουλάρι ο Μυθριδάτης μου κουβαλάει παρέα, | The mule Mithridatis brings me his fellows,

Και βόδι ο Πρύτανης που μουγκανάει γενναία. | And Pritanis, the ox, bravely bellows.'

The Imiskoumbria, 'The Cat on the Roof'

By parodying Snoop's self-referential 'dog' metaphor and defining themselves as a 'donkey', a 'mule' and an 'ox', the Imiskoumbria declare their distinctness, suggesting that the translation of American musical form into the Greek context can never be absolute. Additionally, the use of the augmentative suffix -αρα (-ara) to modify the name of the Athenian suburb from which Mentzelos hails, Χολαργός (Holargós), at

**172**

once serves the purposes of identification and place reference and also indicates an attachment to a different model of locality. It also ironizes the position from which he enunciates his message, since Holargós is an affluent and politically conservative suburb.

An even more radical revision of American form – and, by extension, declaration of parallel status – can be found in the song 'The Bucolic', from the album *Thirty Years of Hits*. 'The Bucolic' is preceded by an introductory segment, titled 'Klatz FM' ('Κλατζ FM'). In this segment, the group's lead rapper, Mentzelos plays the role of a radio DJ spinning *laïká* hits. Talking over a *kalamatianó* – a traditional folkdance rhythm from the south of Greece that features a rapid, lilting melody – he introduces 'The Bucolic' by saying,

(2)  ' *Όποιος δεν έχει ξυπνήσει*    'Whoever hasn't woken up yet,
     *ακόμα, ακούστε αυτό.*'         listen to this.'

                                    The Imiskoumbria, 'The Bucolic'

A sheep bell sounds, and a song follows that features a rap between Mentzelos and Mithridatis. In this case, the rhythmic backdrop for the rap creates the disjunction. By constructing the backdrop around a sample from a *tsámiko* – a folkdance rhythm from northern Greece that features a slow, plodding melody – the Imiskoumbria again highlight the difference between themselves and their American counterparts. At the same time, they introduce an element of self-parody by appealing to traditional stereotypes, operative both inside and outside of Greece, of rural Greek authenticity.

The music of the Imiskoumbria, however, is not merely about difference and identity. It mobilizes difference for specific political purposes. The group's parallel aesthetic status, in other words, also implies a parallel political message. In much the same way that rap music in the United States has mobilized a discourse about the 'authenticity' of Black urban experience to critique American society and raise political consciousness, the Imiskoumbria have created a political discourse about the relation between the 'authenticity' of urban experience in Greece and official versions of 'authentic' Greekness. The content of this discourse emerges most clearly again in 'The Bucolic'. By incorporating samples from folkdance melodies, the song appropriates Greece's musical past and deploys it to satirically highlight the disjunction between past and present musical styles and to critique the tendency to associate Greekness solely with the former.

The song's lyrics continue in this manner, criticizing the Greek nation's 'imagined community' (Anderson, 1983, pp. 6–7) and its culturally essentialist proposition that there is an immutable link between

**173**

Greek culture, the land and the sea. In so doing they call into question a whole range of antecedent cultural production. As Leontis (1995) has argued, the relationship between Greek culture and its *tópos* ('land' or 'landscape') has been at the core of Greek literary production. Additionally, the *tópos* has been integral to the development of the tourist's experience of Greece (Holst-Warhaft, 1997) and theatrical and film genres, namely the *dramatikó idíllio* ('dramatic idyll') and the *foustanéla* (a rural drama featuring shepherds that is named after the traditional white, pleated kilts that the male characters wear). Finally, the *tópos* has been a crucial element of Greek myths of national origin, which emphasize the humble and autochthonous origins of heroes of the 1821 revolution such as Theodoros Kolokotronis, a bandit warrior who acquired wealth by stealing sheep and, after acquiring British military know-how, became a preeminent military leader, and Admiral Konstantinos Kanaris, a navy commander renown for firebombing the Turkish fleet.

In 'The Bucolic', the group argues that if Greek culture were actually inseparable from the Greek *tópos*, modern urban life would smoothly coincide with the national imaginary. Instead, as the lyrics point out, the Greek national imaginary shares little with the cultural matrix in which Greeks live today. The song – which is performed with a simulated rural Greek accent, phonologically indexed by the backing of /o/ to /u/ (e.g., 'furo' (*φουρώ*) for Standard Modern Greek *foro* (*φορώ*) in example 3, and 'ehu' (*έχου*) for *eho* (*έχω*) in example 9), and by final syllable deletion (e.g., '*m*'' (*μ́*) for possessive pronoun *mu* (*μου*) in example 3) – imagines how modern urban Greeks would interpret the world around them if they actually accepted internally and externally generated stereotypes. They would be modern versions of 'Kolokotronis' (Mentzelos) and 'Kanaris' (Mithridatis) dressed in '*foustanélas*' and struggling against their Turkish oppressors.

(3) *Φουρώ τη φουστανέλα μ'*    'I wear my *foustanéla* with my
*τα τσαρούχια μ'τα δυό.*    clogs.'

(4) *Εγώ είμαι ο Γέροντας που*    'Me, I'm the Old Man, the Morean
*είναι του Μοριά,*    (Kolokotronis's nickname),

*Κι ελεύθερος θα είμαι,*    And I'll always be free. You'll
*ποτέ μου με λουριά.*    never rein me in.'

(5) *Εγώ είμαι ο Κανάρης,*    'Me, I'm Kanaris, the famous
*γνωστός πυρπολητής.*    fire-ship skipper.

**174**

| | |
|---|---|
| *Από μικρός το ήξερα πως* | I knew I'd be an arsonist, from |
| *θα'μαι κι εμπρηστής.* | when I was a nipper.' |

The Imiskoumbria, 'The Bucolic'

Their female companions would be named 'Astero' and 'Malamo', after characters from popular dramatic idylls and film *foustanélas*, or 'Bouboulina' after the revolutionary war heroine and archetypal mother of the Greek nation. Playing on a double-entendre – the words for 'kiss' (*φιλάω, filáo*) and 'guard' (*φυλάω, filáo*) in Greek are homophones – the song also highlights the disjunction between past and present attitudes towards women. If viewed through the lens of traditional Greek patriarchy, the vocalist would almost certainly be talking about 'guarding' the two women. Through the lens of contemporary patriarchy, however, he'd probably be talking about kissing them.

(6)  *Φιλάω/φυλάω την Αστέρω.*   'I kiss/guard Astero. I kiss/guard
     *Φιλάω/φυλάω τη Μαλάμω.*   Malamo.'

(7)  *Με την Μπουμπουλίνα*   'With Bouboulina I danced at the
     *χορεύαμε στην ντίσκο.*   disco.'

The Imiskoumbria, 'The Bucolic'

Moreover, their long 'frizzy' hair would serve as a simultaneous tribute to the long-haired fathers of the nation and popular musicians such as 'Kenny G' (example 8) – whose name, conjugated as an ancient third-declension masculine noun, draws an ironic parallel to the forefathers of the nation – as well as latter-day revolutionaries such as the Rastafarians (example 9). Finally, balancing 'a knife' in one hand with 'a cell phone' in the other (example 10), they would circulate around town on 'horses' with 'tax-free license plates' (example 11).[6]

(8)  *Σπαστό είναι το μαλλί μου*   'My hair's all wavy, just like
     *σαν του Kennyta του G.*   Kenny G's.'

(9)  *Έχου το μαλλί μου, την*   'I've got my hair done up in an
     *τρομερή τη Rasta.*   awe-inspiring Rasta.'

(10)  *Στο 'να χέρι το σπαθί, στο*   'In one hand a knife, in the other
     *άλλο το κινητό μου*   my cell phone'

(11) *Και καβαλάω τ'άλογό που*   'And I hop up on my horse,
     *είναι κ'ένα ΑΜΟ.*           which is even tax-free.'

The Imiskoumbria, 'The Bucolic'

Through this juxtaposition of the past and the present, 'The Bucolic' points out the fading relevance of myths of national generation, while, at the same time, exposing the Americanization and often tasteless consumerism of contemporary Greek life. The modern-day Kolokotronis, performed by Dimitris Mentzelos, listens to traditional music by folk music icon Domna Samiou on a 'walkman' (example 12), eats fast food 'hamburgers with . . . chili' (example 12), wears 'glasses' like U-2 singer 'Bono' (example 13), and claims he can draw a pistol faster than Hollywood Western villain 'Lee Van Cleef' (example 14), who became well-known in Greece as a spaghetti-Western stalwart.

(12) *Παίρνω και το γμόκμαν με*   'I take my Walkman playing
     *την Δόμνα τη Σαμιώ.*         Domna Samiou.

     *Τρώω κι ένα χάμπεργκερ*      I eat a hamburger with even
     *με περισσό το τσίλλι.*        more chili.'

(13) *Και θα'χω και γυαλί σα*      'And I'll be wearing glasses, just
     *τον μπέγκερεμπέκερε Bono.*   like Bono.'

(14) *Ρε, φάτε χώμα, ρε. Εγώ*      'Eat my dust, man, 'cause I'm the
     *είμαι ο Chief.*              Chief.

     *Τραβάω και πιο γρήγορα*      I'm quicker on the draw than
     *από τον Lee Van Cleef.*     even Lee Van Cleef.'

The Imiskoumbria, 'The Bucolic'

When he is not planning confrontations with the Ottoman fleet, Kanaris, performed by Mithridatis, 'dances in the disco with Bouboulina' (example 7), listens to Greek rock music, and brags about his sexual prowess (example 15).

(15) *Στις καρδιές των κοριτσιών*  'In the hearts of the girls, I'm the
     *εγώ, την πρώτη νιότη.*        favourite lad.

     *'Όλες περιμένανε ν'*          They all expected to fall in love
     *αγαπήσουνε νησιώτη.*          with the island man.

     . . .                         . . .

     *Ακούγαμε Φατμέ: 'Την*        We listened to "I Get Off on
     *βρίσκω με το ρίσκο,'*         Danger," the album by Fatme
                                   [Greek rock band]

**176**

| Και η Φατμέ, η τουρκάλα, | And Fatme, the Turkish girl, |
|---|---|
| με γούσταρε πολύ. | was really into me.' |

The Imiskoumbria, 'The Bucolic'

Through these juxtapositions of past and present, the song exposes how the power of the nation as an imagined community has been weakened by the expansion of supranational economic and cultural systems. The infirmity of the nation and the bankruptcy of its revolutionary ideology are perhaps most apparent in Kanaris's closing refrain, which plays on the similarities between the Greek words for dandruff, 'πιτυρίδα' (*pitiríδa*), and for gunpowder, 'πυρίτιδα' (*pirítiδa*):

(16)  Εμένα το μαλλί μου    'As for me, there's no dandruff in my
      δεν έχει πιτυρίδα.       mop.

      Με θέλουν αρχηγό ολοί   All the guys in the flagship want me
      στην ναυαρχίδα.         at the top.'

The Imiskoumbria, 'The Bucolic'

By invoking the language of dandruff commercials and advertising strategies – imported from the United States – that play on the fear of public embarrassment caused by bodily imperfections, the chorus points out how adherence to the dictates of American-style consumer culture has bankrupted the revolutionary power that the act of imagining the nation once contained. The new revolutionaries, the Imiskoumbria thus suggest, must be able to transcend the grammar of style that has been imposed from without. They must, in other words, adopt a hip-hop sense of culture, time and place, which, in keeping with Pennycook's critical philosophy of transgression, seeks to enact 'a continuous questioning of how we come to be as we are, how our ways of understanding have been set, and how this could look differently if we started to think otherwise' (2007, p. 56).

For the Imiskoumbria, then, rap music is ultimately a parallel political language, a language that, in spite of its ostensibly foreign origins, allows them to lay claim to their local cultural specificity and articulate a new, if incomplete and at times ambiguous, vision of Greekness. In spite of their emphasis on claiming a viable sense of Greekness, however, the Imiskoumbria refuse to view rap music as a vehicle for a strictly nationalist politics. They refuse to replace the older topographic imaginings of Greece that they satirize, which are rooted in Greek revolutionary nationalism, with a new Neo-Hellenic *tópos*. Instead, they imagine a new cosmopolitan political sensibility that seeks both to confront the broader geopolitical entities that constrain Greek identity

**177**

and to broaden the horizon of what it means to be Greek by doing away with entrenched biases and opening Greek culture up to the world.

## 4.2 Race and racism in Greek culture

The second of these goals, broadening the horizon of what it means to be Greek, means, among other things, rethinking the politics of race in Greece. Until quite recently, official Greek culture defined Greece as one of the most ethnically unified populations in the world. Although recent census data has acknowledged the presence of a million immigrants living in Greece, through the 1990s census data defined 98 per cent of the citizenry as ethnically Greek and Orthodox Christian (Clogg, 1992, p. 233). The assertion of ethnic and religious homogeneity, however, hides the diversity of contemporary Greece, which contains substantial Albanian, Philippine, Eastern and Western European, Pakistani, Afghani and African populations, as well as a variety of diasporic Greeks. Since the twentieth century, Greece has taken in diasporic populations from Asia Minor, Egypt, the Black Sea regions of Turkey and the Soviet Union, Romania, Yugoslavia, Bulgaria and Albania. Additionally, many emigrants to Germany, the United States and Australia, have opted to return.

The assertion of national homogeneity also ignores the extent to which representations of cultural diversity, through American and Western European mass media products and advertising campaigns have become part of the terrain of Greek popular culture.[7] The Imiskoumbria address this state of affairs, particularly the resistance of official culture to cultural pluralism, in the song 'Hip Hop Won't Stop', asserting that rap music is misunderstood because of entrenched biases:

(17) Και όλοι προτιμάνε τα    'And everyone prefers the
κουκούτσια απ' τα πεπόνια,    honeydew and its seed,

Αλλά κι απ' τα καρπούζια    Though they claim eating
πρόβλημα δεν έχουν.    watermelon's not an evil deed.

Απλά απ' την μαυρίλα    It's the blackness [of the
γουστάρουν να απέχουν.    pits] from which they would
    recede.'

The Imiskoumbria, 'Hip Hop
Won't Stop'

Using this elaborate metaphor, which plays on the difference in colour between honeydew and watermelon seeds and the comparative edibility of the former, the Imiskoumbria thus chide two groups: (1) those who claim not to be racist but nonetheless want to keep their distance

**178**

from people of colour and (2) those who are nostalgic for traditional rock and roll music, which is rooted in African-American musical traditions, but are unwilling to give hip hop a chance.

Their race politics, however, is not one of simple advocacy. In 'The Cat on the Roof', the group critique other Greek rap artists who imitate the conventions of American rap more closely and attempt to promote themselves as a purer, more politically astute form of hip hop. In the words of Mentzelos,

(18) *Κι έχεις την εντύπωση*   'And you've got the notion when
*μαύρα οτάν τα βάφεις,*   you paint things black,

*Ευθύς πως είσαι ποιητής,*  Straight away you're a poet like
*ο μέγιστος Καβάφης.*    the illustrious Cavafy.'

                    The Imiskoumbria, 'The Cat on the Roof'

The attitude towards difference that they thus promote champions (1) the ability to appreciate other cultures without patronizing them and (2) the ability to borrow from other cultures and traditions without abandoning all notions of a cultural core as they set about reimagining Greek identity.

## 4.3 Tourism, neoliberalism, and the European Union

Broadening the horizon of Greekness also means rejecting both externally generated stereotypes and internalized complicity with those stereotypes. The process of shedding stereotypes, however, is not simply a therapeutic expansion of the self for the Imiskoumbria. Instead, it is implicitly political. The Imiskoumbria attempt, in Bhabha's (1994) terms, to 'disrupt' the 'authority' of political and economic discourses about Greece by 'disclosing the ambivalence' of these discourses for Greece's citizenry and establishing the foundation for an 'insurgent counter-appeal'. Their mechanism for doing this is 'fetishism', a term which normally evokes connotations of magic objects and seemingly irrational devotion, but which, in this context, might be best understood as conscious strategy, a means of deploying the trope of metonymy to the point where it becomes preposterous and ruptures the discourse, thus revealing the need for an emergent counterdiscourse.[8] As will be shown, the Imiskoumbria deploy fetishism to rupture political and economic discourses that fix Greek subjects as (1) objects of the tourist gaze, (2) participants in the agricultural semi-periphery of the European Union and (3) passive consumers of American mass media products.

**179**

As Clogg has noted, 'rapidly rising standards of living in Western Europe, coupled with the development of mass air travel and much improved internal communications . . . led to tourism reaching a "take-off" stage by the late 1950s' (1992, p. 149). At a macroeconomic level, tourism has been a boon for Greece. It has provided a badly needed source of foreign currency reserves, helped stabilize the country's balance of payments, and contributed to integration within the European Union. Socially, culturally and psychologically, however, tourism has produced mixed results. It has helped undermine traditional institutions and notions of community and forced Greeks to encounter and even market stereotyped understandings of their culture (Tsartas, 1989). The development of the tourist economy, in other words, has reinforced images of Greece that are generated through the prism of the Other. The tourist's gaze has defined modern Greeks in terms of a conglomerate of putative traits including: their ancient inheritance, their sexual prowess, their mythical bond to the sea, their disorganization and chaos, their artistic temperament, and finally, their picturesque primitiveness. The last trait, picturesque primitiveness, is often characterized for tourists by the image of the small-scale farmer with a donkey, an image that has been used extensively to promote Greece's tourism industry and that still plays a role in contemporary tourism, where donkey rides are frequently offered as novelties and to help tourists ascend to archaeological sites.

In this context, the Imiskoumbria's decision to define themselves in 'The Cat on the Roof' as a 'donkey', a 'mule' and an 'ox' is a strategic one (example 1). The group not only uses mimicry, as was previously explained, to establish their parallelism with – and by extension their difference from – American gangsta rap. Operating through stylistic parallelism, they employ fetishism to point out the absurdity of the way the tourist economy has penetrated everyday Greek life and self-conception. By invoking a metonymic shift in which they become the animals with which the discourse of tourism associates Greek culture, the Imiskoumbria demonstrate the extent to which tourism impacts Greek self-conception by alienating the culture from the contemporary world in which it functions. At the same time, however, they also celebrate the resilience of Greek identity and suggest that adopting a hip-hop sense of culture, time and place can serve as an antidote to the psychological damage of the tourist economy. In the introductory track on *Thirty Years of Hits*, the self-titled 'Imiskoumbria', Mithridatis describes how his conversion to hip-hop consciousness saved him from the vapidity of a life that conforms to the norms of the tourist economy.

**180**

(19) *Ήμουνα και γω στη*        'I was living in Mykonos as a
     *Μύκονο ζωγράφος.*         painter.

     *Έκανα πορτραίτα σαν να*    I drew portraits, moving like a
     *ήμουν χορογράφος,*        dancer,

     *Και έφτιαχνα κολιέ με*     And I created necklaces, with
     *χάντρες μπιχλιμπίδια.*     beads and baubles.

     *Έγραφα ονόματα σε μύδια*   I wrote names, on oysters and on
     *και σε στρείδια.*         mussels.'

                            The Imiskoumbria, 'Imiskoumbria'

Before he 'took the microphone' and began to rap with Mentzelos, he existed in a touristic purgatory as an 'artist' in Mykonos, the most heavily travelled of the Greek islands, making trinkets for the tourist economy. As the song continues, rap proves to be a liberating act of self-creation:

(20) *Έπαιρνα το μικρόφωνο*     'I took the microphone and started
     *και έπαιζα κρυφτό.*       to play out of sight.

     *Και να ο Μεντζελάκι!*      And then came Mentzelaki! Then
     *Να ο Μεντζελάκι!*         came Mentzelaki!

     *Και μου είπε με φούρια,*   And he told me with haste, to play
     *να παίξουμε με φούρια,*    music with rapidity.

     *Να παίξουμε μαζί, και*     He said, 'Let's play together', and
     *να οι Ημισκούμπρια.*      thus The Imiskoumbria.'

                            The Imiskoumbria, 'Imiskoumbria'

Hip hop, in other words, liberates self-expression from the routinization and stereotypes of the tourist economy and thus reinvigorates the possibilities of group identity, as manifested by the birth of the Imiskoumbria.

In the remainder of this song, the group expand their critique of Greece's position within the European Union by examining the way Greece's local economy has been altered by membership in the European Union and the expansion of neo-liberal trade relations. Greek membership in the European Union – an entity that emerged out of the Anglo-American vision for the post-World War II organization of Europe – accelerated the development of the agricultural and the retail/service sectors of the economy. In so doing, it generated wealth, but also created tremendous turmoil. By easing restrictions on transnational capital flows and liberalizing trade, the European Union allowed American and European agribusiness and multinational corporations to make inroads in the Greek economy. The result has been the displacement of small-scale farmers and neighbourhood merchants. The former are being undermined by falling commodity prices and a system of nation-based production quotas, and the latter are being undersold and out-advertised by multinational retail chains.

The Imiskoumbria address the role of the European Union in the Greek economy, but not through the traditional political language of realism. Their songs, in fact, have little to say about the economic plight of the average person. Instead, they attempt to address the plight of the nation as a whole, which has been relegated, both in actuality and discursively, to the agricultural semi-periphery of the European Union. In 'Imiskoumbria', Mentzelos defines himself as a recovering agronomist, who is saved by rap music:

| | |
|---|---|
| (21) *Οταν αποφάσισα να πω το παραμύθι,* | 'The moment I decided to tell the fairy story, |
| *Κανείς δεν μου 'χε πει πως θα είμαι με τον Μίθι.* | No one told me that I'd be teamed with Mithridati. |
| *Και σπούδαζα αγρότης σε κάμπους και λιβάδεια.* | I was studying as a farmer in the field and in the pasture. |
| *Έπαιρνα τρακτέρ και έβγαινα τα βράδυα* | I went out at nights, riding on my tractor, |
| *Παρέα με τα μπρόκολα, ντομάτες, κολοκύθια,* | Hanging out with broccoli, zucchini, and tomatoes, |
| *Καρπούζια, και αχλάδια που έγιναν ρουβίθια.* | Watermelons and pears, which turned into garbanzos.' |
| | The Imiskoumbria, 'Imiskoumbria' |

Fetishization in this passage occurs at two junctures. The first is when Mentzelos, who elsewhere describes himself as an urban denizen of the middle-class Athens suburb of Holargos (example 1), adopts the persona of the farmer. By transcribing his real urban experiences (i.e., going out at night with his gang of friends) into a rural setting, the track's lyrics create a false metonymic relationship in which 'farmer' is substituted for the broader category of 'Greek citizen'. This first moment of fetishization is reinforced by a second, in which the farmer's companions are defined as different types of agricultural produce. By deploying fetishization in this manner, the Imiskoumbria undermine the stability of political and economic discourses – in which both European Union and Greek officials and experts participate – that define Greece in terms

**182**

of its agricultural production. The track thus ridicules the tendency to establish an identity between Greece and its agricultural products and effectively makes the argument that discourses about Greece's economic future should not be defined by the products it presently exports.

A similar strategy of disruption through the disclosure of ambivalence is deployed with regard to the presence of American popular culture products. In 'Apollonian Bod' ('Απολλώνεια Κορμάρα'), for example, the Imiskoumbria address the arrival of American-style fitness centres and body images. The track, which is set against a backdrop of light jazz, begins with the tourist season approaching. Mentzelos looks in the mirror and realizes he is not ready to display himself on the beach. He decides to go to the 'sacred space' of the gym, a description that evokes the connection between physical, intellectual and spiritual education in the gymnasiums of antiquity, in order to transform himself into a muscle-bound hunk.

(22) *Το γυμναστήριο είναι ένας*   'The gymnasium is a sacred
    *χώρος ιερός.*   space.

   . . .           . . .

*Και εγώ με μία άνεση θα το*   And with a studied ease, I'll
*παίξω με τα χέρια.*   give it [the barbell] nine lives.

*Στήθος, πόδια, πλάτη, θα*   Chest, legs, back, I can swallow
*καταπιώ μαχαίρια,*   knives,

*Γιατί είμαι ο Σβαρτζενέγκερ*   Cause I'm the Schwarzenegger
*γιατί είμαι ο Συλβέστρος,*   yes, I am the Sylvester,

*Και τρώω τον Τουϊ΄τισμό*   And I eat the Tweety Bird
*γιατί είμαι ένας μαέστρος.*   'cause I am a master.'

                        The Imiskoumbria, 'Apollonian
                        Bod'

In this passage, the group introduces fetishism by displaying their virtuosity at negotiating the cosmos of American popular culture. Beginning with an English-language pun that conflates Sylvester Stallone and Sylvester the Cat through a false synecdoche that links Arnold 'Schwarzenegger' to 'Sylvester' and then 'Sylvester' to the 'Tweety Bird', the song proceeds to critique the habitual consumption of American popular culture by suggesting the existence of a mind so inundated by external popular culture products that it wants to adopt an alien body aesthetic, modelled on Hollywood stars such as Schwarzenegger and Stallone, in order to be identified with the alien culture it consumes. A metonymic relationship is established in which

American popular culture images and ideas are substituted for Greek self-perception, and a visceral, confused, and ultimately ridiculous way of thinking emerges. The personas that Mentzelos and Mithridatis adopt see themselves as both quintessentially Greek (Apollonian, another evocation of the ancient gymnasium) and American (Schwarzenegger and Stallone). While working out, they fantasize about their desirability in a mixture of Greek and English.

(23) *Κι έτσι εδώ που βρίσκομαι και χτίζω το κορμί*   'So here I am, building the body,

*Μα όχι με μπετά, σαν το μπετατζή*   But not out of concrete like the concrete worker.

*Θα γίνω υποψήφιος και φίλε μη γελάς*   I'll become a candidate and, friend, don't you snicker

*Εμένα θα εκλέξουνε για Μίστερ της Ελλάς*   They're going to elect me, Greece's next Mister.'

The Imiskoumbria, 'Apollonian Bod'

Meanwhile, a female voice praises their musculature, cooing:

(24) *Ξέρω ότι είσαι σφίχτης.*   'I know you're tight. I know that
*Ξέρω ότι είσαι* strong.   you're "strong."

*Και τραβάς τα ζόρια άμα λάχει* all night long.   I know you'll pull your weight, if it happens, "all night long,"

*Mr. Sphincterman*   Mr. Sphincterman'

The Imiskoumbria, 'Apollonian Bod'

The heteroglot language practices here – the use of borrowings ('Mister', 'strong') and calques ('*χτίζω το κορμί*' lit. 'building the body', and '*σφίχτης*, lit. 'tight') – are significant. They are common in the group's songs, but they are never used in an unreflective manner. Instead, they almost always highlight the absurdity of the cross-cultural encounters they depict. Here, the clarification of '*χτίζω το κορμί*' or 'building the body' by specifying 'but not out of concrete' defamiliarizes the calque, pointing out its ridiculousness in Greek. A similar mechanism is initiated through the intentionally inopportune translation of the Greek word for 'tight' or 'firm' ('*σφιχτός*, sfikhtós) as the female vocalist defines Mithridatis as 'Mr. Sphincterman', a bilingual pun that works in both Greek ('*σφιγκτήρας*, sfinktíras) and English.

**184**

The myth of bodily perfection – as expressed through the ritual of lifting weights in the 'sacred space' (example 22) of the gymnasium – is thus punctured as Mentzelos and Mithridatis are revealed to be self-obsessed Sphinctermen who are deflated through a culminating burst of flatulence.

The lesson of Mentzelos's experiences as Mr. Sphincterman is clear. Engagement with American popular cultural forms, though an unavoidable part of contemporary Greek existence, cannot be accomplished in an unmediated, visceral manner. It requires a detailed knowledge of the form and history of American popular culture products. Rap music, because it incorporates elements of *bricolage* and possesses an implicit historical sensibility, is an ideal medium for negotiating the presence of American popular culture products. It provides a historical vantage point and method from which to envision another society and begin articulating a critique of the role that American-centred global economic forces and Americanized culture play in shaping modern Greece and the world.

## 5 Absent audiences and the politics of rap in Greece

For the Imiskoumbria, rap music has the potential of becoming an international political language, one that simultaneously addresses both local and global concerns and is based on respect for cultural difference. Although aware of the global origins of the genre, the group's musical and lyrical choices indicate that rap music, for them, is an American form and, as such, part of the unequal cultural flows that lay at the core of the machinery of United States imperialism. At the same time, however, the group recognizes that the form is redefining itself as it spreads around the globe. As a result, they refuse to define 'Americanness' or even 'African Americanness' as the sign of rap-music authenticity. Though students of the history of rap music, they define themselves in terms of political affinity rather than political fealty. In other words, they acknowledge their debts to American rap music and see themselves as part of a common struggle, but also evince a willingness to criticize those elements within American rap music that detract from the political power of the genre.

Specifically, the Imiskoumbria often attack those aspects of American rap music that define difference in negative terms. They are particularly critical of music that gives vent to certain types of sexist proclivities. In 'Cat on the Roof' they employ self-irony to critique the emphasis – present in some American and some Greek rap music – on male sexual

**185**

prowess. The lyrics on their first album, they jokingly reason, must have been:

(25) *Βλακείες στην ουσία* 'In essence nonsense,

*αφού δεν αναφέρανε* since they didn't even mention a single
*ούτε μια συνουσία* sexual convergence.'

The Imiskoumbria, 'The Cat on the Roof'

The use of the word *συνουσία* for the act of sex is noteworthy here, since it represents an archaic usage drawn from Classical Greek and pokes fun at the perceived pseudo-seriousness of sexual conquest raps. Another song, 'The Man of the House' ('Ο κύρης του σπιτιού'), targets the institution of patriarchy.

(26) *Που γύριζες, κοκόνα μου, κι* 'Where were you, princess?
*είσαι αργοπορημένη;* And why so late?

*Έλυνες ασκήσεις και πάλι* Doing homework again with
*με την Άννα;* Anna? [Have I got that straight?]

*Κοίτα εδώ που σου μιλώ και* Don't look at your mother. Look
*μη κοιτάς τη μάνα.* at me when I'm speaking.

*Σους, σιωπή και σώπαινε!* Shush, silence! I'm the one
*Εγώ μιλάω τώρα.* who's doing the talking.

. . .  . . .

*Που' ναι το παλικάρι μου* Where is my lad who himself is
*άργησε κι αυτός;* a little late.

*Αλλά με καμιά γκόμενα θα* Probably out snuggling up with
*είναι αραχτός.* a date.

*Έτσι εμπειρίες να μην είναι* Good for him, he needs some
*του κουτιού.* practice

*Γιατί αυτός θα γίνει ο κύρης* Because someday soon he's
*του σπιτιού.* going to take my place.'

The Imiskoumbria, 'The Man of the House'

Instead of replicating rap music that celebrates male virility and denigrates female fidelity, they opt to parody Greek patriarchy. The song highlights the frequently unequal treatment of sons and daughters within the Greek family with regard to sexual morality, academic achievement and housework. Whereas the sexual promiscuity of the son is tolerated and even encouraged by the father, the daughter is viewed as property to be controlled and forcibly restrained if necessary. This is not to say that female sexuality never suffers the sharp tongue of the group or that sex is never celebrated. Rather, it is to note that the Imiskoumbria are equal opportunity offenders and that men are as likely as women to be the targets of their ire.

The political message of the Imiskoumbria is based on an inclusive vision of their audience. It does not seek to eliminate difference, but rather to build bridges across barriers. Although their primary audience, given the centrality of the Greek language and the history of Greek popular music to their rap, is a national one, they do not appeal to their listeners solely as national subjects. Instead, the group premises its music on the existence of a shared corpus of texts that stretches across geopolitical borders. By incorporating a barrage of intertextual references to American popular culture, the Imiskoumbria invite the Greek audience to conceptualize itself as part of a broader, international audience that stretches from the Americas to Asia, Oceania, Africa and Europe and shares the experience of external involvement in local cultural, economic and political life. Not all of the barriers the Imiskoumbria encounter, however, are easily transcended. Particularly troubling is the barrier of language. Since English is nearly universal as a second language in Greece, Greek audiences are able to decode American rap music. The reverse is not true. The broader audience that the group posits is ultimately an imaginary audience, a projection of desire for an expanded political community.

In many ways, the desire for an absent audience that resonates within the music of the Imiskoumbria can be explained in terms of Frederic Jameson's notion of the 'geopolitical unconscious', which he defines as 'a collective effort at trying to figure out where we are and what landscapes and forces confront us in a late twentieth century whose abominations are heightened by their concealment and their bureaucratic impersonality' (1995, p. 3). Through a related process which Jameson terms 'cognitive mapping', the geopolitical unconscious attempts to 'refashion national allegory into a conceptual instrument for grasping our new being-in-the-world' (ibid.). The Imiskoumbria, to the extent that they debunk the role of the *tópos* in the construction of Greek identity and actively refashion traditional national allegories to fashion a new sense of Greekness, conform to Jameson's model. Their project, however, does not strike me as, in any way, 'unconscious'. On the contrary, their manipulations of national allegory exist entirely at the level of intentionality. They aim in entirely conscious ways to refashion national allegory in order to build cognitive, psychological and ultimately ontological bridges between groups of people whose sense of culture as a local entity is undermined by the increasing

**187**

presence of supranational political and economic institutions and their agendas. Instead of describing their project as 'unconscious', I would argue that their project is incomplete. It requires something external, a supplement. The success of their project is undermined by the hegemony of the English language and the one-way dynamics of cultural flows. In order to succeed, their project – and other similar projects around the world – requires the development of new modes of translation and criticism and new projects for the creation of cross-cultural meaning that are capable of finding points of solidarity in the struggle against global cultural homogenization.

## 6 Conclusion

This study has attempted to demonstrate the utility of Bhabha's (1994) notions of mimicry and fetishization, as well as the concept of a United States empire (Kaplan, 1993; Pease, 1993), in studying the political significance of rap music outside the United States. Through mimicry and fetishization, the Imiskoumbria articulate a complex, heteroglot critique that targets the central role the United States has played in the construction of the contemporary world order through its global military presence, its insistence on neoliberal trade laws, and the saturation of world markets with its popular culture products. In the process, they generate a hybrid, poetic reconfiguration of Greek identity that allows them to lay claim to their local cultural specificity and articulate a new vision of Greekness based on an emerging cosmopolitan political sensibility that seeks both to broaden the horizon of what it means to be Greek and to confront the broader geopolitical entities that constrain Greek identity. Their ability to do the latter, however, is constrained by the boundaries of language. The emergence of the type of global political discourse that their music seems to call for requires the creation of new modes of translation and criticism and new projects for the creation of cross-cultural understanding that are capable of building alliances across borders and barriers.

## Notes

1. Testimonials to the influence of Public Enemy on the evolution of rap music in Greece may be found in Iosifidis (2000, p. 129), Papadimitriou (1996, pp. 4–6), Dreez (2001) and Imiz Biz Entertainment (2001).
2. The root of the word *laïkí* is *laós*, 'the people'. Traditional *laïkí* music can be thought of as roughly analogous to North American country music. Its contemporary variant, *elafrá* ('light') *laïkí*, bears little resemblance to its predecessor. In terms of composition and lyrical content, it is more comparable to Western pop music.

3. The Larisa-based group Microphone Snipers, which boasts both Greek and Albanian members, did a significant number of live performances from 1999 to 2005, but never landed a recording contract (Microphone Snipers, 2008). More recently, Athens-based Albanian rapper Aldri Milo has begun to attract some attention via web-published videos (Contis, 2008). In general, however, the Greek rap scene is almost entirely Greek dominated (Androutsopoulos and Scholz, 2003, p. 465).

4. The Truman Doctrine, articulated on 12 March 1947, pledged that the United States would lead the fight to contain Communism. It was specifically directed at Greece and Turkey, which were perceived as vulnerable to Soviet expansionism. It served as the vehicle through which the United States intervened in the Greek Civil War of 1946–1949 by funnelling military and economic aid to the recognized government of the country, the centre-right coalition, which ultimately defeated EAM–ELAS, the leftist coalition that had played a key role in resisting the Axis Occupation.

5. George Clinton's two bands Parliament and Funkadelic were instrumental in the evolution of funk music in the 1970s. Bootsy Collins became Clinton's bass player in 1972 . The bass style he developed was one of the signatures of the funk sound.

6. The reference to tax-free license plates refers to a loophole in the tax system that allows repatriating Greek emigrants to return with larger and more expensive cars without paying penalties.

7. Greek television has a long history of broadcasting American programming that purports to represent the cultural diversity of the United States: *Julia*, *The Rookies*, and *I, Spy* in the 1970s; *F.A.M.E.* and *Hillstreet Blues* in the 1980s; and *Miami Vice* and *The Fresh Prince of Bel Air* in the 1990s. Additionally, television and urban billboards regularly feature advertising campaigns by corporations such as Benetton, Nike and Reebok that attempt to create culturally diverse corporate images.

8. Bhabha (1994, pp. 74–75) adapts the term fetishism from Freud to describe the dynamics of racial stereotypes within colonial discourse. He argues that 'the fetish represents the simultaneous play between metaphor as substitution (masking absence and difference) and metonymy (which contiguously registers the perceived lack). The fetish or stereotype gives access to an "identity" which is predicated as much on mastery and pleasure as it is on anxiety and defense, for it is a form of multiple and contradictory belief in its recognition of difference and disavowal of it'. My definition of fetishism follows the general contours of Bhabha's thought on the term. As I define it, however, fetishism operates as more of a self-conscious discursive strategy as opposed to an organic upwelling of subconscious desire.

## Discography

Imiskoumbria (1996), *Thirty Years of Hits* (*Τριάντα χρόνια επιτυχίες*). Athens, Greece: FM Records.

Imiskoumbria (1997), *The Disk You Advertise* (*Ο δίσκος που διαφημίζετε*). Athens, Greece: FM Records.

# References

Alim, H. S. (2009), 'Straight outta Compton, straight aus München: global linguistic flows, identities, and the politics of language in a Global Hip Hop Nation', in H. S. Alim, A. Ibrahim and A. Pennycook (eds), *Global Linguistic Flows: Hip Hop Cultures, Youth Identities, and the Politics of Language*. New York: Routledge, pp. 1–22.

Anderson, B. (1983), *Imagined Communities: Reflections on the Origin and Spread of Nationalism*. New York: Verso.

Androutsopoulos, J. (2007), 'Style online: doing hip-hop on the German-speaking Web', in A. Peter (ed.), *Style and Social Identities. Alternative Approaches to Linguistic Heterogeneity*. Berlin, NY: de Gruyter, pp. 279–317.

Androutsopoulos, J. and Scholz, A. (2003), 'Spaghetti funk: appropriations of hip-hop culture and rap music in Europe'. *Popular Music and Society*, 26, 4, 463–478.

Appadurai, Arjun (1996), *Modernity at Large: Cultural Dimensions of Globalization*. Minneapolis: University of Minnesota Press.

Baker, Jr., H. A. (1993), *Black Studies, Rap, and the Academy*. Chicago: University of Chicago Press.

Bhabha, H. (1994), *The Location of Culture*. New York: Routledge.

Brennan, T. (1994), 'Off the gangsta tip: a rap appreciation, or forgetting about Los Angeles'. *Critical Inquiry*, 20, 4, 663–666.

Brown, T. (2006), '"Keeping it real" in a different 'hood: (African-)Americanization and hip hop in Germany', in D. Basu and S. J. Lemelle (eds), *The Vinyl Ain't Final: Hip Hop and the Globalization of Black Popular Culture*. London: Pluto, pp. 137–150.

Chuck D. with Jah, Y. (1997), *Fight the Power: Rap, Race, and Reality*. New York: Delacorte Press.

Clogg, R. (1992), *A Concise History of Greece*. New York: Cambridge University Press.

Condry, I. (2001), 'A history of Japanese hip-hop: street dance, club scene, pop market', in T. Mitchell (ed.), *Global Noise: Rap and Hip Hop Outside the USA*. Middletown, CT: Wesleyan University Press, pp. 222–247.

—(2006), *Hip-Hop Japan: Rap and the Paths of Cultural Globalization*. Durham, NC: Duke University Press.

Contis, A. (2008), 'Second generation citizens'. *The Athens News*, 28 November 2008, p. A14.

Dreez, D. (2001), *Dr. Dreez and Emeez Homepage*, 'History', <www.geocities.com/ SunsetStrip/Garage/9140/dreez/historyhtm>, accessed 15 January 2001.

Durand, A.-P. (2003), *Black, Blanc, Beur: Rap Music and Hip-Hop Culture in the Francophone World*. Lanham, MD: Scarecrow Press.

Dyson, M. E. (1997), *Between God and Gangsta Rap: Bearing Witness to Black Culture*. New York: Oxford University Press.

Fernando, Jr., S. H. (1994), *The New Beats: Exploring the Music, Culture, and Attitudes of Hip-Hop*. New York: Anchor.

Fink, R. L. (2006), 'Negotiating ethnicity and authenticity in Tokyo's Club Harlem', in D. Basu and S. J. Lemelle (eds), *The Vinyl Ain't Final: Hip Hop and the Globalization of Black Popular Culture*. London: Pluto, pp. 200–209.

Gilroy, P. (1993), *The Black Atlantic: Modernity and Double Consciousness*. New York: Verso.

Hatzipantazis, T. (1977), *Η Αθηναϊκή Επιθεώρηση*, Τόμος Δεύτερος [*The Athenian Revue*, Volume Two]. Athens: Ekdhotiki Ermis.

Helenon, V. (2006), 'Africa on their mind: rap, blackness, and citizenship in France', in D. Basu and S. J. Lemelle (eds), *The Vinyl Ain't Final: Hip Hop and the Globalization of Black Popular Culture*. London: Pluto, pp. 151–166.

Hesmondhalgh, D. and Melville, C. (2001), 'Urban breakbeat culture: repercussions of hip-hop in the United Kingdom', in T. Mitchell (ed.), *Global Noise: Rap and Hip Hop Outside the USA*. Middletown, CT: Wesleyan University Press, pp. 86–110.

Holst-Warhaft, G. (1997), 'Song, self-identity, and the neohellenic'. *Journal of Modern Greek Studies*, 15, 2, 232–238.

Imiz Biz Entertainment (2001), 'Βιογραφία, επεισόδιο 2' [*The Imiskoumbria Homepage*, 'Biography, episode 2'], <www.imiskoumbria.gr>, accessed 15 January 2001.

Iosifidis, K. (2000), *To graffitti στην Ελλάδα 2: το χρώμα της πόλης* [*Graffiti in Greece 2: The Color of the City*]. Athens: Ekdhosis Akti-oksi.

Jameson. F. (1995), *The Geopolitical Aesthetic: Cinema and Space in the World System*. Bloomington, IN: Indiana University Press.

Kaplan A. (1993), '"Left alone with empire": the absence of empire in the study of American culture', in A. Kaplan and D. E. Pease (eds), *Cultures of United States Imperialism*. Durham, NC: Duke University Press, pp. 3–21.

Kaya, A. (2001), *'Sicher in Kreuzberg': Constructing Diasporas: Turkish Hip Hop Youth in Berlin*. Bielefeld: Transcript Verlag.

Kelley, R. D. G. (1996), 'Kickin' reality, kickin' ballistics: gangsta rap and postindustrial Los Angeles', in W. E. Perkins (ed.), *Droppin' Science: Critical Essays on Rap Music and Hip Hop Culture*. Philadelphia: Temple University Press, pp. 117–158.

Kolovos, Y. (2000), 'Χιπ–χοπ: η ρίμα του μένους' ['Hip-Hop: The Rhyme of Wrath']. *Καθημερινή* [*Kathimerini*], 14 May, 48.

Krims, A. (2000), *Rap Music and the Poetics of Identity*. New York: Cambridge University Press.

Leontis, A. (1995), *Topographies of Hellenism: Mapping the Homeland*. Ithaca, NY: Cornell University Press.

Lipsitz, G. (1994), *Dangerous Crossroads: Popular Music, Postmodernism and the Poetics of Place*. New York: Verso.

Low Bap Foundation (2008), *Low Bap Foundation Homepage*, 'Active Member', <http://www.lowbap.com/gr/artistdetails.asp?artistsid=2>, accessed 11 July 2009.

Maxwell, I. (2001), 'Sydney stylee: hip-hop down under comin' up', in T. Mitchell (ed.), *Global Noise: Rap and Hip Hop Outside the USA*. Middletown, CT: Wesleyan University Press, pp. 259–279.

Microphone Snipers (2008), *Microphone Snipers, Official Web Site*, <http://www.micsnipers.com/>, accessed 10 July 2009.

Mitchell, T. (2001a), 'Fightin' da Faida: the Italian posses and hip-hop in Italy', in T. Mitchell (ed.), *Global Noise: Rap and Hip Hop Outside the USA*. Middletown, CT: Wesleyan University Press, pp. 194–221.

Mitchell, T. (2001b), 'Kia kaha! (Be strong!): Maori and Pacific Islander hip-hop in Aotearoa-New Zealand', in T. Mitchell (ed.), *Global Noise: Rap and Hip Hop Outside the USA*. Middletown, CT: Wesleyan University Press, pp. 280–305.

—(2003), 'Doin' damage in my native language: the use of "resistance vernaculars" in hip hop in France, Italy, and Aolearoa/New Zealand', in H. Berger and M. Carroll (eds), *Global Pop, Local Language*. Jackson: University Press of Mississippi, pp. 3–17.

—(2006), 'A modern day corroboree – Wire MC'. *Music Forum*, 12, 4, 26–31.

Papadimitriou, D. (1996), 'Active Member'. *Rock: Μηνιαία επιθεώρηση της Ελληνικής ανεξάρτητης σκηνής* [*Rock: Monthly Review of the Greek Independent Music Scene*], 5, 46, 4–6.

Pease, D. E. (1993), 'New perspectives on U.S. culture and imperialism', in A. Kaplan and D. E. Pease (eds), *Cultures of United States Imperialism*. Durham, NC: Duke University Press, pp. 22–38.

Pennay, M. (2001), 'Rap in Germany: the birth of a genre', in T. Mitchell (ed.), *Global Noise: Rap and Hip Hop Outside the USA*. Middletown, CT: Wesleyan University Press, pp. 111–133.

Pennycook, A. (2007), *Global Englishes and Transcultural Flows*. New York: Routledge.

Pennycook, A. and Mitchell, T. (2009), 'Hip Hop as dusty foot philosophy: engaging locality', in H. S. Alim, A. Ibrahim and A. Pennycook (eds), *Global Linguistic Flows: Hip Hop Cultures, Youth Identities, and the Politics of Language*. New York: Routledge, pp. 25–42.

Prévos, A. J. M. (1996), 'The evolution of French rap music and hip hop culture in the 1980s and 1990s'. *The French Review*, 69, 5, 713–725.

—(1998), 'Hip hop, rap, and repression in France and the United States'. *Popular Music and Society*, 22, 2, 67–84.

—(2001), 'Postcolonial popular music in France: rap music and hip-hop culture in the 1980s and 1990s', in T. Mitchell (ed.), *Global Noise: Rap and Hip Hop Outside the USA*. Middletown, CT: Wesleyan University Press, pp. 39–56.

—(2003), 'Two decades of rap in France: emergence, developments, prospects', in A.-P. Durand (ed.), *Black, Blanc, Beur: Rap Music and Hip-Hop Culture in the Francophone World*. Lanham, MD: Scarecrow Press, pp. 1–21.

Rose, T. (1994), *Black Noise: Rap Music and Black Culture in Contemporary America*. Hanover, NH: Wesleyan University Press.

Samuels, D. (2004), 'The rap on rap: the "black music" that isn't either', in M. Foreman and M. A. Neal (eds), *That's the Joint: The Hip-Hop Studies Reader*. New York: Routledge, pp. 147–153.

Spady, J. G., Alim, H. S. and Meghelli, S. (2006), *Tha Global Cipha: Hip Hop Culture and Consciousness*. Philadelphia: Black History Museum Press.

Toop, D. (1984), *Rap Attack: African Jive to New York Hip-Hop*. Boston: South End Press.

Tsartas, P. (1989), *Κοινωνικές και οικονομικές επιπτώσεις της τουριστικής ανάπτυξης* [*Social and Economic Effects of Tourism Development*]. Athens: EKKE.

# 8 Keeping it Native (?): The Conflicts and Contradictions of Cypriot Hip Hop

Evros Stylianou

## 1 Introduction

'Keep it real'. In the three decades since the release of the first rap records, that perennial hip hop imperative has been adumbrated with so many meanings and contexts, to the point where it has become completely clichéd. 'Keep it street', 'stick to what you know', 'do not sell out', 'do not pander', 'do not beat around the bush', 'keep it Black', 'show no fear', 'avoid superfluity', 'do not forget where you came from', 'keep it gangsta', 'never lose face', 'be yourself', 'don't back down', 'express you'. All these statements, and many more besides, have come to define that tricky urban aphorism at one point or another. Outside of the United States, away from its complicated race politics and multitude of hip-hop sub-genres, global hip hop has taken that charge, to 'keep it real', particularly to heart.

Cutler states that: 'Realness or authenticity in hip hop is predicated to a large degree on one's connection to the urban Black experience forcing White middle class young people to establish their authenticity in other ways' (2007, p. 533). In the case of global hip hop one of these ways is undoubtedly the appropriation and adaptation of hip-hop culture to express the unique identities of new locales. Androutsopoulos and Scholz observe that 'Rapping in native speech is the starting point for the genre's reterritorialization' (2003, p. 469). It would appear, then, that for hip-hop scenes finding their feet outside the United States, the idea of 'keeping it real' is inextricably linked to keeping it native.

According to Kelley, on the other hand, 'Contrary to recent media claims, hip hop hasn't "gone global". It has been global, or international at least, since its birth in the very local neighbourhoods of the South Bronx, Washington Heights and Harlem' (2006, p. xi). He goes on to cite the diverse ethnic origins of several early hip-hop innovators and to explain that 'It was born global because it erupted in the midst of a *new stage* of globalization.' Hip hop was born at a time when economic and

**194**

technological forces were beginning to undermine national boundaries like never before, hastening the spread of information, products and of course cultural artefacts (albeit mostly North American). Being itself a product of globalization, both as a cultural outcome of this process and as an item for sale, it seems that hip hop was always bound to spread to all four corners of the globe. Potter notes that 'particularly in the early 90s it is increasingly clear that hip hop has become a transnational, global art form capable of mobilizing diverse disenfranchised groups' (1995, p. 10); while Chang points out that the seeding of hip-hop culture around the world had been actively encouraged by the grass roots, from the very beginning:

> For two decades [Afrika] Bambaataa[1] had been a hip hop ambassador, seeding cities around the world with Universal Zulu Nation chapters and the basic elements. By the end of the century, many of these cities – from Sarajevo to Sydney, Amsterdam to Zanzibar – had been through two generations of hip hop heads with their own defiant youth countercultures. (Chang, 2007, p. 448)

By the end of the last decade of the twentieth century the seeds of hip-hop culture seemed to have been successfully sewn the world over and you would be hard pressed to find an urban centre anywhere in the world without an established (or at least burgeoning) native-tongue hip-hop scene. Born as it was in the midst of ever-accelerating globalization, and having successfully spread from city to city and country to country, the similarities between hip-hop culture and a franchise are clear, each local scene taking its cue from the way American hip-hop artists use beats, rhymes, sampling, graffiti and dance to relocate hip-hop culture and place it within the context of their own urban environment. However, hip hop also exhibits some pronounced differences to franchises: '[Hip hop's] participants are engaging in a symbolic struggle for cultural autonomy, whereby simple imitation of the "mother" culture is rejected in favour of a creative integration of rap into the host culture' (Androutsopoulos and Scholz, 2003, p. 468). This creative integration has taken many forms, and has been helped and hindered by situations that are unique to the native cultures in question.

British hip hop, for instance, has had to contend with sharing the same language as the culturally dominant United States. British rappers initially began by copying the accents they heard in American rap records, partly because those records formed an 'overt reference point for how they should sound when rapping' (Drou, 2007), and partly because their audiences also had the same preconceptions. Trudgill's (1983) analysis of accent imitation in music showed that in the case of British pop music artists' imitation of American accents between the

**195**

1950s and 1980s, imitation is rarely perfect, but rather reveals a conflict between emulating the accent of those groups with which they identify and their inherent pride in their own nationality. Nowadays, as far as hip hop goes at least, the pendulum has swung completely the other way with subsequent generations of rappers from the UK finding it absurd not to use their own regional speech in rap. In a documentary about British hip hop, UK rapper Skinnyman had the following to say on the issue of accent:[2]

> [We] embraced our favourite rappers, which were the big main-stream American rappers. The people in the UK would be rapping in an American twang . . . but when they talk to you, to relate to you in a conversation, they go back to the way how I'm speaking now, in a perfect London accent or, you know, in their native accent. A way that we can reflect on the time and the period is when people started shouting out 'keep it real'. If you speak English and every time you go to rap and kick some lyrics you go into this whole new altered ego of an American accent . . . Is that really real? Or is that as fake as it can get? You know? Does some American kid wanna hear us do some bad imitation of what he does? I don't think so.

French hip hop has been greatly pushed forward by the 1996 Pelchat amendment that obliges radio stations to play at least 40 per cent French language music during prime time, and of that 40 per cent at least half to be from new artists or new recordings (Hare, 2003, p. 62). This attempt to counter the erosion of national character and bolster the French music industry against foreign imports, has conversely aided what was essentially a foreign cultural product to develop extremely healthy native roots.

Greek hip hop, on the other hand, experiences an ongoing split, with groups aligning themselves with one of two subgenres, '*Skliropiriniko*' (Hardcore) or 'Low-Bap',[3] each with its own ideas as to what Greek hip hop should be, and each with its own armies of loyal fans (see also Hess, this volume). Hardcore is typically upbeat and aggressive in delivery, and Low-Bap is a home-grown variation that doesn't even label itself hip hop, its name hearkening back to the early days of Boom-Bap.[4]

This study will look at the hip-hop scene in Cyprus and how its practitioners are dealing with the process of reterritorialization. Just as all hip-hop scenes face the idiosyncratic obstacles unique to their nation and culture, Cyprus's hip-hop scene is a fascinating case with many influences jostling for dominance and many problems inhibiting its growth. Among these factors are the cultural influence that Greece exerts over Cyprus and the peculiar relationship Cypriots have with their dialect, as well as Cyprus's colonial history. In addition, the Republic of Cyprus's sub-1,000,0000 population[5] places strict restrictions on the growth and economic viability of an emergent culture such as hip hop. These factors have contributed to an interesting dynamic in which Greek Cypriot hip-hop artists are still in the process of negotiating what Cypriot hip hop is. With a miniscule home market and an undervalued vernacular to work with, their relationship with notions of realness, as with one another, is often a belligerent one.

The study's main focus is on the use of the Greek Cypriot dialect (henceforth GCD) in Greek Cypriot rap music.[6] If the use of native speech is essential to reterritorialization, then Cyprus presents a complicated case where the mother tongue is a basilectal[7] form which, while spoken by all Greek Cypriots, can be considered rude and inappropriate in formal situations. Androutsopoulos and Scholz point out that '[r]egional dialects appear more frequently in rap songs in societies in which they are generally vital and prestigious' (2003, p. 473). The GCD can certainly be characterized as vital, being more than an accent, the variety spoken by an entire people. Nevertheless, being a non-standard variety at the periphery of the standard as spoken in Athens, it is not considered prestigious, or sometimes even correct (Papapavlou and Sophocleous, forthcoming). This study explores the language attitudes of Greek Cypriot rap artists, who are in a unique position to comment on the broader language attitudes of the country. Being the creators of a form of oral poetry known for its linguistic experimentation and openness to unofficial vernaculars, as well as its preoccupation with authenticity, their views on how and why they express themselves through rap in the ways they do are as valuable to hip-hop scholars as they are to linguists concerned with language attitudes and identity.

A qualitative approach has been adopted for the study that combines two complementary sources of data: semi-structured interviews with artists who have released either full-length albums or EPs (Extended Plays) in the Greek Cypriot hip-hop scene, and analysis of individual songs selected by the author because they seem to employ certain strategies that attempt to re-cast the GCD as a credible form of hip-hop address. In addition, articles on the subject that have been published in the national press and online have also been consulted.[8] The study will present an overview of the history and dynamics of the Greek Cypriot scene, while also narrowing in on the unique obstacles faced by Greek Cypriot rappers due to language attitudes on the island, and how they may be thought of as coming into direct conflict with the first steps native hip-hop scenes tend to take towards reterritorialization.

## 2 Cyprus and its language situation

Cyprus is a small divided island in the eastern Mediterranean. Since the Turkish invasion in 1974 and the partition of the island that ensued, the northern side (TRNC or Turkish Republic of Northern Cyprus, not officially recognized by the international community) is populated mostly by Turkish troops, Turkish Cypriots and Turkish mainland settlers, whereas the southern side (The Republic of Cyprus) is mostly populated by Greek Cypriots. The language used for official business in the Republic of Cyprus (henceforth referred to as Cyprus) is Standard Modern Greek (henceforth SMG).[9] Greek Cypriots are educated and receive their news as well as all official correspondence in SMG, even though they grow up speaking the GCD, which bears phonological, morphological, syntactic and lexical differences from SMG (Pavlou and Papapavlou, 2004, pp. 248–249, Terkourafi, 2005, pp. 311–317).

The disparities between GCD and SMG have called into question the prudence of forcing children to be educated in a language that differs from the one they speak at home with their families. Pavlou and Papapavlou (2004, p. 249) point out that this policy comes into direct conflict with UNESCO policy stating that students ought to be schooled in their mother tongue. The situation does, however, appear to be changing. Pavlou and Papapavlou refer to official guidelines that would have teachers correcting students not only when using GCD in the classroom, a place reserved for the exclusive use of SMG, but even when pronouncing SMG words with a GCD accent (2004, p. 250). Tsiplakou (2007), on the other hand, describes the official position towards the use of GCD in teaching as one of tolerance, in addition to a general sense of de-stigmatization associated with it (used as anything other than an educational tool).

Official policies naturally have an impact on the attitudes of native speakers themselves. A study of the language attitudes of 11-year old Greek Cypriot children revealed that '[t]he students held very positive values towards Standard Modern Greek in matters of prestige, appropriateness, aesthetics and correctness' whereas '[t]he overwhelming majority of them underestimated the Dialect and considered it "rude", "inappropriate", "peasant" and so forth' (Ioannou, 2004, p. 36). Regardless of the perceived prestige of SMG, the students interviewed said that 'they found it easier to use [the GCD], contrasting it to the "inconvenience" and "confusion" they often felt when they used the Standard' (Ioannou, 2004, pp. 36–37). This sort of data can be thought of as emblematic of the contradictory relationship Greek Cypriots have with their own dialect.

Looking at the other end of Cyprus's student spectrum, 22 first-year students from the University of Cyprus took part in a matched-guise test. The test aimed to understand how the students would judge people who spoke SMG or GCD. The results are extremely interesting, especially when placed alongside the results of the Ioannou study. 'Specifically, the results show that those who use SMG are (a) *more attractive*, (b) *more ambitious*, (c) *more intelligent*, (d) *more interesting*, (e) *more modern*, (f) *more dependable*, (g) *more pleasant*, and (h) *more educated* than those who use the Cypriot dialect' (Papapavlou, 1998, p. 22).

Although this research was conducted more than a decade ago, it should not be too hastily dismissed as the attitudes of many Cypriots can still be thought to be in agreement with these findings. However, it should also be noted that GCD is used on television much more these days, while the prevalence of communications technologies such as the internet and mobile telephony has led to GCD, which has no standardized written form, being used to a great degree online and by SMS. These factors, and a much more visible youth culture on the island, are beginning to undermine older perceptions of GCD (cf. Terkourafi, 2007, pp. 80–81).

Garrett holds that 'language attitudes research shows some clear disadvantages to "correctness"' (2001, pp. 626–631), but it would appear that these disadvantages have not yet manifested themselves within the Cypriot cultural context. As things currently stand, there is certainly a growing sense of pride in GCD, nevertheless there are also some clear disadvantages in its reception by some areas of Cypriot society. Drawing on Moschonas's analysis of Cypriot Greek, who situates it outside SMG as 'an Interior within an Exterior', Terkourafi (2007, p. 74), adds that, when spoken in Greece, GCD constitutes 'an Exterior within an Interior', resulting in a 'schizophrenic' position whereby the GCD is thought of as 'simultaneously Interior and Exterior' (2007, p. 74). This ambivalent understanding, and the way Greek Cypriots themselves vacillate between these two points, are important to bear in mind, especially as hip hop's first question to any fledgling native scene always seems to be, 'who are you?'

## 3 A brief history of hip hop in Cyprus

Hip hop came to Cyprus in dribs and drabs between the mid to late 1980s and early 1990s. An influx of foreign students (many of them from the Middle East, but also several from North Africa and Eastern

Europe) and Cypriots who had grown up abroad, in the UK, the US and Australia, brought cassettes and CDs of American hip hop to the island with them. Local DJs started playing hip-hop songs in discotheques that catered mainly to foreign clubbers, but also to English-speaking locals. The first hip-hop songs recorded in Cyprus were by a group called Βαωμένοι Έσσω (Vaomeni Esso, 'Locked Indoors'). The group formed in 1992 and began by performing comical raps over American hip-hop instrumentals in GCD.

Although Vaomeni Esso are considered the first Greek Cypriot rappers, many of the artists interviewed cite Haji Mike as the first figure to use GCD to rap with. Not a hip-hop artist per se, Haji Mike started recording reggae-influenced music in GCD in London during the late 1980s and early 1990s. He quickly became well known on the island with his evocations of village life from an English-Cypriot perspective in songs like 'Stavroula' and 'O Vrakaman' ('The Vraka-man', from *vraka*, the men's traditional wide black trousers reaching just below the knee). His lyrics featured code-switching between GCD and English commonly observed in the speech of Greek Cypriots raised in English-speaking countries (also affectionately called 'Gringlish').[10]

It was the emergence of hip hop in Greece in the mid 1990s that really set Greek Cypriot imaginations alight, and provided more of a push towards developing a home-grown scene. The influence of the Greek scene cannot be overlooked as for many Cypriot fans and aspiring lyricists it was the first time they had heard hip hop being done in the language of their education. The artists interviewed cite Greek groups such as FFC ('Fortified Concept'), Razastarr, Terror X Crew and Imiskoumbria ('The Semi Sardines') among their influences (see also Hess, this volume).

After the early experiments of Vaomeni Esso, one of their members, Chinese-Cypriot John Wu recorded *Το Φαινόμενο* (*To Fenómeno*, 'The Phenomenon') along with French rapper Issa in 1994. Wu's own verses featured GCD but the album never saw the light of day. This was the last album in which Wu would use GCD to rap with. The Greek Cypriot hip-hop scene's first widely released album was Wu's next project, the solo album *Τελευταίες Μέρες* (*Teleftées Méres*, 'Last Days'), put out as an experiment by the now defunct All Records in 1997. John Wu's *Απαγορευμένες Γνώσεις* (*Apaghorevménes Gnósis*, 'Forbidden Knowledge') followed in 1999, released by All Records in Cyprus and Minos EMI in Greece. It was the first time a Cypriot artist had released a hip-hop album in Greece. All Records then released an EP by Σιωπηλός Αφηγητής (*Siopilós Afigitís*, 'Quiet Narrator') called *Το Τρένο* (*To Tréno*, 'The Train') in 2001 and John Wu's next album *Αόρατος Πόλεμος* (*Aóratos Pólemos*, 'Invisible War') was released in 2003, funded by himself and distributed by All Records. In 2004 independent label Olive Tree Music released *Cyprus Thing*, a double album featuring 'Urban' and 'World Music' created on both sides of the Cypriot divide. Although not strictly a hip-hop album, it featured a number of hip-hop songs. *Συχνότητες* (*Sihnótites*, 'Frequencies') was a self-funded five track EP released by DNA (*Δημιουργοί Νέας Αντίληψης*, *Dimiourgí Néas Antílipsis*, 'Creators of a New Perception') in 2006. The last official hip-hop release on the island at the time of writing is a compilation titled *The Rise of Cyprus Hip hop: The Beginning*, released by All Records in 2007. The album features various rappers from the island as well as several who now live abroad.

From 2000 onwards many groups and individuals stepped out onto the stage. Although many have never released material with a record label, they have all contributed to the dynamic of the Greek Cypriot scene, some of them having distributed CDs on their own. These groups include: HCH (Hardcore Heads), FTW (Fuck the World, or Foretelling Wisdom), IUT (Invisible Underground Threat), AII (consisting of two former members of IUT) – who finally split up leaving only one of their lyricists Mazud DiAngelo active, CyMafia, P.O.T.S. (Part of the Soul), 2J, Oneway, D.R.I.G. and Napa Connection. As far as solo artists go, Πονοκέφαλος (*Ponokéfalos*, literally 'Headache' – originally part of Vaoméni Esso), Kinesiotherapistís, Sergio, Brice, Sniper (originally part of the British So Solid Crew), Uncle Festa (originally part of the British M.U.D. Family), Sofoz MC, Lyrical Eye and Mario Mental are also all members of the scene.

## 4 Language use in official and unofficial releases

Many of the artists interviewed refer to a dichotomy between 'commercial' vs 'underground', which is much the same as you will find in other hip-hop scenes throughout the world. I will instead use the distinction of 'official' vs 'unofficial' – with *official* referring to barcoded, widely distributed, professionally pressed full-length albums and EPs, and *unofficial*[11] reserved for full-length albums and EPs distributed hand-to-hand and online – due to the fact that this study does not concern itself with commercial success or underground posturing, but rather with language attitudes and the process of reterritorialization. On the surface there may seem to be a parallel between commercial/underground, and official/unofficial, however the data has shown that this is not quite so; for example artists such as Mario Mental and Lyrical Eye, who are largely considered to be commercial rappers, have to date put out more unofficially released tracks than official ones. Moreover, it would be inaccurate to equate official with 'rapped

**201**

in SMG' and unofficial with 'rapped in GCD'. While SMG does appear far more frequently in official releases and GCD in unofficial ones, there are also a plethora of unofficial releases rapped in SMG (see Tables 8.1 and 8.2).

**Table 8.1** Language use in officially released albums and EPs

| Official releases (albums and EPs) | | |
|---|---|---|
| **SMG** | **GCD** | **English** |
| Teleutaies Meres – John Wu | | |
| Apagorevmenes Gnosis – John Wu | | |
| To Treno – Siopilos Afigitis | | |
| Aoratos Polemos – John Wu | | |
| Cyprus Thing – Various | | |
| Sihnotites – DNA | Sihnotites – DNA | |
| The Rise of Cyprus Hip-hop – Various | | The Rise of Cyprus Hip-hop – Various |

**Table 8.2** Language use in unofficially released albums and EPs.

| Unofficial releases (albums and EPs) | | |
|---|---|---|
| **SMG** | **GCD** | **English** |
| HCH – HCH | HCH – HCH | |
| Etsi – P.O.T.S. | Etsi – P.O.T.S. | |
| Elysian Fields 1 – Mazud DiAngelo | | |
| Elysian Fields 2 – Mazud DiAngelo | Elysian Fields 2 – Mazud DiAngelo | |
| No Way Back – One Way | | |
| Omonimo – FTW | | |
| Skepsis – FTW | | |
| Epanastatis – FTW | | |
| FTW Mehri Na Pethano – FTW | | |
| Noctuary – FTW | | |

The point to bear in mind is that by looking solely at barcoded releases, one gets an entirely different picture of hip hop in Cyprus, both in terms of GCD use and number of active groups and individuals. As can be seen by comparing Tables 8.1 and 8.2, Greek Cypriot hip hop has more unofficial releases to date than official ones, and far more active performing MCs (Emcees) and groups than the official discography would suggest. This can be put down to the size of the market and the fact that there are not any record labels on the island. The closest thing to a record label, All Records, was more accurately a distribution company that dabbled in home-grown releases from time to time.

Greek Cypriot hip hop's official discography spans the decade between 1997 and 2007. Three of its seven albums were released by John Wu (rapping as either John Wu, or Mastermind) and none of these releases feature GCD on any tracks. The same situation is to be found in *To Tréno* by Siópilos Afigitís. While the *Cyprus Thing* compilation does feature GCD on a number of tracks, none of the hip-hop songs on the compilation are performed in GCD. *The Rise of Cyprus Hip Hop: The Beginning* also features various MCs who either rap in SMG or English, but none in GCD. To date the only official hip-hop release to feature GCD is DNA's self-funded 2006 Frequencies EP, of which only two tracks feature the dialect. This presents us with a situation where the only officially released hip-hop songs to feature GCD in a decade's worth of professionally pressed hip-hop music in Cyprus have come from one group, and amount to 40 per cent of the EP they featured on, which in turn only amounts to around 14 per cent of the overall official discography of Cyprus's hip-hop scene.

The situation is entirely different when looking at unofficial releases. All five tracks on HCH's self-titled 2003 EP feature GCD (as well as SMG and code-switching between the two). *Έτσι* (*Etsi*, which roughly translates as 'So' or 'Like This'), the 2007 full-length album by P.O.T.S., also features GCD on all the lyrical tracks. Mazud DiAngelo's first solo effort, *Elysian Fields 1* (released in 2001) featured only SMG whereas its follow-up, *Elysian Fields 2*, featured two tracks in GCD. Oneway's album *No Way Back* is rapped exclusively in SMG although rapper Nitro from the group has released a solo track in GCD titled 'Εν έσιεις υπόθεση' ('En éshis ipóthesi', which roughly translates as 'You're Hopeless' or 'You're Useless'). On the other hand, all of FTW's five releases – *Ομώνυμο* (*Omónimo*, 'Homonym', 2000), *Σκέψεις* (*Sképsis*, 'Thoughts', 2001), *Επαναστάτης* (*Epanastátis*, 'Rebel', 2002), *FTW Μέχρι Να Πεθάνω* (*FTW Méhri Na Petháno*, 'FTW Until I Die', 2005) and *Noctuary*, 2007 – are rapped in SMG. These five albums significantly tip the balance, making it harder to equate unofficial releases as being primarily in GCD. The same goes for the output of IUT, CyMafia and Mario Mental, leaving Sniper, Uncle Festa and Lyrical Eye, who all rap in English.

## 5 What the artists have to say

Interviews were conducted by the author with the following artists: Haji Mike, John Wu, MegaHz, Magos, Mazud Diangelo, Zivana, Ponoke-falos, and Sofoz MC. The interviews were semi-structured and all lasted longer than an hour. All the interviews were conducted in GCD (with regular unintentional code-switching by the author between GCD and English), with the exception of Haji Mike who was interviewed in English.

As was to be expected, the opinions of the artists interviewed were closely in accord with their own chosen modes of expression. Rappers who use GCD almost exclusively, could not understand why Greek Cypriot MCs would choose to express themselves in any other way, especially in a medium such as hip hop that places a high premium on colloquial speech. A common theme running through these interviews was the notion of authenticity: rappers who use GCD failed to see the use of SMG by Greek Cypriots in rap as authentic, but viewed it rather as a 'bad copy' of what Greek rappers already do far better. They also stated that rappers who chose to rap in SMG were making a clear commercial decision, and they saw its use as an attempt to appeal to a wider Greek audience, as well as to bypass the attitudes towards GCD held by many Greek Cypriots.

Ponokéfalos was particularly confounded by the idea that Cypriots who choose to rap in SMG do so because it is the language of their education and so comes more naturally to them than GCD (all translations my own):

> Is it possible for them to speak Cypriot all day and it to come easier for them in Greek? Is it possible? Are they putting us on? You take what's in your head and put it down on paper, if I have in my mind '*touton to prama en m'areski*' [GCD for: I don't like this thing], when I write it on paper am I going to write '*afto to prama den mou aresi*'? [same phrase in SMG]. If you have something in your mind do you voice it in Greek? I don't get it . . . Basically they know that if they put out music in Cypriot, people are going to make fun of them, and no one wants to be made fun of, they also want to sell.

When asked how he felt about the use of GCD in Cypriot hip hop, Mágos, DJ, producer, and rapper with the group HCH, had the following to say on the matter:

> It's simple, you rap how you speak, especially in Cyprus where the dialect is under pressure, to rap in Greek sounds fake to me, almost always. We've got the Athenian dialect that has the prestige and the lower dialect that is stigmatized. In Cyprus, as soon as someone is presented with a microphone, they automatically revert to [Standard] Greek . . . It's also embedded in us, it's the commercial concern to do with appealing to a larger Greek market, but it's also inside us, that if I'm going to put myself out there to sing a song and say something important I don't use it [the dialect], I use it when I'm going to order a beer or something, but not if I'm going to speak publicly. Many people used to do one track in Cypriot, for laughs, and if they're going to say something serious, they'll do it in Kalamaristika [Greek Cypriot slang for SMG].

Many of the persons interviewed, especially Ponokéfalos and Mágos, narrowed in on a perception of Cypriots not being comfortable with who they are. Like Terkourafi (2007, cited above), they also mentioned the word 'schizophrenic' when discussing the way Cypriots are more comfortable addressing others and being addressed in GCD, but at the same time feel somewhat ashamed of it.

In an article published in the national newspaper *O Politis* ('The Citizen'), P.O.T.S., writing in GCD, expressed their own reasons for using the dialect in their music:

> We live in Cyprus and our tongue matches in Cypriot.[12] We've learned to think, to speak and express ourselves in Cypriot and this is why you hear Cypriot in our songs. Many believe that Cypriot is a joke . . . Most Cypriots have complexes and undervalue them-selves, believing that they are more polite when they speak Greek and English. It's fashionable to constantly imitate others. We have departed from this way of thinking and imprisonment.

Rappers who rap exclusively in SMG took an altogether less pole-mical stance on the subject. They did not see the idea of 'keeping it real' as necessarily synonymous with using GCD in rap. When pushed, given examples of the 'nativeness' of other international hip-hop scenes, and the obstacles that scenes such as the British one (in the form of the culturally dominant American accent) have had to overcome, they answered by reminding the interviewer that the Greek language is taught in schools, is the language of the Greek Cypriot media and as such is also native to Cyprus. For them the idea of 'keeping it real' was not aligned to the use of GCD; rather, it meant that everyone should just be themselves and not attempt to dictate to anyone else what form their expression should take.

Zivana, one of the MCs with FTW regarded his decision to use SMG over GCD as being one of individual choice:

> Expression is expression, the way you feel it comes out better. Personally for me I feel it comes out better in Greek, and I don't consider that a disadvantage, language is language and it expresses that which you want it to say, I believe it's a personal choice for each individual.

John Wu on the other hand, who began rapping in GCD but whose output since 1997 has been solely in SMG, admitted that for him it was a commercial concern:

> I chose the Greek language so I could have a broader audience, plus the fact that Cypriots laugh when they hear the dialect of the island, but Greek is a bit more serious, so I started doing it in Greek, keeping the Cypriot stuff for myself, just for fun, for me, and just rapping it to my friends to show how different it sounds.

Other rappers who use both SMG and GCD were unwilling to equate 'realness' with the exclusive use of GCD but understood the conflict in not using everyday speech in rap. Nevertheless it was apparent in these interviews that these artists, along with the ones who chose to rap exclusively in SMG, were more concerned with authenticity in the content of their lyrics rather than the form. Sofoz MC, who has not released any albums or EPs to date, but is well known as a performer in both SMG and GCD, was also made uncomfortable by the notion of 'keeping it real' having to do with the choice of language:

> Keeping it real is not a matter of language, I believe it's a matter of how each person expresses themselves, for example I may speak Cypriot but because of education I've learnt to write my lyrics in Greek, no-one can come along and say 'that doesn't express you' . . . We are still under Greek influence, we receive our schoolbooks from Greece. There *is* a small rebellion happening and it started from hip hop, which is very important . . . There has to be a standard, we could make a standardized Greek-Cypriot dialect,[13] but no one has taken that initiative, it's not my job to do, but it's my job to promote it before it happens.

Rappers who have used both varieties to rap with seemed the most troubled by concerns of 'realness' and the fact that elsewhere nativization almost always involves the use of local patterns of speech. All of the artists interviewed understood how hip-hop culture has spread throughout the world but also seemed caught up in the general language attitudes of the country, painfully aware that these attitudes are the same ones that will be used to judge their music.

Zambian-Cypriot MC, Mazud DiAngelo expressed his own dilemma when writing songs:

> I'm torn between both as far as the dialect goes. I've tried the Cypriot dialect and Greek, over the last few years I was a bit confused as to which I should rap in, because if you were going to rap in proper Cypriot no one would understand anything . . . I think it's harder to write in Cypriot, to write something with meaning . . . As soon as someone calls it 'peasant', they leave it there, they won't get involved with it.

MegaHz was also somewhat troubled by the possibility of using the GCD: 'Cypriot is a far harsher dialect, and the crowd is not used to hearing it, it sounds too heavy to them, it sounds peasant.' HCH's Zack explained his own reasons for using GCD in an interview the group gave in 2006:

> When I first wrote lyrics in Greek, I felt like I was fooling myself, I didn't feel like Zack, I felt I was being someone else, so I tore them up and started writing in Cypriot. The way we're talking now, and I believe it's good because it touches the other person, they understand you better.[14]

The question of whether to use, or not to use the dialect penetrates to the core of much that has remained unexamined in Cypriot life. Hip hop presents a rare instance where Cypriot artists are forced to confront Cyprus's language situation head on in a way that many other arts or genres of music do not require. Hip hop demands honest and uncontrived expression and this is, I think, where the conflict lies in Cypriot rap. A perfect example of hip hop's demands on expression is that no-one will bat an eyelid if they hear a British rock group singing in an American accent, but a British rapper trying to sound like he's from Queens Bridge won't be given the time of day. This is where Cyprus differs: the fact that its people oscillate between identification with the dialect and feeling embarrassed about it has had a stultifying effect not only on the arts in Cyprus, but also on popular culture and indeed on Cypriot identity itself.

One thing that was interestingly absent from all the interviews was the perception of Cypriot as an accent as well as a dialect, since the considerable overlap between SMG and GCD, logically, should not rule out Cypriot pronunciation of SMG words and phrases. Regardless of whether Cypriots choose to distance themselves from what may be considered a peasant vocabulary, it doesn't explain why artists who rap in

SMG also avoid pronouncing Greek words with a Cypriot accent. None of those artists interviewed who use SMG were able to answer this question convincingly – instead their answers indicated that they regarded the two varieties as mutually exclusive.

## 6 Where we're at: a look at several Cypriot tracks

This section will look a little closer at the 'Cypriot track', that playful experiment that Mágos alluded to in his interview as a way Cypriot rappers have tended to experiment with GCD. The aim of narrowing in on the Cypriot track is to try and understand the stylistic techniques employed by artists in subject matter, sonic accompaniment and delivery to make a basilectal form such as GCD sound appealing to their audiences. Five tracks have been selected: 'Μόδα' ('Módha', 'Fashion') by HCH, 'Funky Κάττος' ('Funky Káttos', 'Funky Cat') by P.O.T.S., 'Κυπριακή Πραγματικότητα' ('Kypriakí Pragmatikótita', 'Cypriot Reality') by DNA, '84 Boom' by Mazud DiAngelo and 'Εν Έσιεις Υπόθεση' ('En Eshis Ipothesi', 'You're Useless') by Nitro. The analysis in this section is similar to that carried out by Androutsopoulos (2003) on a selection of Greek hip-hop songs; however, the focus here will be on how these tracks differ in their efforts to reappropriate the GCD as a credible hip-hop language. As with all poetry, much of the vitality and wit is lost in direct translation, as are the rhyme schemes, but a balance has been attempted between faithful translation and coherence.

While only ever recording one EP, HCH regularly pop up in discussions about Cypriot hip hop as early innovators. Mágos is mentioned by many of the artists interviewed as a particularly capable producer and DJ who makes hip hop the 'proper way', with sampler and turntables rather than PC software. The crew is also repeatedly cited as having been involved in all four elements of the culture; their initial crew also comprised members who were involved in graffiti as well as breakdancing. Their self-titled EP is actually rapped in both SMG and GCD, with some lyricists favouring one variety over the other and code-switching to GCD. Musically the EP is influenced by the Greek hardcore sound, specifically by Terror X Crew; the tracks are noisy, often dissonant, clearly punk inspired, but unmistakably hip hop. In 'Módha' a traditional Cypriot fiddle weaves in and out of the rest of the distorted sonic accompaniment, a single musical thread linking the piece back to some sort of Cypriot heritage.

Pavlou (1996 and 2001, cited in Pavlou, 2004, p. 17) observes that almost all advertisements on Greek Cypriot television that feature GCD begin and end with a voice speaking in SMG. This so called 'voice of authority' also frames 'Módha', the opening track of the EP, but is manipulated and recontextualized by Mágos, who scratches the words *Παρακαλώ ξυπνήστε μας* ('Please wake us up'), using them to frame the central message of the song: that fashion, and phoney café culture are destroying modern life by commodifying everything. Quite appropriately, the sample is taken from a record that teaches SMG. The same Greek voice closes the track saying: *Το καπαρέ κλείνει τα μεσάνυχτα* ('The cabaret closes at midnight'). The second and third verses of the song, performed by Zack and Mágos in GCD, are a startling display of the expressive possibilities of GCD. As is frequently the case with non-standard varieties in general, Cypriots often talk about how satisfying it is to swear in Cypriot, it being far harsher-sounding, more guttural than SMG. These two verses are a perfect example of that rougher sound both MCs consciously playing on the dialect's more confrontational possibilities. The second verse opens with

(1) *Εν ούλλα ένα ψέμα τζιαι μιαν υποκρισία*  'Everything is a lie, everything is hypocrisy

*όπου γυρίσεις όπου δεις η ίδια μαλακία*  Wherever you turn, wherever you look you see the same crap

*ούλλοι εν με τα στενά ούλλοι με Gabbana*  Everyone is in tight [pants] everyone wears [Dolce and] Gabbana

*ούλλοι αποφασίσασιν να κάμουν την πουτάνα*  Everyone's decided to play the whore.'

HCH , 'Módha'

And further on:

(2) *Γιατί έτσι σας εμάθαν με τού'ν την νοτροπία*  'Because that's how they've taught you, with this way of thinking

*Σαν τα αρνιά που ειν έτοιμα να πάσιν στα σφαγεία*  Like lambs that are ready to go to the slaughterhouse

*Γαμημένη κοινωνία, ούλλοι θέλουν να φκάλουν ριάλλια*  Fucked-up society, everyone wants to make money

*Ούλλοι εν πλεγμένοι μες σε βρώμικα κανάλια*  Everyone entangled in dirty channels

*Τραγουδιστές, ηθοποιοί, τραγουδίστριες, παραγωγοί,*  Singers [masc.], actors, singers [fem.], producers

**209**

| *Ακόμα τζιαι τη μάναν τους πουλούσιν μερικοί* | Some would even sell their mother |
| *Έγιναν ούλλα καπαρέ, τζιαι τα κλαπ τζιαι τα καφέ* | Everything's become a stripjoint, and so have the clubs and the cafes.' |

HCH, 'Módha'

Zack employs the Cypriot vernacular ruthlessly to cut down all the corrupt influences he perceives around him; he does so with anger and fire, rather than a considered social critique, playing on existing preconceptions of the dialect as heavy and vulgar to present himself as an angry outsider to trendy society. The moment he has finished uttering the line equating clubs and cafes with brothels, Mágos takes the mic and further ups-the-ante, making it clear that he actually finds himself in one of these establishments. From this point onwards he becomes increasingly more aggressive, sexually harassing a woman, taunting a man, and threatening to burn the place down.[15]

| | | |
|---|---|---|
| (3) | *Έλα κούκλα μου έλα κούκλα μου μωρό μου* | 'Come my doll, come my doll, my babe |
| | *Έλα κάτσε το κωλούιν σου μες τα μούτρα μου* | Come sit your little bottom on my face |
| | *Μάνα μου νιώθω έτσι ένα σπάρκωμα πάνω μου* | Oh mother, I feel such horniness on me |
| | *Ε πουτάνα μου, το private, την ρουφκιάνα μου* | Hey my whore, the private, my roufkiana |
| | *Εν τάραμα, εν ούλλα συνάλλαγμα* | It's crazy, everything's a transaction |
| | *Κάμνετέ μου ούλλοι πεζοδρόμιο στα καφέ αντί στο 'Αγαλμα* | You're all street-walking at the cafés instead of the Statue |
| | *Είσαι άθρωπος εσού όξα πελάτης; α;* | Are you a man or a customer? Huh? |
| | *Έλα τζέρνα μας κάτι* | Come, buy us something |
| | *Λαλούσιν για αγάπη, εννά τα πιάμε;* | They're talking about love, are we going to go steady? |
| | *Ίντα 'ν που λαλείς εννά σας φάμεν!* | What do you say? We're going to eat you!' |

HCH, 'Módha'

**210**

Mágos presents the listener with a stereotype of coarseness, scratching beneath the surface of innocuous modern Cypriot culture as portrayed by the media, purposefully roughing it up and unearthing the native. The character he plays in 'Módha' is a character most Cypriots will be familiar with, but he doesn't just present the listener with a comic sketch or careful containment of this figure as Cypriot television often does; he sets that character loose in a modern, style-conscious, Euro-friendly environment. He also interestingly aligns the character with the rough and ready hip-hop persona, finding the two to have some essential connection, but also with the Greek Cypriot dialect, and presents himself as a threat to fashion, popular culture, glitz and glamour.

P.O.T.S., on the other hand, take an entirely different approach to their music. Their album *Etsi*, while still completely in line with the D.I.Y. ethos found in HCH's work, uses humour, cut and paste sampling, and a microphone stance that can only be characterized as informal, to address their public. Their tracks often leave the listener waiting for a verse to begin as layers of samples and musical abstractions give way to vocal booth chit-chat and in-jokes. When the two MCs, Fuckit and Archangelos, finally begin to rhyme, the result is also inimitably Cypriot, but much friendlier than anything by HCH. They effortlessly and without a hint of self-consciousness use colloquial speech in humorous rhymes about Greek Cypriot society, easing the audience in by befriending them and making them smile. Their debut album is extremely reminiscent of early De La Soul[16] (specifically *Three Feet High and Rising*), and blends the techniques of that young De La Soul sound with the irreverence of Greek hip-hop group Imiskoumbria, presenting GCD as a perfect vehicle for light-hearted and witty verses that win you over first and then make you think.

In the eighth track of the album 'Funky Káttos' they play on the literal and slang connotations of the lexical item *káttos* (GCD for 'cat'), consciously blurring the lines between the human and feline worlds. Each MC takes on the persona of a local stray cat and proceeds to describe his daily experiences in the neighbourhood, dozing in the shade and trying to get fed by the local housewives. The song plays with cultural stereotypes, such as the laid back Cypriot attitude and indolent highly sexed lifestyle, transforming these notions into the daily experience of a cat relaxing by day, and his nocturnal antics while on the prowl for a mate by night. As with most of the album, the song, in true hip-hop style, is a cultural collage, juxtaposing wedding march samples with jazz piano, saxophone, scratching, nursery rhymes and heavy metal (these stylistic variations are announced throughout the song by the utterance αλλαγή!

**211**

(*alagi!*, 'change!' or 'switch!'). The song also employs code-switching into English, as in the following example by MC Fuckit:[17]

(4)  *Τζιαι όταν τελειώνω που τες*   'And when I finish from my
     *βρώμικές μου business*         dirty business

     *Κάμνω break να φάω Kit-Kat*   I have a break to have a Kit-Kat'

                                    P.O.T.S., 'Funky Káttos'

P.O.T.S. often present the listener with popular culture references that will immediately be understood by Cypriot listeners, such as the scenario of a cat hanging around Zorpas, a well-known bakery franchise on the island, in the hope that it will find a bite to eat. As the song progresses the lyrical switches between the feline and human worlds disappear and guest rapper Felix makes a critique of Cypriot culture at large, along similar lines to 'Módha' (examples 1–3 above), but with an entirely different approach. Having gained the attention of their listeners with funny, friendly rhymes, popular culture references, and a smorgasbord of sounds, they finally go in for the kill:

(5)  *Σκλάβοι στη μόδα τζιαι σε κάθε*   'Slaves to fashion and every
     *επιχείρηση*                       kind of business

     *Ρε κάττες αντιδράστε, εγινήκετε*  'Hey cats react, you've
     *διαφήμιση*                        become a commercial

     *Σκλάβοι στα λεφτά, δουλειά,*      Slaves to money, work, God,
     *Θεός, κομματοποίηση*             party politics

     *Πού εν η δημοκρατία, εν είμαστεν*  Where is democracy? We're
     *βλάκες, πάρτε το είδηση*         not stupid, take note'

                                       P.O.T.S., 'Funky Káttos'

The piece concludes with:

(6)  *Τράβα πίσω που τες μάζες*   'Pull back from the masses like
     *όπως κάμνουμεν τζιαι μεις*   we do

     *Πιασ' τα σωστά τζιαι τα*     Take the rights and the wrongs
     *λάθη τζιαι αμφισβήτα τα*     and question them to see
     *να δεις*

     *Δεξιά αριστερά μια*          Right or left only hypocrisy will
     *υποκρισία εννά μείνει*       remain

     *Φερ' τα μίλια σου μελέτα*    Pull up your socks study yourself
     *τον εαυτό σου που εννά*      instead of judging!'
     *κρίνεις*

                                   P.O.T.S., 'Funky Káttos'

This last line is shouted at the listener in mock hardcore style reminiscent of the delivery already explored in 'Módha' and emphasized by audio effects, but is immediately smoothed out and addressed by Fuckit who responds: *E παιδί μου, χαλάρωσε* ('Hey mate, relax').

DNA as already mentioned is the only hip-hop group on the island to have officially released tracks in GCD. 'Kypriakí Pragmatikótita' ('Cypriot Reality') is one of the two tracks from their 2006 *Frequencies* EP that features the use of GCD throughout and is perhaps the most widely known 'Cypriot track'. In 'Cypriot Reality', DNA sample a traditional Zeibekiko instrumental by Cypriot-born composer Manos Loizos, called 'Evdokía'.[18] The track is up-tempo, necessitating a far quicker delivery by Decayer and MehaHz who spit rapid verses over thumping beats, bouzouki loops and scratching. Unlike the other tracks being discussed here, the song seems not to have a core concept, but rather has both MCs switching between lyrical bravado, critique on hip hop and Cypriot culture, while liberally seasoning their verses with words and phrases from the GCD. The best way to describe what takes place in 'Cypriot Reality' is to quote a line by MegaHz:

(7) *Εν ο Decayer τζιαι ο MegaHz*   'It's Decayer and MegaHz
    *κάμνουν καρκασιαλίκι*     mucking around.'

                    DNA, 'Kypriakí Pragmatikótita'

*Καρκασιαλίκι* (*karkashallikki*) is colloquial for 'noise', 'fuss'. The choice of this word is perfect here as it is also inimitably Cypriot. This is precisely what both MCs are doing on 'Cypriot Reality'; a conceptually loose musical free-for-all where their producer Mush creates the space for both MCs to play with the GCD, hopping from notion to notion in stream of consciousness style as many hip-hop songs are known to do. So with this approach you have Decayer saying:

(8) *Είμαι μοδάτος αλλά λαλώ*   'I'm stylish, but I say down with
    *κάτω το κράτος*           the state

    . . .                   . . .

    *Τζιαι θα βάλλω φωθκιά*   And I'll set fire to the school
    *κάθε χρόνο στο σχολείο*   every year

    *Πέρκι κρούσει πιον το*     Hopefully the decrepit thing
    *γέριμο τζ' έκαμα τη λαχείο*  burns down and I'll have won
                    the lottery

    . . .                   . . .

    *Έτσι περίπου έχουν τα*    That's roughly how things are in
    *πράγματα στη νέα κοινωνία*  the new society

**213**

*Ούλλα εν χωσμένα πίσω που*   Everything is hidden under a
*μιαν πατανία*   blanket.'

DNA, 'Kypriakí Pragmatikótita'

One of Mazud DiAngelo's two Cypriot tracks to date, '84 Boom', takes a completely different route to ingratiating itself with the listener, being both an anti-drug song and a parody of one at the same time. Instead of hortatory sermonizing on the evils of using illicit substances, Mazud presents them as rather played-out and boring, judging their users as sad followers toying with their own mental health. But these conclusions are only drawn after he makes it clear that he himself has dabbled extensively: [19]

(9)  *Ε ναι ρε κουμπάρε εδοκίμασα*   'Well, yeah man I've tried
*τζ 'εγώ ναρκωτικά, εδοκίμασα*   drugs as well, I've tried as
*τζ 'εγώ (μα ποιά;)*   well (Which ones?)

*Εν εκατάλαβα πάντως ίντα 'ν*   I don't get why everybody
*που κάμνουν παναΰρι*   makes such a big deal

*Ήμουν πέντε μέρες τά νγκα*   For five days, boing-boing,
*τούνγκα αππηητούρι*   I was jumping up and down

*Το μόνον που θυμούμαι ήταν*   All I remember was happiness
*σίλια ευτυχία*   going at a thousand

*(Αλλά τζείνον πρέπει*   (But that must've been the
*να 'ταν το Βάλιουμ πιστέφκω*   Valium I believe personally).'
*προσωπικά)*

Mazud DiAngelo, '84 Boom'

Indeed the honesty of his advice and what he would consider an illicit substance are all called into question before the song even begins, and at each interval between the choruses, when the sound of him and his companions falling about laughing echoes through the speakers. The way he confronts the listener also goes beyond the informalities of hip-hop address. The home-made sound of the song, its head-throbbing synths, the intermittent fits of laughter, the focus on a very specific group of young men born in 1984 who served their military service in series B, as well as the way he uses the GCD as if speaking directly to someone in the room with him, are all features that create a sense of solidarity with the listener, something that would have been impossible to pull off with a Cypriot audience if he had chosen to rap in SMG. Another technique he uses, that most young Cypriots will be very familiar with, is the simple two-line chorus that is shouted in much the

**214**

same way as a football chant is, and is repeated frequently throughout to demand recitation:

(10) *Ογδοντατέσσερα βήτα ως*    'Eighty-four B all the way to
    *τζιαι το εφτά, έμαθαν οι*    seven, the kids have all learnt
    *μητσιοί τα ναρκωτικά*    about drugs

    *Ογδοντατέσσερα βήτα ως*    Eighty-four b all the way to
    *τζιαι το εννιά εννά μείνουσιν*   nine, they're all going to be
    *ούλλοι με ψυχολογικά*    left with psychological issues.'

Mazud DiAngelo, '84 Boom'

Finally we come to 'En Eshis Ipothesi' ('You're Useless'), a singular Cypriot hip-hop track that may never be repeated. The idea was shared with rapper Nitro by Ponokéfalos, who gave him a copy of 'Brooklyn Zoo' in the hope that he would use GCD to create something similar to the unique sound of American rapper Ol' Dirty Bastard.[20] This is precisely what Nitro went on to do and the result is rather compelling. The reason 'En Eshis Ipothesi' is such an interesting track is the fact that it has been conceived and purposefully executed as a cultural hybrid. It recognizes certain perceived stereotypical attributes of GCD, such as its harsh sound, low prestige, rudeness and vulgarity, and marries them with the ever distinctive style and technique of the late Ol' Dirty Bastard, who is also famous for exhibiting all of the above traits. His lyrical style can also be described as drunken: words are sometimes slurred, often moving in and out of sync with the beat, his pitch is strangled and jumps wildly depending on how much force a statement is uttered with. The mixture of these unexpected changes of pace and pitch creates the sense of someone quite threatening and slightly unhinged, causing Bradley to describe Ol' Dirty as a 'clown prince' (2009, p. 123) and his style as 'predictability of the unpredictable' (2009, p. 199). Nitro does well to point to this, finding the style ideal for voicing all those vitriolic antagonisms GCD seems to be able to produce so convincingly and with such ferocity. The song is essentially a battle track, its sole purpose being to devastate the person or persons Nitro's scorn is aimed at.[21] This is precisely what he accomplishes, cramming more Cypriot colloquialisms, pronunciations, and insults per bar than almost anyone who has come before in Cypriot hip hop. In fact, listeners who do not even speak the language but who have a certain degree of hip-hop proficiency will instantly recognize the track as inspired by Ol' Dirty Bastard.

Like all good hip hop, 'En Eshis Ipothesi' uses the global to give voice to the local, the track being stuffed full of very specific local references. Among these, the image of being head-butted by a *Zita* (a motorbike police officer), Fontana juices, the Limassol suburb of Ekali and Limassol's dried-out Germasoia river.

(11) *Να φκεις πάνω; Κάτσε κάτω*   'Trying to step up? Sit down
     *ρε μεν φάεις τον πάτσο ρε*   before you get slapped

     *Που τον κόσμον που*   By the crowd who've paid,
     *επκιέρωσεν, εν σε ζήτησεν*   they didn't ask for you

     *Ακόμα εν έμαθες τίποτε*   You still haven't learned anything

     *Γι'αυτό κάτσε έσσω σου, φά*   So stay at home, eat your
     *τα cornflakes σου*   cornflakes

     *Γέμωσε τες κόλλες σου με του*   Fill your pages with your
     *κλάμα σου, άκου σου!*   tears, listen to you!

     *Θέλεις τζιαι μικρόφωνον;*   And you want a microphone?
     *Μάθε πρώτα ίνταλος άφκει*   First learn how to turn the
     *το μαυροσκότεινο*   cursed thing on

     *Ξαπόλα το!*   Let go of it!'

                          Nitro, 'En Eshis Ipothesi'

In true Ol' Dirty style, Nitro concludes the track by repeating the same words over and over again, with slight variation. Speaking directly to inferior MCs he says: [22]

(12) *Αχάπαρε MC 'ντα 'ν που*   'Clueless MC what the devil do you
     *θκιάολο θέλεις;*   want?'

     *Ζιλικούρτι να φκάλεις,*   *Zilikourti* on you! You're hopeless!'
     *εν έσιεις υπόθεση*

                          Nitro, 'En Eshis Ipothesi'

In conclusion, the 'Cypriot track' still seems to be something of a novelty in Cypriot hip hop, with artists experimenting with ways to circumvent attitudes towards GCD and get their listeners on board. A variety of tactics are employed to this end: befriending and entertaining the listener with the use of story-telling, insider language and local references, as in the case of P.O.T.S., Mazud DiAngelo and to some extent Nitro; focusing on the creation of a strong rhythmic backbone conducive to the dance-floor, and using this as a vehicle for experimental word-play, as in the case of DNA; proving GCD's expressiveness by using it in a traditional hip-hop test of lyrical skill, the battle, as in the case of 'Eneshis Ipothesi'; or, finally, applying uncompromising punk sensibilities and rubbing it in the face of the listener as HCH have

**216**

been shown to do. The styles and techniques are many but the goal is one: to reprogram the listener into not only accepting GCD as a hip-hop language, but also seeking it out and actively demanding it.

## 7 Final thoughts

While researching this study I started compiling a list of official and unofficial releases, and was utterly bemused by the poverty of native speech in Cyprus's official hip-hop discography. It seems to directly fly in the face of that oldest of hip-hop mainstays: that you should express yourself in the way you do in everyday life, unguarded, and never edit yourself for the benefit of your audience. Not only this: you should also, in the act of producing cultural artefacts, give credence and weight and validity to everything that can be expressed as local. This is what I understand to be the essence of keeping it real. Of course Cyprus's language (and indeed cultural) situation is far more complex. Cyprus is an ancient place, but a relatively new state, having only just emerged from the yoke of a myriad of colonial powers into the divided island you see before you today.[23] Modern Cyprus has been born in the midst of enormous global changes and influences that are constantly challenging the idea of what Cypriotness really is.

As Ioannou (2004) and Papapavlou (1998) have demonstrated, native speakers, from a young age, regard the use of GCD as more comfortable and natural to them, even though they clearly state that they also regard it as inappropriate and rude. These perspectives are what have helped shape the dynamics of that official hip-hop discography. If GCD was as desirable and fashionable a vernacular as, say, African American English (AAE) is, I doubt there would be a question in the minds of Cypriot lyricists when putting their pens to their rhyme books, regardless of how they have been educated or in which language variety their mail arrives. Then again, in the case of AAE, it is really the rappers who have helped make this so, something which has still to occur in the case of GCD.

It also has to be noted that the present situation must create a strange conflict in the mind of the Cypriot listener. While it is likely that much of the Cypriot population will regard lyrics recited in GCD as peasant, or even vulgar, it would also seem that the adoption of SMG by Cypriot hip-hop artists, in an attempt to neutralize these negative perceptions, may also amputate certain key features that their work should have. Hip hop has always been about immediacy, about addressing the youth of your community first. But how can this be done convincingly when the way you address them instantly marks you out as foreign to them? How can you get in with them if you refuse to speak their lingo?

Tsiplakou et al. (2006) point out that to Greek Cypriots SMG remains: 'a level of standardizing speech deemed appropriate for use only with SMG speakers, and otherwise open to criticism if used with in-group members' (reported in Terkourafi, 2007, p. 81). Since these in-group members are precisely the audience of the hip-hop artist in question, how is that constant oscillation between the Interior and the Exterior to be bridged? These are questions still being wrestled with by Cyprus's hip-hop community and it will be fascinating to see what answers they eventually provide. As Hebdige presciently pointed out three decades ago, coincidentally at the same time the first rap records were emerging from the inner cities of New York, '[i]f we emphasize integration and coherence at the expense of dissonance and discontinuity, we are in danger of denying the very manner in which the subcultural form is made to crystallize, objectify and communicate group experience' (1979, p. 79).

Today you will find GCD used in writing more than ever before, but not in newspapers or even in the arts: the place you are most likely to find the greatest amount of GCD used on a regular basis is on the internet and on people's mobile phones. As I type this, thousands of conversations are being conducted in GCD by SMS, instant messaging, forum and blog posts (ironically most of these are typed in Roman characters). This can only give us a clue as to the vitality of GCD, but whether or not this vitality will ever be reflected elsewhere remains to be seen. Hip hop, as I understand it, ought to be ahead of the curve, it should break new ground and sow seeds. In the above respect Cypriot hip hop has largely failed to reflect Cypriot experience. The fact that GCD up until now has had little or no place in Cypriot hip hop's official discography says precious little about its vitality as a dialect, though it speaks volumes about the cultural mores of the moment and the unwillingness of today's hip-hop artists to challenge them.

It will be very interesting to observe how Cyprus's language situation will evolve in the near future, and indeed whether its burgeoning hip-hop scene will reflect or challenge these changes. It is unlikely that the youth will ever stop putting rhymes to beats, but the ways in which they do so will be fascinating to observe as a new generation of hip-hop kids pick up the mic and attempt to address one another.

## Notes

1. Afrika Bambaataa is often referred to as the 'Godfather' of hip-hop culture and 'Master of Records'. He was instrumental in the early development of hip hop and its propagation throughout the world. He founded the Universal Zulu Nation in the 1970s, managing to involve many former gang

members in an attempt to inspire a sense of community, getting them to channel their energies into other, more productive enterprises. These included organizing cultural events and bringing together the various arts, such as dance and graffiti, which were later to become the elements of hip-hop culture.

2. Mattison, S. *Isle of Rhyme aka Bare Means A Lot – Part 2 of 3*, 06 May 2007, (<http://www.youtube.com/watch?v=rmWvKgRj7Ao&feature=channel>, accessed 29 August 2009).

3. Low-Bap is a musical off-shoot of Greek hip hop that began to emerge in the mid 1990s as hip-hop culture really began to take root in Greece. Low-Bap is characterized by slower tempos and heavier beats, often acoustic instrumentation and an emphasis on socially and politically aware, as well as poetic lyrics. Its founder, Greek rapper and producer B. D. Foxmoor, is also the founding member of the group Active Member, Low-Bap's main exponent.

4. Boom-Bap is simply the sound of the heavy bass drum, and thick snare that characterizes many early hip-hop records. Many people refer to Boom-Bap as the original, old-school hip hop. The term was popularized by KRS-One's seminal first solo album, *The Return of the Boom-Bap*, released in 1993.

5. The exact figure of 789,300 refers only to residents of the Republic of Cyprus's government controlled area. Source: *Demographic Report 2007*, Statistical Service of the Republic of Cyprus. <http://www.pio.gov.cy/mof/cystat/statistics.nsf/All/A99C11748F366966C22575D300315734?OpenDocument&sub=1&e=>, accessed 10 July 2009.

6. Throughout this chapter, I use the term Greek Cypriot Dialect (GCD) to refer to the variety of Greek spoken natively in Cyprus. Although researchers have placed this at various points along the language-dialect continuum, I regard it as a dialect as do most Cypriots, and a lot of the existing literature on the subject refers to it as such. For a recent analysis of the relationship of the Cypriot variety of Greek to Standard Modern Greek (SMG), see Terkourafi (2007).

7. Although the GCD is not the outcome of creolization, it has undergone multiple processes of language contact and koineization (for a historical overview, see Terkourafi, 2005). As a result, a spectrum ranging from basilectal (most local) to acrolectal (approximating the Athenian Standard) varieties are spoken on the island, while the situation today has been described as a 'post-diglossic' continuum (Tsiplakou et al., 2006). I use 'basilectal' here to highlight the non-standard and low-prestige aspects of the GCD as opposed to SMG.

8. www.hiphop.com.cy provides an archive where many of these articles can be found. It is also a resource providing information on all things involving hip hop in Cyprus. At the time of writing all five tracks discussed in this study are available for free download from this site.

9. According to the Constitution of 1960 that established its independence, the Republic of Cyprus has two official languages, Greek and Turkish. However, the variety of Greek intended is not specified (at the time, *Katharevousa*, the High variety, was in official use in Greece), while, since the 1974 invasion

and *de facto* division of the population that followed, the use of Turkish has been limited to some official state documents, such as passports and identity cards.

10. Cyprus is a former British colony; as a result the UK has a large Greek Cypriot population.

11. The term 'unofficial' makes the task of compiling a comprehensive list of these releases problematic at best, but the situation can be thought of as no different to the limited edition vinyl releases (often limited to as little as 500 copies) that have been the life-blood of other scenes throughout Europe in the past – the difference here consisting in the absence of a vinyl-buying public or many options of distribution.

12. The word 'match' in GCD is τσαττίζει (*chattízi*), which also refers to a traditional Cypriot form of improvisational oral poetry called τσαττιστά (*chattistá*), P.O.T.S. seem to be using the word consciously here to draw attention to parallels between traditional Cypriot culture and hip hop. For an in-depth look at *chattistá*, see Doukanari (1997).

13. On the emergence of Cypriot Standard Greek see Arvaniti (in press), and for discussion see Terkourafi (2007, pp. 81–83).

14. Συνέντευξη απο τους HCH. ('HCH Interview', March 2006), <http://www.hiphop.com.cy/interviews/hch.html>, accessed 18 August 2009.

15. Ρουφκιάνα (*roufkiána*) is more commonly used in the masculine as ρουφκιάνος (*roufkiános*) and is generally thought to be a person of dubious moral standing, an informer, or quite literally someone who sucks. 'Private' in the same line refers to sexual services in a private room, while the 'Statue' below refers to a popular spot where prostitutes congregate in the capital, Nicosia.

16. De La Soul are an American hip-hop group famous for their playful, intricate lyrics that tend to steer clear of hip-hop clichés such as drugs, guns and violence. Their first album *Three Feet High and Rising* was released in 1989, produced by Prince Paul it featured eclectic sampling and off-beat subject matter and is now hailed as a hip-hop classic.

17. The second line in example (4) is a reference to a popular European ad campaign for the candy bar Kit Kat.

18. Ζεϊμπέκικο (*zeibekiko*) is an urban improvisational dance common in Greece and areas around the world with large Greek populations. It is danced by one man (or, most recently, woman) at a time, and is considered an intensely personal dance where people can express their individuality. It may also include performing feats such as standing on a glass of wine or a chair or fireplace, or picking up a table, adding a sense of braggadocio and humour.

19. Αππηητούρι (*appiitúri*, glossed here as 'boing boing') is a small hopping insect.

20. 'Brooklyn Zoo' is Ol' Dirty Bastard's debut single from his solo album *Return to the 36 Chambers*. He was a member of the New York collective the Wu Tang Clan that still remain one of the most memorable hip-hop crews to date. Ol' Dirty died in 2004 of a drug overdose.

21. Battle tracks are typically composed of energetic, antagonistic verses, used in hip-hop music as displays of lyrical dexterity and quick-wittedness. They have evolved from the typical bravado that is found on many hip-hop songs into a specific type of hip-hop track, focused solely on intelligent use of insults and word play. The battle-verse has developed parallel to MC battles which are live improvisational displays of these skills. Often two rappers who have a 'beef' with one another will fight it out by releasing battle songs, specifically geared at making the other look ridiculous. As with many live battles, the audience decides who wins.

22. Ζιλικούρτι (*zilikourti*) is thought to have entered GCD from Turkish (Hadjiioannou, 1996, p. 66) and is quite a severe curse, one of the insults to really have retained all of its original vehemence in the Cypriot dialect, although not many people know exactly what it means. Usually it is used as a very vulgar way of telling someone to shut up; it curses the recipient to catch a plague-like disease that permanently shuts them up.

23. Cyprus became a republic in 1960, after fighting to free itself from British colonial rule. Escalating tensions between its Greek and Turkish communities, and an attempt by Greek Cypriot nationalists (backed by Greece's military junta) to overthrow the republic's first president Archbishop Makarios, and to unify the island with Greece, led to the Turkish invasion of 1974 and division of the island.

# References

Androutsopoulos, J. (2003), 'Ο ραψωδός που θέλεις να φτάσεις: γλωσσικές στρατηγικές πολιτισμικής οικειοποίησης στο ελληνόφωνο rap', ['The poet you want to reach: linguistic strategies of cultural appropriation in Greek rap'], in *Proceedings of the 6th International Conference of Greek Linguistics*, pp. 18–21.

Androutsopoulos, J. and Sholz, A. (2003), 'Spaghetti funk: appropriations of hip hop culture in Europe'. *Popular Music and Society*, 26, 4, 463–479.

Arvaniti, A. (in press), 'Linguistic practices in Cyprus and the emergence of Cypriot Standard Greek'. *Mediterranean Language Review*.

Bradley, A. (2009), *Book of Rhymes: The Poetics of Hip Hop*. New York: Basic Civitas.

Chang, J. (2007), *Can't Stop Won't Stop: A History of the Hip hop Generation*. New York: Ebury Press.

Cutler, C. (2007), 'Hip hop language in sociolinguistics and beyond'. *Language and Linguistics Compass*, 5, 1, 519–538.

Doukanari, E. (1997), 'The Presentation of Gendered Self In Cyprus Rhyming Improvisations: A Sociolinguistic Investigation of Kipriaka Chattista in Performance'. Unpublished PhD dissertation, Georgetown University.

Drou, N. (2007), 'Yanking it (or "pimps don't fake accents")', *UKHH.COM: Original UK HipHop*, 27 February. <http://www.ukhh.com/features/articles/yanking_it/yanking_it.html>, accessed 4 June 2009.

Garrett, P. (2001), 'Language attitudes and sociolinguistics'. *Journal of Sociolinguistics*, 5, 4, 626–631.

Hadjiioannou, K. (1996), *Ετυμολογικό λεξικό της Ομιλούμενης Κυπριακής Διαλέκτου* ['Etymological Dictionary of the Spoken Cypriot Dialect']. Nicosia: Tamassos.

Hare, G. (2003), 'Popular music on French radio and television', in S. Cannon and H. Dauncey (eds), *Popular Music in France from Chanson to Techno: Culture, Identity, and Society*. Aldershot UK: Ashgate, pp. 57–76.

Hebdige, D. (1979), *Subculture: The Meaning of Style*. New York: Routledge.

Ioannou, E. (2004), 'On language and ethnic identity among Greek Cypriot students'. *The Cyprus Review*, 16, 1, 28–51.

Kelley, R. D. G. (2006), 'Foreword', in D. Basu and S. J. Lemelle (eds), *The Vinyl Ain't Final: Hip Hop and the Globalization of Black Popular Culture*. Ann Arbour, Michigan: Pluto Books, pp. xi–xvii.

Papapavlou, A. N. (1998), 'Attitudes toward the Greek Cypriot dialect: sociocultural implications'. *International Journal of the Sociology of Language*, 134, 15–28.

Papapavlou, A. and Sophocleous, A. (forthcoming), 'Language attitudes and folk perceptions towards linguistic variation', in M. Karyolemou, P. Pavlou and S. Tsiplakou (eds), *Studies in Language Variation – European Perspectives II*. Selected papers from ICLaVE 4. Amsterdam: John Benjamins.

Pavlou, P. (2004), 'Greek dialect use in the mass media in Cyprus'. *International Journal of the Sociology of Language*, 168, 101–118.

Pavlou, P. and Papapavlou, A. (2004), 'Issues of dialect use in education from the Greek-Cypriot perspective'. *International Journal of Applied Linguistics*, 14, 2, 243–258.

Potter, R. A. (1995), *Spectacular Vernaculars: Hip hop and the Politics of Postmodernism*. New York: State University of New York Press.

Terkourafi, M. (2005), 'Understanding the present through the past: processes of koineisation on Cyprus'. *Diachronica*, 22, 2, 309–372.

—(2007), 'Perceptions of difference in the Greek sphere: the case of Cyprus'. *Journal of Greek Linguistics*, 8, 60–96.

Trudgill Peter (1983), 'Acts of conflicting identity. The sociolinguistics of British pop-song pronunciation', in P. Trudgill (ed.), *On Dialect: Social and Geographical Perspectives*. Oxford: Blackwell, pp. 141–160.

Tsiplakou, S. (2007), 'Language variation and critical pedagogy: correlations and educational implications', in I. G. Matsagouras (ed.) *Classroom Literacy: Functional, Critical, and Scientific*. Athens: Grigoris, pp. 466–511 (in Greek).

Tsiplakou, S., Papapavlou, A., Pavlou, P. and Katsoyannou, M. (2006), 'Levelling, koineization and their implications for bidialectism', in F. Hinskens (ed.), *Language Variation: European Perspectives: Selected papers from the Third International Conference on Language Variation in Europe (ICLaVE 3)*, Amsterdam: John Benjamins, pp. 265–276.

# 9 Hip Hop, Ethnicity and Linguistic Practice in Rural and Urban Norway

Endre Brunstad, Unn Røyneland and Toril Opsahl

## 1 Introduction

Several studies have made connections between hip hop and globalization (Mitchell, 2001; Klein, 2003; Androutsopoulos and Scholz, 2003; Penny-cook, 2007), placing particular emphasis on the dialectics between the global and the local (Lull, 1995; Androutsopoulos, 2006; Dyndahl, 2008). This chapter will delve into global-local relations as they have developed in Norwegian hip hop during the 2000s. Since 2000, Norwegian hip hop has been characterized by a strong Norwegian-language scene. At the same time, English is also used, and we find an abundance of English loanwords and code-switching, as well as references to the American basis for hip hop. One interesting feature of Norwegian hip hop is its connections to rural lifestyles and rural dialects. Some hip-hop artists such as Side Brok have achieved success by using aesthetic elements connected to Norwegian rurality. Considering the traditional affinity between hip hop and urban lifestyle with its street culture and ghettos, rural hip hop is a rather remarkable phenomenon (cf. Klein, 2003, p. 22). On the other hand, we have seen the emergence of ethnically mixed urban hip-hop groups, particularly in Oslo, making use of various languages in their lyrics, though with Norwegian at the core. For some of these groups, such as Minoritet1, this linguistic practice appears to be part of a self-conscious development of a new, Norwegian multiethnolectal speech style. Moreover, this linguistic phenomenon is not restricted to performers. A significant connection seems to exist between the linguistic practices found among adolescents in multilingual settings in Oslo and affiliation to hip-hop culture.

These two expressions of hip hop in Norway – rural hip hop on the one hand and urban, multiethnic hip hop on the other – indicate a multifaceted way of how hip hop has spread and become localized, and thereby also how it is to be regarded as an aspect of globalization. Both of the approaches in this chapter will focus on the way language

**223**

stylization creates new forms of linguistic identification together with new forms of activities and new sets of linguistic features.

In the next section we briefly discuss some general relations between hip hop and globalization and present four notions of globalization to which the global-local relations are of relevance. Following that, we outline some of the developments regarding hip hop in Norway and give examples of how Norwegian rap relates to global text cultural frames of rap. The use of dialects is considered in this context and an analysis of rural hip hop is provided with specific emphasis on the group Side Brok. From rural hip hop, we turn our focus to multilingual urban hip hop and the emergence of new speech styles. Here we consider various examples drawn from an ongoing study of linguistic practices in multilingual settings in Oslo and analyse the lyrics of two hip-hop crews. We argue that hip hop has a significant influence on the formation of a Norwegian multietholectal speech style. Finally, we suggest that glocalization is a highly valuable concept for the study of the transformation and local adoption of hip hop, but at the same time we emphasize the need for a broader understanding of this concept.

## 2 Hip hop and globalization

In Norway, as in other Nordic countries, there has been a public debate on issues relating to language globalization (meaning the relationship between languages of the Nordic countries and linguistic flow). If we look at the general understanding of globalization as it is reflected in this debate, we may identify four areas of concern in which we also find some general notions of globalization itself: (1) globalization as diffusion; (2) globalization as global fight; (3) globalization as multiculturalism and (4) globalization as glocalization (Brunstad, 2006). As ideal types (in the Weberian sense) these four notions may be fruitful as entrances for studying the relationship between hip hop and globalization.

The notion of globalization as 'diffusion' suggests that a global language culture is developed just once, from one source, and then spread to the rest of the world by transmission from people to people. This general view on cultural development is, in its extreme form, considered 'dead' (Barnard, 2000, p. 183). The reason for this is, first of all, the general insight from anthropology and cultural studies that the same ideas and phenomena may be invented by different groups of people. Furthermore, cultural phenomena may change radically as a result of the transmission process. However, diffusionist approaches have in fact been revitalized by globalization theory and its focus on cultural flow around the world (Barnard, 2000, p. 54). Also, critical approaches to cultural hegemony and domination may contain aspects of diffusionism. This is the case, for instance, when The Norwegian Language Board gives suggestions for more comprehensive language planning in its report *Norsk i hundre*: 'Globalization is basically a one-way-process in which concepts and products developed within an Anglo-American cultural sphere are spread to the rest of the world' (*Språkrådet*, 2005, p. 13, our translation). With respect to hip hop, diffusionist views are found in studies focusing on the roots of hip hop, claiming that all types of hip hop around the world actually are derived from African American culture (Bozza, 2003, p. 130). According to this view, African American culture is considered to be *the* original and authentic hip hop. Such a view is also found in Norway and is referred to in, e.g., Opsahl's discussion of the African American oral traditions (Opsahl, 2000). However, the essential link between hip hop and African American culture has been challenged by studies focusing on the local transformation of hip hop around the world (Mitchell, 2001).

The idea of globalization as a 'global fight' stems from the diffusionist view, but furthermore suggests that in order to survive, local or national language culture ought to resist globalization in terms of diffusion from an Anglo-American culture and the monolingual spread of the English language (Phillipson, 1999, p. 274). This view is based on an understanding of globalization without resistance as more or less equivalent to imperialism, colonialism and hegemony. From a political point of view, the so-called anti-globalization movement is first of all critical to the global spread of neo-liberalism. In this movement we also find hip-hop artists. One example is the Norwegian group Gatas Parlament which has a clear left-wing statement and has been prominent in different political activities since its formation in 1993. Their 2006 song 'Antiamerikansk dans' ('Anti-American dance') attracted a lot of attention as it was connected to a video and a website, www.killhim.nu ('kill him now'), which claimed to collect money in order to assassinate US President George W. Bush.

Mitchell (2001, pp. 21–22) argues that the use of local and regional speech in hip hop may also play a role in the global fight. As a form of 'resistance vernacular' (Potter, 1995), this speech is 'in opposition to a perceived U.S. cultural imperialism in rap and hip hop' (Mitchell, 2001, p. 22). If we also accept Potter's view that hip hop's best way of addressing social resistance 'takes place on the level of language' (1995, p. 17), the best way of analysing the political potentiality of hip hop lies in analysing the way language is used. From this point of view, it is also relevant to take into account new cultural and linguistic forms in which both the global and the local are changed, as is the case with multi-ethnolectal speech styles within hip hop.

**225**

The notion of globalization as 'multiculturalism' may be summarized as 'living together separately'. Ideologically, it is based on political support for cultural, ethnic and linguistic variation (within a demographic setting such as a nation-state, a region, or a city) and it is connected to particular attention to the Other's integrity, that is, the idea that each language culture has the right to live side by side with the global language culture, e.g., by bilingualism or by specialization to pre-assigned domains. With respect to hip hop, multiculturalism is often connected to the role of subcultures in postmodern societies. An interesting aspect of subcultures, as it is outlined by Hebdige (1979), is that they are oriented towards activities that are not localized in time and space: their focus is on style and style-related practice and behaviour (cf. Preisler, 1999a, p. 117). It is also through style that subcultures have an impact on mainstream culture. The notion of English 'from below' (Preisler, 1999a; 1999b), for instance, suggests that English is spread from subcultures like hip hop to mainstream culture because of their status and style. The general role of subcultures is also of interest with respect to the role of hip hop in the development of multiethnolects. However, one effect of multiculturalism's focus on diversity and each culture's autonomy is that cultures are often being regarded – at least implicitly – as incommensurable, ignoring the changing of their boundaries and the mixing of cultures and languages in which new identities and new forms of practice are created.

Finally, much attention has been paid over the last few years to Roland Robertson's (1995) concept of 'glocalization'. This concept portrays globalization as a dynamic process combining elements of the global and the local with regards to both language culture and linguistic elements. Connell and Gibson (2003, p. 328), however, argue that the term 'glocal' indicates a rather static relation between the global and the local and prefer the terms 'fluidity' (which refers to the global flow of music) and 'fixity' (which refers to spaces, tradition and local expressions). Pennycook supports Connell and Gibson and labels the term 'glocal' as 'trite' (2009, p. 328). From our point of view, we need to see the relations between global and local in a broader sense, as a process of fixity and fluidity, as a process of change, which also gives possibilities for new forms of identification.

## 3 Hip hop and regionality in Norway

The starting point of hip hop in Norway is quite easy to identify, namely the summer of 1984 when the movie *Beat Street* was shown at Norwegian cinemas. Then hip hop emerged, first as breakdance and graffiti culture. As breakdancing went out of fashion and graffiti was banned

**226**

by the police, hip hop increasingly became a subculture composed of a limited but hardcore fan base. In this setting, a small Norwegian rap scene emerged. This scene was (with some exceptions) linguistically dominated by English. The artist Diaz explained this by pointing out American culture as the frame of reference:

> When we started there was not talk about other than English texts. The whole culture functioned in English – from graffiti to the b-bending. All words, expressions and moves were in English and were not understood by others than those who kept on with it. It is after all an American culture we are doing, so it's no wonder that we use English. (Diaz, 2000)

In this early period, Norwegian hip hop indicates a rather straight-forward cultural diffusion from the United States of America. Norwegian rap performers such as Tommy Tee and A-Team, used English as their language and American rap was the norm.[1] In spite of some rap in Norwegian both in the 1980s and the 1990s, leading figures of hip hop in Norway did not consider it as serious compared to English (Holen, 2004, p. 41). Some members of the hip-hop community also thought Norwegian was inadequate linguistically; it was too 'choppy' to 'flow' and had too many hard consonant sounds, they claimed (Hole, 1997, p. 57). Such views died out at the beginning of the twenty-first Century when rap in Norwegian had its breakthrough (Hole, 1997, p. 57). Young rap artists interviewed in the period from 2003 to 2009 obviously did not see the consonant sounds of Norwegian as a significant problem (e.g. Brunstad, interview with Gest & Runar Gudnason). References to problems with consonant sounds should therefore be regarded as rationalizations of an established state of affairs.

Around 2000, Norwegian rap went through a phase of 'Norwegiani-zation'. At that time, several artists started using Norwegian as their medium of rapping, instead of English. At the same time we saw the emergence of hip-hop scenes outside Oslo with artists using their own dialects and rapping about their own experiences. Most prominent was the group Tungtvann ('Heavy Water') from the town Bodø in the North of Norway. As pointed out by Danielsen (2008), Tungtvann used many of the same rhetorical tools as American hardcore rap, such as Ice Cube and Public Enemy, but instead of rapping about being marginalized as Black and poor in the USA, Tungtvann were rapping about their members' own experience as geographically and socially marginalized, coming from the Norwegian periphery. Tungtvann also played on stereotypes about people from the North of Norway: that they drink, swear and have more sex than people in other areas of Norway. In this context, Danielsen (2008) has drawn a parallel between the traditional stereotypes about men from the North of Norway (as 'rough', 'barbarian' and 'sexual') with stereotypical beliefs in Black culture, suggesting that the success of Tungtvann (as a pioneer of mother tongue rap in Norway) may also be connected to these recontextualized attributes of African American culture. Tungtvann used their members' own local dialect in the lyrics, such as in their 2002 song 'Pøbla' ('Rabbles'):

(1) *Æ har trakka mine egne*   'I have gone my own, since I was
   *spor, sia æ va en neve stor,*  a little boy (lit. "small as a fist"),
   *stått inne færr det æ har*   stand in for what I have done, no
   *gjort uansett ka æ gjør*    matter what I do'

Tungtvann, 'Pøbla'

In this passage (as it is printed in Tungtvann's album *Mørketid*, 2002), the written form is close to the North Norwegian dialect which means that it has several non-standard elements both with regard to morphology and phonology. The personal pronoun *æ* ('I') is dialectal for standard *jeg* (in Norwegian *Bokmål*), and similarly with *sia* for *siden* ('since'), *va* for *var* ('was'), *ka* for *hva* ('what'), and *førr* for *for* ('for').

## 3.1 Aspects of textual norms and language use in Norwegian rap

Drawing on studies of rap texts from five different European countries, Androutsopoulos and Scholz (2002, p. 10) developed a model for text cultural norms of rap. According to this model, there are seven dominating topics (self-presentation, scene discourse, social critique, contemplation, love/sex, party/fun, and dope) and seven speech act patterns captured in two groups, 'actionality' (self-referential speech, listener-directed speech, boasting, and dissing) and 'localizing' (place/time references, identification, representing). Although that study is now a few years old, their model remains useful to analyse Norwegian rap from 2000 onwards.

Based on a sample of 50 rap texts, we see some clear patterns. The dominating speech act pattern in Norwegian rap, as in rap everywhere, is self-referential speech, just as self-presentation is the dominating topic of rap texts, as in Side Brok's: *Ej heite Thorstein Hyl den tredje* ('My name is Thorstein Hyl the third'). Self-referential speech is also connected to scene discourse with references to the crew of the hip-hop artist, as well as to friends and antagonists such as in Karpe Diem's references to the East and West of Oslo (examples below) and in Tungtvann's critical references to commercial interests within the music scene as in their 2002 track 'Bransjehora' ('Industrial Whores'). Listener-directed speech is also prominent, as in Side Brok's (2004) *alle folka ned på*

**228**

*golve / rist med raua di og dans ned på golve* ('all the people down on the floor / shake your ass and dance on the floor'), as is boasting, as in *dei veit at ej he ørsta stål i ondebrellå* ('they know I got Ørsta steel in my underpants'), again from Side Brok (2006). Boasting is often connected to irony but its effect may be disputable. This is the case when it comes to boasting about sexual conquest of women such as the following line from Tungtvann's 2000 release, 'Jenta fra ifjor' ('The girl from last year'):

(2)  *Trine, Line, Kine og Karoline,*  'Trine, Line, Kine og Karoline,
     *alt de har til felles e kjønns*  all they have in common is my
     *sykdomman mine*  venereal diseases'

Tungtvann, 'Jenta fra ifjor'

This kind of boasting is related to sexism in American hip hop – especially within gangsta rap – in which women often are connected to themes such as prostitution and presented as fake and manipulative, while men are portrayed as players/pimps (Larsen, 2006, p. 53). Such a way of stylizing women has actually been supported by the leading Norwegian hip-hop magazine *King Size*, which claimed that it was part of the genre, and that feminist critics did not understand the irony of hip hop (Brunstad, 2006. p. 52). This view, however, has also been problematized within hip hop itself (ibid.). Asked if it was acceptable to label Black people as 'nigger slaves', the artist Don Martin answered 'of course not'; therefore it should not be acceptable to label women as 'whores', he claimed (Don Martin, 2004). The discussion on this issue, which peaked between 2003 and 2004, may be regarded as an example of the process of indigenization[2] in Norway, and shows that the stylized sexism found in African American gangsta rap was, at least in its pure form, not credible in a society such as Norway in which equality between women and men is highly valued. This, however, does not mean that sexism is non-existent in current Norwegian hip hop. Such modified stylization is interesting in view of what feminists have called a 'pornification' of the public sphere, especially through media and advertising.

The fourth pattern within the actionality group of speech acts patterns, dissing, is not as prominent in Norwegian hip hop (however see section 5 below), perhaps because Norway is a small country and many of the rappers are familiar to each other.

When it comes to localizing speech act patterns, 'place/time references' are quite frequent. The Bergen group Spetakkel (2003) refer to '5005', the zip code for the part of Bergen where the members of Spetakkel came from. Groups like Klovner i Kamp (2001) refer to Tåsen, a part of Oslo, Fremmed Rase (2007) refer to Trondheim, Side Brok (2004, 2006) to Ørsta, Jaa9 and OnklP (2003, 2004) to Lillehammer, and Minoritet1 (2008) to the eastern side of Oslo. The second act of localizing, 'identification', is connected to the ideals of closeness and authenticity in hip hop. This again is frequent in Norwegian hip hop and closely connected to self-presentation (see above). The third act, 'representation', is also frequent, as in Tungtvann's 2002 song 'Ekte menneske' ('Real people') where they refer to themselves as representatives for the whole 'slum' of their area, or their 2000 track 'Reinspikka hip hop' ('Pure hip hop') where the members are 'Representatives from where the midnight sun never goes down'. As with place/time references, representational speech may be regarded as an aspect of the recontextualization process of American hip hop in which we also find references to places, etc.

With respect to topics, direct social critique has not been as prominent in Norwegian rap as, for instance, in French rap (Prévos, 2001). Instead, the dominant topics have been the rapper himself and scene discourse together with love/sex and partying. That does not mean that there has been no politically oriented rap (cf. Gatas Parlament, 1994, 2001, 2004). Rather, social critique has been expressed in more subtle ways (e.g., through references to geographical, social, ethnic and linguistic marginality). We may say that the political potentiality actually lies in the way hip hop is stylized at the level of language (cf. Potter, 1995, p.17; our analysis of Karpe Diem in section 4.3).

The model of text cultural norms as connected to speech act patterns is important for understanding why Norwegian and its dialects have such an important place in Norwegian rap. Text cultural norms clearly seem to underline notions of 'credibility', 'authenticity', 'self experience' and 'belonging to a local place' as cultural values within hip hop. Following these values means that a Norwegian teenager is more likely to rap in Norwegian than in English – and to do so in his own dialect of Norwegian. The role of dialects in Norwegian rap is connected to the general status of dialects in Norway (Røyneland, 2009). Asking members of the Bergen group Spetakkel why they were using the Bergen dialect, they answered: 'Why not? What else should we have done? Rapping in Eastern Norwegian? No, that would just be ridiculous. We would not have been taken seriously' (e.g. Brunstad, interview with members of the group Spetakkel, A-laget and Tungtvann).

In the hip-hop community it seems important to portray the transition from English to Norwegian as part of an internal development within hip hop itself. Several artists have referred to Sweden as a source of inspiration in this respect (Brunstad, interviews with the artists). Artists such as The Latin Kings and Petter showed that it was possible

**230**

to do good hip hop in Swedish and also to have commercial success doing so. In this context it is also worth taking into account the point that membership in subcultures is often interpreted as a conquest (Preisler, 1999a). This comes up in personal interviews when performers explain how they got into hip hop. According to this narrative, the performers discovered and then conquered hip hop, and in this process they found themselves becoming part of hip hop through the Norwegian language. In addition, artists explain how hip hop is conquering them and the rest of society. In the excerpts below, the use of the verb *relatere til* ('to relate to') is revealing in this respect:

> *Plutselig begynte det å komme et par grupper på norsk og det var liksom sånn der, oj, det hørtes, det kan vi relatere til, det kan vi ta inntil oss mye lettere.*
> 'Suddenly a couple of groups appeared, using Norwegian and it was like, oh, it sounded, that is something we can relate to, we can get into this much easier.'
> (Brunstad, interview with Khnokle & Martinez)

> *Med en gang vi gjorde den låten live – vi var på Gimle skole, for 3-400 mennesker – det var akkurat som de relaterte seg mye mer. Du fikk en mye bedre feeling med publikum.*
> 'At once, when we did that song live – we were at Gimle school with about three, four hundred people – it was like they related much more. You got a much better feeling with the audience.'
> (Brunstad, interview with Gest)

> *For at folk kan relatere seg mer til den norske rappen, i Norge då.*
> 'Because people then may relate more to Norwegian rap, in Norway, then.'
> (Brunstad, interview with Khnokle & Martinez)

Norwegian in these examples is considered more 'felt' due to the fact that one can 'relate to' real life through a suitable language. One informant underlines this by saying that 'Nobody's being shot at a driveway in Norway'; therefore it is not felt as 'real' to be rapping in English about killings when you are living as a teenager in suburban or rural Norway.

Norwegian hip hop contains a lot of loanwords, such as 'battle', 'breaking', 'deal', 'DJ', 'chicks', 'writer', 'wannabe', 'muthafucka', 'bitch' (Graedler and Johansson, 1997). Furthermore, we find code-switching between English and Norwegian, often as tag-switching such as 'Fuck it, *mann, du vet ka æ snakka*' ('Fuck it, man, you know how I speak', by *Tungtvann* in their 2000 song 'Undergrunn'). There is also switching between sentences and between parts of texts such as by Karpe Diem (see section 4.3). If we look at the fan core on the internet, one interesting example of code-switching is found in an internet discussion at the website Bergenhiphop.com from the signature Mc Pantha:

(3) TEXTDamn . . .
*Denne festivalen er akkurat det Bergen trenger,*
*Alle mc'ees må samles, fuck the beef!!*
*glem hvem som disset hvem, We gotta show love in the name of*
*hip hop – og det er det KN og klicken prøver å gjøre her, stå på*
*KN, jeg støtter deg 100% ut . . . hvis det er noe jeg kan hjelpe*
*med, så er det bare å ta kontakt, Mc Pantha.*

TEXT**Damn** . . .
This festival is just what Bergen needs
All MCs got to get together, **fuck the beef!!**
forget who was dissing who, We gotta show love in the name
of hip hop – and that is what KN and his crew is trying to do;
keep up the good work, KN, I support you 100% . . . if there is
anything I can do to help, just let me know, MC Pantha.

In this passage we find sentence internal code-switching between English and Norwegian in a context that is Norwegian. The first code-switch, 'TEXTDamn', indicates frustration with the discussion. By saying 'fuck the beef', MC Pantha encourages the one being criticized in this debate not to worry about the complaints, and, through code-switching, gives the impression that there is an internal alliance among people who share this view. The phrase 'We gotta show love in the name of hip hop' bears associations to African American preaching styles (as in, 'We gotta show love in the name of Jesus'). African American culture is used here as a resource, a cultural background with which young people in Norway are familiar through film. Several young informants have claimed that if they were to use English as their medium of rap, it would have been African American English. This does not mean that they will actually do so, and we find no tendency of doing so in Norwegian rap done in English. That young people *say* so is nonetheless characteristic of the special status African American culture does have in hip hop across the globe.

## 3.2 Side Brok and rural hip hop

At the beginning of the 2000s, several of the new hip-hop artists using Norwegian as their language came from the geographical periphery of Norway and made references to this periphery. Following up this trend, the group Side Brok from the village of Hovdebygda in the West of Norway became the most prominent performers of 'rural rap'. Side Brok was rapping about being a Norwegian *rånar* (a Norwegian version of 'redneck' or 'hillbilly'), drinking homemade liquor, and driving their car from one village to the other, as in their 2004 track '1, 2, 3, fyre':

(4)  *Frå vik te volda, volda te vik* — 'From Vik to Volda, Volda to Vik

*å glide heile helga e et jevla slit* — gliding all the weekend is a damn toil

*men nåken må nå gjer det, alle kan lære det* — but somebody has to do it, everyone can learn it

*alt en trenge e en bil og bensinpenge* — all you need is a car and money for gas

*og ei femme . . . eller fem* — and a femme . . . or five

*og en sjåfør så aldri skal heimgjen* — and a driver that never will go home again

*me trenge å bevege oss, aldri stå stille* — we need to move, never stand still

*ront og ront som ei vinylrille* — round and round as in a vinyl record

*me he bilstereo med gode bass* — we have a car stereo with good bass

*og på baksete e der alltit plass* — and in the back there is always a seat

*te ekstra kjekse, ekstra heimeguta* — for extra chicks, extra home boys

*fleire passasjera enn hurtigruta* — more passengers than the Hurtigruta

*fyll på, me trenge litt trengsel* — bring in, we need some crowding

*for snart e det fem nye daga med lengsel* — because soon there are five new days of longing'

Side Brok, '1, 2, 3, fyre'

In this text passage, the geographical places are identified, such as 'Vik' and 'Ørsta', and Side Brok also uses the dialect of these two villages. The cultural setting is also identified with the *rånar* culture of the area (crowded cars, a car stereo with a bass drumming). By overdoing this setting, though, Side Brok makes it a parody of the *rånar* culture,

**233**

especially with the main character of Side Brok's text, Thorstein Hyl, performed by the leader of the group, Runar Gudnason.[3] By using such a character in many of their songs, the authenticity of the group's performance does not need to be connected to Runar Gudnason himself, rather to how likely it is for the character Thorstein Hyl to act in a specific way.

Generally speaking, interpreting parody involves the performers discrediting a cultural practice and positioning themselves outside or above the scene of this cultural practice (Coupland, 2001, p. 175). Such an outside position, however, is not as simple in the case of Side Brok. First, the group are using the dialect of this area as a general tool of communication, not just as an instrument of parody. Even though Side Brok are exaggerating traditional dialectal speech, such as in the nasalized pronunciation of the vowel /a/, this exaggeration is sympathetic to the speech community in question; the nasalized pronunciation is actually regarded as 'old-fashioned' within this culture and is used at local revues to stylize old bachelors from the countryside. In this sense, Side Brok use parody to focus, in Bakhtin's (2000) terms, the 'heteroglossic' character of the dialect, and this again underlines a cultural and linguistic inside position. Secondly, the performers are not depicted as just narrow-minded or stupid. The last sentence of the passage, 'soon there are five new days of longing', gives a rather philosophical view on the behaviour being performed. In this context, the term metaparody is of interest (Clarke and Hiscock, 2009, p. 257; Coupland, 2001, p. 175, with reference to Morson, 1989, p. 67). According to Morson (1989), metaparody references, and is antithetical to, other texts (and cultural practices), but does not intend to have higher semantic authority than the original text (or cultural practice): 'The effect of metaparodic representation is often that audiences laugh *with* rather than *at* performer's representations' (Coupland, 2001, p. 175). The same kind of parodic performance is found by Clarke and Hiscock in their analysis of a New Foundland rap group, Gazeebow Unit:

> Like many regionally based rap artists round the world in the first decade of the twenty-first century, and in partial response to the multileveled and somewhat paradoxical credo of 'keepin' it real,' Gazeebow Unit have constructed a globally congruent and locally responsive performance, utilizing at both the musical and rhetorical levels the global form of hip hop, mixed with local linguistic stylizations and replete with metaparodic (Morson, 1989) and dynamic ambiguity. (Clarke and Hiscock, 2009, p. 258)

The irony and experimentation of Side Brok, especially through the central figure of Thorstein Hyl, was not accepted by all in the Norwegian

**234**

hip-hop community, especially not by all younger parts of the fan core. Some believed that Side Brok was not serious about hip hop, and there has been a lot of discussion on hip-hop websites about this issue (such as the main Norwegian website www.hip-hop.no). The rap duo Jaa9 and OnklP also dissed Side Brok in their (2005) 'Skills Misse Baren' ('Bar of divorces') on such a premise. To understand this kind of criticism, we need to take into account the discussion on the identity of hip hop in Norway at that time.

Hip hop had gone from subculture to being accepted by mainstream commercial interests. New performers had appeared, together with new forms of expression and possibilities for commercial success. The identity of hip hop was changing, which again made young people confused. On Norwegian hip-hop websites at the time we find several discussions on what was 'real' in hip hop, and especially among younger adolescents we find rather conservative notions of what was 'real' (Brunstad, 2005). Reactions against Side Brok within hip hop were first of all directed towards their irony and experimental style. Here we see interesting similarities to the public reactions to the Newfoundland rap group Gazeebow Unit discussed earlier (Clarke and Hiscock, 2009).

What about Side Brok's references to a rural lifestyle? As several studies have pointed out, the global stereotype of the hip hopper has been a person (a male African American) living in a big city, most likely in a ghetto (Klein, 2003, pp. 24–30). Klein and Friedrich (2003) underline that hardly any other youth culture has been so affined to urbanity as is the case with hip hop, at least in its early decades. As a contrast we have often found the nerdy White boy from a suburban area trying to fit in with these stereotypes, such as the main character in The Offspring's (1998) song and music video 'Pretty Fly (For A White Guy)'. Typically here, the suburban 'White guy' is a wannabe who is on to hip hop because it is trendy. Rurality has been quite out-of-the-way in hip hop. The general stereotypes of hip hop and hip hop's affinity to urbanity, however, have been called into question within hip hop itself. During the last decade, hip hop in the Southern region of the USA, often labelled Dirty South, has expanded with many associations to rural living (see Cramer and Hallett, this volume). As is the case with the Dirty South, rural rap in Norway has been regarded as 'unsophisticated' by some of the urban media. It has also been labelled as 'an exuberant, profanity-laden musical style' which is also the way *Britannica Online* defines the Dirty South (referring to the artist Ludacris).

Rural hip hop is a complex phenomenon considering the position of 'rurality' and rural culture in a period of globalization and late modernity. During the last decades, the distinction between urban and rural areas has become somewhat blurred in terms of work, living

**235**

conditions, access to technology, media use, mobility, etc. In addition, diversity of lifestyles, culture and interests is no longer a phenomenon connected exclusively with larger cities. When Side Brok are ironic towards traditional rural culture in their rap, the reception of listeners from rural areas is not just that of 'recognition'. These listeners do have both knowledge of, and a certain distance from, traditional rural culture; they are aware of the heteroglossic character of Norwegian rural and suburban areas. Furthermore, when it comes to school, media, shopping and leisure activities, youth from rural areas are familiar with urban life and themselves wander and switch between different living areas and life styles.

Rural hip hop in Norway illustrates some general aspects related to the localization of hip hop with processes such as deterritorialization, hybridization and indigenization (cf. Lull, 1995). The importance of rural hip hop may also say something about Norway as a society in which the geographical and linguistic periphery plays a more prominent role than in many others. Still, though, the periphery is peripheral and thereby marginal. From such a perspective, rural hip hop may function as a 'resistance vernacular' (Potter, 1995, p. 68). Examples of such a 'resistance vernacular' can also, however, be found in urban hip hop, especially among multilingual hip-hop performers. In the next section, our focus shifts from rural to urban Norwegian hip-hop practices. In particular, we will scrutinize what seems to be a connection between hip hop and the emergence of new, Norwegian multiethnolectal speech styles.

## 4 Hip hop and the formation of a Norwegian multiethnolectal speech style

> *hip hop er ikke noe du gjør, det er noe du lever*
> 'hip hop isn't something you do, it is something you live'
> *('Anders', Norwegian/Moroccan boy from Oslo)*

'Anders', one of the respondents in an ongoing study of linguistic practice among adolescents in multilingual and multicultural parts of Oslo, makes the above statement in a videotaped conversation with a schoolmate. When asked by the interviewer whether he is interested in hip hop, he responds emphatically: *jeg lever hip hop . . . hip hop er livsstilen min* ('I live hip hop . . . hip hop is my lifestyle'). As we will see below, he is not the only respondent in this study who identifies with hip-hop culture.

The study in question is part of the national UPUS-project (*Utviklingsprosesser i urbane språkmiljø*, 'Developmental processes in urban linguistic environments').[4] Of particular interest to this study is the emergence of new ways of talking in Norwegian: so called multi-ethnolectal speech styles (Clyne, 2000; Quist, 2000). The study of such styles was initiated by Kotsinas (1988) in Stockholm, Sweden, and has since been detected and described in a number of European cities (Auer and Dirim, 2004; Cheshire et al., 2008; Fraurud and Bijvoet, 2004; Kallmeyer and Keim, 2003; Nortier, 2001, 2008; Quist, 2000, 2005; Rampton, 1995, 1998; Torgersen et al., 2006). Prior to the UPUS-project, there had not been any comprehensive study of this phenomenon within a Norwegian context apart from studies of lexical loans from immigrant languages (Aasheim, 1995; Drange, 2002). The aim of the UPUS-project is to describe the emergence of a Norwegian multi-ethnolectal speech style on several linguistic levels as well as shedding light on functional aspects of this speech style.

In the UPUS/Oslo-project we are currently developing a corpus of spoken data from approximately 90 adolescents between 13 and 23 years. Our fieldwork is concentrated on local communities with a relatively high proportion of immigrants[5] and in translocal settings such as central youth clubs, theatre, dance and other leisure activities.[6] All of the adolescents were born and raised in Norway. Currently the UPUS/Oslo corpus consists of responses by 56 adolescents from multilingual areas in Oslo.

'Anders', the respondent mentioned at the start of this section, is a young boy from Oslo with mixed parental background. He claims to use a multiethnolectal speech style and says the following about this way of speaking:[7]

> *jeg er blitt fått lært at det er heter 'gebrokkent' da (.) men jeg vil se på det som en dialekt . . . jeg har ikke noe navn for det jeg har b – jeg f – ser på det som en refleksjon av mangfold og fellesskap . . . det her er vår dialekt . . . minoriteten*
>
> 'I have been taught that it is called "broken" like (.) but I want to look at it as a dialect . . . I don't have a name for it I have – I view it as a reflection of diversity and "togetherness" . . . this is our dialect . . . the minority.'

The multiethnolectal speech style is one of several styles in his linguistic repertoire (cf. Svendsen and Røyneland, 2008). Apart from being a proud user of the multiethnolectal speech style, 'Anders' is highly engaged in hip-hop culture, not only as a consumer of rap music and hip-hop fashion, but also as a rap-artist. We believe that this combination of hip-hop affiliation with the use of a multiethnolectal speech style is not coincidental.

**237**

## 4.1 Multilingual Oslo

Traditionally, Oslo has been socially divided into two parts: the Western part, which used to be the upper and middle class area; and the Eastern part, which used to be the industrial, working class area. Today, we find more or less the same division, despite an ongoing process of gentrification in the Eastern area as a result of industry having been moved to a large extent out of town. The East–West opposition, nevertheless, is still very much alive and many of the same stereotypes and prejudices are connected to the two areas, as for instance 'posh' (West) versus 'punk' (East). Moreover, an additional ethnic dimension seems to have been established, namely 'Norwegians' versus 'foreigners' (cf. Sandberg, 2005). Approximately 25 per cent of Oslo's population are classified as migrants, and most of them live in the suburban areas in the Southern and North-Eastern parts of Oslo and in the inner city – in short, in the Eastern part. When asked to describe the adolescents in the part of the city where she lives, 'Linn', a young girl from the Eastern part of the city, says:

> *det er veldig sånn gangsteraktig hvis du skjønner . . . sånn der slåsskamp eller det va'kke (.) det var mye slåsskamp før rundt her på N1 (.) så har det roa seg og så kom det igjen . . . for jeg har loka veldig mye på Oslo S før (.) og da var det sånn derre røyka hasj (.) banka folk (.) ingen skulle leke deilig og bla bla bla bla bla liksom*
>
> 'it is very like gangster if you know . . . like fights or it wasn't (.) there were a lot of fights before around here at N1 [in Old Oslo] (.) so it has cooled down and then it came again . . . because I have been hanging around a lot at Oslo S [the central station, downtown] (.) and then it was like smoking grass (.) beating people up (.) no one should play gorgeous and bla bla bla bla kind of.'

Here we see an example of self promotion where the majority culture's stereotype of 'gangster' and 'the dangerous immigrant' is invoked, and hence how the opposition between East and West has been invested with traits of ethnicity. 'Linn', however, has a Norwegian family background. Traditional Oslo East features combined with some multiethnolectal features and youth slang mark her speech. She reports having 'street kid style': she listens to hip hop, RnB and rap. Considering the question, 'what is the best thing about being young in Oslo?' she and her friend both express great pride in being from the Eastern part of the city. Furthermore they state a clear preference for minority boys:

'Kine': *det beste hva er det beste?*
'Linn': *kebaben (.) guttene*
'Kine': *guttene e ikke norske gutter*

**238**

'Linn': *nei pakkiser*
'Kine': 'the best what is the best?'
'Linn': 'the kebab (.) the boys'
'Kine': 'the boys eh not Norwegian boys'
'Linn': 'no Pakistanis.'

The foreigner–Norwegian-opposition is apparently not merely connected to minority background. A symbolic connection between the
Eastern side of Oslo and foreignness seems to have taken form, and
hence a general picture of the East as a minority-ethnic part of the
city (Sandberg, 2005, p. 37; 2008; Hårstad, forthcoming; Aarsæther,
forthcoming).

## 4.2 Signs of hip hop among adolescents in multilingual Oslo

One core research question within the UPUS/Oslo-project has been
whether certain individuals or groups of individuals play a particularly
prominent role in the creation and spread of multiethnolectal speech
styles. In the course of our study it has become apparent that hip hop
seems to play a decisive role in the adolescents' lives and, as suggested
above, possibly also in the creation and formation of these new multiethnolectal speech styles (Opsahl and Røyneland, 2008). A similar
connection has been documented among East African youth in Canada
(Ibrahim, 1998) and Eastern European immigrants in the US (Cutler,
2008). These studies show that both first and second-generation immigrants as well as native-born youth are drawn to hip hop's defiant
symbolism. According to Cutler (2008, p. 8), 'hip hop culture and
Black culture more broadly offer more attractive models for identity-
formation than the surrounding White mainstream culture'. The result
has been the emergence of a hip-hop flavoured speech style among
urban and suburban youth across North America. This speech style
contains many linguistic variants that are also found in vernacular
African American English (AAE).[8] However, the users of this speech
style are not necessarily trying to project a single type of ethnic or
hip-hop identity:

> Hip hop offers up a range of social, cultural, and linguistic resources
> that anyone can experiment with, and immigrant youth in parti-
> cular seem drawn to the possibilities for self-definition that these
> symbolic resources can offer. This is evident in verbal interactions
> at both the linguistic and discursive level as they negotiate a place
> in their adopted homeland. (Cutler, 2008, p. 8)

The significance of hip-hop culture in multicultural environments in
present-day Oslo is apparent in the conversation between two teenage

boys, 'Lukas' and 'Mike', recorded at a suburban youth club. Both 'Mike' and 'Lukas' have African family backgrounds (Ethiopian and Nigerian, respectively), but they were born and raised in Oslo. Their conversation is rather slow and lifeless at first. It is only when they start talking about music, playing music, singing and even dancing, that the conversation lights up. The whole world serves as a frame of reference and we are reminded of the fact that these young boys are global citizens: 'Mike' brings in the African hip-hop scene through references to the well known song 'African queen' by *2face Idibia* and he also mentions another African artist who sings in 'your language', that is 'Lukas's' language (Yoruba). The USA is present through a discussion of the voice of the hip-hop artist Lil' Wayne. 'Lukas' starts singing the rapper 2Pac's song 'Dear Mama'. They also rather mockingly discuss a friend's lack of English skills when he tries to rap. The rapping and singing is brought about in parallel with discussions of everyday topics like the players at their local soccer team. It seems that hip-hop music is a rich source of meaningful references for these boys. The music is literally what turns their conversation alive.

This corresponds well with 'Anders's' claim: 'hip hop isn't something you do, it is something you live'. He proclaims to 'live' hip hop, and adds that 'among adolescents it is quite popular with hip-hop style and like that'. This view is clearly supported by our findings. However, only a minority of the hip-hop affiliated adolescents in our data actually participate in hip-hop practices such as 'graffing', b-boying, DJ-ing and MC-ing. Most of them display their affiliation by dressing in a hip-hop manner and listening to rap music. In the questionnaires we gave our respondents, we ask them about their style and taste in music. When analysing the answers of 56 respondents, it became clear that 88 per cent of the boys (N = 34) and 68 per cent of the girls (N = 22) cited hip-hop fashion as their preferred style and rap as their preferred music. These findings clearly illustrate the important role that hip hop plays in these young people's lives. But why is this so? One line of explanation, we hope to show, lies in one of the central characteristics of hip hop: that it allows its practitioners to express and mediate both local and global aspects of cultural identity (as outlined in section 2).

By the same token, hip-hop culture is a fruitful site of investigation if we want to further develop new knowledge of linguistic practices used in multilingual urban areas in Norway today. As pointed out by Knudsen (forthcoming), central features characterizing rap music, such as borrowing phrases, rhythms and beats, sampling and mixing, reappropriation, transformation and improvisation, may be seen to have close parallels to the practice and development of the urban multi-ethnolectal speech styles. These styles are characterized by a high degree of lexical borrowings from a number of different languages (cf. Opsahl et al., 2008) and of phonological, morphological and syntactic elements which deviate from the 'standard language' (Svendsen and Røyneland, 2008; Opsahl and Røyneland, 2009; Opsahl and Nistov, forthcoming; Røyneland, in preparation). As discussed by Jaspers (2008) and Cutler (2008), this linguistic practice may be interpreted as an objection and affront to standard language ideologies insisting on the need for immigrants to use the standard language for their own benefit. This subversive element remains even though it is true that hip hop today is also big business. Local adaptations and inventions ensure that the co-option remains incomplete, and hip hop continues to be surrounded by a resilient resistance mythology:

> Hip hop is a culture of resistance, its language a *resistance vernacular* which 'deploys variance and improvisation in order to deform and reposition the rules of 'intelligibility' set up by the dominant language' (Potter, 1995, p. 68, original emphasis).
>
> In this vocal expression of defiance and protest, language use is strategic. Rap lyrics connote defiance, and to emphasize this performers apparently set out to bend and break standard language rules in much the same [way] as they challenge rules of society and established principles of making music. (Knudsen, forthcoming)

In his exploration of the 'hip-hop vernacular' in the USA, Potter (1995, p. 64) suggests that linguistics can provide a model for the tactics and effectiveness of hip hop's cultural resistance movement. Knudsen (forthcoming) asks whether it might be relevant to raise the question the other way around: 'that the codes and constructing principles underlying hip hop style and rap music can serve as a model for the "tactics" of linguistic development', in view of the spread of hip-hop culture to multilingual environments outside Anglophone countries. Without assuming that such 'tactics' imply conscious planning on the part of individual agents, we would like, in what follows, to pursue precisely this line of thought, taking primarily a closer look at the rap element of hip-hop culture.

## 4.3 Multilingual urban hip-hop groups rapping in Norwegian

Two Norwegian-rapping hip-hop groups with minority background in particular have achieved notable success in the course of the last decade: Karpe Diem and Minoritet1 (and more recently Forente Minoriteter, 'United Minorities').

Karpe Diem formed in 2000, and have since released two albums: *Rett fra hjertet* ('Straight from the heart', 2006), and *Fire vegger*

**241**

('Four walls', 2008).[9] The group had its breakthrough in 2006 with an album portraying cool authenticity and cool marginality. In January 2009 they received a prestigious music award for the best hip-hop album released in Norway in 2008.

We will have a closer look at one of their rap lyrics from their 2005 release, 'Fjern deg!' ('Get lost!'). This song is actually not included on either of the two albums, but the video is available on the group's home page www.karpediem.no. In these lyrics we find a powerful example of the way in which distinct local aspects of identity, such as the complex opposition between the Eastern and Western parts of Oslo, are placed in a larger context of ethnicity, marginality and (ironic) self portrayal. Here is an example from the first verse:

(5) *Joe Budden style baby: Pump,* 'Joe Budden style baby: Pump,
*pump it up* pump it up

*Oslogutta digger tracken, du* The Oslo guys dig the track,
*gir blaffen og ler av`n* You don't care and laugh of it

*Hva vet du om falafel og* What do you know about
*kebab på t-banen?* falafel and kebab on the Tube?

*Jævla nørd pakk sammen* Bloody nerd pack up or throw
*eller kast alt* it all away

*Jeg er ingen thug men det her* I'm not a thug but this is my
*er min asfalt* asphalt

*Så bare pass på at du er en* Just make sure that you are a
*mann* man

*Når du tester de som kjenner* When you test those who know
*hver due ved navn* every pigeon by name

*Kara gruer seg til brune gutta* The guys dread the brown guys
*skrur på sjarm* turning on their charm

*Helt ærlig: Fjern deg, du* Honestly: Get lost, You look
*ser`ke ut for faen* like hell'

Karpe Diem, 'Fjern deg!'

In these lines kids from the East are ironically portrayed as dangerous and virile gangsters who challenge and threaten posh, nerdy kids from the West. In opposition to Western kids, Eastern kids are cool and street-wise, they have street credibility. Their ethnicity and minority status is evoked with reference to food ('falafel and kebab') and colour ('brown guys'). Their macho standing is explicit; they claim not only popularity among the girls ('pigeons') but also ownership. Eastern kids defend their home turf. Conforming to a characteristic trait of hip hop, the

**242**

second verse raises explicitly political issues, containing elements of social critique and expressions of international solidarity:

(6) *For det er vi som er de som er*    'Cause it's we who are those
     *for peace mann så:*      that are for peace man so:

     *Shake that ass; for Palestina og*    Shake that ass; for Palestine
     *bistand*      and foreign aid

     *vis mamma hvem som er i mot*    Show mummy who's against
     *okkupasjonen og*      occupation and

     *Shake that ass; mot Bondevik*    Shake that ass; against
     *og co*      Bondevik'[10]

                   Karpe Diem, 'Fjern deg!'

Throughout the song there are many elements of self and other stereo-typing where differences between Eastern and Western kids are emphasized. Whereas Eastern kids are associated with qualities that tend to be connected to African American youth culture, such as coolness, street smartness, and a tough and more physical kind of masculinity, Western kids are connected to characteristics often associ-ated with hegemonic middle-class Whiteness. The last verse displays a parody of the White majority posh adolescents' supposed view of minority kids.

According to Coupland (1991, p. 345), stylization involves perform-ing non-current-first person persona by phonological and related means, sometimes in play or parody. An example of this is the styliza-tion of adolescents from the Western part of Oslo through the use of voiced *z* in place of unvoiced *s*, as in *mizter, lizm, avizn* ('Mister', 'like', 'the newspaper'):

(7) *Pliz mann, du kan`ke si*    'Please man, you can't say that
     *sånn uten reason lizm*      without reason like

     *Mizter lizm lest om hiphop*    Mister like read about hiphop in
     *i avizn*      the paper

     *Det er rap, break, graph og*    It is rap, break, graph and
     *turntablelizm, lizm*      turntablelism, like'

                    Karpe Diem, 'Fjern deg!'

Throughout, the lyrics are characterized by an abundance of English loan words and phrases in English: 'fake', 'pissed', 'thug', 'peace', 'rap-kids', 'practice', 'backstage', 'peace', 'beef', 'break', 'graph', 'wack bitch', 'Joe Budden style baby', 'Pump, pump it up', 'Shake that ass', 'check this'. Moreover, Norwegian noun and verb suffixes are applied to

English nouns and verbs: '*track-en*' ('the track'), '*kick-er back*' (kick-s back). In addition to these code-mixing and code-switching practices, there are several examples where spelling norms of the standard language are broken. In the various transcripts of hip-hop lyrics available on the internet, the voiced *z* mentioned above is visible through conscious misspellings of both English and Norwegian words: 'pliz', 'wizdom', 'Mizter', 'Make luv in the backseat', lizm (Standard Norwegian (henceforth SN) for *liksom*, 'like'), *avizn* (SN: *avisen*, 'the newspaper'). Elements typical of spoken Norwegian, such as contractions, are also reflected in the spellings *kan`ke disse`em* (SN: *kan ikke disse dem*, 'you can't diss them') alongside the use of slang words which lack counterparts in the standard written language: *lættis* ('heavy laughter'), *disse* ('diss'). Hence, the written versions of hip-hop lyrics also may be said to deform the standard language.

The blending of English and Norwegian is one illustration of how the global and the local are co-present in Karpe Diem's lyrics. Both text and video, moreover, offer descriptions of stereotypical features of Norwegian multicultural society; references to the Norwegian government are juxtaposed with references to American reality rap and to gangsta rap (e.g., 'Joe Budden' and 'MCs that are like G's'). The Asian perspective is brought in through mention of belly dance and *Bangla* ('those who dance bellydance', 'This is Bangla for those who like rap'). The Western classical music canon is brought in visually with a white ballerina featured in the video. This aural and visual fusion of elements gives an opportunity to embrace the diversity of both one's local community and the global community of which one is a part.

The same role of a bridge between the global and the local may, to some extent, also be filled by the use of a multiethnolectal speech style, a point made quite clear by another multiethnic hip-hop crew in central Oslo, Minoritet1.[11] This group pitches itself as user and producer of a new variety of Norwegian; known alternatively as *Norsk 2* or *Norsk 3*, *asfaltspråk* or *gatespråk* ('Norwegian 2 or 3', 'asphalt language' or 'street language'), labels employed by the group members themselves. This pan-ethnic music collective consists of 15 boys and one girl with highly varied ethnic backgrounds: Iraq, Morocco, Somalia, Bosnia, Pakistan, Lithuania, Uganda, Kurdistan and Norway. These performers strongly emphasize their minority status both through their lyrics and the band name itself: Minoritet1. In Norwegian, this name may be understood as 'minority number one' or as 'the minority' since the pronunciation of the numeral is homonymous with the definiteness suffix *-en*. Their shared experience with the challenges and difficulties associated with their minority position is put forward as the important glue that keeps the group together.

During the autumn of 2007, four key members of Minoritet1 were portrayed in a six-episode TV documentary, *Glatte gater* ('Slippery streets'), on the national broadcasting channel (NRK). The series and the group members received considerable media attention. In early 2008 four members left Minoritet1 to form their own group Forente Minoriteter (United Minorities). In the autumn of 2008, this group released the album, *99% ærlig* ('99% honest'). The crew and their work on this album were the subject of a successful feature length documentary released at the same time and under the same title. The use of a multiethnolectal speech style has become a trademark of all these performers. As noted by Knudsen (forthcoming) they 'take pride in promoting their own "street language", marking themselves as "different" and positioning themselves locally', and hence they make no attempt at downplaying or hiding non-Norwegian accent or 'devious' grammar. Two of the Forente Minoriteter crew members even translated Romeo and Juliet into so-called 'Kebab-Norwegian' (a term much appreciated by the media, but by and large regarded as a pejorative term by the users themselves, cf. Svendsen and Røyneland, 2008, pp. 68, 70). The translated play *Romeo og Julie in Rap!* was staged at the Nordic Black Theatre in autumn 2007, and a sequel was performed the following year.[12]

An important debate within hip hop relates to the notions of authenticity, street credibility and anti-commercialism. Given the considerable attention and success different group members and the groups as such have enjoyed in recent years, their credibility might be placed in question. Minoritet1, however, make and distribute their music within an underground non-commercial network, and the goal of their musical practice is primarily live shows. In their lyrics they describe the difficult, challenging life of the urban street environment. Indeed, 'underground' is a key metaphor for the group (as elaborated by Knudsen, forthcoming). They promote their music as underground rap from the core of the city – locating this in the Eastern part of Oslo:[13]

(8) *Hey hey Lillebror, hey*
*Lillebror slapp av nå hey*
*lady junior nå må du fortelle*
*dem hva du har å si få det*
*frem la dem få høre hvem du*
*er representerer østkanten*
*og den nordafrikanske*
*sirkuselefanten som alltid*
*lever uttafor kanten . . .*

'Hey hey Baby Brother [artist name] cool down hey lady junior now you must tell them what you have to say get it out let them hear who you are represent the Eastside and the North African circus elephant that always lives outside the edge . . .'

Minoritet1

**245**

In this extract, various aspects of the members' sub-cultural capital are summed up. Their identity as both local and global citizens is brought together as they invoke 'the Eastside' of Oslo and the 'North African circus elephant', and their status as a marginalized minority is clearly indicated.

Through their lyrics Minoritet1 show a great deal of linguistic creativity. Their rap is an arena for constructing, mixing, testing, accepting or rejecting lexical items from different languages. With Norwegian at the core they introduce English hip-hop expressions, lexical items from different minority languages (often with a slang function and taboo words), they twist Norwegian words and mix words from different languages (as shown in Knudsen, forthcoming). In this sense rap is an important arena for innovation, testing and spread. Also in their everyday linguistic practice, as displayed in the TV and feature length documentary, they display a multicultural, urban identity through the use of the hip-hop vocabulary. Their speech style, however, is not only marked by the use of certain words, but also distinctive at other linguistic levels such as phonology, morphology and syntax.

These latter features, some of which are also displayed in their rap – particularly phonetic and prosodic ones – are congruent with those found in the UPUS-material.[14] Here the link between the multi-ethnolectal speech style and hip hop was frequently made explicit; for instance, when our respondent 'Anders' is asked to illustrate the multiethnolectal style he responds by rapping:

| | |
|---|---|
| 'Anders': | *(.) eeh for språk og ordtrykk vent da (.) jeg kan rappe en tekst for deg (.) jeg vedder på du ikke skjønner det* |
| Interviewer: | *ja gjør det* |
| 'Anders': | *ok ja* |
| Interviewer: | *(.) gjør det* |
| 'Anders': | *hva skjer'a bahme har du sett Zæh si at han er en skikkelig kæh hvorfor det? han skylder meg cash fra no' stash som vi tæsja fra noen kæber som trengte læg fordi vi trengte næt du vet hvordan det er (.) svartingliv (.) det sleipe smil noen ganger det går schpa noen ganger det går skikkelig (xxx) men ekte svartinger backer hverandre opp samarbeider om å lete etter muligheter til neste jackpot (.) skjønner hva jeg mener (.) det er sånn ok greit vil ikke gå (.) utdype teksten men hvert fall dem som skjønner dem skjønner dem som skjønner ikke trenger ikke å skjønne skjønner hva jeg mener* |
| 'Anders': | *'(.) eeh for language and word stress wait (.) I can rap a text for you (.) I bet you don't understand it'* |

| | |
|---|---|
| Interviewer: | 'yes do that' |
| 'Anders': | 'ok yes' |
| Interviewer: | '(.) do that' |
| 'Anders': | 'what's up bahme ("friend") have you seen Zæh tell him that he is a real kæh (?) why? because he owes me cash from some stash which we tæsja ("stole") from some kæber ("girls") which needed læg (?) because we needed næt (?) you know how it is (.) Blacks, life (.) the slippery smile sometimes it goes schpa ("good") sometimes it goes really (xxx) but genuine Blacks are backing each other cooperating looking for possibilities to the next jackpot (.) see what I mean (.) it is like ok good I won't go (.) explain the text but at least those who understand they understand those who understand not need not to understand see what I mean.' |

As we can see, the improvised rap of 'Anders' not only references ethnicity and the marginalized and difficult situation of minority adolescents in Oslo, but also their solidarity and mutual support. Many of the adolescents we have interviewed point to prosodic features such as speech rhythm and stress as perhaps the most prevalent feature of the multiethnolectal speech style. It is reported to sound more staccato, harder, faster and more aggressive than 'normal' Norwegian (Svendsen and Røyneland, 2008, pp. 71, 72). The way in which 'Anders' talks throughout the extract above could indeed be described as staccato. In his rap there are several words that will not be found in a Norwegian dictionary. There are a series of loan words from English, such as 'cash', 'stash', 'back-er' (with the Norwegian present tense suffix *–er*) and loan words from other languages; *bahme* (Kurdish: 'friend'), *tæsja* (Berber: 'stole'/'fooled', with the Norwegian past tense suffix *–a*), *kæber* (Berber and Arabic: 'girls' originally 'prostitute', with the Norwegian plural suffix *–er*), *schpa* (Berber: 'good'). There are also some words and phrases we had difficulty in understanding, but when asking 'Anders' to help us, he said: 'The street is to be told, not to be sold.' In the very last comment after the rap, 'Anders' states that this is a language for the initiated: 'those who don't understand, they don't need to understand'. As adult researchers we are obviously not the main target audience of this rap; however, kids in multilingual environments in Oslo have no problem understanding what's going on.

By virtue of their position in multiethnic youth communities, urban hip-hop performers seem to have a significant influence on the formation and particularly the propagation of a new urban, Oslo-based, multiethnolectal speech style. Hip-hop lyrics may well be an important

**247**

scene for the creation and spread of lexical features, but what about other distinctive linguistic features of everyday linguistic practice in multicultural youth communities:[15] can they be traced in these lyrics? Except for some sequences in 'Anders's' rap, few instances of the distinctive morphological and syntactic features that we find elsewhere in peer conversations were present in the speech of the Minoritet1 group members during the television show and feature documentary. This might be due to the fact that the rap lyrics are artistic artefacts, although to some extent improvised. They have a syntax of their own, not necessarily reflecting everyday language use at all linguistic levels. Still, they deserve our attention as an important factor in young people's lives. As we have shown above, hip-hop music was what brought the conversation between 'Mike' and 'Lukas' to life; many young boys and girls in multilingual Oslo identify with hip-hop music, style and culture.

We have seen that the linguistic practices in ethnically mixed urban hip-hop groups appear as a self-conscious development of a new multiethnolectal speech style. This is particularly salient in Minoritet1 and Forente Minoriteter, groups who promote themselves by the use of 'street language', 'Kebab-Norwegian' or 'Norwegian 2'. As to the question of where this language comes from, 'Anders' illustratively answers:

> det kommer jo ut ifra e nye kulturer og (.) sånn ikke sant (.) og på en måte e (.) felleskapet har (.) utvikla det språket der . . . det er fellesskapet som (.) liksom vi tar og vi gir til hverandre for det er det vi har og (.) det har blitt et språk ut av det
> 'It comes from new cultures and (.) like you know (.) and in a way eh (.) the community has (.) developed that language . . . it is the community that (.) like we take and we give to each other because it's what we've got and (.) it has become a language.'

## 5 Concluding remarks

Rural hip hop and urban, multiethnic hip hop in Norway illustrate some general aspects of how a global cultural phenomenon may be localized in terms of language, style, poetic forms and themes. We began this chapter by pointing out four notions of globalization to which the global-local relations of hip hop may be significant: globalization as diffusion, globalization as a global fight, globalization as multiculturalism, globalization as glocalization. Even though our analysis of hip hop in Norway has emphasized glocalization, this does not mean that the other notions are irrelevant. Our focus on localization processes means that our perspective has much in common with the interpretation of globalization as 'glocalization', at least in a broad sense of the term. From our point of view, hip hop is by no means only an American or global culture but is being transformed as it develops new forms locally. At the same time, hip hop *is* a global culture in that hip hoppers relate their notions of what is 'real' to text cultural norms and attitudes that are indeed global, e.g., by recontextualization. Even though processes of glocalization have certainly eased the connections between urban African American culture and hip hop around the world (cf. Mitchell, 2001), that does not mean that these connections are irrelevant. However, the process of glocalization implies that local adaptations will not be confined to the cultural resources implicit in these connections.

The diffusionist perspective does not apply well to how hip hop has developed in Norway. This perspective does not take into account that there may be different sources of inspiration, at different times, and that there is a dialectic fluidity of cultural impulses that is rather complex. It may, though, say something about how Norwegian hip hop developed in its earliest stage, in the 1980s.

When it comes to the notion of globalization as a 'global fight', our analysis of how Norwegian rap may be understood as 'resistance vernaculars' provides an interesting perspective, because it brings to the fore the political potentiality of hip hop in its use of language and style. On the other hand, we ought to be aware that hip hop, with its hybridity and cultural and linguistic loans, is not characterized by linguistic and cultural purism directed to other languages or cultures. Anglicisms and borrowings from other languages are not regarded as a problem.

The notion of globalization as 'multiculturalism' focuses on the parallel existence of cultural diversity and gives insight into the subcultural aspects of hip hop. Our analysis of multiethnolectal speech style in Oslo shows that hip hop with its subcultural style has an influence on other groups, both linguistically and culturally. However, the notion of multiculturalism cannot explain the processes through which hybrid subcultures such as hip hop are created and how they change.

By contrast, the glocalization perspective highlights exactly these processes. Hence it is a fruitful perspective to take to the analysis of hip hop in Norway, providing, we maintain, the best general view on the dynamic relations between globalization and hip hop. However, it is also necessary to take into consideration notions of fluidity and fixity as aspects of the multifaceted transformation process to which hip hop is connected. Therefore, the need for a broader understanding of the concept of glocalization is another aspect we wish to emphasize.

**249**

## Acknowledgements

The research related to a Norwegian multiethnolectal speech style is in part based on studies conducted by the Oslo group of the national UPUS-project (Linguistic development in urban environments), funded by grants from the Norwegian Research Council. We wish to express our gratitude to the other researchers in the project, Ingvild Nistov, Bente Ailin Svendsen and Finn Aarsæther, and last but not least, to the adolescents who participated in our study.

The research related to rural hip hop and globalization is in part based on studies made within the framework of the research project "The New Norwegian", funded by grants from the Norwegian Research Council.

## Notes

1. The use of English, though, does not mean that the small Norwegian hip-hop scene was simply a mirror image of the American one. In the 1990s, several Norwegian hip-hop artists were obviously influenced by British Hip hop, 'Britcore', with artists such as *Gunshot and Silver Bullet* (Holen, 2004, p. 76).
2. According to Lull (1995, p. 155), indigenization is a step before reterritorialization (cf. Androutsopoulos and Scholz, 2003, p. 468).
3. *Thorstein Hyl* actually represents an allusion to an American hip-hop artist, *Tirstin Howl The 3rd* (with whom they collaborated on an album).
4. See <http://www.hf.uio.no/iln/forskning/forskningsprosjekter/upus/>, accessed February 2009.
5. Specifically, 43 per cent in the Southern, suburban area and 33 per cent in the old part of Oslo (Statistics Norway, 2009).
6. For more details about our data and corpus see Svendsen and Røyneland (2008), Svendsen (forthcoming).
7. Transcripts are close to orthographic. (.) denotes a brief pause; longer pauses are timed in seconds, i.e., (1.0). Inaudible strings are marked by (xxx). Single parentheses denote paralinguistic traits, such as laughter or include comments whereas – denotes interruptions. '. . .' marks small omitted parts.
8. For a comprehensive list of features see Cutler (2008, p. 13).
9. The group has three members: *Magdi* (Magdi Omar Ytreeide Abdelmaguid) of Egyptian/Norwegian descent, *Chicosepoy* (Chirag Rashmikant Patel) of Indian descent, both born 1984, and *DJ Marius Thingvald* of Norwegian descent.
10. Kjell Magne Bondevik was Prime Minister of Norway at the time of the recording.
11. See Knudsen (2009) for a comprehensive description of the group and its lyrics.
12. This, however, is not a uniquely Norwegian phenomenon; see, for instance, *The Bombitty of Errors*, an English-language hip-hop adaptation of Shakespeare's *The Comedy of Errors*.

13. See <http://www11.nrk.no/urort/Artist/Minoritet1/default.aspx>, accessed February 2009.
14. See for instance Svendsen and Røyneland (2008), Opsahl and Nistov (forthcoming), Røyneland (in preparation).
15. Discussed in Svendsen and Røyneland (2008), Opsahl and Nistov (forthcoming).

## Interviews

Brunstad, E. (2003–2009), Audiotaped interviews with hip-hop artists.
UPUS (2004–2008), Videotaped interviews and peer conversations

## Discography

Fremmed Rase (2007), *Varsko her.* Album.
Gatas Parlament (1994), *Autobahn til Union.* EP.
Gatas Parlament (2001), *Holdning over underholdning.* Album.
Gatas Parlament (2004), *Fred, Frihet and Alt Gratis.* Album.
Jaa9 and OnklP (2003), *Bondegrammatikk.* Bootleg.
Jaa9 and OnklP (2004), *Skills Misse Baren.* EP.
Karpe Diem (2005), *Fjern deg!* Video: <www.karpediem.no>, accessed 10 August 2009.
Karpe Diem (2006), *Rett fra hjertet.* Album.
Karpe Diem (2006), *Fire vegger.* Album.
Klovner i kamp (2001), *Bjølsen Hospital.* Album.
Minoritet1 (2008), *99% ærlig.* Album.
NRK ('Norwegian Broadcasting Corporation') (2007), *Glatte gater.* TV documentary about members of Minoritet1.
The Offspring (1998). *Americana.* Album.
Side Brok (2002), *Side Brok.* EP.
Side Brok (2004), *Høge brelle.* Album.
Side Brok (2005), *Side Brooklyn.* EP.
Side Brok (2006), *Kar me kjøme frå.* Album.
Spetakkel (2003), *Spetakkel.* Album.
Tungtvann (2000a), *Reinspikka hip hop.* EP.
Tungtvann (2000b), *Nord og ned.* Album.
Tungtvann (2002), *Mørketid.* Album.

## References

Aarsæther, F. (forthcoming), 'The use of multiethnic youth language in Oslo', in P. Quist and B. A. Svendsen (eds), *Multiethnolects in Urban Scandinavia.* Multilingual Matters.
Aasheim, S. (1995), '"Kebab-norsk": framandspråkleg påverknad på ungdomsspråket i Oslo'. Master thesis, Oslo: University of Oslo.

Androutsopoulos, J. (2006), 'Hip hop and language: vertical intertextuality and the three spheres of pop culture', in P. Dyndahl and L. A. Kulbrandstad (eds), *High Fidelity Eller Rein Jalla? Purisme som problem i kultur, språk og estetikk* Hamar: Oplandske Bokforlag, pp. 161–188.

Androutsopoulos, J. and Scholz, A. (2002), 'On the recontextualization of hip hop in European speech communities: a contrastive analysis of rap lyrics'. *PhiN: Philologie im Netz*, 19, 1–42. <http://web.fu-berlin.de/phin/phin19/p19t1.htm>, accessed 20 September 2009.

—(2003), 'Spaghetti funk: appropriations of hip hop culture and rap music in Europe'. *Popular Music and Society*, 26, 4, 463–479.

Auer, P. and Dirim, I. (2004), *Türkisch sprechen nicht nur die Türken: über die Unschärfebeziehung zwischen Sprache und Ethnie in Deutschland*. Berlin: de Gruyter.

Bakhtin, M. (2000), 'From the prehistory of novelistic discourse', in D. Lodge (ed.), *Modern Critcism and Theory. A Reader*. London: Longman, pp. 105–136.

Barnard, A. (2000), *History and Theory in Anthropology*. Cambridge: Cambridge University Press.

Bozza, A. (2003), *Whatever You Say I Am. The Life and Times of Eminem*. London: Bantam.

*Britannica Online*. Available online at: <www.britannica.com>, accessed 10 August 2009.

Brunstad, E. (2005), 'Identitet og purisme i ein hipphopp-diskusjon', in P. Dyndahl and L. A. Kulbrandstad (eds), *High fidelity eller rein jalla? Purisme som problem i kultur, språk og estetikk*. Hamar: Oplandske Bokforlag, pp. 147–160.

—(2006), 'Globalisering og språkleg mangfald', in H. Sandøy and K. Tenfjord (eds), *Den nye norsken? Nokre peilepunkt under globaliseringa*. Oslo: Novus, pp. 40–72.

Cheshire, J., Fox, S., Kerswill, P. and Torgersen, E. (2008), 'Ethnicity, friendship network and social practices as the motor of dialect change: linguistic innovation in London'. *Sociolinguistica*, 22, 1–23.

Clarke, S. and Hiscock, P. (2009), 'Hip hop in a post-insular community. Hybridity, local language, and authenticity in an online Newfounland group'. *Journal of English Linguistics*, 241–261.

Clyne, M. (2000), 'Lingua franca and ethnolects in Europe and beyond', in *Sociolinguistica*, 14, 83–89.

Connell, J. and Gibson, C. (2003), *Sound Tracks: Popular Music, Identity and Place*. London: Routledge.

Coupland, N. (2001), *Style: Language Variation and Identity*. Cambridge: Cambridge University Press.

Cutler, C. (2008), 'Brooklyn style: hip hop markers and racial affiliation among European immigrants in New York City'. *International Journal of Bilingualism*, 12, 1 and 2, 7–24.

Danielsen, A. (2008), 'Iscenesett marginalitet? Om regional identitet i nordnorsk hip hop', in M. Krogh and B. Stougaard Pedersen (eds), *Hiphop i Skandinavien*. Århus: Aarhus Universitetsforlag, pp. 201–218.

**252**

Diaz, (2000), Interview with Diaz and Tommy Tee. *Stress Magazine.* <http://www.stress.no/magazine.asp?Nid=607andcat=10>, accessed 20 September 2009.

Don Martin (2004), 'F.E.M.I.N.I.S.T.'. *Dagbladet,* 8 June 2004. <http://www.dagbladet.no/kultur/2004/06/08/399913.html>, accessed 20 August 2009.

Drange, E.-M. (2002), 'Fremmedspråklige slangord i norsk', in E.-M. Drange, U.-B. Kotsinas and A.-B. Stenström (eds), *Jallaspråk, slanguage og annet ungdomsspråk i Norden.* Kristiansand: Høyskoleforlaget, pp. 9–18.

Dyndahl, P. (2008), 'Norsk hip hop i verden. Om konstruksjon av glokal identitet i hiphop og rap', in M. Krogh and B. Stougaard Pedersen (eds), *Hiphop i Skandinavien.* Århus: Aarhus Universitetsforlag, pp. 103–125.

Fraurud, K. and Bijvoet, E. (2004), 'Multietniskt ungdomsspråk och andra varieteter av svenska i flerspråkiga miljöer', in K. Hyltenstam and I. Lindberg (eds), *Svenska som andraspråk: i forskning, undervisning och samhälle.* Lund: Studentlitteratur, pp. 389–417.

Hårstad, S. (forthcoming), 'Performing "dangerousness" linguistically: the case of the "bad Norwegian" on the streets of Trondheim', in J. N. Jørgensen, et al. (eds), *Jugendsprache – Youth Language. Proceedings from the 5th Jugendsprache Conference 2008* [working title]. Cambridge Scholars Publishing/Copenhagen Studies in Bilingualism.

Hebdige, D. (1979), *Subculture: The Meaning of Style.* London: Routledge.

Hole, G. (1997), 'Verbale skittkastere eller poetiske avantgardister?' MA Thesis. Department of Sociology, University of Oslo.

Holen, Ø. (2004), *Hiphop-hoder – fra Beat Street til bygde-rap.* Oslo: Spartacus.

Ibrahim, A. (1998), 'Hey, Wassup Homeboy? Becoming Black: Race, Language, Culture, and the Politics of Identity'. PhD dissertation, Department of Curriculum, Teaching and Learning, University of Toronto.

Jaspers, J. (2008), 'Problematizing ethnolects: naming linguistic practices in an Antwerp secondary school'. *International Journal of Bilingualism,* 12, 1 & 2, 85–104.

Kallmeyer, W. and Keim, I. (2003), 'Linguistic variation and the construction of social identity in a German-Turkish setting. A case study of an immigrant youth group in Mannheim, Germany', in J. Androutsopoulos and A. Georgakopoulou (eds), *Discourse Constructions of Youth Identities.* Amsterdam: John Benjamins, pp. 29–46.

Klein, G. (2003), *Is this real? Die Kultur des HipHop.* Frankfurt am Main: Suhrkamp.

Klein, G. and Friedrich, M. (2003), 'Globalisierung und die Performanz des Pop', in K. Neumann-Braun, A. Scmidt and M. Mai (eds), *Popvisionen. Liks in die Zukunft.* Frankfurt am Main: Suhrkamp, pp. 77–102.

Knudsen, J. S. (forthcoming), '"Playing with words as if it was a rap game": street language in a multiethnic hip hop crew', in P. Quist and B. A. Svendsen (eds), *Multiethnolects in Urban Scandinavia.* Multilingual Matters.

Kotsinas, U.-B. (1988), 'Rinkebysvenskan – en dialekt?', in P. Linell et al. (eds), *Svenskans Beskrivning* 16. Linköping: Tema Kommunikation, Universitetet i Linköping, pp. 264–278.

Larsen, J. K. (2006), 'Sexism and Misogyny in American Hip-Hop Culture'. Master thesis. Oslo: University of Oslo, <http://www.duo.uio.no/sok/work. html?WORKID=40242>, accessed 20 September 2009.

Lull, J. (1995), *Media, Communication, Culture: A Global Approach*. Cambridge: Polity Press.

Mitchell, T. (ed.) (2001), *Global Noise. Rap and Hip Hop Outside the USA*. Middletown, Connecticut: Wesleyan University Press.

Morson, T. (1989), 'Theory of parody', in G. S. Morso and C. Emerson (eds), *Rethinking Bakhtin*. Evanston, IL: Northwestern University Press, pp. 63–86.

Nortier, J. (2001), '"Fawaka, what's up?" Language use among adolescents in Dutch monoethnic and ethnically mixed groups', in A. Hvenekilde and J. Nortier (eds), *Meetings at the Crossroads: Studies of Multilingualism and Multiculturalism*. Oslo: Novus forlag, pp. 61–72.

—(2008), 'Ethnolects? The emergence of new varieties among adolescents'. *International Journal of Bilingualism*, 12, 1–5.

Opsahl, C. P. (2000), 'Blant mikrofonriddere og plateryttere. Selvpresentasjon i norsk hip hop'. *Kirke og kultur*, 3. <http://www.carlpetter.com/texts/ mikrofonriddere.htm>, accessed 29 September 2009.

Opsahl T. and Nistov, I. (forthcoming), 'On some structural aspects of Norwegian spoken among adolescents in multilingual settings in Oslo', in P. Quist and B. A. Svendsen (eds), *Multiethnolects in Urban Scandinavia*. Multilingual Matters.

Opsahl, T. and Røyneland, U. (2008), 'Hip hop and the formation of a Norwegian multiethnolectal speech style'. Paper presented at Jugendsprache. The Fifth International Conference on Youth Language. 27–29 March 2008, Copenhagen.

—(2009), 'Osloungdom – født på solsiden eller i skyggen av standardtalemålet?'. *Norsk Lingvistisk Tidsskrift*, 27, 1, 95–120.

Opsahl, T., Røyneland, U. and Svendsen, B. A. (2008), '"Syns du jallanorsk er lættis, eller?" – om taggen [lang=X] i NoTa-Oslo-korpuset', in J. B. Johannessen and K. Hagen (eds), *Språk i Oslo. Ny forskning omkring talespråk*. Oslo: Novus, pp. 29–42.

Pennycook, A. (2007), *Global Englishes and Transcultural Flows*. London: Routledge.

—(2009), 'Refashioning and performing identities in global hip hop', in N. Coupland and A. Jaworski, *The New Sociolinguistic Reader*. Basingstoke: Palgrave Macmillan, pp. 326–340.

Phillipson, Robert (1999), 'Voice in global English. Unheard chords in Crystal loud and clear [Review of D. Crystal, English as a global language.]'. *Applied Linguistics*, 20, 2, 265–276.

Potter, R. A. (1995), *Spectacular Vernaculars: Hip Hop and the Politics of Postmodernism*. Albany, NY: State University of New York Press.

Preisler, B. (1999a), *Danskerne og det engelske sprog*. Roskilde: Roskilde Universitetsforlag.

—(1999b), 'Engelsk ovenfra og nedenfra: Sprogforandring og kulturell identitet', in N. Davidsen-Nielsen (ed.), *Engelsk eller ikke engelsk? That is the Question*. Copenhagen: Gyldendal, pp. 39–64.

Prévos, A. J. M. (2001), 'Postcolonial popular music in France: rap music and hip hop culture in the 1980s and 1990s', in T. Mitchell (ed.), *Global Noise. Rap and hip hop Outside the USA*. Middletown: Wesleyan University Press, pp. 39–56.

Quist, P. (2000), 'Ny københavnsk "multietnolekt": Om sprogbrug blandt unge i sprogligt og kulturelt heterogene miljøer', in *Danske Talesprog* Bind 1. København: C. A. Reitzels Forlag, pp. 143–212.

—(2005), 'Stilistiske praksisser i storbyens heterogene skole – en etnografisk og sociolingvistisk undersøgelse af sproglig variation'. PhD dissertation. Nordisk Forskningsinstitut, Avd. for dialektforskning. København: Københavns Universitet.

Rampton, B. (1995), *Crossing: Language and Ethnicity Among Adolescents*. London: Longman.

—(1998), 'Language crossing and redefinition of reality', in P. Auer (ed.), *Code-switching in Conversations*. London: Routledge, pp. 290–320.

Robertson, R. (1995), 'Glocalization: time-space and homogeneity-heterogeneity', in M. Featherstone, S. Lash and R. Robertson (eds), *Global Modernities*. London: Sage, pp. 25–44.

Røyneland, U. (2009), 'Dialects in Norway: catching up with the rest of Europe?' *International Journal of the Sociology of Language*, 196/197, 7–31.

—(in preparation), 'Phonological characteristics associated with the Norwegian speech of adolescents in multilingual and multicultural communities of practice in Oslo'. A subproject to UPUS-Oslo.

Sandberg, S. (2005), 'Stereotypiens dilemma. Iscenesettelser av etnisitet på "gata"'. *Tidsskrift for ungdomsforskning*, 5, 2, 27–46.

—(2008), 'Get rich or die trying', *Tidsskrift for ungdomsforskning*, 8, 1, 67–83.

Språkrådet (2005), *Norsk i hundre. Norsk som nasjonalspråk i globaliseringens tidsalder*. Oslo: Språkrådet. <http://www.sprakradet.no/upload/9832/norsk_i_hundre.pdf>, accessed 29 September 2009.

Statistics Norway (2009), <http://www.ssb.no/english/>, accessed 20 January 2009.

Svendsen, B. A. (forthcoming), 'Linguistic practices in multilingual urban contexts in Norway: an overview', in P. Quist and B. A. Svendsen (eds), *Multiethnolects in Urban Scandinavia*, Multilingual Matters.

Svendsen, B. A. and Røyneland, U. (2008), 'Multiethnolectal facts and functions in Oslo, Norway'. *International Journal of Bilingualism*, 12, 1 & 2, 63–83.

Torgersen, E., Kerswill, P. and Fox, S. (2006), 'Ethnicity as a source of changes in the London vowel system', in F. Hinskens (ed.). *Language Variation – European Perspectives. Selected Papers from the Third International Conference on Language Variation in Europe (ICLaVE3)*, Amsterdam, June 2005. Amsterdam: Benjamins, pp. 249–263.

UPUS/OSLO (2009), *Corpus of spoken language in multilingual areas in Oslo*. Under development by I. Nistov, T. Opsahl, U. Røyneland, B. A. Svendsen and F. Aarsæther, transcription assistants: I. I. Ims, H. Haug and Y. Sandanger. <http://www.hf.uio.no/iln/forskning/forskningsprosjekter/upus/english/>, accessed 19 January 2008.

# 10 From Chi-Town to the Dirty-Dirty: Regional Identity Markers in US Hip Hop

Jennifer Cramer and Jill Hallett

## 1 Introduction

Long considered a form of rebellion to both mainstream music and ideology, hip hop has emerged as a powerful tool for the construction of social identity. Pennycook (2007, p. 14) argues that hip hop is a vehicle for the '"global spread of authenticity" – a culture of being true to the local, of telling it like it is'. If this is true, we can expect that hip-hop lyrics, in representing the local culture, can be considered a strong indexer of regional affiliation. This chapter shows how hip hop perpetuates local indices of identity, while at the same time maintaining roots of solidarity within the local communities of origin.

The selection of particular words associated with a particular region in the lyrics of hip-hop music establishes in-group solidarity, while excluding those unaffiliated with the region. These regional markers of identity follow a natural progression from the East Coast–West Coast rivalry prevalent in the 1990s and have now branched out to include the Midwestern and Southern United States. By exploring the same questions posed by Le Page and Tabouret-Keller (1985) in their seminal work on identity markers, this chapter aims to discover how these new indices of identity are currently under development along the lines of regional affiliation.

Regional identity is indexed by mention of local foods, town names, and other lexical items to effectively convey in-group solidarity and out-group exclusion (Morgan, 1993, 2001). In this chapter, we examine the tactics used by hip-hop artists in the Southern and Midwestern regions of the United States to identify with groups in their communities. We argue that particular lexical uses aid these artists in their attempts at in-group solidarity and successful identity construction.

**256**

This chapter is organized as follows. In Section 2, we present some background information on hip hop and identity, exploring in particular the theory of identity as described by Le Page and Tabouret-Keller (1985). Section 3 is a brief historical account of the rise of hip hop in the Midwestern and Southern United States. We discuss the methods for data collection and analysis in Section 4. Section 5 is a presentation of the results. The discussion of those results can be found in Section 6. Section 7 provides some preliminary conclusions and areas for further research.

## 2 Hip hop and identity

Scholars are increasingly turning to hip hop as a viable and valuable source for linguistic inquiry (Cutler, 2007). In particular, many scholars have been interested in the appropriation of hip hop by youth far-flung from the genre's original locus (e.g., Perullo and Fenn, 2003; Osumare, 2001; Mitchell, 2003; Alim et al., 2009). Pennycook (2007) discusses the importance of artists' negotiation of local identities with the ever-more global medium of hip hop. A great deal of scholarly attention has been devoted to understanding the spread of hip hop in its variant forms across the globe, including South America (Roth-Gordon, 2009), Asia (Pennycook, 2007), Africa (Omoniyi, 2006, 2009; Higgins, 2009) and Oceania (Mitchell, 2001).

The examination of global hip hop has resulted in important insights regarding the real-time distribution, appropriation and nativization of music, culture and language from hip hop's roots in the United States. However, the spread of hip hop *within* the United States has been given far less attention, except, perhaps, in the context of female rappers' advances to the hip-hop scene (Goodall, 1994; Haugen, 2003). This chapter aims to show what American hip hop has learned from global hip hop, particularly as it pertains to the shaping of the global medium of hip hop to meet local needs, desires and expressions of identity.

In our examination, we look to the lexical choices made by hip-hop artists to understand identity construction. This area is not completely unstudied in the realm of hip hop. The importance of the 'Word' is made clear in Morgan (2001). She claims that '[i]n Hip Hop, the "Word" is both the Bible and the law; a source of worship and competition' (2001, p. 204). Additionally, Morgan (1993) points to the cultural capital a hip-hop artist wields when using particular words. As such, the selection of particular words can be a powerful tool in the construction of identity. Morgan further points to the local importance of lexical choices by stating that 'urban African American life is not simply represented in relation to in-group intersubjectivities, but through

**257**

cultural symbols and sounds, especially linguistic symbols, which signify membership, role and status' (2001, p. 205). She discusses the cultural insider/outsider positions of young African Americans with respect to established practices of hip hop, resulting in 'a significant reclamation and restructuring of African American language practices by youth who have, for the first time in urban African American communities, intentionally highlighted and re-constructed regional and local urban language norms' (2001, p.188). Accordingly, lexical choices made by artists to affiliate with certain cities and regions serve to establish in-group solidarity.

These types of choices might be better understood within the context of an example. During her fieldwork on urban youth language in Los Angeles, Morgan (2002) encountered a hip-hop group called Project Blowed. When one of their crew members won a rap battle, their fans shouted 'Westside!' The rappers themselves also employ such regional names in their rhymes, and when rappers from the East Coast school of rap encountered the different style on the West Coast, they chose not to change, in order to be 'true to the East' (2002, p. 111). Thus, these uses of lexical items indicating regional affiliation establish solidarity with their region and the people who live there.

Morgan (2001, p. 190) lists certain criteria for membership in and representation of the hip-hop nation: 'purchase of recordings, memorization of rap lyrics, freestyle practice, loyalty to crews and/or individuals, and publication of lyrics and artists' biographies on rap web sites'. To this list, we would add 'intertextual competence', as understanding of lexical references of locality such as those described above and those detailed in our study are part of what establish a listener as 'in' or 'out' in terms of group membership.

This intertextual competence is rather important in the construction of regional identity in hip hop. Morgan (2002) found that as rappers became the main focus in hip hop and disc jockeys (DJs) no longer held centre stage, around the time when 'Rapper's Delight' hit the airwaves (Chang, 2005), geographic identity became increasingly important. Local and regional affiliation establishes groups; cognitive competence in types of representation constitutes membership. Lexical items, syntax and phonology all contribute to the indexing of local stylistic variants.

Though regional hip hop has received very little scholarly attention, certain linguistic features associated with these regional styles have been pinpointed. Morgan (1993) claims that aspects of phonology, such as /t/ deletion/glottalization or syllable deletions, differentiate rappers from the East and West Coasts. Alim (2009) discusses hip hop's linguistic influence insofar as certain regional phonological features have

**258**

become at least salient, visible, and possibly available for other regions via hip hop. Highlighting linguistic features then enables rappers from a particular region to establish an identity within the hip-hop community. Alim (2009) offers examples of St. Louis and Deep Southern linguistic features making their way into the language of speakers from other regions. This inter-regional linguistic awareness, Alim argues, somewhat diffuses the artificial dichotomy of prestige vs non-prestige varieties of English (2009, pp. 215–216).[1]

At the epicentre of our discussion of hip hop's local lexical indices lies the notion of identity. This term has been defined by numerous scholars in varying disciplines. One clear definition, presented by Bucholtz and Hall (2005), states that '[i]dentity is the social positioning of the self and other' (2005, p. 586). A key feature of identities is that they emerge in interaction, and, in the case of hip-hop artists, identities emerge through the medium of their music.

Though identity has been studied through many different lenses, the work of Le Page and Tabouret-Keller (1985) on 'acts of identity' provides an appropriate framework for our discussion of regional identity marking in US hip hop. The goal of their work was to capture the ways in which linguistic performance is connected to the emergence and creation of particular identities. The populations examined in their research included groups in which 'the vernacular behaviour of most of the population has been looked down on, stigmatized, in comparison with a linguistic standard set by the educational system which has acted as a yardstick for formal social acceptability and prestige' (1985, p. 5). One could easily argue that hip hop also falls into this category, and thus is appropriately analysed using their framework.

We can consider the ways in which people speak as 'acts of projection', according to Le Page and Tabouret-Keller (1985). This notion of 'projection' can be best understood in the authors' own words:

> [T]he speaker is projecting his inner universe, implicitly with the invitation to others to share it, at least insofar as they recognize his language as an accurate symbolization of the world, and to share his attitude towards it. By verbalizing as he does, he is seeking to reinforce his models of the world, and hopes for acts of solidarity from those with whom he wishes to identify. The feedback he receives from those with whom he talks may reinforce him, or may cause him to modify his projections, both in their form and in their content. To the extent that he is reinforced, his behaviour in that particular context may become more regular, more focussed; to the extent that he modifies his behaviour to accommodate others it may for a time become more variable, more diffuse, but in time the behaviour of the group – that is, he and those with whom he is

**259**

> trying to identify – will become more focused. (Le Page and
> Tabouret-Keller, 1985, p. 181)

From this understanding, we can see that the 'acts of identity' the authors refer to point to notions of social alignment and, one could argue, audience and referee design (Bell, 2001).

However, our ability to reach the level of focus discussed here is constrained. The following are the four constraints outlined in Le Page and Tabouret-Keller's work:

(i)    we can identify the groups
(ii)   we have both adequate access to the groups and ability to analyse their behavioural patterns
(iii)  the motivation to join the groups is sufficiently powerful, and is either reinforced or reversed by feedback from the groups
(iv)   we have the ability to modify our behaviour.
                            (Le Page and Tabouret-Keller, 1985, p. 182)

The first constraint is simple; in order to identify with some group, we have to know who belongs to that group and how that group is delimited. The example presented by the authors discusses how a child can, rather early in life, identify his mother and father as part of a group to which he belongs – although group identification is arguably a lot more complex when it comes to people of mixed descent (Le Page and Tabouret-Keller, 1985, p. 182).

Access requires that we can meaningfully interact with these groups – and the amount of access will determine the degree to which one can be part of the group. In Le Page and Tabouret-Keller's research, the focus seems to be on routes of communication and transportation as providing access. In an age of globalization, the access seems limitless, particularly in the world of hip hop. Ability to analyse behaviour deals with an individual's capacity for learning the patterns (particularly linguistic ones) present in a group (Le Page and Tabouret-Keller, 1985, pp. 183–184).

Motivation for group affiliation, which Le Page and Tabouret-Keller have called the most important of these constraints (1985, p. 184), is the oft-cited cause for a person choosing to adopt or eschew a particular linguistic variant. This motivation is linked to the idea of group solidarity; however, it is important to note that motivations can be mixed. For instance, the language of the home may have certain intimacy connotations, but still be devalued because another variety is the language of economic success.

Finally, the ability to modify one's (linguistic) behaviour requires that an individual be able to identify the patterns (following from the

**260**

second constraint) and to approximate them in a way that is accepted by the legitimated group members. This concerns how people learn to accommodate to others, focusing on the idea that a person beyond a certain age (i.e., the critical period) has a harder time modifying linguistic behaviour. Older individuals, according to the authors, require greater motivation in order to effectively modify their behaviour (Le Page and Tabouret-Keller, 1985, pp. 186–187).

According to Le Page and Tabouret-Keller, speakers are constrained by these four points in their identity-building process. In this chapter, we consider how hip-hop artists in the relatively understudied Southern and Midwestern hip-hop scenes are also constrained by these four points, looking specifically at the ways in which regional groups are identified and how access and behaviour modification are established. The case of Southern and Midwestern hip hop is an interesting site for identity construction, particularly in light of the media-hyped East Coast–West Coast rivalry of the 1990s (see Section 3 for further discussion). In our analysis of the data, we will return to Le Page and Tabouret-Keller's framework to discuss how hip-hop artists use lexical choices to construct their regional identities.

This overview points to the linguistic complexity of hip hop as it has evolved. It is clear that the question of identity plays a huge role in how hip-hop artists construct a song, an album and a persona. This chapter explores one instance of this identity construction: the construction of regional identity through the choice of regionally significant words. But in order to appreciate the reasons why a regional identity might be one of the many identities hip-hop artists have in their repertoires, we need to explore why region is important in US hip-hop culture.

## 3 The emergence of regional hip hop

The emergence of hip hop in the Midwestern and Southern United States can be best understood by examining the path that hip hop has taken in the United States, from its roots in Jamaican political unrest and in racial disquiet in the Bronx, New York (Chang, 2005). In this section, we briefly discuss how hip hop in the Midwest and South is a product of the rich history hip hop has in this country.

In the late 1960s, DJ Kool Herc moved from Jamaica to the Bronx. It was there that he made a name for himself as a DJ, and where his parties gave rise to hip-hop culture. Along with Grandmaster Flash and Afrika Bambaataa, he laid the groundwork for hip hop's future success. At the time hip hop was very local; most of the parties were held in South Bronx. It was not until after these DJs were already established that hip hop even ventured out of the borough. In the early 1980s, artists like

Run DMC, the Beastie Boys and LL Cool J emerged from Queens, but hip hop was still virtually confined to New York City (Chang, 2005).

Hip hop's genesis in New York meant that the East Coast scene dominated the genre until the early 1990s, when artists like Eazy E. and N.W.A. broke out on the West Coast. The music was different; it was no longer solely about 'The Message'. Many artists turned their sights more and more towards the gangster life: guns, drugs, sexual promiscuity. And, again, hip hop was associated with a locality. West Coast rap centred around South Central Los Angeles. N.W.A.'s 'Straight Outta Compton' was an anthem to locality. Chang claims that after the release of this album, 'it really was all about where you were from' (2005, p. 321).

Death Row Records, a West Coast record company headed by Suge Knight, was established as a rival to New York's Bad Boy Records, which featured artists like Sean 'Puffy' Combs, Nas, Jay-Z and DMX. A rivalry developed between the coasts, with artists taking their 'beefs' to the recording studio, incorporating 'disses' into their rhymes.[2] This rivalry culminated in the unsolved murders of Tupac Shakur (a West Coast rapper) and Notorious B.I.G. (an East Coast rapper) within six months of each other in 1996 and 1997, respectively (George, 1998).

In the latter half of the 1990s, after the fallout of the rivalry, record producers started to take notice of the rather large hip-hop movement in the Southern United States. This movement and genre is often referred to by the Southern hip-hop community as the 'Dirty South', a nickname that originated in a Goodie Mob song of the same name (Sarig, 2007; Goodie Mob, 1995). According to Sarig, the term is used as 'shorthand for the region's rap flavor' and points to 'the rowdier Southern hip-hop that was to come' (2007, p. 138). Born out of 'Southern rap' in places like Memphis, Atlanta, Houston and others, this 'third coast' hip hop (Sarig, 2007) developed in direct response to the East Coast–West Coast rivalry. In order to break away from the conflict, record labels needed to find a new market. They found it in Atlanta, a market that had been previously ignored (Cutler, 2007). And they found more than a new market; hip hop found a new home in the South. Sarig (2007), citing the recent large number of 'Billboard 100' number one hits by Southern rappers, claims that New York hip-hop artists began to feel like the underdogs.

What is interesting about the development of hip hop in the South is that, while seemingly born out of the other two coasts, the South also provided its own influence. Miami had the Miami Bass sound; Memphis was home to the blues; Houston saw a mix of soul, blues and gangster rap. These different sounds came together to form a larger conception of Southern hip hop. Groups like 2 Live Crew, Arrested

Development, Goodie Mob and others helped shape this conception, often drawing on Southern family values and the state of the New South to immortalize the Southerner in song (Sarig, 2007).

After Southern artists found success, hip hoppers from other regions, most notably the Midwest, began promoting their music with a particular regional connection. For instance, Nelly, a St. Louis-based rapper, has been described as having 'reduced his life story to a geographical fact: he comes from St. Louis' (Sanneh, 2002, p. 1). According to Alim (2009, p. 215), Nelly and the St. Lunatics 'were among the first rappers to represent St. Louis, Missouri on an (inter)national scale'. With Nelly as the apparent leader, the rise of hip hop in the Midwest has been characterized as 'the next Dirty South':

> Thanks to the Nelly-Eminem juggernaut, 2002 has turned out to be a banner year for Midwestern music as major labels begin to take unprecedented notice of St. Louis . . . Chicago and other cities scattered through the overlooked heartland. Thanks to the rise of the Southern sound epitomized by Atlanta artists like OutKast and Ludacris, regional rap is all the rage – and the region at the center of the map right now is, both culturally and geographically, miles from hip-hop's traditional East and West Coast strongholds. Even if St. Louis isn't the next Atlanta, the Midwest is already being touted as the next Dirty South. (Chonin, 2002)

Having established the path that led to the development of Midwestern and Southern varieties of hip hop, we can turn to the ways in which these artists index their regional affiliation through lexical choice in their songs.

## 4 The current study

This study focuses on how regional identities are established by rappers in the Midwestern and Southern United States. Specifically, we want to explore how rappers index local/regional affiliation through lexical choice and how these lexical choices serve to exclude non-members. Our hypothesis is that exclusion takes place through in-group references to entities of local importance, such as local events, food, neighbourhoods, etc. However, since no rapper can make a career out of selling just to the in-group, references to well-known landmarks and cities aid in reaching out to a larger audience. We were also concerned with the ways in which local affiliations contribute to the construction of regional hip-hop identities. By indexing non-coastal references specific to their respective regions, we suggest that Midwestern and Southern rappers create locally relevant hip hop that exemplifies regional authenticity.

For this study, we examined the lyrics of several songs written by artists claiming regional affiliation with either the Midwest or the South. For each artist, we selected two to three songs to analyse. When possible we selected songs that express some regional affiliation in the title. Regional markers in the title provide an initial context within which regional identity might more likely be expressed; however, the data will reveal that regional identity marking does not occur solely in this initial context. The lyrics were taken from www.azlyrics.com, a popular site for song lyrics.[3] Table 10.1 lists the artists and songs analysed in this study. The original analysis only consisted of the first seven artists. As will become clear in the analysis, more Midwestern artists were examined, in order to establish that the original results for the Midwestern artists were not unique. In each set of lyrics, we searched for words that fall into the following categories: cities/states, sports/schools, explicit to the region, foods, specific local reference, people, and other regional references. These categories were developed based on the authors' personal experience with regional hip hop as well as a preliminary examination of the data.

The first category, cities/states, includes references to place-names that might be found on a map (i.e., 'Atlanta', 'Chicago'), as well as nicknames that have gained wider understanding or are rather simple to decipher (i.e., 'A-town' for Atlanta, 'Chi-town' for Chicago). The category of sports/schools includes references to local sports teams (i.e., 'Braves' for Atlanta Braves baseball, 'Bulls' for Chicago Bulls basketball) and area schools. Explicit references to region are those that specifically name a regional affiliation, either as a noun (i.e., 'the South', 'the Midwest') or as a modifier (i.e., 'Southern hospitality'). The category of foods encompasses references to the cuisine of a particular region, including also specific products from particular states or regions (i.e., 'peaches' from Georgia). Specific local references are those that are more obscure; these references generally designate very specific local landmarks (i.e., names of housing projects and local hangouts) as well as names of streets and area nicknames that would be difficult to know without familiarity with the area. We also included a category for references to people from the area (i.e., 'Redd Fox' is from St. Louis). Finally, we included a 'catch-all' category called 'other regional reference', which serves to categorize words that carry regional importance but do not easily lend themselves to categorization (i.e., 'confederate flags', 'country living').

Only the first mention of a word in each song was tallied, to avoid finding an inordinate amount of references in a song that features repetition of a regional reference in the chorus. To verify the meanings of certain words, the authors used www.urbandictionary.com.[4]

**264**

**Table 10.1** Artists and songs analysed

| Artist | Regional affiliation (specific location) | Song (album) |
|---|---|---|
| Ludacris | South (Atlanta) | 'Georgia' (*ATL Soundtrack*, 2006); 'Southern Hospitality' (*Back for the First Time*, 2000) |
| Nappy Roots | South (Kentucky) | 'Awnaw' (*Watermelon, Chicken, & Gritz*, 2002); 'Kentucky Mud' (Watermelon, Chicken, & Gritz, 2002) |
| OutKast | South (Atlanta) | 'Southernplayalisticadillacmuzik' (*Southernplayalisticadillacmuzik*, 1994); 'Two Dope Boyz [In a Cadillac]' (ATLiens, 1996) |
| Kanye West | Midwest (Chicago) | 'Drive Slow' (*Late Registration*, 2005); 'Homecoming' (Graduation, 2007) |
| Nelly | Midwest (St. Louis) | 'St. Louie' (*Country Grammar*, 2000); 'Country Grammar' (*Country Grammar*, 2000) |
| Common | Midwest (Chicago) | 'Chi-City' (*Be*, 2005); 'Southside' (*Finding Forever*, 2007) |
| Twista | Midwest (Chicago) | 'Art & Life [Chi-Rock]' (*Kamikaze*, 2004); 'No Remorse' (*Adrenaline Rush*, 1997) |
| Streetz & Young Deuces | Midwest (Milwaukee) | 'Just Asking You' (*Money Marathon*, 2008); 'Get it Done' (*Get it Done 12"*, 2008) |
| D12 | Midwest (Detroit) | 'D12 World' (*D12 World*, 2004) |
| Bugz | Midwest (Detroit) | 'Can't Nobody/Detroit Detroit' (*These Streets EP*, 1999) |
| Bugz, Bizarre, Shane Capone, and 5150 | Midwest (Detroit) | 'Cruel Intentions' (*Damaging Words*, 2001) |
| Rhymefest | Midwest (Chicago) | 'Dynomite [Going Postal]' (*Blue Collar*, 2006) |
| P.O.S. | Midwest (Minneapolis) | 'Half Cocked' (*Audition*, 2006) |

**265**

Once the results were tabulated for each region separately, Midwestern and Southern hip-hop artists' regional indexing strategies were compared.

# 5 Results

## 5.1 The South

The following states are typically included in descriptions of the South: Texas, Louisiana, Mississippi, Alabama, Tennessee, Kentucky, Georgia, Florida, South Carolina, North Carolina, Virginia, Maryland and West Virginia. Hip hop has flourished in many different locales within these areas, but it has been most successful in major metropolitan cities like Atlanta, Houston and Memphis.

Lexical references to the South in the lyrics of Southern rappers can be found in Table 10.2. Looking at the raw numbers, we see that the artists in this study make use of all of our categories relatively consistently (with the exception of sports/schools). Ludacris uses more total references (N = 47) than the other two artists, with references to Southern foods occurring most frequently. References to food are the most common category for all artists. These references include 'collard

**Table 10.2** Categorization of Southern Data

| Artist – song | Cities/states | Explicit regional reference | Specific local reference | Other regional reference | Sports/schools | Foods | People | Total |
|---|---|---|---|---|---|---|---|---|
| Ludacris 'Georgia' | 10 | 1 | 2 | 4 | 6 | 12 | 3 | 38 |
| Ludacris 'Southern Hospitality' | 0 | 2 | 0 | 1 | 0 | 5 | 1 | 9 |
| Nappy Roots 'Awnaw' | 1 | 0 | 1 | 4 | 0 | 0 | 2 | 8 |
| Nappy Roots 'Kentucky Mud' | 0 | 1 | 6 | 8 | 0 | 0 | 3 | 18 |
| OutKast 'Southernplaylisticadillacmuzik' | 3 | 5 | 2 | 4 | 0 | 4 | 8 | 26 |
| OutKast 'Two Dope Boyz' | 1 | 1 | 4 | 0 | 0 | 1 | 1 | 8 |
| Total | 15 | 10 | 15 | 21 | 6 | 22 | 18 | 107 |
| Percent | | 14.0 | 9.4 | 14.0 | 19.6 | 5.6 | 20.6 | 16.8 | 100 |

greens', 'grits' and 'chitlins', all stereotypical Southern foods, as well as references to specific regional products, like 'peaches' from Georgia and 'bourbon' from Kentucky. Nappy Roots lyrics contain many references to other Southern cultural notions, like 'roosters' on farms, 'confederate flags', and 'country' lifestyles, which are categorized under the heading of 'other regional reference'. This category served as the second most frequent category, which might be expected as it serves as our 'catch-all'.

## 5.2 The Midwest

The Midwest encompasses Illinois, Indiana, Iowa, Ohio, Michigan, Missouri, Wisconsin and Minnesota. Major hip-hop artists from the Midwest typically get their start in major cities, like Chicago, St. Louis and Detroit. Artists such as Nelly (St. Louis) and Kanye West (Chicago) have achieved local, national and international acclaim. Table 10.3 shows the breakdown of the different types of localized lexical items for the Midwestern artists, by song.

**Table 10.3** Categorization of Midwestern Data I

| Artist – song | Cities/states | Explicit regional reference | Specific local reference | Other regional reference | Sports/schools | Foods | People | Total |
|---|---|---|---|---|---|---|---|---|
| Nelly 'St. Louie' | 1 | 0 | 8 | 0 | 0 | 0 | 3 | 12 |
| Nelly 'Country Grammar' | 2 | 0 | 3 | 0 | 0 | 0 | 0 | 5 |
| Kanye West 'Drive Slow' | 1 | 0 | 3 | 0 | 1 | 0 | 0 | 5 |
| Kanye West 'Homecoming' | 2 | 0 | 1 | 0 | 0 | 0 | 0 | 3 |
| Common 'Chi City' | 2 | 0 | 0 | 0 | 0 | 0 | 0 | 2 |
| Common 'South Side' | 4 | 0 | 2 | 0 | 0 | 0 | 0 | 6 |
| Twista 'Art & Life' | 2 | 0 | 9 | 0 | 0 | 0 | 0 | 11 |
| Twista 'No Remorse' | 1 | 0 | 2 | 0 | 0 | 0 | 0 | 3 |
| Total | 15 | 0 | 28 | 0 | 1 | 0 | 3 | 47 |
| Percent | 31.9 | 0 | 59.6 | 0 | 2.1 | 0 | 6.4 | 100 |

As shown in Table 10.3, Midwestern hip-hop artists tend to emphasize the names of their cities ('St. Louie', 'Chi-Rock') and focus on local references, including items such as shopping malls and street gangs. We see no explicit mention of region, or of unifying regional items (such as the 'country' experience mentioned by the Southern artists).

More than half of these indices of local identity by artists from St. Louis and Chicago are comprised of specific local references such as St. Louis's O'Fallon neighbourhood and Chesterfield Mall, and Chicago's Stones (street gang), West Side neighbourhood, and Lake Michigan. However, songs from the two cities differ in lexical identity construction in that the St. Louis artist refers to well-known people from the city (i.e., 'Cedric the Entertainer', 'Redd Foxx'), whereas the Chicago artists make no mention of famous people. Both groups mention cities and states (Nelly: 'St. Louie', 'the Lou'; Chicago artists: 'Chi-City', 'Chi-Roc'), though Chicago artists use these references more frequently.

A brief examination of other Midwestern cities' rappers shows that if we had originally included a wider range of artists, we might have found more explicit regional references like 'Midwest'. Table 10.4

**Table 10.4** Categorization of Midwestern Data II

| Artist – song | Cities/states | Explicit regional reference | Specific local reference | Other regional reference | Sports/schools | Foods | People | Total |
|---|---|---|---|---|---|---|---|---|
| Streetz & Young Deuces 'Just Asking You' | 0 | 0 | 1 | 0 | 0 | 0 | 0 | 1 |
| Streetz & Young Deuces 'Get It Done' | 1 | 0 | 0 | 0 | 0 | 0 | 0 | 1 |
| D12 'D12 World' | 0 | 0 | 0 | 0 | 0 | 0 | 1 | 1 |
| Bugz 'Can't Nobody' | 1 | 0 | 1 | 0 | 0 | 0 | 0 | 2 |
| Bugz et al 'Cruel Intentions' | 1 | 0 | 4 | 0 | 0 | 0 | 0 | 5 |
| Rhymefest 'Dynomite' | 0 | 0 | 2 | 0 | 0 | 0 | 0 | 2 |
| P.O.S. 'Half Cocked' | 1 | 2 | 2 | 1 | 0 | 0 | 1 | 7 |
| Total | 4 | 2 | 10 | 1 | 0 | 0 | 2 | 19 |
| Percent | 21.1 | 10.5 | 52.6 | 5.3 | 0 | 0 | 10.5 | 100 |

shows how some additional Midwestern artists index their local and regional affiliations. Like the other results from the Midwest, local references made up the majority of lexical indexing of locality. Again, there is no mention of foods from the region. However, unlike the other Midwest data, there is some explicit reference to region, from one song: P.O.S.'s 'Half-Cocked'. Two adjacent lines in this song mention 'the Middle West' and 'the heart land'. A covert reference is contained in 'Our nights are colder right?' Otherwise, the Midwestern data from the second round of collection follow much in line with those of the first round.

## 5.3 Comparison

Overall, it seems fair to say that Midwestern artists use local references in lexical choice more than they use any other strategy for indexing local identity, using explicit names of cities or states as a secondary strategy about half as often. These two strategies alone account for roughly 90 per cent of the data in the first round of Midwest hip-hop examination, and more than 70 per cent in the second round. These findings contrast starkly with the lexical indexing of locality for Southern artists, whose distribution scatters with much more consistency across the categories.

# 6 Discussion

Let us begin the discussion of the data by examining how these artists can be described as creating a regional identity through the lens of Le Page and Tabouret-Keller's (1985) constraints on acts of identity. We must look at individual artists to see how this identity is portrayed. We begin by examining more closely the lyrics of the song 'Georgia' by the Southern rapper Ludacris. With respect to Le Page and Tabouret-Keller's (1985) first constraint, it is clear from the title of this song that Ludacris has identified a particular group to identify with. To identify with other Georgians, Ludacris must discover what is important to people in that group. In one stanza, Ludacris makes reference to three Georgia sports teams ('Dirty Birds', a nickname for the Atlanta Falcons football team; 'Bulldawgs', the mascot for the University of Georgia athletics; 'be brave', covert reference to Atlanta Braves baseball). Ludacris's references suggest that sports are important to the particular group of Georgians with whom he wants to identify.

He also needs access to the group. Despite having been born in Illinois, Ludacris has been one of the most successful artists from the Dirty South, which seems to indicate that he has the access. The motivation could be record sales, however many Southerners develop a strong connection to the region, which may be more of a motivation for indexing a Southern identity. Having been an outsider originally may have driven Ludacris to establish his Southern identity clearly in his songs.

Finally, when we talk of modifying behaviour, we need evidence that his behaviour is different in other contexts. The only evidence of such is that Ludacris does not rap about Georgia in all of his songs. Thus, this particular song represents a concerted effort to index a Southern (or at least Georgian) identity.

For Midwestern artists, the acts of identity we observed are not realized in the same way. Kanye West's 'Homecoming' (2007) epitomizes Chicago artists' treatment of their city. Listeners can easily identify the subject of the song (made explicitly clear by the line, 'If y'all don't know by now, I'm talking 'bout Chi-town'), and thus the group with which West affiliates. West's access to the group is undeniable: Chicago supports its artists and West's Chicago upbringing is often the subject of media attention. His childhood on Chicago's south side affords him access to the city's well-known features (such as Lake Michigan) as well as features known better to locals (not exploited in this song, but in others such as 'Drive Slow').

The motivation underlying acts of identity distinguishes these two artists: Kanye West was extremely well-known when his album 'Homecoming' was released; thus, the motivation to gain a specific Chicago following was not necessary. In order to maintain his hometown supporters without alienating non-Chicago audiences, his references needed to be general enough to be inclusive to the out-group. The only references to Chicago in 'Homecoming' are the terms 'Chi City' and 'Chi-town' and the obvious natural feature, Lake Michigan.

We know West has the ability to modify his behaviour; he already has. In 2005, Kanye West was already wildly popular in Chicago, but was just bursting onto the national/international scene. 'Drive Slow' came out at this time, making references to specific south side Chicago features such as a specific street corner ('79th and May') and a local school ('Calumet High School'). In the two years between the release of 'Drive Slow' and 'Homecoming', West attained a much wider audience, so his references became more inclusive, referring to 'Chi-town' and 'Lake Michigan' instead of using more specific, local lexical items.

We can see a similar pattern with Nelly, whose entire *Country Grammar* album is laden with highly specific references to St. Louis.[5] Interestingly, of the two songs analysed here, *Country Grammar* was the success story, catapulting the artist to fame. This song mentions three neighbourhoods in St. Louis (Jennings, U-City, Kingsland), but otherwise only references 'St. Louis' and 'The Lou', two obvious references to the city (another obvious reference in Nelly's repertoire is his backup group, the 'St. Lunatics'). A glance at singles on later albums did not reveal overt or implicit references to St. Louis. Again, what is obvious is accessible; as there does not seem to be a cohesive Midwestern regional identity in hip hop, Nelly and other Midwestern artists can only take their local identities so far before losing their audiences.

Our examination of Southern and Midwestern hip-hop artists' means of indexing identity confirms our hypothesis that regional affiliation is achieved through the use of specific lexical choices. These artists connect with the in-group through references to specific local events, foods, neighbourhoods, etc. that are unknown to the larger audience. However, to attract those unfamiliar with the very specific local affiliations the artists strive for, they also include references to well-known cities and landmarks.

Nevertheless, the ways in which Southern and Midwestern artists index their local identities differ. While the Southern artists use almost all of our pre-established indexing categories, Midwestern artists seem to focus on references to cities and specific local information. This could indicate that the Southern rappers are more inclusive of the larger regional audience. Midwestern artists tend to affiliate with cities, and audiences from these cities appear to be extremely loyal. In order to maintain the large audiences achieved in the home city (such as St. Louis and Chicago), the city must be named. However, in order to succeed beyond the local scene, references must be kept general. The most successful Midwestern artists analysed here, Nelly and Kanye West, do just that. The other Midwestern artists are not as successful beyond their home cities, where audiences still catch the references.

We can return to one of Le Page and Tabouret-Keller's constraints to understand these differences. In identifying groups, Le Page and Tabouret-Keller point to certain clear-cut, easily identifiable groups like 'American' and 'Irish'. These groups, they claim, have at least at some point been associated with a single language and a monolithic culture. One could argue that we find a similar case in the Southern United States. The dialect spoken in the South is one of the most recognizable American dialects. The culture associated with Southernness is also quite salient, including certain foods, religions, sports, etc. But the Midwest seems to be lacking in these respects. Discussions about an overarching Midwestern dialect often result in a decision that the speech is neutral. It also does not seem that one singular salient culture is perceived to be associated with being a Midwesterner. This might explain the lack of cohesiveness in the ways in which regional identification is established among Midwestern hip-hop artists.

**271**

Having established the existence of these regional identities, we must look for some explanations for their creation. Perhaps coastal affiliations made rappers from other regions feel insecure, due to historical slighting by record companies. For Southern rappers, a long-standing tradition of affiliation and pride in the region could explain their desire to identify with that group (Sarig, 2007). For the Midwestern cities, perhaps size of city creates less need for regionality.

It is also important to understand why there are differences between the ways in which Southern and Midwestern hip-hop artists index regional identities. Our methodology did not span a large enough area of the country to get all the answers, but perhaps the insecurity that surrounded the birth of the Dirty South has little influence on Midwest rappers because that variety is more removed from the coastal debates. Additionally, as might be the case with Nappy Roots, if artists come from lesser-known areas or smaller cities, they may be more likely to affiliate on a regional, rather than local, level. Further research in these areas might elucidate some of these questions about regional hip-hop identity construction.

## 7 Conclusions and areas for further research

We can conclude that rappers index their local/regional affiliation lexically through in-group references to the seven categories we examined. But as we have seen, Midwestern and Southern rappers in different cities vary in the construction of their larger regional local affiliations, even within the same region (as in Chicago and St. Louis in the Midwest).

Further research would help clarify the ways in which regional hip-hop identity is established. It would be interesting to see specifically how success on the music charts (national and international) correlates with more obscure local lexical indexing.

Additionally, now that we have established that several regional identities already exist in US hip hop (East Coast, West Coast, Dirty South, and Midwest), we wonder what might crop up next on the rap map. And when a new regional variety appears, how will region and locality be indexed (if at all)? While we cannot speculate which regional varieties will emerge, we think that regionality may become less important. Without a two-coast dichotomy, perhaps some overarching American hip hop will emerge. Or, perhaps the essence of locality will become the city, as it seems to have already in the Midwest.

As researchers expand their studies in Hip Hop Linguistics, they should be constantly on the lookout for multidisciplinary theoretical approaches to round out their research. This study is only an initial foray into what can be inferred from linguistics, sociology and linguistic

**272**

anthropology. Additional incorporation of ideas from musicology, psychology, minority studies, and other areas can only benefit what is already proving to be a field of inquiry with important consequences for how we understand the construct of identity.

## Acknowledgements

The authors would like to thank Marina Terkourafi, the audiences at the November 2007 workshop on 'Language and Hip Hop Culture in a Globalizing World' at the University of Illinois at Urbana-Champaign and at Sociolinguistics Symposium 17 in Amsterdam, and the two anonymous reviewers for all of their helpful comments and suggestions.

## Notes

1. For a summary of the regional forms of hip-hop language, see Cutler (2007).
2. As one reviewer pointed out, the East Coast–West Coast rivalry was perhaps made to be more important than it actually was by the popular press. However, we argue that the media's coverage of the situation originally gave music producers a niche market to play into, thus making a move to other regions an undesirable shift. As the feud escalated, those same producers sought new talent elsewhere, to distance themselves from the conflict.
3. This website is like a wiki, in that anyone can edit lyric entries. It does not seem to be as rigorously edited as Wikipedia, for instance, therefore it is prone to errors. However, the popularity of this site leads us to believe that it is one of the best sources for this kind of data on the internet.
4. This website is organized like a dictionary, with several entries for words that are typically considered slang and therefore would not have appropriate definitions in a standard dictionary. Each entry features a sample sentence as well. Like www.azlyrics.com, this website is a wiki and is prone to error. However, this site is well-known for its wide and up-to-date coverage of current terminology.
5. As one reviewer noted, this album title could seem more like a reference to the South than to the Midwest. Biographies about Nelly indicate that his upbringing was somehow both urban and rural and that this is reflected in his accent, which has been described as being 'as much Southern drawl as Midwestern twang' (Birchmeier, 2009). The album title, then, could be considered to highlight this feature of his accent. Overall, the album seems to be filled mostly with Midwestern (St. Louis) references, not Southern ones.

## Discography

Bugz (1999), 'Can't Nobody/Detroit Detroit', *These Streets EP*. Goodlife Entertainment.

Bugz, Bizarre, Shane Capone, and 5150 (2001), 'Cruel Intentions', *Damaging Words*. Fifth Mile Productions.

Common (2005), 'Chi-City', *Be*. Geffen Records.

Common (2007), 'Southside', *Finding Forever*. Universal Music Group.

D12 (2004), 'D12 World', *D12 World*. Shady Records.

Goodie Mob (1999), 'Dirty South', *Soul Food*. LaFace Records.

Ludacris (2000), 'Southern Hospitality', *Back for the First Time*. Def Jam.

Ludacris (2006), 'Georgia', *ATL Soundtrack*. The Island Def Jam Music Group.

Nappy Roots (2002), 'Awnaw', *Watermelon, Chicken, & Gritz*. Atlantic.

Nappy Roots (2002), 'Kentucky Mud', *Watermelon, Chicken, & Gritz*. Atlantic.

Nelly (2000), 'Country Grammar', *Country Grammar*. Umvd Labels.

Nelly (2000), 'St. Louie', *Country Grammar*. Umvd Labels.

OutKast (1994), 'Southernplayalisticadillacmuzik', *Southernplayalisticadillac-muzik*. Artista/LaFace.

OutKast (1996), 'Two Dope Boyz [in a Cadillac]', *ATLiens*. Artista/LaFace.

P.O.S. (2006), 'Half Cocked', *Audition*. Rhymesayers.

Rhymefest (2006), 'Dynomite [Going Postal]', *Blue Collar*. Allido Records.

Streetz & Young Deuces (2008), 'Just Asking You', *Money Marathon*. Unsigned.

Streetz & Young Deuces (2008), 'Get it Done', *Get it Done 12"*. Unsigned.

Twista (1997), 'No Remorse', *Adrenaline Rush*. Big Beat /Wea.

Twista (2004), 'Art & Life [Chi-Rock]', *Kamikaze*. Atlantic /Wea.

West, K. (2005), 'Drive Slow', *Late Registration*. Roc-A-Fella Records.

West, K. (2007), 'Homecoming', *Graduation*. Roc-A-Fella Records.

# References

Alim, H. S. (2009), 'Creating "an empire within an empire": critical hip hop language pedagogies and the role of sociolinguistics', in H. S. Alim, A. Ibrahim and A. Pennycook (eds), *Global Linguistic Flows: Hip Hop Cultures, Youth Identities, and the Politics of Language*. New York: Routledge, pp. 213–230.

Alim, H. S., Ibrahim A. and Pennycook A. (eds) (2009), *Global Linguistic Flows: Hip Hop Cultures, Youth Identities, and the Politics of Language*. New York: Routledge.

Bell, A. (2001), 'Back in style: reworking audience design', in P. Eckert and J. R. Rickford (eds), *Style and Sociolinguistic Variation*. Cambridge: Cambridge University Press, pp. 139–169.

Birchmeier, J. (2009), 'Full Biography', Nelly | Music Videos, News, Photos, Tour Dates, Ringtones, and Lyrics | MTV. MTV.com. <http://www.mtv.com/music/artist/nelly/artist.jhtml>, accessed 21 May 2009.

Bucholtz, M. and K. Hall (2005), 'Identity and interaction: a sociocultural linguistic approach'. *Discourse Studies*, 7, 4–5, 585–614.

Chang, J. (2005), *Can't Stop Won't Stop: A History of the Hip-Hop Generation*. New York: St. Martin's Press.

Chonin, N. (2002), 'Hip-hop heartland: Nelly and Eminem make the Midwest a rap hot spot'. *San Francisco Chronicle*, Wednesday, 16 October 2002.

<http://www.sfgate.com/cgi-bin/article.cgi?f=/c/a/2002/10/16/DD180076.D TL&hw=hi+hop+heartland&sn=002&sc=668>, accessed 27 January 2009.

Cutler, C. (2007), 'Hip-hop language in sociolinguistics and beyond'. *Language and Linguistics Compass*, 1, 5, 519–538.

George, N. (1998), *Hip Hop America*. New York: Viking/Penguin.

Goodall, N. H. (1994), 'Depend on myself: T.L.C. and the evolution of black female rap'. *The Journal of Negro History*, 79, 1, 85–93.

Haugen, J. D. (2003), '"Unladylike divas": language, gender, and female gangsta rappers'. *Popular Music and Society*, 26, 429–444.

Higgins, C. (2009), 'From Da Bomb to *Bomba*: Global Hip Hop Nation language in Tanzania', in H. S. Alim, A. Ibrahim and A. Pennycook (eds), *Global Linguistic Flows: Hip Hop Cultures, Youth Identities, and the Politics of Language*. New York: Routledge, pp. 95–112.

Le Page, R. B. and Tabouret-Keller, A. (1985), *Acts of Identity: Creole-based Approaches to Language and Ethnicity*. Cambridge, UK: Cambridge University Press.

Mitchell, T. (ed.) (2001), *Global Noise: Rap and Hip Hop Outside the USA*. Middletown, CT: Wesleyan University Press.

—(2003), 'Doin' damage in my native language: the use of "resistance vernaculars" in hip hop in France, Italy, and Aotearoa/New Zealand', in H. M. Berger and M. T. Carroll (eds), *Global Pop, Local Language*. Jackson, MS: University Press of Mississippi, pp. 3–17.

Morgan, M. (1993), 'Hip Hop Hooray!: the linguistic production of identity'. Paper presented at Annual Meeting of the American Anthropological Association, Washington, D.C.

—(2001), '"Nuthin' but a G thang": grammar and language ideology in hip hop identity', in S. L. Lanehart (ed.), *Sociocultural and Historical Contexts of African American English*. Amsterdam/Philadelphia: John Benjamins, pp. 187–209.

—(2002), *Language, Discourse and Power in African American Culture*. Cambridge: Cambridge University Press.

Omoniyi, T. (2006), 'Hip hop through the World Englishes lens: a response to globalization'. *World Englishes*, 25, 2, 195–208.

—(2009), '"So I choose to do am Naija style": hip hop, language, and post-colonial identities', in H. S. Alim, A. Ibrahim and A. Pennycook (eds), *Global Linguistic Flows: Hip Hop Cultures, Youth Identities, and the Politics of Language*. New York: Routledge, pp. 113–138.

Osumare, H. (2001), 'Beat streets in the global hood: connective marginalities of the hip hop globe'. *Journal of American & Comparative Cultures*, 24, 1–2, 171–181.

Pennycook, A. (2007), *Global Englishes and Transcultural Flows*. London: Routledge.

Perullo, A. and J. Fenn (2003), 'Language ideologies, choices, and practices in Eastern African hip hop', in H. M. Berger and M. T. Carroll (eds), *Global Pop, Local Language*. Jackson, MS: University Press of Mississippi, pp. 19–51.

**275**

Roth-Gordon, J. (2009), 'Conversational sampling, race trafficking, and the invocation of the *gueto* in Brazilian hip hop', in H. S. Alim, A. Ibrahim and A. Pennycook (eds), *Global Linguistic Flows: Hip Hop Cultures, Youth Identities, and the Politics of Language*. New York: Routledge, pp. 63–77.

Sanneh, K. (2002), 'The mayor of Nellyville, a floating neighbourhood'. *The New York Times*, 23 June 2002. <http://query.nytimes.com/gst/fullpage.htm l?res=9C03E0DA163FF930A15755C0A9649C8B63&sec=&spon=&pagewant ed=2>, accessed 27 January 2009.

Sarig, R. (2007), *Third Coast: OutKast, Timbaland, and How Hip-Hop Became a Southern Thing*. Cambridge, MA: Da Capo Press.

# 11 Realkeepen: Anglicisms in the German Hip-Hop Community

Matt Garley

## 1 Introduction[1]

In the last decade, a number of linguistic analyses of German-language hip hop have been conducted (among numerous others, Androutsopoulos and Scholz, 2003; Berns and Schlobinski, 2003; Androutsopoulos, 2009). These studies are fundamentally qualitative, and many of them (Androutsopoulos's work being the primary exception) focus solely on rap lyrics, as Androutsopoulos notes in his call for the exploration of (largely) ignored territories in linguistic research on hip hop:

> most language-centered studies on hip hop focus on rap lyrics. Although this focus has yielded many important results so far, it seems to overlook the emic distinction between hip hop as a cultural hyperonym and rap as one of its hyponyms . . . An integrative view on language and hip hop would need to encompass a much wider range of discourse practices, such as talk at work among rappers, writers, and breakers; the discourse of hip hop magazines and broadcast shows; artist-fan communication during live events; and an array of everyday talk and computer-mediated discourse in what is often termed the *Hip Hop Nation*. [emphasis added] (2009, p. 44)

In the present study, I seek to address this gap in research by discussing the role of English borrowings in the German hip-hop fan community, drawing on quantitative analysis of an original corpus collected from a German-language internet hip-hop discussion forum – a large collection of natural language material produced by hip-hop fans. While the exact classification of the borrowed variety of English may be a matter of some debate, my focus will instead be on the forms and social meanings of hip hop-related borrowings. This concentration on quantitative data from hip-hop fans and followers not only answers questions regarding the nature and significance of the linguistic borrowing

**277**

process, but also addresses questions regarding sociolinguistic factors which affect the incidence of borrowing.

This study concerns itself with the following questions: first, how frequently do youth on the cutting edge of this imported subculture engage in the practice of linguistic borrowing? Second, how do these borrowing practices compare to those of non-hip hoppers? Third, what sorts of factors might constrain the use of borrowings in this subculture? Fourth, what sort of formal linguistic and orthographic constraints on borrowing are attested in online hip-hop discussion? Finally, what does borrowing in German hip-hop fans' language reveal about the question of *imitation versus innovation* in terms of global hip-hop culture? As Higgins asks in her study on hip hop-related influences on language in Tanzania:

> Are these youth *crossing* from Tanzanian varieties of English into AAE, borrowing the linguistic and semiotic styles of another culture? Or, are they *appropriating* what may be better described as Global Hip Hop Nation Language to fit their local East African context, their language use resulting in a simultaneously localized, yet global, form of expression . . . ? (2009, p. 95, original emphasis)

In this study, I ask a similar question with regard to German hip-hop fans' language practices.

In addressing these research questions, I discuss the utility of Rampton's (2005) notion of 'crossing', which has been cited and applied extensively in work on global hip hop (Androutsopoulos, 2009 and Higgins, 2009 being two recent examples), calling into question its straightforward application to the analysis of German hip-hop fans' borrowing practices. Through the analysis of my own data, I reveal an orientation towards the (non-present) discourse referent – American and German hip-hop artists – through patterns in the use of borrowing. I account for this orientation by introducing 'crossing avoidance', which relies in this case on Bell's (1991) notion of 'referee design', demonstrating that German hip-hop fans tailor language practices specifically to avoid the pitfalls inherent in linguistic crossing. Finally, I address the question of imitation vs innovation in German hip-hop culture – proposing that neither one description nor the other can alone account for the borrowing patterns found in German hip-hop fans' language use.

I begin by introducing the dataset analysed in Section 2. In Section 3 I put forth a more precise definition of the anglicism and outline the methods used in this study, while in Section 4 I present the results of a number of large-scale analyses alongside a discussion of particular anglicisms found in the corpora, followed by a discussion of the case for innovation in German hip-hop fans' language use. In Section 5,

**278**

I present the results of a closer analysis contrasting fans' discussions of German artists with their discussions of American artists, and present the case for imitation in German hip-hop fans' language use. Section 6 concludes the chapter and summarizes the results.

## 2 The dataset

The German hip-hop scene has gained popularity in leaps and bounds since the late 1980s. One of the most prominent German hip hop gathering points in the last decade has been the website MZEE.com, which presents itself as the *größtes deutschsprachiges Hip Hop medium überhaupt* ('largest German-language Hip-Hop medium anywhere'), a claim borne out by statistics from independent web monitoring company Alexa.com.[2] MZEE.com (*mzee* being the quasi-phonetic transliteration of 'MC' in German)[3] is an online hip-hop fan portal; the title of the main page reads as follows: *MZEE.com: Hip Hop Network (Forum, Dates, Shop, News . . .) HipHop Rap Graffiti Aerosol Writing DJing Breakdance BBoying.*[4] Given the page title, an English-language frontpage might be expected, but this is not the case: apart from the headings on different sections of the site, which are either English borrowings like 'Shop, Newscenter, Special', or else borrowings combining English and German material, like *Jamkalender* ('jam calendar'), the text on the MZEE.com frontpage is predominantly in German.

The MZEE.com forums, with 4.35 million posts, include debate about German and American rap artists and DJs alongside original compositions and discussions of the other forms of expression which comprise hip-hop culture. As is standard for the medium of internet forums and discussion boards, the MZEE.com forums are accessed through a web browser, and constitute an asynchronous form of online communication in which multipartite discussions are carried out in topic-titled discussion 'threads' by users identified with a nickname. Forums like those at MZEE.com are moderated by volunteers, usually veterans of the messageboards, who attempt to enforce the board-specific regulations and keep discussions on topic. Rather than deleting posts and threads, moderators generally wield power by 'locking' threads (allowing no further posts), banning users from the forum temporarily or permanently, or moving discussions from one subforum to another – leaving the use of natural language essentially intact. The forums were chosen for this study because of the potential for capturing German hip-hop fans' use of anglicisms. While the use of borrowings on the MZEE.com staff blogs, interviews and news stories would make for an interesting discussion, these would represent an editorial view – one rigorously constrained by corporate realities. The forums,

**279**

on the other hand, represent a quasi-random sampling of German-speaking fans, volunteering their own views on topics germane to hip-hop culture.

The research presented here is mainly grounded on a by-hand analysis of a small corpus of ten threads from the MZEE.com forum. This corpus, which I will call the 10-thread corpus, includes approximately 24,000 words in 1,000 posts (100 posts per thread) from the years 2007 and 2008 from threads discussing the following German and American artists: (American) G-Unit, Ludacris, Redman, Talib Kweli and Tech N9ne; (German) Curse, Dynamite Deluxe, JAW, Taichi and Westberlin Maskulin. These threads were selected at random from a list of notable artist discussion threads compiled by the users of the MZEE.com forum, and five of each were selected in order to operationalize 'nationality of discourse referent' as a sociolinguistic variable (the reasons for focusing on this variable will become clear in Section 5 below).

Items which the by-hand analysis revealed to be of interest were then further investigated in two large, originally collected corpora. These large corpora are used in the present study for gross comparisons of hip hop-related discussion to standard German discussion and for corroboration of patterns found in smaller samples. The first of these I will refer to as the MZEE corpus, a 17.9 million word corpus comprising 339,436 forum posts, of which the 10-thread corpus comprises a subset; the MZEE corpus essentially mirrors the entire *Hip hop Diskussion* subforum at MZEE.com from 2000 to 2008. It is worth noting at this juncture that it is nearly impossible to ensure that all users of the MZEE.com forums are native German speakers, or that they are furthermore not native English speakers. While such 'noise' certainly exists in the data, the size of the large corpora and the likelihood that the vast majority of MZEE.com forum users are native speakers of some variety of German should serve to mitigate some of these concerns. At the very least, it can be asserted that this dataset represents speakers of German, and furthermore speakers of German who are interested in hip hop.

The second of the large corpora is the *Tagesschau* corpus, a 136.9 million word corpus comprising 1.05 million forum posts collected from the forums at German news site tagesschau.de, which is devoted to news discussion revolving around a daily news report broadcast by the ARD, a consortium of public broadcasters.[5] This corpus, with post dates ranging from 2004 to 2008, is essentially a collection of news discussions revolving around Germany's most popular nightly news program.

# 3 Methods

The present study takes as its starting point the definition of English-to-German borrowings by Onysko (2007), who presented a comprehensive treatment of the subject of anglicisms (English borrowings). Onysko provides a critical discussion of past classifications of anglicisms, and suggests a model involving the transmission of language material from a source language (SL) into a receptor language (RL).

Onysko identifies four primary types of transmission of language material. Straightforward 'borrowing' (the classic examples being loanwords like 'Gang', 'cool' and 'Designer') includes productive uses of borrowing (*Abendshow*,'evening show'; *cruisen*, 'to cruise'; *dealen*, 'to deal'), all of which involve a transfer of form and meaning from SL to RL.[6] 'Conceptual transmission without SL form' involves the novel creation of lexical items on the basis of an SL concept; an example of this would be a calque like *Wolkenkratzer* ('skyscraper', lit.'cloud-scratcher'). The third type of transmission, which Onysko calls 'interference', involves the semantic broadening of an RL lexical item to match the semantics of a similar SL lexical item – in this way, German *realisieren* can mean 'to become aware of' on the basis of English 'realize', a broadening from the original German meaning, 'to make something concrete'.[7] Finally, 'code-switching' is taken to involve the syntactic embedding of SL material – multiword units – in an RL matrix clause. An example of this type of anglicism comes from a German McDonalds ad: 'About this *Frühstücksei lachen ja* the chickens' ('Even the chickens are laughing about this breakfast egg'). This model affords a great deal of flexibility, as it covers a wide variety of instances of language material transfer. For the purposes of the present study, all four types of transmission are considered, but the majority of identifiable anglicisms consist of instances of borrowing (type 1) and code-switching (type 4).

In order to find items of interest for the present analysis, anglicisms in the 10-thread corpus were identified by a trained annotator. In the identification process, certain parts of the text were exempted from anglicism identification: these included quoted song lyrics, names of hip-hop artists, album and song titles, names of record labels, forum posters' usernames, names of TV shows, magazines and movies, and direct quotes from previous posts and outside news sources. The above were exempted from identification because no choice is made by the language user to favour one code over the other: these can be considered a type of 'forced' usage.

After the identification of anglicisms in the 10 threads, anglicisms – individual lexical borrowings including some German words with significantly borrowed/extended meanings – were grouped into types: all occurrences of verb forms of a single verbal lexeme were taken to constitute a type, as were all instances of plural and inflected forms of a noun. Adjectives were also grouped into types, including in each type comparative and superlative forms of the adjective.

At this point, Carstensen and Busse's (1993) *Anglizismen-Wörterbuch* ('Dictionary of Anglicisms') was consulted for matches. This reference was chosen primarily because it is the most complete dictionary of anglicisms in German from 1945 on, but also because it has the particular benefit (with regard to this study) of its year of publication: Carstensen and Busse's corpora extend up to about 1989, when hip hop in Germany had only begun to emerge from the underground – therefore Carstensen and Busse's dictionary is unlikely to include most newer hip hop-related borrowings, assisting in the proper distinction of these potentially hip hop-related borrowings from older (pre-1989) borrowings. Indeed, more than half of anglicisms (423/611 types, or 59%) were found to match in form and general meaning in Carstensen and Busse's dictionary (including straightforward extensions, like 'crew', attested from 1910 with the nautical meaning) and these were exempted from further analysis, as they are not candidates for hip hop-related borrowing/innovation.

It was unproblematic to categorize the majority of the remaining 188 types into one of three categories:

1. *hip hop-related borrowings*, which are group-exclusive or near group-exclusive to the community of hip-hop fans, and which carry rich social meaning ('yo', 'Beef', 'word');
2. *borrowings related to the internet* and other new technologies that appeared post-1993 ('Download'/*downloaden*, 'homepage', 'lol');
3. *borrowings related to some aspect of the music industry*, but which are not exclusively or primarily used in discussions of hip hop ('Release'/*releasen*, 'lyrics', 'Producer').

Several interesting points can be made about the results of this system. Notably, 'Rap', 'Hip Hop', *rappen*, and 'Hiphopper', along with their orthographic variations, were removed from the analysis, as all of these terms appear in Carstensen and Busse (1993). Although these terms are certainly used within the hip-hop community, they are also used in broader societal discourse, by Germans who do not necessarily affiliate with hip-hop culture – these terms, then, are neither group-exclusive nor group-preferential.

For the final part of the analysis, hip hop-related anglicisms of interest (i.e., those with especially high frequencies in the threads analysed) were located in the large corpora to yield comparative counts.

These counts were then weighted by the size of each corpus to yield comparable frequencies. This method of analysis serves to distinguish the borrowings used in the hip-hop corpus by and large from the borrowings found in the standard news corpus, and reveals further cases of interest in the corpora.

# 4 Hip-hop English in the German context: the case for innovation

## 4.1 Examination of the 10-thread corpus

In this section, I present descriptive statistics for the 10-thread corpus from MZEE.com, comparing the results to a similar analysis in Onysko (2007) and, using examples from the dataset, elucidate the type of anglicism which is referred to with the label 'hip hop-specific'.

In his own quantitative type/token analysis, Onysko (2007, p. 114) found the overall proportion of anglicism types to overall word types in the 2000 volume of *Der Spiegel* to be 5.8 per cent, i.e., regardless of the number of instances of an individual lexical item in the text, the number of distinct lexical items which were English borrowings constituted 5.8 per cent of the number of distinct lexical items overall. In the 10-thread corpus analysed here, the proportion of anglicism types to word types overall was found to be slightly higher (6.9%) as shown in Table 11.1.

The present findings, however, differ greatly from Onysko's findings for the 2000 *Spiegel* in the proportion of anglicism tokens to word tokens overall, taking into account the number of instances of a single word form. Onysko (2007, p. 114) found a proportion of 1.11 per cent anglicism tokens to word tokens (straightforwardly, 1.11 per cent of the words in the corpus were anglicisms), but in the 10-thread corpus analysed here this figure is several times higher, at 7.35 per cent. What these two proportions tell us with respect to Onysko's findings is that only a slightly higher proportion of borrowed words from English are used in the MZEE.com forum (6.9%) than in *Der Spiegel 2000* (5.8%),

**Table 11.1** Incidence of anglicisms (new and old) overall in the 10-thread corpus

|  | **Types** | **Tokens** |
| --- | --- | --- |
| 10-thread corpus total nr. of words | 4454 | 23907 |
| Total nr. of anglicisms | 307 | 1755 |
| Percentage of anglicisms/ total nr. of words | 6.9% | 7.35% |

**283**

**Table 11.2** Counts of most frequent hip-hop anglicisms in the 10-thread corpus, divided by thread type

| Threads about American artists | | Threads about German artists | |
|---|---|---|---|
| Anglicism (type) | Count | Anglicism (type) | Count |
| Flow | 11 | Flow | 11 |
| Peace (inc. orthographic variants) | 7 | MC | 11 |
| dissen | 6 | Line(s) | 9 |
| MC | 6 | battlen/batteln | 7 |
| word | 4 | dissen | 7 |
| Diss | 4 | Diss | 5 |
| dope (adj.) | 3 | haten ('to hate') | 4 |

but these anglicisms are used much more frequently (7.35%) in the case of the MZEE.com forum than in *Der Spiegel 2000* (1.11%).

To illustrate the type of anglicisms found in the threads, I present in Table 11.2 a list of the most common hip hop-related anglicisms found in each type of thread, along with the frequency of each within the thread type. None are particularly frequent when compared with non-hip hop-related anglicisms, like 'Album'. 'Album', attested in Carstensen and Busse (1993) from 1966 on, totals 282 occurrences across the 10 threads. I have omitted frequency per 100 words in this case due to the relatively low counts for each item. This table provides examples of the kinds of anglicisms considered hip hop-related in the present research. Explanation of several of the items above (in their English forms) are to be found in this volume's glossary. However, several of the anglicisms listed above merit further discussion.

A number of items, like 'Peace' and *battlen/batteln* ('battle') are found with alternative orthographies – Peace is found as *Piiz* and *Peaz*, both cases exhibiting an orthographic substitution of –z (cf. Androutsopoulos and Scholz's (2003) discussion of –z as an alternative orthography). The processes involved in the case of *battlen* and *batteln* will be addressed later in this section. In addition to orthographic variants, several words displayed productive and creative affixation, i.e., nativization. In addition to *battlen*, one may consider *haten* ('to hate (on)'), which connotes not only a dislike of something, but a specifically irrational and unfounded dislike. One token of the verb found in the corpus comes in a derived adjectival form: *unhatebar* ('unhatable'). These alternative orthographies and productively affixed

**284**

word forms attest to creativity and innovation resulting in morpho-logical assimilation of English borrowings in the language of German hip-hop fans.

## 4.2 Extending the research paradigm to the MZEE and Tagesschau corpora

During the second stage of analysis, the large MZEE.com and *Tagesschau* corpora were searched using Python scripts for the most frequent hip hop-related anglicisms identified by hand in the 10-thread corpus and shown in Table 11.2. The frequency counts obtained in this way apply only to instances of the items as simple (i.e., non-compound) words.[8] However, probable declensions, conjugations, and alternative ortho-graphies of each item were also identified. Note that the counts obtained by this method were adjusted by the corpus size in millions of words to yield frequency per million words in the corpora for each item. These results are presented in Table 11.3.

In discussing Table 11.3, the sheer magnitude by which the occur-rences of every one of these items in the MZEE corpus outpaced the frequency in the Tagesschau corpus is noteworthy. However, it is important not to get carried away in this analysis – there are very strong effects of text genre, probable median age of speakers, and subject of discussion at work. While hip hop and music more generally are occasionally discussed in the Tagesschau corpus, these are far from the most common subjects of discussion. The numbers which are most

**Table 11.3** Occurrence per million words of top 10 hip-hop anglicisms in the large corpora

| Item | MZEE corpus | Tagesschau corpus | Ratio |
|---|---|---|---|
| Flow | 416.9 | 0.8 | 521.1 |
| peace | 797.9 | 5.0 | 159.6 |
| MC | 784.1 | 5.1 | 153.7 |
| Line(s) | 153.8 | 5.2 | 29.6 |
| Diss/Dis | 144.4 | 4.9[9] | 29.47 |
| *dissen* | 269.6 | 0.2 | 1348 |
| *battlen/batteln* (combined) | 67.82 | not found | undef. |
| word | 261.2 | 2.3 | 113.6 |
| dope | 159.7 | 0.8 | 199.6 |
| *haten* | 139.5 | 0.1[10] | 1395 |

**Table 11.4** Occurrence per million words of additional anglicisms in the large corpora

| Item | MZEE corpus | Tagesschau corpus | Ratio |
|---|---|---|---|
| cool | 1244.8 | 280.3 | 4.44 |
| ok/okay | 504.9 | 103.0 | 4.9 |
| real | 478.9 | 70.0 | 6.84 |
| Fan | 298.6 | 28.0 | 10.7 |

meaningful here are the differences in the Ratio column, which are calculated by dividing the frequency per million in the MZEE corpus by the frequency per million in the Tagesschau corpus, yielding a measure of *how much* more each item is used in the MZEE corpus.

In order to get a picture of how frequently other (not necessarily hip hop-related) borrowings are found in the corpora, consider the data in Table 11.4.

'Cool' and 'okay' are older borrowings into German; they are attested in Carstensen and Busse (1993) from 1967 and 1962, respectively, and they are furthermore fairly neutral with regard to field (i.e., they are not, today, lexical items which primarily assess or have to do with music or any other specific field). However, these items still appear 4–5 times more frequently in the MZEE.com corpus than in the Tagesschau corpus. 'Fan', likewise non-hip hop-specific, appears roughly 10 times more often – the difference between the former two items and the latter can be explained by the fact that 'Fan', while common to sports, music and other diversions, is not likely to be used in a discussion of, say, the stock market. 'Real' is included in this table for reference with regard to a special case which I will now discuss, along with *batteln* and *battlen*.

### 4.3 Two case-studies: 'real' and 'battlen/batteln'

In the analysis of the 10-thread corpus, two especially interesting cases came to light. The first involves the item 'real', which while generally pronounced /riːl/ or /ʁiːl/ as its English counterpart in German hip-hop culture, has a cognate in German *real*, /ʁeˈal/ meaning 'concrete' (as opposed to abstract or imaginary), which accounts for the majority of its usage in the news discussion corpus. When checking for occurrences of this item in the MZEE corpus, a surprising reversal of a trend was found. Consider the occurrence of English and German superlative forms of the borrowings listed in Table 11.5.

**Table 11.5** Number of occurrences of German and English superlative suffixes in the MZEE corpus

| Adjective | Number of occurrences | |
|---|---|---|
| | German suffix (-ste) | English suffix (-est) |
| cool | 134 | 7 |
| wack | 52 | 3 |
| dope | 56 | 14 |
| real | *70* | *137* |

**Table 11.6** Number of occurrences of *battle(n)* and *battel(n)* in the MZEE corpus

| Item | Number of occurrences | Item | Number of occurrences |
|---|---|---|---|
| *battlen* | 732 | *batteln* | 205 |
| *gebattlet* | 104 | *gebattelt* | 29 |
| *battlet* | 108 | *battelt* | 35 |
| *Battle* | 4155 | *Battel* | 102 |

As this table indicates, the German superlative suffix *–ste* (omitting even the declined forms) is favoured over the English *–est* in the case of 'cool', 'wack' and 'dope', but, intriguingly, not in the case of 'real'. The explanation I propose is related to the existence of the standard German *real*, /ʁeˈal/ which may make *realste* with the borrowed meaning look awkward to a native speaker with the German ending, and lead a speaker to the avoidance of homonymy with German *real* /ʁiːl/. The alternative orthography *riel* seems to serve a similar function in one instance in the 10-thread corpus, further supporting this homonymy-avoidance explanation.

The second item which merits mention here is the verb *battlen/ batteln*, which appears in two alternative orthographies. This is not unheard of – German infinitives are created by the addition of *–en* to the verb stem. However, when the verb stem ends in /r/ or /l/, the *-e-* is deleted, and the infinitive suffix simply becomes *–n*. Taking an English word like *battle* and treating it as a German verb stem brings up a few orthographic problems: German verb stems rarely or never end in *-e*, and the English word 'battle' phonologically ends in *-l*, making it an easy phonological borrowing with *-n* (it is pronounced in any case as /ˈbatəln/, never /ˈbatlən/). Orthographically, however, there seems to be pressure for it to fall in line with other verbs, many of which end in *-eln*. This causes a sort of orthographic metathesis between the *e* and the *l*.[11] Consider the frequencies in Table 11.6.

**287**

*Battlen, gebattlet* and *battlet* are all conjugated forms of the verb, whereas *battle* is likely to be the noun, but could also be the first-person present singular form of the verb. On the other side, *batteln, gebattelt* and *battelt* are again verb forms, while *battle* must be either a nominal form or a second-person singular familiar imperative. The original, and more foreign-looking, borrowing is the noun *Battle*. After this, *battlen* is analogically created from *Battle*, and mutates orthographically to *batteln* based on its pronunciation. This, however, is nothing new – *recyclen* and *recyceln* have been in complementary distribution in German orthography, and the decision between the two is commonly avoided by the use of the borrowed gerund 'Recycling'.[12]

What is most surprising in this case is the subsequent influence of the altered verb on the orthography of the noun – a development which highlights change in progress in hip-hop fans' language and demonstrates the extensive nativization of many borrowings. The following example (among several others) is found in the MZEE.com corpus:

> 1. *Die Frage bezieht sich auf ein sehr bekanntes Freestyle-Battel in Hamburg!*
> 'The question hinges on a very well-known freestyle battle in Hamburg!'

There is no feasible independent reason for this change in the noun orthography from *Battle* to *Battel*; this appears to be a further analogical formation of the noun on the model of the verb changes discussed above.

The phenomena discussed with reference to Tables 11.5 and 11.6 support the notion of hip-hop culture as a site for innovation and contact-induced change, and suggest that certain linguistic changes related to lexical borrowing may only be visible in orthographic form; i.e., the distinction between *battlen* and *batteln* is moot in spoken German due to phonotactic constraints. Finally, these examples demonstrate a series of incremental changes in the process of nativization with regard to hip hop-specific borrowings, displaying the innovative character of language use within the subculture.

## 4.4 Discussion: anglicisms in the German context

In this subsection, I present what I believe to be the broader social ramifications of the above findings, discussing previous work on anglicisms (not necessarily hip hop-related) and the status of English in German culture. Anglicisms are a prominent issue in the politics of the German language. Onysko notes that opponents of the use of anglicisms perceive English 'as a force that threatens the existence of the German language or that leads to an adulteration of German' (2007, p. 1). He further reports that in order to combat this perceived menace, concerned citizens have formed an organization known as the VDS, or the *Verein Deutsche Sprache* ('German Language Association'). Diethold Tietz, a member of the VDS board of directors, notes:

> the phenomenon of anglicisms does not demonstrate natural changes, but rather a manipulation. Turns of phrase taken from English like 'Sinn machen' [lit. to make sense], 'Es rechnet sich' [it pays for itself], 'realisieren' [broadened from financial meaning] – instead of 'wahrnehmen' [realize] – or concepts like 'Wellness' or 'Handy' *do not attest to natural development*, but rather simply to laziness, ignorance, and the tendency to curry favor. (2004, p. 33; my translation, emphasis added)

However, as a number of researchers on anglicisms in German have noted (cf. Busse, 1993; Yang, 1990; Onysko, 2007), the status of English in Germany is far more complex than simple portrayal as a linguistic bogeyman can capture. Rather, borrowings from English have different and often conflicting indexicalities. I discuss here two studies of English use in German contexts which frame the interpretation of the present results.

Piller (2001) presents an analysis based on Bakhtinian voicing which investigates the use of English in German magazine and TV advertising. On the social meaning of bilingualism in Germany, Piller writes:

> although German advertising may construct both identities of the national Self and of the national Other as multilingual, bilingualism in English and German is set up as the 'natural' option for successful middle-class Germans, while other languages . . . are presented as the languages of the cultural and national Other. (Piller, 2001, p. 155)

Piller's compelling multimodal analysis of advertising makes the point abundantly clear that the advertisements, through the use of language and image, position the reader as part of the business elite – someone for whom (Standard) English bilingualism is the norm – or else as an aspirant to such a position. Crucially, Piller (2001, p. 158) presents her data as a corpus, basing the in-depth analysis of individual advertisements on a brief summary of proportions of ads which include English, and the extent to which English is included. Piller finds that English used by narrators conveys a voice of authority, while English targeted at listeners and viewers orients the addressee towards internationalism, the future, success, sophistication and fun. Contrasting indexicalities of English are presented through non-profit advertising, the most relevant of which is an advertisement from the *Verein Deutsche Sprache*

**289**

criticizing and mocking the overuse of anglicisms; however, this is presented by Piller as a poorly executed challenge from a fringe group in the face of the overwhelming strength of positive English linkages in mainstream advertising.

Grau (2009) investigates the status of English in Germany from a different perspective – through the contact of German teenagers with various forms of English, highlighting the distinction (cf. Androutso-poulos, 2009) which Preisler (1999) makes between 'English from above' (learned and valued in institutional settings) and 'English from below' (learned and valued in leisure time). Discussing various English inputs which teenagers encounter, including advertising and pop music, Grau comes to hip hop, succinctly summarizing one of the most important research findings:

> In analyses of the language used on websites, guest books, and phone-in radio shows for German hip-hop fans, Androutsopoulos (2003a [Androutsopoulos, 2003], b [Androutsopoulos and Scholz, 2003]) and Berns (2003 [Berns and Schlobinski, 2003]) show how words, phrases, and particular characteristics from Black English, such as the ending –z or indefinite [sic] articles tha or da, are used by German youths to identify with the global hip-hop community. Given the type of language in these data, the comment that 'it obvi-ously has not been transmitted through the institutional teaching of English as a Foreign Language' (Androutsopoulos, 2004, p. 93) does not come as a surprise. (Grau, 2009, p. 163)

Grau (2009) finds through her own study that both teachers and students conceive of a mental divide between English learned at school and English learned outside of school, calling for a broader commit-ment to integration in educational materials.

These studies, then, provide a sort of backdrop for the findings of the present research – Germany is a society where a relatively high premium is placed on a form of Standard English, at least. In contrast, however, the perceived inundation and adulteration of German with English borrowings has caused no little concern in some small but vocal circles – as Diethold Tietz's screed above demonstrates. Further-more, multiple (and separate) varieties of English are at work in youth language – suggesting that hip hop acts as a *conduit* for the introduc-tion of a specific, non-standard variety of English into German culture.

In terms of the larger picture of the status of English in German soci-ety, the present study provides distributional support for the notion of multiple Englishes at work in German society, given the vast differ-ences in the frequency of specific borrowings between the MZEE and Tagesschau corpora. Additionally, the types of orthographic changes at work suggest that hip hop-related anglicisms in German are often regularized and nativized according to predictable processes not independent of German linguistic structures and conventions; however, these processes, as the cases of *battle* and *real* demonstrate, may be more complex than expected.

# 5 'Crossing avoidance' and the case for imitation

## 5.1 Results of thread type comparison

I turn here to the key finding of the present study – one which has direct ramifications for sociolinguistic theory. To this point, the analyses presented here have taken the 10-thread corpus as a whole, essentially glossing over the distinction included in the research design between threads discussing American artists and threads discussing German artists. This methodological decision was made in order to facilitate a comparison of the two thread types, not by properties of the speaker/writer or addressee/audience, but rather on a level not often considered by sociolinguists: the discourse referent. Unlike classic sociolinguistic variables like ethnicity, social class, gender, etc., the discourse referent is not a property pertaining to either the speaker or audience. In this section, I show that speakers' language practices vary according to the discourse referent, and moreover that this variation can inform linguists' understanding of some processes behind language style.

To set a point of comparison for the analysis of hip hop-related anglicisms to come, I present in Table 11.7 the relative frequencies in

**Table 11.7** All post-1990 anglicisms in threads about American vs German artists

| Threads about American artists | | | Threads about German artists | | |
|---|---|---|---|---|---|
| Thread name | Count / wordcount | Instances per 100 words | Thread name | Count / wordcount | Instances per 100 words |
| G-Unit | 54 / 2854 | 1.89 | Curse | 55 / 3065 | 1.79 |
| Ludacris | 49 / 2186 | 2.24 | Dynamite Deluxe | 57 / 2756 | 2.06 |
| Redman | 49 / 2023 | 2.42 | JAW | 91 / 2308 | 3.94[13] |
| Talib Kweli | 44 / 1997 | 2.20 | Taichi | 61 / 2292 | 2.66 |
| Tech N9ne | 53 / 2950 | 1.80 | Westberlin Maskulin | 44 / 1476 | 2.98 |
| Total | 249 / 12010 | 2.07[14] | Total | 308 / 11897 | 2.59 |

the 10-thread corpus of all post-1990 anglicisms, i.e., those which were not present in Carstensen and Busse's (1993) dictionary. These frequencies include both internet-related borrowings ('thread', 'post', 'internet') and those related to music in general ('Album', 'Producer', 'Release'/ *releasen*) along with hip hop-related anglicisms. Because the figures presented in Table 11.7 are sample proportions from random samples, I was able to perform an independent 2-sample t-test to determine whether a significant difference in incidence of these 'new anglicisms' exists between the thread types. No significant difference in the incidence of new anglicisms was found: 2-sample $t(5) = 1.47$, $p = 0.20$ ($\alpha = 0.05$).[15] However, upon isolating those borrowings which carry social meaning in the specific domain of hip hop, i.e., those that exhibit strongly group-preferential or group-exclusive use in hip-hop culture, a different result is found (see Table 11.8).

Again, because these are sample proportions from random samples, I was able to perform an independent 2-sample t-test to determine whether a significant difference in incidence of new hip hop-related anglicisms exists between the thread types, and in this case, *a significant difference in the incidence of hip hop-related anglicisms was found*: 2-sample $t(6) = 2.73$, $p = 0.03$ ($\alpha = 0.05$). This indicates that the null hypothesis – in this case, that the proportion of new hip hop-related anglicisms used is equal when users discuss American and German artists – is rejected, i.e., the difference found in these threads can be extrapolated to the population, viz., other online discussions involving American and German hip-hop artists.

**Table 11.8** New hip hop-related anglicisms in threads about American vs German artists

| Threads about American artists | | | Threads about German artists | | |
|---|---|---|---|---|---|
| Thread name | Count / wordcount | Instances per 100 words | Thread name | Count / wordcount | Instances per 100 words |
| G-Unit | 10 / 2854 | 0.35 | Curse | 18 / 3065 | 0.59 |
| Ludacris | 12 / 2186 | 0.55 | Dynamite Deluxe | 15 / 2756 | 0.54 |
| Redman | 8 / 2023 | 0.40 | JAW | 29 / 2308 | 1.26 |
| Talib Kweli | 13 / 1997 | 0.65 | Taichi | 20 / 2292 | 0.87 |
| Tech N9ne | 10 / 2950 | 0.34 | Westberlin Maskulin | 16 / 1476 | 1.08 |
| Total | 53 / 12010 | 0.44 | Total | 98 / 11897 | 0.82 |

The conclusion is that German hip-hop fans, then, are avoiding the use of hip-hop borrowings carrying rich social meaning when discussing American artists: threads about American artists were found to contain significantly fewer tokens of hip hop-related borrowings, although the proportion of new borrowings overall was comparable.

## 5.2 Discussion: referee design and crossing avoidance

To explain this finding, I propose that fans' use of fewer hip hop-specific anglicisms when discussing American artists constitutes a style-shift in the sense discussed in Bell (2001), whereby the forum users are distancing themselves from the social meanings and inherent claims to authenticity which are attendant to hip hop-related borrowings when assessing the originators of those borrowings (or, at the least, members of the community where these borrowings originated).

There are numerous valid criticisms of Bell's (2001) audience design framework.[16] One extension of the framework, however, is quite useful in the present analysis, and its specific applicability to the situation outlined above is not fully duplicated in other sociolinguistic frameworks, i.e., the relevant generalizations afforded by this piece of the audience design theory cannot as faithfully be captured by another existing theory. Initiative style-shifts, which correspond with Bakhtin's (1981) 'stylization', are explained by Bell as instances where:

> the individual speaker creatively uses language resources often from beyond the immediate speech community, such as distant dialects, or stretches those resources in novel directions . . . it usually draws on existing if distant resources and remakes them. (2001, p. 147)

Bell summarizes initiative style-shifts in two of his programmatic points for audience design theory:

> *8: As well as the 'responsive' dimension of style, there is the 'initiative' dimension . . . where the style-shift itself initiates a change in the situation rather than resulting from such a change.*
>
> *9: Initiative style-shifts are in essence 'referee design,' by which the linguistic features associated with a reference group can be used to express identification with that group.* (2001, pp. 146–147; original emphasis)

Bell (2001, p. 147) further notes that this reference group is not necessarily (and often is not) present in the speech situation, indicating that speakers are choosing a style not tailored to their audience, but rather one associated with a non-present third party.

**293**

Appealing to this notion of 'referee design' is a crucial step in capturing the sociolinguistic situation in which the present phenomena arise. There are undoubtedly numerous influences governing or prompting the individual language user's use of linguistic styles and features in varying contexts – however, in this case the discourse referents, American and German hip-hop artists, serve as both elements of the sociolinguistic context and reference groups which influence speech styles.

Nevertheless, this analysis – without the addition of another crucial element – does not suffice to provide an explanation for the data. German fans are not strictly using the speech styles of German and American artists in the respective threads to identify with these artists, as would be expected under referee design. Rather, fans are modifying their language use as if these non-present actors were present. For an explanation of this process, I turn to 'crossing'.

Rampton's (2005) notion of 'crossing' has played a role in a number of recent accounts of hip hop-related language in sociolinguistic situations around the globe (cf. Androutsopoulos, 2009; Cutler, 2009; Higgins, 2009). 'Crossing' essentially describes the use of language that is somehow 'other' than the code that would be expected – a code that 'belongs' to members of another group. Rampton describes it as follows:

> Crossing, in contrast [to classical accounts of code-switching], focuses on code-alternation by *people who aren't accepted members of the group associated with the second language they employ.* It is concerned with switching into languages that aren't *generally* thought to belong to you. (Rampton, 2005, pp. 270–271; emphasis added)

This definition creates a conflict with regard to the data used in the present study. It is clear from the markers of 'innovation', i.e., nativization and regularization of borrowed items, that – to the extent that German hip-hop fans consider themselves members of a community – they have appropriated this borrowed code as their own. Crucially, though, *the related codes of hip hop belong to more than one group*, and this is one of the features of hip-hop language which contributes to its richness in terms of sociolinguistic analysis.

By Rampton's definition above, hip-hop fans are engaging in crossing when using hip hop-related anglicisms. The limitation of this definition, however, is that it fails to account for this multiplicity of groups who might evaluate the language. Members of the German hip-hop community would likely not evaluate this language use as crossing – this is the code, after all, which negotiates membership within that community. However, American hip-hop artists and fans might negatively evaluate this use of language as crossing, and German hip-hop fans' unwillingness to be considered as engaging in crossing accounts for the restricted use of these anglicisms when discussing American artists – i.e., crossing is contextually assessed, not only by the audience, but pre-emptively, so to speak, by the speaker as well.

I define the phenomenon captured in Table 11.8 as 'crossing avoidance' – a term which could also apply to more common situations in which the 'rightful owners' of a speech style are present and interlocutors choose not to cross in order to evade negative evaluation. Rampton mentions a similar phenomenon known as 'refusal':

> 'Refusal' . . . [is] a way of avoiding the experience of anomaly that crossing entails. Where there is a common lingua franca, this may present no difficulties, but in other circumstances, this can have significant political dimensions. In consequence of 'permanently experienced frustration' in their negotiation with German-speaking bureaucracy, Hinnenkamp describes a disaffection among 'Gastarbeiter' that increases with their L2 proficiency and can culminate in refusal to use the 'host' society's means of communication. (Rampton, 2005, p. 277)

While the first sentence of this citation rings true for the phenomenon discussed here, the sociolinguistic sketch used as an illustration, as well as the term 'refusal', make clear that the phenomenon Rampton refers to arises from resentment or disaffectation. Crossing avoidance, then, is related to 'refusal', but can involve a variety of motivations for not engaging in the practice of crossing.

This is a special case of crossing avoidance – one in which the avoidance of crossing is tied to the non-present discourse referent. This 'self-consciousness' which arises in the discussion of American artists constitutes an acknowledgement that, on some level, the use of hip hop-related anglicisms by German fans is a form of 'imitation' of language belonging to another group. By way of comparison, consider Androutsopoulos's discussion of 'short, formulaic switches into English', like 'word' and 'Straight up Hip Hop', which he considers instances of crossing:

> To be sure, such crossing practices are not uncontested; appropriating superficial features of African American English to construct hip hop identities may be rejected as 'fronting,' in the U.S. context and elsewhere. . . . However, the crucial point seems to be their identity target: Does the use of Hip Hop English by German Hip Hoppers lay a claim to African American identities? (Androutsopoulos, 2009, pp. 58–59)

Androutsopoulos (2009) proposes that, rather than laying a claim to African American identity, these instances of crossing instead involve a 'stepping out of' a German identity. While Androutsopoulos's analysis may be essentially correct, the phenomenon discussed in this section suggests that this 'stepping out of' a German identity is not felicitous in every case, precisely because of the perceived dangers of laying claim to an identity which is unachievable – this could result in an allegation that the crosser is making fun of precisely that group which he/she is perceived as enacting.

## 6 Conclusion

In this chapter, I address questions about borrowing in the context of the German hip-hop fan community, answering a call by Androutsopoulos (2009) for an increased focus on research in what he calls the 'tertiary sphere' of hip hop. In addition, I incorporate methods from text and corpus linguistics, combining qualitative analysis with quantitative analysis to address sociolinguistic questions.

The primary concern of this chapter is whether German hip-hop fans' use of anglicisms qualifies as mere imitation of American hip-hop culture, or rather an innovation whereby hip-hop culture is fully appropriated and (g)localized. By considering the frequency and type of anglicisms found in the corpora, I find evidence that hip hop-related borrowings are used in the hip-hop forum studied more frequently than in Onysko's (2007) study of *der Spiegel 2000*, and that these borrowings are often extensively localized and nativized to fit (*batteln*) or avoid conflict with (*realest*) German paradigms. I find additional evidence indicating that anglicisms related to hip-hop culture constitute a form of Preisler's (1999) 'English from below' by comparing frequencies of particular anglicisms from a hip-hop forum and a news discussion forum.

The key issue at stake in the present study is one with ramifications for sociolinguistic theory – the question essentially being whether borrowings in the German hip-hop context can be considered a form of Rampton's (2005) 'crossing'. I conclude here that 'crossing' is a multiply-evaluated phenomenon which involves not only the audience but also the speaker as judges of what constitutes crossing, a situation which can lead to crossing avoidance. Returning to Higgins's (2009) study, cited in this chapter's introduction, we find a similar sentiment:

> Of course, whether crossing leads to inauthenticity or not depends on the interpretation of the linguistic performance by members of situated linguistic communities. Among African Americans, Tanzanians who use terms like *nigga* as a way to refer to their friends may well come off as inauthentic poseurs. However, Tanzanian youths

who are greeting one another in shout-outs, or who are attending a rap concert in Dar es Salaam, use this same word to establish a claim to a particular Tanzanian identity. (Higgins, 2009, p. 97)

It is precisely this difference in interpretation which is captured in the present study for German hip-hop fans. While Higgins's conclusions suggest an unproblematic case of successful identity construction using Global Hip Hop Nation Language in Tanzania, the results presented in this study lead me to suggest that the situation is not so clear-cut for the German hip-hop fans represented in this study: German fans do exhibit an awareness of crossing and its possible negative assessment, and style-shift accordingly – engaging in 'crossing avoidance', despite the fact that the group most likely to give this negative assessment is not directly involved in the discourse. In this way, German hip-hop fans display their awareness of anglicisms in the German hip-hop community as *both* imitation and innovation – and I suggest that the complete divorce of the former from the latter, that is, a straightforward claim that the use of English borrowings in this context constitutes only one or the other, is implausible.

## Notes

1. 'Props' to: Dr Marina Terkourafi, Dr Jannis Androutsopoulos, and two anonymous reviewers for their extensive and helpful comments on earlier versions of this chapter and critical references; Dr Tania Ionin for double-checking the t-tests; Liam Moran for help with corpus collection; Sarah Hjeltness for assisting with the compilation of the anglicism list; Christoph Baumeister for assistance with annotation and encyclopedic knowledge of German hip hop; and the attendees of the Workshop on Language and Hip-Hop Culture in a Globalizing World and Illinois Language and Linguistics Society 1: Language Online for helpful comments on this research.
2. As of 15 February 2009, Alexa.com <http://www.alexa.com> ranked MZEE. com at 19,989th (lower number indicates higher ranking), above its two largest competitors in Alexa's German-language hip-hop portals category. These two competitors, hiphop.de and rap.de, were ranked 30,296th and 43,323rd respectively. Source: <http://www.alexa.com/browse?CategoryID=861556>, accessed 24 January 2010.
3. Perhaps not incidentally, *mzee* is Swahili for 'respected/dignified elder' or 'ancestor'. It is not known whether the website's founders were aware of this reading as well, but this definition is not entirely incompatible with the earned respect which qualifies one to be an MC in hip-hop culture (see Berns and Schlobinsky, 2003, for an illustrative example). This qualifies as an example of Pennycook and Mitchell's (2009, p. 40) discussion of the 'multiple, copresent, global origins' of Global Hip Hop.
4. MZEE.com (http://www.mzee.com), accessed 6 February 2009.

**297**

5. *Arbeitsgemeinschaft der öffentlich-rechtlichen Rundfunkanstalten der Bundesrepublik Deutschland* (Consortium of public-law broadcasting institutions of the Federal Republic of Germany).
6. Examples taken from Onysko's (2007, pp. 361–376) index of anglicisms.
7. Onysko uses the term 'interference' slightly differently from how the term is used in the fields of psycholinguistics and second language acquisition.
8. Because many borrowings, especially shorter ones, may be 'found' inside of other words when searching within words (e.g., an unfettered search for 'rap' would bring up *strahlentherapeutisch* ('actinotherapeutic'), *choreographieren* ('to choreograph'), or *Raphiabast* ('raffia'), along with many more common words which have nothing to do with rap) this is an unfortunate necessity until I obtain access to or build a parser for German and borrowed compounds. It would also be possible to search the results by hand to remove bad hits, but the size of the corpora in use prohibits this method of filtering.
9. The acronym 'DIS', Deutsche Institution für Schiedsgerichtsbarkeit ('German Institution for Arbitration') accounted for 94 per cent of these instances.
10. All 15 instances were misspellings of *hatten*, a form of 'to have' and an auxiliary verb.
11. Thanks go to an anonymous reviewer for help with the correct analysis of this phenomenon.
12. *Recyceln* is the prescriptively preferred form – see: <http://www.korrekturen.de/wortliste/recyclen.shtml>, accessed 20 September 2009.
13. The thread about JAW remains a slight outlier throughout this analysis, with a higher rate of anglicisms than many others; an explanation of this finding is outside the scope of this paper and remains a topic for further research.
14. Note that because this figure is the incidence per 100 words of new anglicisms for all five threads, it is calculated from the word count of all five threads, and thus does not represent the sum of the values above it.
15. Values presented here are two-tailed; we have no reason to hypothesize that either type of thread would have more new anglicisms than the other.
16. See Coupland (2007) for a cogent summary of both the framework and the criticisms.

# References

Androutsopoulos, J. (2003), 'Jugendliche Schreibstile in der Netzkommunikation: zwei Gästebücher im Vergleich', in Eva Neuland (ed.), *Jugendsprachen – Spiegel der Zeit*. Frankfurt a.M.: Lang, pp. 307–321.

—(2004), 'Non-native English and sub-cultural identities in media discourse', in H. Sandøy (ed.), *Den fleirspråklege utfordringa* [*The Multilingual Challenge*]. Oslo: Novus, pp. 83–98.

—(2009), 'Language and the three spheres of hip hop', in H. S. Alim, A. Ibrahim and A. Pennycook (eds), *Global Linguistic Flows: Hip Hop Cultures, Youth Identities, and the Politics of Language*. New York: Routledge, pp. 43–62.

Androutsopoulos, J. and Scholz, A. (2003), 'Spaghetti funk: appropriations of hip-hop culture and rap music in Europe'. *Popular Music and Society*, 26, 489–505.

Bell, A. (1991), *The Language of New Media*. Oxford, Cambridge, MA: Blackwell.

—(2001), 'Back in style: reworking audience design', in P. Eckert (ed.), *Style and Sociolinguistic Variation*. West Nyack, NY: Cambridge University Press, pp. 139–169.

Berns, J. and Schlobinski, P. (2003), 'Constructions of identity in German hip-hop culture', in J. Androutsopoulos and G. Georgakopoulou (eds), *Discourse Constructions of Youth Identities*. Amsterdam, Philadelphia: J. Benjamins, pp. 197–219.

Busse, U. (1993), *Anglizismen im Duden*. Tübingen: Niemeyer.

Carstensen, B. and Busse, U. (1993), *Anglizismen-Wörterbuch: Der Einfluß des Englischen auf den deutschen Wortschatz seit 1945* (3 vol.). Berlin: Walter de Gruyter.

Coupland, N. (2007), *Style: Language Variation and Identity*. Cambridge: Cambridge University Press.

Cutler, C. (2009), 'You shouldn't be rappin', you should be skateboardin' the X-games: the co-construction of whiteness in an MC Battle', in A. Ibrahim, H. S. Alim and A. Pennycook (eds), *Global Linguistic Flows: Hip Hop Cultures, Youth Identities, and the Politics of Language*. New York: Taylor & Francis, pp. 79–94.

Grau, M. (2009), 'Worlds apart? English in German youth cultures and in educational settings'. *World Englishes*, 28, 2, 160–174.

Higgins, C. (2009), 'From da bomb to *bomba*: Global Hip Hop Nation language in Tanzania', in H. S. Alim, A. Ibrahim and A. Pennycook (eds), *Global Linguistic Flows: Hip Hop Cultures, Youth Identities, and the Politics of Language*. New York: Routledge, pp. 95–112.

Onysko, Alexander. (2007), *Anglicisms in German: Borrowing, Lexical Productivity, and Written Codeswitching*. Berlin: Walter de Gruyter.

Pennycook, A and Mitchell, T. (2009), 'Hip hop as dusty foot philosophy: engaging locality', in H. S. Alim, A. Ibrahim and A. Pennycook (eds), *Global Linguistic Flows: Hip Hop Cultures, Youth Identities, and the Politics of Language*. New York: Routledge, pp. 43–62.

Piller, I. (2001), 'Identity constructions in multilingual advertising'. *Language in Society*, 30, 2, 153–186.

Preisler, B. (1999), 'Functions and forms of English in a European EFL country', in Bex, Tony, and Richard Watts (eds.) *Standard English: The Widening Debate*. London: Routledge, pp. 239–267.

Rampton, B. (2005), *Crossing: Language & Ethnicity among Adolescents*, (2nd edition). Manchester, UK; Northhampton, MA: St. Jerome.

Tietz, D. (2004), 'Der Klügere spricht Deutsch', in *Rettet die deutsche Sprache: Beiträge, Interviews und Materialien zum Kampf gegen Rechtschreibreform und Anglizismen*. Berlin: Junge Freiheit Verlag GmbH & Co., pp. 32–42.

Yang, W. (1990), *Anglizismen im Deutschen: am Beispiel des Nachrichten-magazins Der Spiegel*. Tübingen: Niemeyer.

# 12 'She's so Hood': Ghetto Authenticity on the White Rapper Show

Cecelia Cutler

## 1 Introduction[1]

*Ego Trip's (White) Rapper Show* was a television reality show that aired across the United States of America on the cable station VH1 in early 2007.[2] The show was created by five male hip-hop journalists of colour known as the Ego Trip and was presented as a contest to discover the next great 'White rapper'. The promotional trailer for the show asks, 'Who will step up to become hip hop's next great White hope? – 'Cause lord knows, it's lonely at the top' (image of White rapper Eminem in Jesus robes).[3] Audition tapes were solicited from interested rappers across the United States and a select number of these were invited to audition in person on camera. In one of these auditions, a young White woman called 'Nomi' is asked by the former White rapper and host, MC Serch, what she got out of the experience growing up in the affluent, overwhelmingly White town of Waterford, Connecticut.

> (1) Nomi: What did I get out of my neighborhood? Raw, real life experiences. My neighbors are – FIERCE! I see it real, I see it raw.

MC Serch replies with a big smile, 'Wow, I didn't know it was that hard in Connecticut. That's great!' Nomi does not make it past the audition stage, but this clip sets up a discourse in the show about where real hip hop (and by extension, real hip hoppers) come from, pitting the contestants against one another in a prolonged competition to connect themselves to a received version of the core hip-hop experience. The show's creators (the Ego Trip crew) and its White host (MC Serch) are all connected to a particular time and place in the history of hip hop (New York City and the 1980s) and feel it is their duty to instil in the audience a respect for this 'Old School' style as well as who they consider the founding rappers of hip hop to be, and the places (in the Bronx) that they consider to be pivotal in hip hop's creation.[4]

Authenticity is a theme that runs through many studies of language, identity and hip-hop culture across disciplines (Alim, 2004; Armstrong, 2004; Hall and Bucholtz, 1995; Cutler, 2007, 2009; Gordon, 2005; Hess, 2005; McLeod, 1999; White, 2006). Bucholtz and Hall (2005) describe authenticity as 'the ways in which identities are discursively verified', which is distinct from authentication, 'a social process played out in discourse' (Bucholtz and Hall, 2005, p. 601). In some instances, the term authenticity refers to the legitimacy of one's claim to a particular ethnic identity and the ability of individuals to pass as legitimate members of a particular ethnic group (Hall and Bucholtz, 1995). It may also have a social dimension relating to the specific criteria set up by a community of practice or subculture. Indeed, various music scenes from rock to country to rap each seem to have their own definitions (Davison, 2001, p. 263, cited in Armstrong, 2004, p. 6).

In hip-hop culture, great value is placed on being true to oneself, one's local allegiances and territorial identities, and one's proximity to an original source of rap (Armstrong, 2004, p. 6; McLeod, 1999). Rickford and Rickford (2000) write that the expression 'keepin' it real' is a mantra in hip-hop embodying the idea that people should be true to their roots, and not 'front' or pretend to be something they are not (Rickford and Rickford, 2000, p. 23). 'Fronting' was ultimately what led to the downfall of Vanilla Ice, the White rapper whose claims to come from a Black ghetto neighbourhood in Miami were exposed as fabrications.

Another component of authenticity in US hip-hop culture (and one that poses a challenge to many middle and upper middle class White youth who affiliate with hip hop) involves socioeconomic, ethnic and cultural proximity to the urban African American community where hip hop is created, i.e., 'the street' or 'the center of hip-hop cultural activity' (Alim, 2004, p. 390). Establishing a connection to the street is an extremely important part of how African American rap artists authenticate themselves. Consequently, many White middle class hip hoppers try to play up their connections to some imaginary 'ghetto' by forming crews and engaging in certain 'gang' style activities or pretending they have no money (cf. Sales, 1996; Cutler, 2002).

Another way in which some White rappers and hip hoppers try to authenticate themselves is through foregrounding their status as poor Whites (cf. Eminem), thus establishing a connection to blackness by referencing a common disempowerment (White, 2006). The various semantic dimensions of authenticity discussed above are summarized in the following table, adapted from McLeod (1999, p. 139). Not included in McLeod's original is the talent/skill dimension (author's

**301**

**Table 12.1** Claims of authenticity

| Semantic dimensions | Real | Fake |
|---|---|---|
| Social-psychological | Staying true to yourself | 'Selling out', i.e., following mass trends |
| Racial | Black | White |
| Political-economic | The underground | Commercial |
| Gender-sexual | Hard | Soft |
| Social locational | The street | The suburbs |
| Cultural | The Old School | The mainstream |
| Talent/skill | Ability to write and perform clever rhymes; ability to freestyle and battle spontaneously | 'bites' or steals lyrics from other rappers; inability to freestyle and battle. |

addition), an arguably important part of any rap artist's self-presentation. Hess (2005) notes that the ability to rap and freestyle 'live' is 'one of a set of cultural values by which the artist's authenticity is judged' (Hess, 2005, p. 299). Table 12.1 summarizes the semantic dimensions on which claims of authenticity can be made.

Building on this work, the present chapter examines how *Ego Trip's (White) Rapper Show* fulfils a gate-keeping as well as an educational function for the viewers. It also explores processes of identity formation and the authenticating strategies that the contestants use to construct themselves as 'real'. Along these lines, it examines the stances a female contestant on the show ('Persia') takes towards her rival 'John Brown' and towards her own utterances during a particularly ribald scene in the first episode of the show. Stances encompass the methods (e.g., linguistic or other) that speakers employ to create and signal relationships with their utterances and interlocutors (Johnstone, forthcoming). Another way to define it is 'the display of evaluative, affective, and epistemic orientations in discourse' (Bucholtz and Hall, 2005, p. 595). Persia, along with the other contestants and creators of the show, is engaged in an identity project which emerges through her linguistic and discursive practices in interaction.

Following Bucholtz and Hall's (2005) framework, particularly the principles of Indexicality and Relationality, the chapter focuses on Persia's interactional use of particular syntactic and lexical markers, the content of her statements, and her challenge to John Brown to engage in a 'battle' and how they work together to authenticate her and to construct her as socially real. The Indexicality Principle states that:

> Identity relations emerge in interaction through several related indexical processes, including: (a) overt mention of identity categories and labels; (b) implicatures and presuppositions regarding one's own or others' identity position; (c) displayed evaluative and epistemic orientations to ongoing talk, as well as interactional footings and participant roles [i.e., stances]; and (d) the use of linguistic structures and systems that are ideologically associated with specific personas and groups. [i.e., styles] (Bucholtz and Hall, 2005, p. 594)

The overt mention of identity categories and labels such as 'White' or 'Black', the 'circulation of such categories within ongoing discourse, their explicit or implicit juxtaposition with other categories, and the linguistic elaborations and qualifications they attract (predicates, modifiers, and so on) all provide important information about identity construction' (Bucholtz and Hall, 2005, p. 594). Implicatures and presuppositions are indirect ways of instantiating identity, involving the use of coded or indirect language (e.g., the word 'hood' or 'ghetto') to convey subtle cues to particular listeners. Stance involves the linguistic strategies speakers use to 'position themselves and others as particular kinds of people', (e.g., 'real', 'White trash', etc.) and style refers to the 'repertoire of linguistic forms associated with personas or identities' (Bucholtz and Hall, 2005, p. 595).

A second principle, The Relationality Principle, is also at work in Persia's identity construction as well as in the motives behind the show's creation. It holds that identities are 'intersubjectively constructed through several, often overlapping, complementary relations', including adequation/distinction, authentication/denaturalization, and authorization/illegitimation (Bucholtz and Hall, 2005, pp. 598–603), and stems from the idea that 'identities are never autonomous or independent but always acquire social meaning in relation to other available identity positions and other social actors' (Bucholtz and Hall, 2005, p. 598).

The term adequation is about positioning groups or individuals as alike (e.g., poor Whites and poor Blacks). It involves dismissing differences that may be 'irrelevant or damaging' and foregrounding 'similarities viewed as salient' (Bucholtz and Hall, 2005, p. 599). The counterpart of adequation, distinction, depends on 'the suppression of similarities that might undermine the construction of difference' (Bucholtz and Hall, 2005, p. 600). Authentication and denaturalization, are the 'processes by which speakers make claims to realness and artifice, respectively' (Bucholtz and Hall, 2005, p. 601). The first focuses on how 'identities are discursively verified' and what kinds of language and language speakers count as authentic for a given purpose (Bucholtz and Hall, 2005, p. 601). The second is concerned with how 'assumptions regarding the seamlessness of identity can be disrupted' (Bucholtz and Hall, 2005, p. 601). Authorization entails the local or translocal 'affirmation or imposition of an identity through structures of institutionalized power and ideology' whereas illegitimation speaks to the ways in which identities are 'dismissed, censored, or simply ignored by these same structures' (Bucholtz and Hall, 2005, p. 603).

We can see adequation and distinction at work in the discursive strategies Persia employs to liken herself to an urban, outspoken Black female and to distinguish herself from the other White contestants on the show. Authentication and denaturalization are evident in her discursive and stylistic efforts to construct herself as a 'real' MC and John Brown as a 'fake'. Authorization and illegitimation are visible in the workings of the show itself, the motives of its creators (The Ego Trip crew), the rules they lay down about who is licensed to use particular words, and in the messages being directed at the audience (presumably mostly White) about who can be 'real' in hip hop. It is through the analysis of identity work at these multiple indexical levels that we can arrive at a fuller understanding of identity formation on the show and the individual identity projects of the show's contestants, particularly that of Persia.

## 2 Overview of the show

### 2.1 Reality TV

So-called 'reality television' has been enormously popular in recent years with well over 400 different shows airing in Anglophone countries alone since the 1990s, with several more airing worldwide.[5] Sparks (2007) identifies a combination of factors that led to the rise of reality TV shows: they are relatively cheap to produce; there is no need to pay writers or actors, no rehearsals, and no need for elaborate sets. In a blistering Marxist critique of the genre, Sparks (2007) claims that people are drawn to reality TV by the enormous liberating potential associated with celebrity status (i.e., freedom from the drudgery of an ordinary job and the enormous attention heaped upon the individuality of celebrities as opposed to everyday individuals). Thanks to the numerous iterations of reality shows like *Big Brother* and *Survivor* and the minor celebrity status attained by particular participants, viewers are highly attuned to the possibility of leading a life of leisure and consumption as opposed to labour (Sparks, 2007).

Critics say that the term 'reality television' is somewhat of a misnomer. Such shows frequently portray a modified and highly controlled form of reality (Johnson-Woods, 2002). Participants are put in exotic locations or abnormal situations, sometimes coached to act in certain ways by off-screen handlers, and events on screen are often manipulated through editing and other post-production techniques. Furthermore, the shows are often highly scripted; contestants are chosen more for their looks and personalities than for their talent, and screenwriters cynically plot out scenarios that will pit contestants against one another.

Nevertheless, some reality TV shows have aspects of a social experiment (Smith and Wood, 2003) and may even attempt to get viewers to think critically about certain social issues (e.g., *Black.White*, 2006 on FX; *Frontier House*, 2002 on PBS; *Shalom in the Home*, 2006 on TLC), potentially offering a view into the lives of people in very different situations from those of the viewers. *Ego Trip's (White) Rapper Show* has some aspects of this more socially conscious subgenre and a close examination of outtake interviews with the creators (the 'Ego Trip' crew) makes it clear that they had a social and political agenda in creating the show.[6]

## 2.2 The setting

*Ego Trip's (White) Rapper Show* (henceforth WRS) is set in the South Bronx, the commonly recognized birthplace of hip hop in the 1970s (Chang, 2005). The show was shot during the summer of 2006 and aired from January through March of 2007. Ten White male and female contestants from all over the country were selected from hundreds of aspiring MCs to demonstrate their lyrical talent and knowledge of hip-hop culture for the chance to win $100,000. In hip hop, an MC (emcee) or 'master of ceremonies' raps (performs rhymes) against the backdrop of a beat provided by the DJ or disc jockey. The contestants are brought to a warehouse in the Bronx called 'Tha White House' where they live communally; the house also serves as the primary set for the show where rap contests and meetings with the host and other invited guests take place and where the contestants can be filmed during their down time.

In each of the eight episodes, the host, MC Serch (a White MC from the interracial 1980s group '3rd Bass') comes by the house and introduces the White rappers to hip-hop luminaries like Grandmaster Flash, and sites in the Bronx where hip hop emerged (1520 Sedgewick projects,

Cedar Park, etc., the Rucker playground).[7] Typically the contestants are divided into teams and presented with a challenge in which they have to demonstrate their rapping skills, or some aspect of their hip-hop knowledge. The losing team is then faced with an elimination challenge and the weakest competitor among them then is kicked off the show.

## 2.3 The contestants

The ten finalists chosen to be on the show include three young White women and seven young White men, all in their 20s, from diverse regions of the country including one from the United Kingdom. Each has a short bio on the VH1 website ('Cast Bios') with a link to a personal MySpace page where they can promote their careers, sell merchandise, and correspond with fans. Table 12.2 provides basic biographical information about each contestant.

It seems likely that the contestants were chosen because they represent easily accessible White American ethnic stereotypes. Great care is taken to strengthen these associations in the first few episodes through carefully edited clips. The male rappers include a hard-drinking, small town, southern 'good old boy' (100 Proof), a bespectacled, tie-wearing

**Table 12.2** Ten contestants chosen to be on *The (White) Rapper Show*

| Stage name (legal name) | Age | Gender | Origin |
|---|---|---|---|
| 100 Proof (Chuck Baker) | 28 | Male | Blue Mound, Texas |
| Dasit (David Shinavar) | 29 | Male | Toledo, Ohio |
| G-Child (Gina Morganello) | 21 | Female | Allentown, Pennsylvania |
| John Brown (Greg Kaysen)[8] | 26 | Male | Davis, California; Brooklyn, New York |
| Jon Boy (John Wertz) | 25 | Male | Reedville, Virginia |
| Jus Rhyme (Jeb Middlebrook) | 27 | Male | Austin, Minnesota; Los Angeles, CA |
| Misfit Dior (Laeticia Guzman) | 27 | Female | London, UK; Brooklyn, New York |
| Persia (Rachel Mucerino) | 25 | Female | Far Rockaway, New York |
| Shamrock (Timothy Rasmussen) | 23 | Male | Atlanta, Georgia |
| Sullee (Bobby Sullivan) | 21 | Male | Boston, Massachusetts |

'nerd' from the Midwest (Dasit), an affluent, self-promoting entrepreneur (John Brown), a clean-cut Christian rapper (Jon Boy), and a PhD student in ethnic studies (Jus Rhyme). The three female rappers are Misfit Dior, a pretty blonde originally from London, her oversized, in-your-face counterpart Persia who grew up in a predominantly African American neighbourhood in Queens, NY, and G-Child, a working class 'burnout' and devotee of the disgraced, has-been White rapper Vanilla Ice. Finally, there is Shamrock, a 'jock' from Atlanta with a huge golden grill over his teeth, and Sullee, a working class Irish-American from Boston whose father is allegedly a petty mob leader. The extent to which any of these individuals has actual rapping skills or any involvement in a local hip-hop scene seems less important than the entertainment value each of them can potentially provide.

The 'jock' and 'burnout' constructs are developed fully in Eckert (1989) and refer to oppositional social categories found in typical American high schools. Teenagers who orient towards the 'jock' identity tend to be more middle class and embrace the institutions of the school (sports, school government, etc.), whereas 'burnouts', generally working class, adopt an oppositional stance towards school and towards 'jock' culture. 'Nerds' on the other hand (studious, but socially awkward types) reject both 'jock' and 'burnout' orientations while asserting White or even 'hyperWhite' identities (Bucholtz, 2008).

The limited biographical information provided on the show makes it difficult to determine the extent to which any of the contestants actually identifies as a 'jock', 'burnout', 'nerd' or any other category. The bios on the VH1 website give some hints in this regard ('Cast Bios'). Shamrock is described as a 'high school athlete', but in an interview clip on the show, he describes how he was homeschooled through fifth grade because he had a cleft lip and had to undergo multiple surgeries, only later finding his identity through 'sports' and 'music' ('Shamrock on his Childhood'). G-Child and Dasit may fit the 'burnout' and 'nerd' categories more neatly. In her rap about the theme 'White trash' during the elimination round in Episode 3, G-Child describes how she and her friends engage in burnout-type activities like hanging out on rooftops and 'smokin cigs to pass the time, cause we can't do shit right' ('Elimination Challenge'). Referencing a nerd identity, Dasit's bio describes him as 'a dude who looks like an office worker gone postal' ('Cast Bios'). The reference to these widely recognizable social categories on the show points to their ubiquity and longevity in the American psyche, but we are simply not given enough ethnographic detail to assume that any of the competitors actually conform with any particular social category.

## 2.4 The Ego Trip crew

Ego Trip consists of five young men of colour with journalism backgrounds: Elliott Wilson, Jeff Mao, Sacha Jenkins, Brent Rollins and Gabriel Alvarez. From 1994–1998, the group published a magazine that dealt with issues of race while disguised as a magazine about hip hop.[9] Describing the magazine, Kleinfeld writes,

> They invented a white owner, one Theodore Aloysius Bawno, who offered a message in each issue, blurting his bigoted views and lust for Angie Dickinson. His son, Galen, was a Princeton-educated liberal who professed common cause with blacks. But in truth, he was an unaware bigot, as Mr. Wilson says he feels so many young whites are. (Kleinfeld, 2000, p. 6)

Exploring what the Ego Trip crew is about and its motives is crucial for understanding what the White rapper show is trying to accomplish. The VH1 website that accompanies the show includes a large number of short interviews with the Ego Trip crew. It is evident from these outtakes that the Ego Trip intended for the show to be a forum for educating the mainly White audience about the received version of hip-hop history, focusing on its African American roots in the Bronx and some of its male founders (Grandmaster Flash, Kurtis Blow, Melle Mel, Fat Joe, and others), as well as about some of the contradictions of Whites' participation in hip hop. The Ego Trip have a stake in guarding the gates of the hip-hop nation (Kleinfield, 2000) and the show is a symbolic attempt to define who can gain entrance and what knowledge is required in order to be member. With an average of over one million viewers in the 18–34 age group so highly coveted by television marketers during the first three episodes, the show had the potential to get its message out to a large number of young people (Fitzgerald, 2007).[10]

The creators of the show claim they want to dispel the myth that White rappers inherently lack credibility. In the preview outtakes ('Preview Extras: Tha Interrogation'), Sacha Jenkins, a member of Ego Trip, states that the whole Ego Trip crew had a certain fascination with White rappers because they appear to be trying to be 'something that they're not'. The title of the show certainly implies that the creators are trying to discover White rappers with real talent. In the preview that was aired to promote the WRS, MC Serch introduces the show as a chance for White rappers to demonstrate their 'love and knowledge' of hip hop as well prove 'their lyrical prowess' ('White Rapper: New Series Preview'). But the real motive is to establish a set of ground rules for Whites who want to be part of hip hop. These include acknowledging that hip hop is part of the cultural heritage of Black people, acknowledging the preeminent role of the Bronx in the birth of hip hop, paying tribute to hip hop's founding rap artists as well as places in hip hop's history. In the outtakes, Brent Rollins of the Ego Trip crew says that if hip hop is going to be 'gentrified' by White youth, it is imperative that young White people 'learn about its origins' ('Roundtable: South Bronx'). Acknowledging hip hop's rootedness in the Bronx and in the African American community, in addition to possessing the requisite skill to write clever rhymes and perform them, are the ways in which White rappers, and by extension the mainly White audience, are 'instructed' they can 'be real'.

# 3 Analysis

## 3.1 Whiteness as a marked category

The WRS is an interesting site for analysing questions of authenticity precisely because of the contested nature of White participation in hip-hop culture, the conglomeration of artists and fans who produce and consume the products of hip-hop culture: rapping, DJ-ing, graffiti art and break dancing. In mainstream American culture, White people usually do not have to think about their skin colour or worry about conforming to socially prescribed behaviours in the ways that people of colour often do. DuBois (1903), Spears (1998) and others have written extensively on the double consciousness that affects Black Americans and which forces them to see themselves through the eyes of Whites. But on the WRS, it is the White contestants who are continually reminded of their whiteness and are made to see themselves to some degree through the eyes of Black hip-hop authorities (embodied by guest judges like Prince Paul, Grandmaster Caz, Kwamé, Little X). In the Episode 1 outtakes ('Rountable: The N Word'), Sacha Jenkins of the Ego Trip says that the show is a 'conversation about race . . . in the hands of white people', implying that part of the goal is to get White viewers to understand what it is like to be racialized and objectified.

Often, overt references to whiteness are made via naming and labelling (Indexicality). The contestants are housed in an old warehouse building dubbed 'Tha White House' complete with bunkbeds, a garbage can labelled 'White trash', and other props chosen to give a sort of trashy urban loft vibe. The use of hip-hop orthography with regards to the determiner 'tha' in 'Tha White House' seems to index the cultural backdrop of the show and contrast it with the ethnicity of the contestants – a house reserved for White rappers in the Bronx is certainly marked – as well as create an ironic contrast between the real White House in Washington, D.C. where supreme power rests, and the powerless Bronx where 'Tha White House' is located. Periodically the contestants receive a video message from the host, MC Serch, played on a giant jar of mayonnaise. They are alerted to the message with a voice that says, 'You've got mayo', a play on America Online's ubiquitous email reminder 'You've got mail', but also a reference to the hip-hop expression 'to have mayo' which refers to White people who lack melanin in their skin.

In other instances, the contestants are forced to address whiteness more directly by actually rapping about it. In Episode 3 during the elimination challenge, the contestants on the losing team must take a slice of white bread from a bag with themes like 'white power', 'white trash', 'white wash' and 'white guilt' and go into the 'Ice Ice Chamber' (a sort of isolation tank and play on Vanilla Ice's 1989 hit song 'Ice Ice Baby') and write a 16 line rap about their topic. Two competing interpretations of whiteness emerge in Shamrock's and Sullee's rhymes. Shamrock whose theme is 'white guilt' writes about how being White gets him off the hook for shoplifting and driving a fast car whereas a young Black man would face very different consequences. In response to the theme 'white power', Sullee, expresses indignation at the idea that whiteness confers any advantage on him, saying that it is not about race, but rather economic status. The overt and indirect references to 'whiteness' in these multiple instances (Tha White House, 'you've got mayo', the Ice Ice Chamber, white guilt, white trash, white wash and white power) draw attention to whiteness as marked within the hermeneutics of hip hop, contrasting it with normative blackness (Boyd, 2002).

### 3.2 Competing forms of authenticity in interaction: Persia versus John Brown

The audition process for the WRS has already set up an interesting dialectic between competing dimension of hip-hop authenticity: social-locational vs gender/sexual and social psychological. Throughout the show, we learn that some of the rappers – with the exception of John Brown, the self-professed 'King of the burbs' – claim to come from pretty rough circumstances. Persia says she was 'homeless' at one time; Shamrock says he came from 'nothin'; Sullee says that his dad was in prison when he was young and G-Child is self-professed 'white trash'. They use their putative class origins throughout the show in order to excuse or explain their behaviour and as a way to try to authenticate themselves in a culture that privileges blackness and urban 'street' origins (Alim, 2003). Highlighting social traits that connect Whites and Blacks can be classified as a form of Adequation (Bucholtz and Hall, 2005).

**310**

Asserting a connection to blackness through poverty follows the tradition of the infamous White rapper, Eminem who proudly touts his 'trailer trash' identity. According to White (2006), Eminem is able to establish a relationship to constructions of authenticity within hip-hop culture through the coding of himself as 'white trash', a pejorative term referring to lower class Whites, which in turn connects him to blackness by suggesting that 'whites can be excluded and disenfranchised in much the same way as other non-white communities and groups' (White, 2006, p. 72). Indeed, this is a dimension that the creators seem eager to explore in the show. Brent Rollins confesses that he, like many other African Americans, grew up believing that all White people 'had it easy' and only later came to believe that poor White people are just like poor Black people ('The White Rapper Show is Born').

Persia, a self-chosen moniker that indexes a non-White and somewhat exotic female identity, is a young White woman who distinguishes herself from the other White competitors as someone who was socialized among Black people in a rough part of New York (Far Rockaway, Queens).[11] As we can see in her bio (below), Persia flouts her 'hood' credentials as her ticket to legitimacy as a rapper.

> Repping Far Rockaway, Queens to the fullest, the no-nonsense queen of tough talk bites her tongue for no one. As talented as she is confrontational, Rachel Mucerino, otherwise known as Persia, takes pride in embodying the rough, gritty attitude of old school New York. This is in stark contrast to her smooth-as-hell singing ability that complements her sharp-as-razors raps. The product of a hectic life growing up, 25-year-old Persia has walked the line between right and wrong and has emerged as a rising star (A rising star who prefers to call herself 'That Bitch'). (Cast Bios)

Persia's bio authenticates her by locating her in a Black neighbourhood (Social-Locational), connecting her to 'Old School' New York (Cultural), and by referencing her talent as a singer (Talent/skill). Finally, the fact that she self-identifies as a 'bitch' may be an attempt to lay claim to some of the more positive connotations this term can have in hip hop. It also works via implicature to suggest Black femaleness. Although scholars of hip hop have debated the widespread use of the word 'bitch' and 'ho' (from 'whore') in the lyrics of Black male rappers and their misogynist connotations (Potter, 1995; Perry, 2004; Perkins, 1996), Keyes (2004) writes that 'bitch' can have positive, empowering meanings such as an 'aggressive or assertive female who subverts the authority of men' (Keyes, 2004, p. 200).

By the end of the first episode, Persia, a rotund young woman with a large mop of dark curls and with a flair for loud colours, emerges as

**311**

the main protagonist in the show. She has shown a natural ability to relate to the local Black community in a 'meet and greet' around the south Bronx. She has also demonstrated her prowess at performing spontaneous 'freestyle' raps in front of appreciative Black audiences on the street and has garnered the respect of some of her fellow contestants such as G-Child who remarks, 'She's so hood! She's perfect for this hip-hop game' ('Rappin' in the hood').

Earlier in the first episode, Persia chooses her main rival, John Brown. By openly proclaiming his affluent, suburban California origins, John Brown indexes the social-psychological dimension of authenticity in that he is trying to represent himself truthfully (McLeod, 1999). He also fully embraces a kind of hyper capitalism embodied in the hip-hop expression 'I'ma get mine' and characteristic of entrepreneurial rappers who came up in the late 1990s such as Puff Daddy (Gaunt et al., 2008, p. 13). He is the leader of a movement and brand called 'Ghetto Revival', which he reminds the audience of constantly throughout the series by punctuating the end of every utterance with 'Ghetto revival, baby! Hallelujah, holla back!' John Brown also refers to himself as the 'King of the Burbs' ('Cast Bios') which he defines as being all about 'SATs, SUVs, and keg parties' – metonyms of American, upper middle class, suburbia and the college experience.[12] Persia is the utter contrast having grown up in a rough part of Queens – Far Rockaway – and makes no secret of the fact that she thinks John Brown is a fake and thus not a true representative of hip hop.

These two characters emerge in the first episode as representatives of competing versions of the authentic White rapper; they are repeatedly chosen to head up opposing teams and have already had a few verbal run-ins. Towards the end of Episode 1, the contestants are sitting around 'Tha White House' having drinks. Persia challenges John Brown to a freestyle battle – something that every MC is supposed to be able to do. She follows him around the house, trying to provoke him into battling her, finally resorting to waving her dildo (which is pixilated out of the image) in his face. Persia hurls insults at John Brown and questions his integrity and his masculinity by calling him a fake and a 'bitch', but he refuses to engage her. The increasing use of 'bitch' to refer to men was noted in a recent *New York Times* article (Heffernan, 2005). Calling a male 'bitch' is particularly insulting because it implies not weakness and femininity, but also possible sexual domination by another man (as commonly occurs in male prisons), contrasting with the positive connotations it can have when used in hip hop by women to describe themselves (Keyes, 2004).

**312**

### 3.3 Persia's challenge to John Brown

Persia's challenge to John Brown is to engage in a 'battle', a hip-hop performance genre in which two people agree to a verbal duel instead of a physical fight. The opponents each get a chance to 'diss' one another using spontaneous rhymes for a fixed length of time and the surrounding spectators then judge whose rhymes were better, thus diffusing the conflict. In hip-hop culture, MCs are supposed to be able to freestyle and battle spontaneously, and John Brown's unwillingness suggests that he either does not possess the skills or that he does not take Persia seriously. By challenging him, Persia is trying to expose him as a 'fake' MC, as well as authenticate herself by demonstrating her verbal skills. Sullee's threat to fight John Brown to defend Persia's honour during the confrontation is wholly inappropriate in the context of an MC battle and points to the likelihood that he was not socialized among urban African American hip hoppers. In (2), we see a transcript of the interaction.[13] John Brown has just uttered something inaudible but presumably insulting at Persia and Sullee jumps up from the table and begins threatening John Brown with physical violence. Shamrock tries to hold Sullee back and Persia shoves him away, pointing her finger at John Brown.

(2) Persia challenges John Brown to a battle; Episode 1, Ch. 6: 26:38[14]

| | |
|---|---|
| Persia: | This Ø how I'mo show ((you)) – This Ø how I'mo show the ((motherfuckin')) world he Ø a bitch! |
| Sullee: | Exactly! //louder// Exactly! |
| | **//camera cuts to post hoc interview with Shamrock//** |
| Shamrock: | *That's when like she disrespected him straight up.* |
| | **//camera cuts to Persia waving dildo in John Brown's face//** |
| | //Persia walking towards John Brown; John Brown retreating// |
| | **// camera cuts to Sullee running at John Brown//** |
| Sullee: | Exactly! |
| Persia: | Ø you gonna battle? You got a dick in your face. Ø you gonna battle? |
| | **//camera cuts to post hoc interview with Shamrock//** |
| Shamrock: | //smiling guiltily// *Persia brings out a dildo and put it on that man's mouth! Like* //shrugs// *that's – that's' it!* |
| | **//camera cuts back to Persia waving dildo in John Brown's face//** |
| John Brown: | //protecting face; retreating// All right. All right. |

| Persia: | Ø you gonna battle? Ø you a real **nigga**? You got a ((dick)) in your face. Ø you gonna battle? |
| | **//camera cuts to Persia's post hoc interview//** |
| Persia: | //speech stylized in a more standard direction// *I* [a:] *honestly wanted to push him by any means possible to battle me.* |
| | **// camera cuts back to Persia waving dildo in John Brown's face//** |
| Persia: | Are you gonna battle? |
| John Brown: | |Girl! |
| Persia: | You Ø a dude right? Any dude that have [-AGR] a dick in his face will man up. |
| | **// camera cuts to Persia's post hoc interview//** |
| Persia: | //speech stylized in a more standard direction// *I* [a:] *was thinkin', this is how I'm* [a:m] *gonna test him 'cause everybody I* [a:] *know would just crack me.* |
| | **// camera cuts back to Persia and John Brown//** |

## 3.4 Sociolinguistic identity analysis

We can analyse this scene using Bucholtz and Hall's (2005) Indexicality and Relationality Principles to show how Persia works to construct herself as an authentic hip-hop persona. From the beginning of the confrontation, she invokes a knowledgeable, epistemic stance (Bucholtz and Hall, 2005) as a hip-hop insider with the authority to show the 'motherfuckin' world' that John Brown is a 'bitch'. Persia's attempt to battle John Brown is cut with posthoc interviews about the event with some of the other contestants (e.g., Shamrock) as well as herself in addition to interview outtakes with the show's creators. Shamrock's comments and facial gestures signal his orientation towards the encounter as bemused spectator and sympathizer with Persia.

These carefully edited excerpts function as metanarratives in Bauman's terms (1986), contextualizing the event with the perceived objective of the show as well as the personal agendas each competitor brings with him or her. Persia explains that she attacked John Brown in order to frame him as a fake MC and a wimp. In terms of participant roles, Persia positions herself as a representative and protector of the other contestants and of hip hop itself who is determined to expose 'posers' and 'wannabes'. She tells us that any of the 'real' men she knows would have smacked her for waving a dildo in their faces, implying that John Brown lacks the requisite masculinity to be a 'real' man. Boyd (2002) writes that there is a 'strong sense of physicality and sensuality that informs society's definition of black masculinity' (p. 122) and a 'detached, nonchalant sense of being' that is the 'antithesis of what would be described as white masculinity' (Boyd, 2002, p. 118). In Persia's mind, John Brown's failure to respond to her taunting in a physical way or to at least step up to the challenge of a battle is evidence that he fails to live up to the standards of Black masculinity and is therefore not a suitable representative of hip hop. She, in contrast, positions herself as someone who is ready and willing to battle, making her a legitimate representative of hip-hop culture.

When John Brown responds, he addresses not Persia, but rather the wider audience – TV viewers, and record company representatives. He advises them not to sign any of his competitors (especially Persia) because they would be a financial 'liability', once again indexing his stance as a modern-day capitalist rapper with an eye to the market ('Uh-oh, someone said the n-word'). In his interview, he objectifies Persia's outburst from the perspective of someone with commercial interests who wants to promote a 'good look' in order to sell a product. Here, he is product and he is effectively trying to sell himself and his Ghetto Revival brand to a potential buyer in the record industry or wider hip-hop market. He contrasts his image with that of Persia, a large, outspoken, fearless woman, framing her as someone who will scare away marketers and potential consumers.

In terms of style, Persia demonstrates a degree of linguistic and verbal competence that sets her apart from any of the other participants. In addition to copula absence, a lack of subject verb agreement, and third person verbal /s/ absence, Persia stylizes her speech by using some of the characteristic phonological, intonational and morphosyntactic features of vernacular African American English (AAE).

Some of the other competitors demonstrate that copula absence is part of their linguistic repertoires, but use it only in performing raps: Shamrock omits the copula when quoting a Black friend in his rap about 'white guilt' in Episode 3, and in Episode 4, John Brown, Jon Boy and Sullee write a song called 'She Ø a stunner' (She's a stunner).[15] Persia, on the other hand, uses copula absence throughout her confrontation with John Brown and also on a few isolated occasions in conversation. Referring to the losing team during a dinner with Black rapper Juelz Santana, Persia says, 'That four lost the competition so they Ø over there, doin' our laundry' ('My Dinner with Juelz Santana'). An analysis of her speech in the scene transcribed in (2) and (3) indicates that her performance style contains frequencies of copula absence that are similar to the performance style of African American female rap artists such as Eve (Alim, 2002).

Alim (2002) looks at copula variation in the lyrics and interview data he collected with two rappers, Eve and Juvenile. As we might expect, both artists had higher rates of absence in their lyrics than in

**315**

**Table 12.3** Persia's use of AAE features (battle style)

| Feature | Frequency | No. of tokens |
| --- | --- | --- |
| Copula absence (is) (D/C+D) | 60% | N = 5 |
| Copula absence (are) (D/C+D) | 77% | N = 13 |
| Ø Agreement | 36% | N = 11 |

their interviews (60.9 per cent 'is' deletion; 93.2 per cent 'are' deletion; Alim, 2002, p. 296).[16] The data from the emotionally charged scene in (2) and (3) illustrate that, at least with respect to copula absence, Persia's performance approaches the frequencies found in the lyrics of an African American female rapper (see Table 12.3).

Indeed, Persia's social experience resembles that of the White woman documented in the work of Sweetland (2002) who was socialized in a Black community in Cincinnati, Ohio and who possesses both the linguistic competence and the social license to use AAE syntax in ways that native speakers do. Persia's speech is also notable for its lack of subject–verb agreement and for its AAE intonational features, wide pitch range, raspy voice and falsetto voice, all of which make it conceivable for her to pass linguistically as an African American woman. To borrow Sweetland's expression, Persia appears to be an 'authentic speaker' of AAE both in terms of her ability to pass linguistically, but also in terms of the lexical choices she makes and the stance she takes towards her use of these choices. Taken together, Persia's phonological, morphosyntactic, lexical and intonational style markers serve to demarcate the interaction as a performance and differentiate it from the way she styles her speech in more formal settings where she restricts her speech stylization to monophthongal realizations of /ay/ and postvocalic /r/-lessness.

Persia's use of AAE morphosyntax, her claims to a ghetto identity, and her challenges to John Brown's masculinity as a rapper constitute stance taking moves. Effectively, she is claiming the Racial (blacknesss), Gender-sexual (hard), Social locational (the street), Cultural (old school), and Talent/skill (ability to freestyle/battle) dimensions of authenticity listed in Table 12.1. By taking an epistemic stance as an insider and judge of who is 'real', she is setting herself apart not only from John Brown, but from all of the other contestants, none of whom can lay claim to the range of authenticating dimensions that she does. As shown below, she also does this in her choice of lexis.

At the lexical level, Persia makes use of hip-hop expressions like 'bitch', 'peoples', 'they' (in place of 'their'), 'stupid ass' and 'nigga'.

There have been enormous debates in hip hop about the use of the last of these – the so-called 'N-word', its various meanings and who is allowed to say it (Smitherman, 2000). Smitherman (2000) writes that while it is true that among Blacks, the word has a unique /r/-less pronunciation ('nigga'), and a variety of meanings, only one of which is negative, and that it has become more acceptable for Black people to use it in the public arena since the advent of hip-hop culture, it is still unacceptable for a White person to use the term. This generalization may be extended to any non-African American person judging by the controversy that erupted when the pop singer Jennifer Lopez, who is of Puerto Rican descent, used the N-word in her song 'I'm Real' (written by African American rapper Ja Rule). Among the most vocal critics were African American radio hosts Star and Buc Wild (from New York's Hot 97 Star and Buc Wild Morning Show) who vehemently oppose non-African Americans using the term (Alonso, 2003). The White rapper Eminem has also stated publicly that he would never use the N-word.

Persia's use of the N-word and the comments she makes in her own defence (shown in excerpt 3 below) index her insider status in the Black community. In an interview clip following the incident, she reports that she uses the terms 'among her Black friends', who presumably accept her as part of their peer group as well as their speech community. Elliott Wilson of the Ego Trip observes that she is using it in an 'N-I-G-G-A' way – not an 'N-I-G-G-E-R' way, meaning that she is pronouncing it the way Black people do and that she is using it in a positive or neutral sense, rather than as a racial epithet with its requisite rhotic pronunciation ('Roundtable: The N-Word'). He also notes that although Persia feels licensed to use the N-word around her Black friends, she fails to realize that it may be offensive to others ('Roundtable: The N-Word').

The next excerpt, which follows directly on the heels of (2), shows how Persia's rampant use of the N-word in her attack against John Brown is treated by the show's most politically aware contestant, Jus Rhyme.

(3) Persia challenges John Brown to a battle; Episode 1, Ch. 6: 26:38
(continued)

| | |
|---|---|
| Persia: | //walking down the hallway in pursuit of John Brown// You's [-AGR] a ((fuckin')) bitch, yo. Niggas is [-AGR] ready to knock you out – |
| | **//cut to John Brown chewing lip; cut back to Persia//** |
| Persia: | – and lose they [POSS] whole chance – because you's [-AGR] a bitch. |
| | **//camera cuts to John Brown//** |
| John Brown: | Let's get it poppin'! |

| Persia: | //cynical tone// Oh, now we Ø about to get it poppin', right? You want to fight but you don't want to battle. **//camera pans to Persia//** |
|---|---|
| Persia: | Only because you want the **nigga** //referring to Sullee// to hit you first and go home, right? But you know, this is ((some rap shit)). You don't want to battle. You just want the **nigga** to hit you first. |
| Jus Rhyme: | ⎪Persia. Persia. |
| Persia: | ⎪You Ø a bitch! **//camera cuts to Jus Rhyme lying on bunkbed//** |
| Jus Rhyme: | Would you mind please not using the N-word, 'cause it bothers me. **//cut to Jus Rhyme's post hoc interview//** |
| Jus Rhyme: | *The N-word is not appropriate for people to use – It can be ((a)) hurtful word.* **//cut to Persia and Jus Rhyme//** |
| Persia: | Yeah, well life sucks and there ain't no doors on this room. |
| Jus Rhyme: | I know, I'm just sayin', would you . . . |
| Persia: | //louder// ⎪Yeah, well life sucks and ((they)) ain't no doors on this room! **//camera pans to Persia//** |
| Jus Rhyme: | All right. |
| Persia: | It ain't personal. How Ø you takin' it? **//cut to Jus Rhyme's post hoc interview]** |
| Jus Rhyme: | *My friends are predominantly black and Latino and I'm offended – at her saying the word.* **//cut to Persia and Jus Rhyme//** |
| Jus Rhyme: | I know, I'm just saying, the use – your use of the N-word = //SUBTITLES APPEAR ON SCREEN: I KNOW, I'M JUST SAYING YOUR USE OF THE N-WORD BOTHERS ME. |
| Persia: | //angrily//⎪Yeah, well I grew up in the **hood**= |
| Jus Rhyme: | =bothers me. |
| Persia: | ⎪=and we ain't – no color. Everybody's my **nigga**, right there! |
| Jus Rhyme: | O.K. |
| Persia: | So whoever the fuck takes disrespect, it's they [POSS] ((fuckin')) problem. Wherever they Ø from, they can't say it in front of they [POSS] peoples, that's they [POSS] problem. Everybody's my **nigga**, and I'm somebody's **nigga** right now. |

Within the Black community, the N-word can have a variety of meanings, some of which are positive or neutral (Major, 1994; Smitherman, 2000). Smitherman (2000) writes that it can express personal affection ('He my main nigga'), describe someone who is culturally Black

**Table 12.4** Persia's use of the N-word during attack on John Brown

| Token | Connotation |
|---|---|
| Ø you a real **nigga**? | Positive; someone who is true to themselves and doesn't 'front' or pretend to be something they're not. |
| **Niggas** is [-AGR] ready to knock you out and lose they whole chance. | Neutral; any (presumably) male person, but could refer to an unspecified female person as well. |
| Only because you want the **nigga** to hit you first and go home, right? | Neutral: referring to the White contestant Sullee |
| You just want the **nigga** to hit you first. | Neutral: referring to the White contestant Sullee |
| Yeah, well I grew up in the hood and we ain't – no color. Everybody's my **nigga**, right there! | Positive: meaning something like friend or partner. |
| Everybody's my **nigga**, and I'm somebody's **nigga** right now. | Positive: By saying that everyone is a *nigga*, including her, Persia is trying to show that she's not using the word in its restricted negative sense, but rather a positive one. |

('Niggas is beautiful, baby'), refer to any Black person as a stand-in noun ('Niggas was runnin' all over the place'), or express disapproval of a person's actions ('The nigga ain't shit') (Smitherman, 2000, pp. 362–363). As we see in Table 12.4, Persia has access to the different meanings of the word and uses it in a variety of ways, none of which is negative (all of the tokens occur in the scene transcribed in excerpts (2) and (3) above). Persia initially uses the expression 'real nigga' in a positive sense, referring to someone who is authentic and who stands for something – all qualities that she feels John Brown lacks. She then uses the term in a neutral sense in referring to the other White contestants on the show ('*Niggas* is [-AGR] ready to knock you out . . .') and then in referring to Sullee ('Only because you want the "nigga" to hit you first . . .'). The last three tokens, delivered in an angry, huffing voice ('Everybody's my "nigga", right there!; Everybody's my "nigga", and I'm somebody's "nigga" right now') are used in a highly positive, inclusive ingroup way.

When Jus Rhyme, a doctoral student in ethnic studies, asks her not to use the 'N-word' because he feels that 'it's not appropriate', Persia retorts, 'There ain't no doors on this room' – how Ø you takin' it?, meaning that she thinks it is acceptable to use the N-word if there are not any Black people around to hear it and/or when it is not meant to be a racial epithet. In another short interview clip following the incident, Persia says that she never uses the N-word in a malicious manner, but because she uses it around her friends, 'it's bound to happen' ('Serch lays down the law'). She's clearly aware of the different meanings that it can have based on who says it and how it is meant (cf. Smitherman, 2000), but asserts her right to use this word as shown in (4). It is in this particular instance that we see Persia emphatically taking the stance of an insider and aligning herself with blackness through the implicature of the statement 'we ain't no color'. We also see adequation (suppression of social difference) at work in her use of the inclusive pronoun 'we' which groups her with other, presumably Black people in the 'hood' and implies that there is no difference (in terms of skin colour) between them (Bucholtz and Hall, 2005).

(4) 'Yeah, well I grew up in the hood and **we** ain't – no color. Everybody's my **nigga**, right there!'

The utterance is delivered with an emphatic raspy voice and AAE phonology (the monophthongization of 'I' and 'my', /r/-lessness in 'color', and 'there', and particularly the realization of /h/ in 'hood' as a velar fricative ([x]). Although this last item may not derive from any previously documented feature of AAE, it does seem to be a way for Persia to place special emphasis on the word 'hood', making it especially salient for anyone listening.

The Ego Trip had anticipated this moment and were prepared to deal with it. In the outtakes (Roundtable: The N-Word), Gabriel Alvarez explains that 'you can't do a show like *Ego Trip's (White) Rapper Show* without thinking about White people using the N-Word' ('Roundtable: The N-Word'). MC Serch then explains that the position of the Ego Trip was that any use of the N-word on the show 'would not be tolerated'. By highlighting the problem and asserting their right not to tolerate it, as well as previous references to their 'Old School' roots, The Ego Trip authorize themselves as arbiters and authorities of hip-hop culture.

The next day, MC Serch gathers the rappers for a special meeting. Because of her repeated use of the word 'nigga' during the altercation, MC Serch obliges Persia to wear a special 'bling' (flashy, ostentatious jewellery) – an enormous metal placard on an oversized metal chain with 'N-Word' stamped on it – for the rest of the day while the whole cast goes to play miniature golf. He addresses her use of the N-word in terms of the national audience, saying that the word does not 'flow around the country' in places like Mississippi, Tallahassee and Birmingham ('Roundtable: The N-Word'). Elliott Wilson concedes that, while it may be possible for someone like Persia to use the N-word in 'her environment', she (and by extension the White hip hoppers in the audience) need to recognize that using it anywhere else is offensive to Black people ('Roundtable: The N-Word'). The scene cuts to Jus Rhyme who explains that 'There was a time in history when those chains were real and they were on black people, so what are you really doing if you use that word and you claim to represent hip hop?' Persia accepts her guilt and after the golf game she breaks down in tears, admitting that she may have hurt people by her use of the N-Word (though she does not mention John Brown as being one of them). It is interesting to note here that Persia's use of the word 'bitch' during the confrontations with John Brown in contrast to the N-word receives no attention whatsoever, despite the sexist and misogynist connotations it has in the context of the interaction. Nor is either word censored, unlike 'motherfucker' or 'fuckin' which are 'bleeped out' and appear as subtitles rendered partially with symbols on the screen (e.g., motherf*****).

Persia seems like she's on course to win the show, but is eliminated unexpectedly in Episode 6, much to the chagrin of the host MC Serch who breaks down in tears. The episode starts off by having the remaining rappers (Jus Rhyme, Persia, John Brown, and Shamrock) complete the 'thug challenge' obstacle course which involves stealing three bags of groceries in a shopping cart, smashing a piñata and collecting two dollars worth of dimes, running to a store, exchanging the dimes for lock cutters, stealing a bike, and returning back to Tha White House. Jus Rhyme wins the challenge, but Persia collapses and is hospitalized briefly for dehydration. At elimination, the rappers are required to write a 'thug' version of an old nursery rhyme. Persia stumbles on her rhyme halfway through, and when MC Serch tells her to get back up and try again, she refuses. The judges concur that even though her rhymes are better than many of the others, her failure to finish and refusal to try again mean that she must go. The enormous symbolic potential of a White female rapper winning out over a group of White male rappers is ultimately derailed by a physical contest about who can be the most 'thuggish'.

## 4 Conclusion

The scenes described above can help to address some of the questions raised in this volume, in particular how authenticities are produced and reproduced through semiotic forms of expression, how the application of notions of authenticity legitimates some individuals, and not others, and whose interests are served by the assessment of others' authenticity.

**321**

Persia constructs herself as an authentic hip-hop persona by establishing a cultural affiliation with blackness via implicature and adequation. She talks about coming from the 'hood', calls herself 'bitch' in her bio, refers to herself as a 'nigga' in (3), and uses the inclusive pronoun 'we' in (4) ('Yeah, well I grew up in the hood and we ain't – no color'). She further authenticates herself by adopting a knowledgeable insider stance through the evaluative expressions she makes towards John Brown by calling him a 'bitch', and questioning his integrity and manhood ('Ø you a real nigga?'). Finally, in terms of style, she employs syntactic features of AAE such as Ø copula, and lack of subject–verb agreement, in addition to a range of phonological features and lexical items to reinforce her connection to the 'hood'.

There is also an identity project at work in the show. The Ego Trip and the host, MC Serch, use their 'Old School' status as a way to assert their authority and license to judge who is 'real' and what the received history of hip hop should be. The foregrounding of whiteness in the title of the show, and its frequent mention throughout the show in overt and indirect ways ('Tha White House', 'You've got mayo', etc.) all constitute a strategy of distinction, making the audience aware of the fact that whiteness is marked and problematic in the hip-hop world view. Hegemonic whiteness and its privileged position as the unmarked, unnamed, normative category are challenged by the show's insistence on calling it out, making fun of it, and making White rappers rap about it.

Previous work on *Ego Trip's (White) Rapper Show* has accused it of promulgating essentialized re-presentations of blackness. During a roundtable discussion about the WRS among a group of musicologists that took place in 2007 in Boston, Miles White equates the re-presentations of blackness on the show with minstrelsy, implying that the White rappers on the show are performing blackness in ways that reproduce and promulgate White stereotypes about how Black people behave (White, 2008; cf. Gaunt et al., 2008, Lott, 1993). Shohat (1995) reminds us that while dominant groups need not worry too much about being adequately represented, 'representation of underrepresented groups is, within the hermeneutics of domination, overcharged with allegorical significance' (Shohat, 1995, p. 170). This is certainly another way to examine Persia's identity project and one that goes beyond the scope of this chapter, but it raises interesting questions about how much control the Ego Trip were given and the degree to which commercial interests may subvert efforts to challenge whiteness while failing to problematize damaging stereotypes about Black people.

**322**

## Notes

1. I would like to thank Jacquelyn Rahman for the invitation to speak at Miami University and Marina Terkourafi for organizing the workshop on *Language and Hip-Hop Culture in a Globalizing World* which inspired me to work on this topic. I am also very grateful to Marina Terkourafi for her efforts in editing the present volume, and for the insightful comments on this chapter she and others have given me on earlier versions of this chapter. Finally, I would like to thank Jeff Mao for granting me permission to quote from *Ego Trip's (White) Rapper Show* and for his helpful corrections of my transcript.

2. According to Purcell (2007), the parentheses around *White* in the title of the show (*Ego Trip's (White) Rapper Show*) suggest that the message of the show is not only directed at aspiring White rappers, but the larger audience of rap fans.

3. Eminem emerged in 1999 under the tutelage of the Black rapper and producer Dr Dre and was the first White rapper to achieve a level of success and fame comparable to contemporary Black rappers such as Nas and Jay-Z.

4. Bogdanov et al. (2003) writes that for rappers who emerged in the 1980s, 'Old School' usually refers to artists who came from the late 1970s and early 1980s such as Kurtis Blow, Grandmaster Flash & the Furious Five, the Sugar Hill Gang, the Treacherous Three, Afrika Bambaataa and Kook DJ Herc. During the Old School period, lyrics tended to be light-hearted and frivolous, contrasting notably with violent and/or misogynist lyrics associated with the 'gangsta rap' period of the 1990s.

5. List of Reality Television Programs from *Wikipedia*, the free encyclopedia. <http://en.wikipedia.org/wiki/List_of_reality_television_programs>, accessed 1 December 2008.

6. An outtake is a portion of a work (usually a DVD version of a film) that is not included in the work's final, publicly released version. The outtake interviews with members of the Ego Trip crew were not aired on VH1, but were available on the VH1 website while the show was being aired.

7. According to Gonzalez (2007), the housing project at 1520 Sedgewick was one of the places where hip hop was created. DJ Kool Herc held parties in the common room starting in 1973, using sound system and turntable technology that rapidly spread to the surrounding streets and playgrounds.

8. John Brown, the MC, may have named himself after the White, southern abolitionist by the same name (1800–1859) who was hanged for inciting a slave insurrection and for the murder of five White pro-slavery Southerners. If indeed this was the contestant John Brown's intention, it suggests that he sees himself as some kind of modern day liberator. <http://en.wikipedia.org/wiki/John_Brown_(abolitionist)>

9. *Ego Trip Magazine.* <http://en.wikipedia.org/wiki/Ego_trip_(magazine)>, accessed 1 December 2008. The Ego Trip have also collectively published two books, *Ego Trip's Book of Rap Lists* (Jenkins et al., 1999), and *Ego Trip's Big Book of Racism!* (Jenkins et al., 2002).

10. Television ratings are tracked by the age of the viewers. Viewers aged 18–34 constitute the most sought after age group for the marketers who pay for advertising on television programs because they are thought to be forming their lifelong purchasing habits.
11. According to the *New York Times*, Far Rockaway is 47.3 per cent Black (Far Rockaway Queens: Data Report): <http://realestate.nytimes.com/community/far-rockaway-queens-ny-usa/demographics>, accessed 1 December 2008.
12. The SAT or Scholastic Aptitude Test is a standardized test for college admissions in the United States. One's score on the SAT (based on 1600 points) is one way that college admissions boards rate potential applicants. SUVs or Sport Utility Vehicles are large, four-wheel drive vehicles, the largest of which (Hummers, Cadillac Escalades, etc.) became status symbols due to their enormous size and luxury features in the late 1990s and early 2000s. Keg parties are very common events in the fraternities (young men's clubs) found on American college and university campuses. They involve the consumption of large quantities of beer from a 'keg' or half barrel available at a beer distributor.
13. Part of this interaction can be viewed online on the VH1 website: <http://www.vh1.com/video/play.jhtml?id=1549458&vid=127122>, accessed 24 January 2010.
14. Transcription conventions: (( )) inaudible or questionable utterance; // laughs// = stage directions; italics = off screen utterances; Ø = copula absence; ALL CAPS = increased volume; [-AGR] = lack of subject–verb agreement; [POSS] = possessive pronoun Bold text = feature or word pertinent to the analysis.
15. In his rap about 'white guilt', Shamrock distinguishes himself morpho-syntactically when he drops the copula in voicing his Black friend in the last line: 'Got caught shopliftin' man, Ain't fuckin' funny. I was stressin' like hell, would I be all right'. My Black friend said, 'Yeah, Shamrock, you Ø white!' Shamrock chooses to demonstrate his knowledge of copula absence only when quoting his Black friend. It is through this subtle, linguistic cue that Shamrock asserts his linguistic competence as well as his respect for an unspoken ethnolinguistic boundary.
16. Copula absence can be tallied in a number of ways. This analysis employs Labov Deletion (Labov, 1969) which is calculated by tallying the deleted and the contracted forms of 'is' and/or 'are', putting the total number of deleted forms in the numerator (D), and dividing it by the sum of the deleted (D) plus the contracted forms (C), i.e., $D/(C + D)$.

# Videography

*Black. White* (2006), FX, 8 March 2006–12 April 2006. Los Angeles, CA.
*Blaze Battle* (2000), Home Box Office. (Broadcast on 2 November). Blaze-battle world championship. New York, NY.
'Cast Bios' (2007), *The White Rapper Show: Official Web site*: <http://www.vh1.com/shows/dyn/white_rapper/series_characters.jhtml>, accessed 1 January 2009.

'Elimination Challenge' (2007), *The White Rapper Show*: Official website: <http://www.vh1.com/video/play.jhtml?id=1550485&vid=129031>, accessed 1 January 2009.

Mok, K. (Producer) (2007), *Ego Trip's (White) Rapper Show*, VH-1. New York, NY. 8 January–26 February 2007.

'My Dinner with Juelz Santana' (2007), *The White Rapper Show: Official Web site*: <http://www.vh1.com/video/play.jhtml?id=1550590&vid=129026>, accessed 1 January 2009.

'Rappin' in the hood' (2007), *The White Rapper Show: Official Web site*: <http://www.vh1.com/video/play.jhtml?id=1549458&vid=127120>, accessed 1 January 2009.

'Roundtable: South Bronx' (2007), *The White Rapper Show: Official Web site*: <http://www.vh1.com/video/play.jhtml?id=1549361&vid=127088>, accessed 1 January 2009.

'Roundtable: The N-Word', (2007). *The White Rapper Show: Official Web site*: <http://www.vh1.com/video/play.jhtml?id=1549361&vid=127086>, accessed 1 January 2009.

'Serch lays down the law', (2007). *The White Rapper Show: Official Web site*: <http://www.vh1.com/video/play.jhtml?id=1549458&vid=127123>, accessed 1 January 2009.

*Shalom in the Home*, (2006). TLC. Launched 4 March, 2006. New York, NY.

'Shamrock on his childhood', (2007). *The White Rapper Show: Official Web site*: <http://www.vh1.com/video/play.jhtml?id=1549361&vid=126935>, accessed 1 January 2009.

'Preview Extras: "Tha Interrogation"', (2007). *The White Rapper Show: Official Web site*: <http://www.vh1.com/video/play.jhtml?id=1549004&vid=126388>, accessed 1 January 2009.

'The White Rapper Show is Born', (2007). *The White Rapper Show: Official Web site*: <http://www.vh1.com/video/play.jhtml?id=1549004&vid=126201>, accessed 1 January 2009.

'Uh-oh, someone said the n-word', (2007). *The White Rapper Show: Official Web site*: <http://www.vh1.com/video/play.jhtml?id=1549458&vid=127122>, accessed 1 January 2009.

'White Rapper: New Series Preview', (2007). *The White Rapper Show: Official Web site*: <http://www.vh1.com/video/play.jhtml?id=1548682&vid=125712>, accessed 1 January 2009.

# References

Alim, S. (2002), 'Street-conscious copula variation in the hip hop nation'. *American Speech*, 77, 3, 288–304.

Alim, H. S. (2003), 'We are the streets: African American language and the strategic construction of a street conscious identity', in S. Makoni, G. Smitherman and A. Ball (eds), *Black Linguistics*. New York: Routledge, pp. 40–59.

—(2004), 'Hip Hop Nation Language', in E. Finegan and J. Rickford (eds), *Language in the USA*. New York: Cambridge University Press, pp. 387–409.

Alonso, A. (2003), 'Won't you please be my nigga: double standards with a taboo word'. *Streetgangs Magazine*. <http://www.streetgangs.com/magazine/053003niggas.php>, accessed 29 May 2009.

Armstrong, E. G. (2004), 'Eminem's construction of authenticity'. *Popular Music and Society*, 27, 3, 335–355.

Bauman, R. (1986), *Story, Performance and Event: Contextual Studies of Narrative*. Cambridge: Cambridge University Press.

Bogdanov, V., Woodstra, C., Erlewine, S. T. and Bush, J. (2003), *All Music Guide To Hip-hop: The Definitive Guide to Rap and Hip-hop*. San Francisco: Backbeat Books.

Boyd, T. (2002), *The New H.N.I.C.* New York: New York University Press.

Bucholtz, M. and Hall, K. (2005), 'Identity and interaction: a sociocultural linguistic approach'. *Discourse Studies*, 7, 4–5, 585–614.

Chang, J. (2005), *Can't Stop Won't Stop*. New York: St. Martin's Press.

Cutler, C. (2002), 'Crossing over: white youth, hip-hop and African American English'. PhD Dissertation. New York University.

—(2007), 'Hip hop language in sociolinguistics and beyond'. *Language and Linguistics Compass*, 5, 1, 519–538.

—(2009), 'You shouldn't be rappin', you should be skate boardin' the X-games: The co-construction of whiteness in an MC Battle', in A. Ibrahim, H. S. Alim and A. Pennycook (eds), *Global Linguistic Flows: Hip Hop Cultures, Youth Identities, and the Politics of Language*. New York: Taylor & Francis, pp. 79–94.

Davison, A. (2001), 'Critical musicology study day on "authenticity"'. *Popular Music*, 20, 2, 263–264.

DuBois, W. E. B. (1903), *The Souls of Black Folk*. <http://www.bartleby.com/114/>, accessed 27 July 2007.

Eckert, P. (1989), *Jocks & Burnouts: Social Categories and Identity in the High School*. New York: Teachers College Press.

Fitzgerald, T. (2007), 'VH1's (White) Rapper, the new sitcom: Kids living in a house and playing the fool'. 31 January. <http://www.medialifemagazine.com/cgi-bin/artman/exec/view.cgi?archive=483&num=9857>, accessed 1 June 2009.

Gaunt, K., Keyes, C. L., Mangin, T. R., Marshall, W. and Schloss, J. (2008), 'Roundtable: VH1's (White) Rapper Show: intrusions, sightlines, and authority'. *Journal of Popular Music Studies*, 20, 1, 44–78.

Gonzalez, D. (2007), 'Will gentrification spoil the birthplace of hip-hop?' *The New York Times*, 21 May. <http://www.nytimes.com/2007/05/21/nyregion/21citywide.html>, accessed 1 June 2009.

Gordon, L. R. (2005), 'The problem of maturity in hip hop'. *The Review of Education, Pedagogy, and Cultural Studies*, 27, 4, 367–89.

Hall, K. and Bucholtz , M. (eds) (1995), *Gender Articulated: Language and the Socially Constructed Self*. London: Routledge.

Heffernan, V. (2005), 'Epithet morphs from bad girl to weak boy'. *New York Times*, p. E8.

Hess, M. (2005), 'Hip-hop realness and the white performer'. *Critical Studies in Media Communication*, 22, 5, 372–89.

Jenkins, S., Wilson, E., Mao, C. M., Alvarez, G. and Rollins, B. (1999), *Ego Trip's Book of Rap Lists*. New York: St. Martin's Press.

—(2002), *Ego Trip's Big Book of Racism!* Los Angeles: Regan Books.

Johnson-Woods, T. (2002), *Big Bother: Why did that Reality-TV Show Become Such a Phenomenon?* St. Lucia, Qld.: University of Queensland Press.

Johnstone, B. (forthcoming), 'Stance, style, and the linguistic individual', in A. Jaffe (ed.), *Stance: Sociolinguistic Perspectives.* Oxford University Press.

Keyes, C. (2004), *Rap Music and Street Consciousness.* Champaign, IL: University of Illinois Press.

Kleinfeld, N. R. (2000), 'Guarding the borders of the Hip Hop Nation'. *New York Times*, 6 July. <http://www.nytimes.com/2000/07/06/us/guarding-the-borders-of-the-hip-hop-nation.html?sec=&spon=&pagewanted=6>, accessed 1 December 2008.

Labov, W. (1969), 'Contraction, deletion, and inherent variability of the English copula'. *Language*, 45, 715–762.

Lott, E. (1993), *Love and Theft: Blackface Minstrelsy and the American Working Class.* Oxford: Oxford University Press.

Major, C. (1994), *Juba to Jive: A Dictionary of African-American Slang.* New York: Penguin Books.

McLeod, K. (1999), 'Authenticity within hip-hop and other cultures threatened with assimilation'. *The Journal of Communication*, 49, 4, 134–150.

Perkins, W. (1996), *Droppin' Science: Critical Essays on Rap Music and Hip Hop Culture.* Philadelphia: Temple University Press.

Perry, I. (2004), *Prophets of the Hood: Politics and Poetics in Hip Hop.* Durham & London: Duke University Press.

Potter, R. (1995), *Spectacular Vernaculars: Hip-hop and the Politics of Postmodernism.* Albany, NY: State University of New York Press.

Purcell, R. (2007), 'Rapping about guilty pleasures'. *News and Notes*, 23 March. National Public Radio. <http://www.npr.org/templates/story/story.php?storyId=9097615>, accessed 3 May 2009.

Rickford, J. and Rickford, R. (2000), *Spoken Soul: The Story of Black English.* New York, NY: John Wiley & Sons.

Sales, N. J. (1996), 'Teenage gangland'. *New York Magazine.* 16 December, 29, 49, 32–9.

Shohat, E. (1995), 'Performing in the postcolony: the plays of Mustapha Matura', in R. De La Campa, E. A. Kaplan and M. Sprinker (eds), *Late Imperial Culture.* London: Verso, pp. 166–178.

Smith, M. J., and Wood, A. F. (eds) (2003), *Survivor Lessons: Essays on Communication and Reality Television.* Jefferson, NC: McFarland & Company, Inc., Publishers.

Smitherman, G. (2000), *Talkin' That Talk: Language Culture, and Education in African America.* New York: Routledge.

Sparks, C. (2007), 'Reality TV: the Big Brother phenomenon'. *International Socialism*, 114. Issue: 114. <http://www.isj.org.uk/index.php4?id=314&issue=114>, accessed 1 December 2008.

Spears, A. (1998), 'Language use and so-called obscenity', in S. Mufwene, J. R. Rickford, G. Bailey and J. Baugh (eds), *African-American English.* New York: Routledge, pp. 226–250.

Sweetland, J. (2002), 'Unexpected but authentic use of an ethnically-marked dialect'. *Journal of Sociolinguistics*, 6, 4, 514–536.

White, M. (2008), 'The (Black) Boy Shuffle: internalizing, externalizing, and naturalizing the black male body double'. *Journal of Popular Music Studies*, 20, 1, 44–78.

White, R. (2006), 'Behind the mask: Eminem and postindustrial minstrelsy'. *Journal of American Culture*, 25, 1, 65–97.

# Glossary of Hip-Hop Terms

**Backpacker** (n.): a fan of **underground hip-hop** music, sometimes perceived as a poser or elitist

**Battle** (n.): a performance competition between **MCs** or (**crews** of) **breakdancers/b-boys**, **graffiti** artists, and other groups associated with hip-hop culture aiming to outperform the opponent by a display of skill assessed by an audience

**Battle** (v.): to engage in such a competition

**B-boy** (v.): to dance to **break beats** in the style associated with hip-hop culture; typical moves include **moonwalking** and **headspins** (also **break** or **breakdance**)

**B-boy** (n.): one who engages in this style of dance (also **breaker** or **breakdancer**)

**Beef** (n.): a grudge or rivalry

**Bite** (v.): to steal significant portions of lyrics, typically memorable **rhymes**, from another **rapper**

**Black** (adj.): pertaining to African American culture, often extended metaphorically to a group perceived outside the dominant power structure. The concept **Black** in **hip hop** is typically associated with style, agility, creativity, authenticity, and being electrifying and cutting-edge

**Bling** (n.): flashy, ostentatious jewellery and decoration

**Boast** (v.): a self-referential speech that involves praising oneself in lyrics

**Break** (n.): any segment of music (usually four measures or less) that could be sampled and repeated

**Break** (v.): see **b-boy** (v.)

**Break beat** (n.): the sampling of **breaks** such as drum loops, and using them as the rhythmic basis for hip-hop and rap songs

**Breakdance** (v.): see **b-boy** (v.)

**Crew** (n.): a group of **hip hoppers**, usually rappers or **break-dancers/b-boys**, who perform together regularly

**Crunk** (adj.): good, fine; under the influence of drugs or alcohol

**Da/Tha** (art.): the

**Dirty South** (n.): a nickname for the artists and style of music produced by hip hoppers in the southern United States (alternative spell. **durrty**)

**Dis(s)** (v.): to verbally attack or humiliate (from 'disrespect')

**DJ** (v.): to produce music by mixing pieces from one or more tracks, often including the practice of **scratching** vinyl albums

**DJ** (n.): a person who produces music in this way

**Dope** (adj.): cool

**Flow** (n.): the rhythm and timing of a hip-hop song, usually attributed to the skilful combination of beats and rhymes of the DJ and MC

**Fly** (adj.): awesome, cool, pretty

**Freestyle** (v.): to perform a spontaneous **rap**, unplanned lyrics

**Freestyle** (n.): a rap performance that involves unplanned, spontaneous composition of lyrics

**Front** (v.): to portray oneself or one's abilities as different or better than they are perceived by others—the opposite of **keepin it real**

**Gangsta** (n.): one who participates in ghetto and/or gang life and activities associated with such a life

**Gangsta** (adj.): characteristic of possessing or demonstrating one or more attributes associated with ghetto and/or gang life; cool

**Gangsta rap** (n.): a style of rap that portrays ghetto life, characterized by violence, criminal activity, and urban ghetto experiences

**Hard** (adj.): authentic, tough, muscular

**Hate (on)** (v.): to insult or verbally attack another; to be jealous

**Homeboy** (n.): friend, neighbour, companion (also **homey** or **homie**)

**House** (v.): to have a major success; to beat in competition; to dominate

**Ice** (n.): diamonds and other expensive jewellery

**330**

**Isht** (n.):   a euphemistic misspelling of shit, with the same uses and meanings (also **ish**).

**Ghetto** (n.):   an urban neighbourhood characterized by poverty

> **Ghetto** (adj.):   pertaining to such a neighbourhood; of questionable quality
>
> **Ghetto pass** (n.):   figurative or literal approval of a non-Black person (or a now-successful Black person) from Black Americans (or the hip-hop music industry); the street cred of someone known for **keepin it real**

**Graffiti** (n.):   images or lettering, often including the artist's 'signature', spray-painted on property (typically subway trains or buildings)

**(Hip Hop) Head** (n.):   a person who participates in various aspects of **hip-hop** culture

**Headspin** (n.):   a **breakdance** move in which a person balances on their head while rotating along the vertical axis of their body

**Hip hop** (n.):   a culture or identity that is expressed through particular language and lifestyle practices, usually embraced by youth, and often associated with African American culture and rap music; practices include: music (**rap**, **DJ-ing**, **MC-ing**), dance (**breakdancing/b-boying**), art (**graffiti**), fashion, sociopolitical worldview centred around notions of authenticity and shunning the mainstream

> **Hip-hop** (adj.):   pertaining to hip hop
>
> **Hip Hop Linguistics (HHLx)**:   an interdisciplinary approach to language and language use within the **HHN** with particular emphasis on the creation and practices of new varieties of **HHNL**
>
> **Hip Hop Nation (HHN)** (n.):   the broader (inter)national **hip-hop** community who share (aspects of) a common lifestyle, language style, and worldview
>
> **Hip Hop Nation Language (HHNL)** (n.):   a variety of English used by **hip hoppers** that builds on and extends the grammar and lexicon of African American English

**Hip hopper** (n.):   one who participates in **hip-hop** culture, particularly performance aspects, such as music and dance

**Hiphopography** (n.):   an emic approach to the study of **hip-hop** culture that combines the methods of ethnography, biography, and social and oral history, and aims to break down the hierarchical relationship between the 'researcher' and the 'researched'

**Hood** (n.):   home neighbourhood or turf

> **Hood** (adj.):   having attributes associated with a **ghetto**

**Hype man** (n.):   a hip-hop performer responsible for backup **rapping** and singing, and increasing an audience's excitement with call-and-response chants

**Keep it Real** (v.):   to represent oneself, one's abilities and one's background as authentic

**Lamp** (v.):   to take one's ease, to chill

**MC** (n.):   Master of Ceremonies; one who performs **rap** lyrics to the music provided by a **DJ**; can also connote skill and experience at doing this

> **MC** (v.):   to perform **rap** lyrics

**Mix** (v.):   to combine beats and rhythms, previously recorded material, and/or other instrumentation on a **track**

**Moonwalk** (v.):   a **breakdancing** technique creating the appearance of the dancer gliding while staying on the same spot.

**Name** (v.): to refer to oneself and/or other **crew** members during a performance or recording

**Old School** (adj.):   pertaining to the early waves of **hip-hop** artists from the 1970s and 1980s

**Peace**:   a parting salutation common in **hip-hop** culture

**Pimpin** (adj.):   cool, fashionable, **fly**

**Playa** (n.):   a competitive person who can command respect in their community by the extent of his or her 'game'; one who participates in **hip-hop** culture

**Rap** (n.):   a spoken style of lyrical performance characterized by rhythmic speech and/or singing

**Real** (adj.):   authentic or truthful

**Represent** (v.):   to acknowledge oneself as an appropriate representative of a certain group, usually with reference to a **crew**, a neighbourhood, or other locally important group (NB: **represent** can be used both transitively and intransitively)

**Rhymes** (n.):  **rap** lyrics

**Rocks** (n.):  diamonds; crack cocaine

**Sample** (v.):  to incorporate portions of previously recorded material into a new **track**

**Scratch** (v.):  a **mixing** technique that involves quick back and forth movement of a vinyl record as an enhancement to the **tracks** being mixed

**Shout out** (n.):  a positive acknowledgment or message, often offered up in a public setting in front of a wider audience

**Street** (n.):  the sphere of authenticity in **hip hop**

> **Street** (adj.):  having qualities pertaining to authentic **hip-hop** culture

**Tha** (art.):  see **Da**

**Thug** (adj.):  criminal or threatening

**Tip drill** (n.):  an unattractive person, male or female, esp. one used for sex or money

**Twist (someone's) cap** (v. phr.):  to kill someone; to beat, outwit, or get the better of someone (also twist (someone's) cap back)

**Underground** (adj.):  pertaining to an artistic scene not recognized or published by mainstream outlets

**Wack** (adj.):  of poor quality, inauthentic

**White** (adj.):  pertaining to mainstream American culture, often extended metaphorically to a group perceived as the controllers of socioeconomic and/or political power. The concept White in hip hop is typically associated with blandness, awkwardness, lack of creativity, lack of authenticity, and being unfashionable

**Whoadie** (n.):  a casual, familiar form of address for a friend

**Word** (adv.):  an exclamation used as a sign of agreement

**Yo**:  a greeting; a contracted form of 'your'; an informal address term

# Index